We held a studio-wide weight loss competition. The goal: lose 5 kg in a month. The results: amazing! I'm down to 65.4 kg!! Woooot! Who da man?! Bang the drums and toot the horns! Exercise really does matter! Well, it's diet and exercise. And don't forget the exercise!! But now I'm up to 66.5 kg again... Hmm, time to exercise, because I'm maintaining this weight no matter what!

—Mitsutoshi Shimabukuro, 2010

Mitsutoshi Shimabukuro made his debut in **Weekly Shonen Jump** in 1996. He is best known for **Seikimatsu Leader Den Takeshi!** for which he won the 46th Shogakukan Manga Award for children's manga in 2001. His current series, **Toriko**, began serialization in Japan in 2008.

TORIKO VOL. 9
SHONEN JUMP Manga Edition

STORY AND ART BY **MITSUTOSHI SHIMABUKURO**

Translation/Christine Dashiell
Adaptation/Hope Donovan
Touch-Up Art & Lettering/Maui Girl
Design/Matt Hinrichs
Editor/Alexis Kirsch, Hope Donovan

TORIKO © 2008 by Mitsutoshi Shimabukuro
All rights reserved. First published in Japan in 2008 by SHUEISHA Inc., Tokyo.
English translation rights arranged by SHUEISHA Inc.

Printed in Canada

Published by VIZ Media, LLC
P.O. Box 77010
San Francisco, CA 94107

10 9 8 7 6 5 4 3 2 1
First printing, April 2012

www.viz.com

THE WORLD'S
MOST POPULAR MANGA

SHONEN JUMP
www.shonenjump.com

Story and Art by Mitsutoshi Shimabukuro

TORIKO

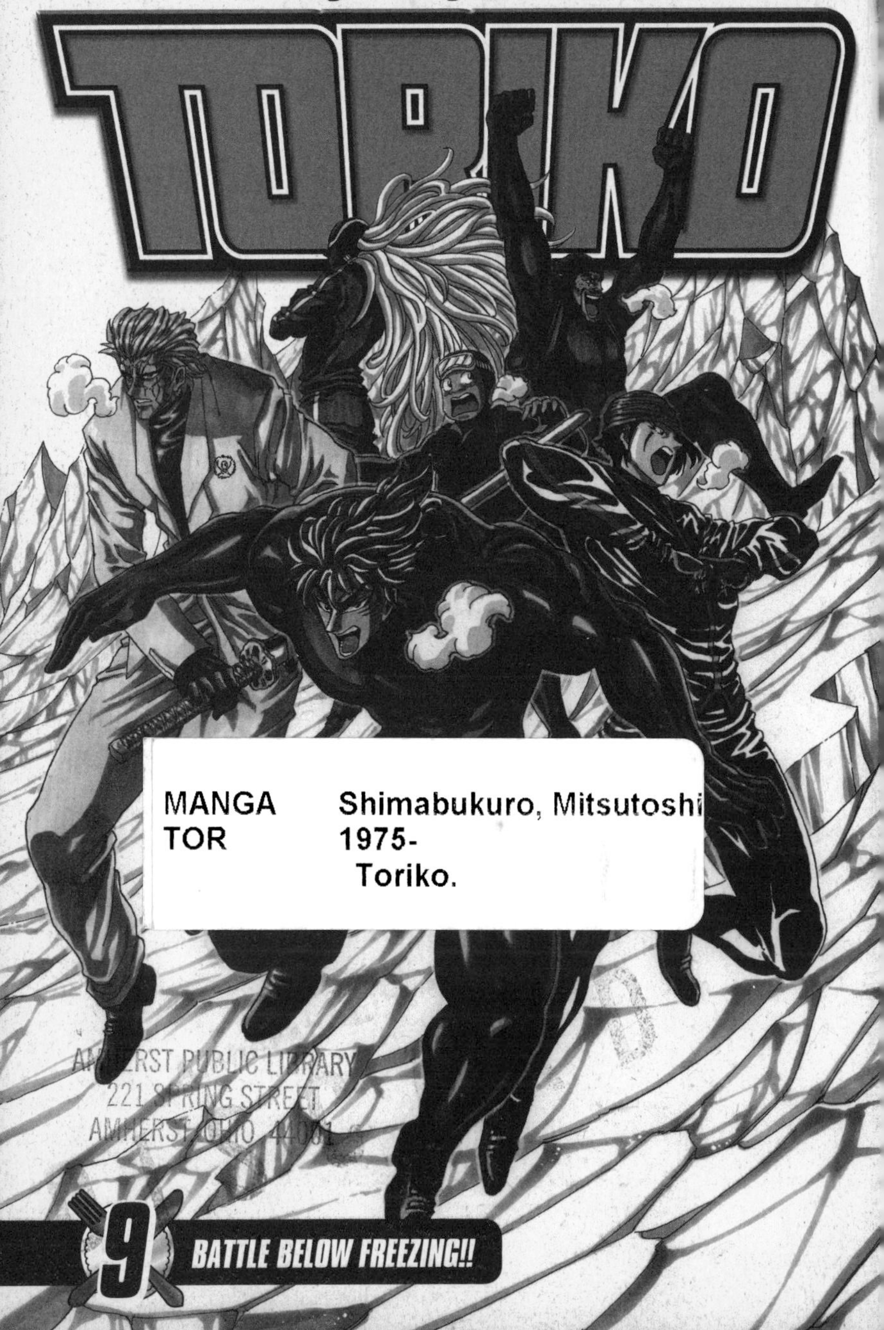

9 BATTLE BELOW FREEZING!!

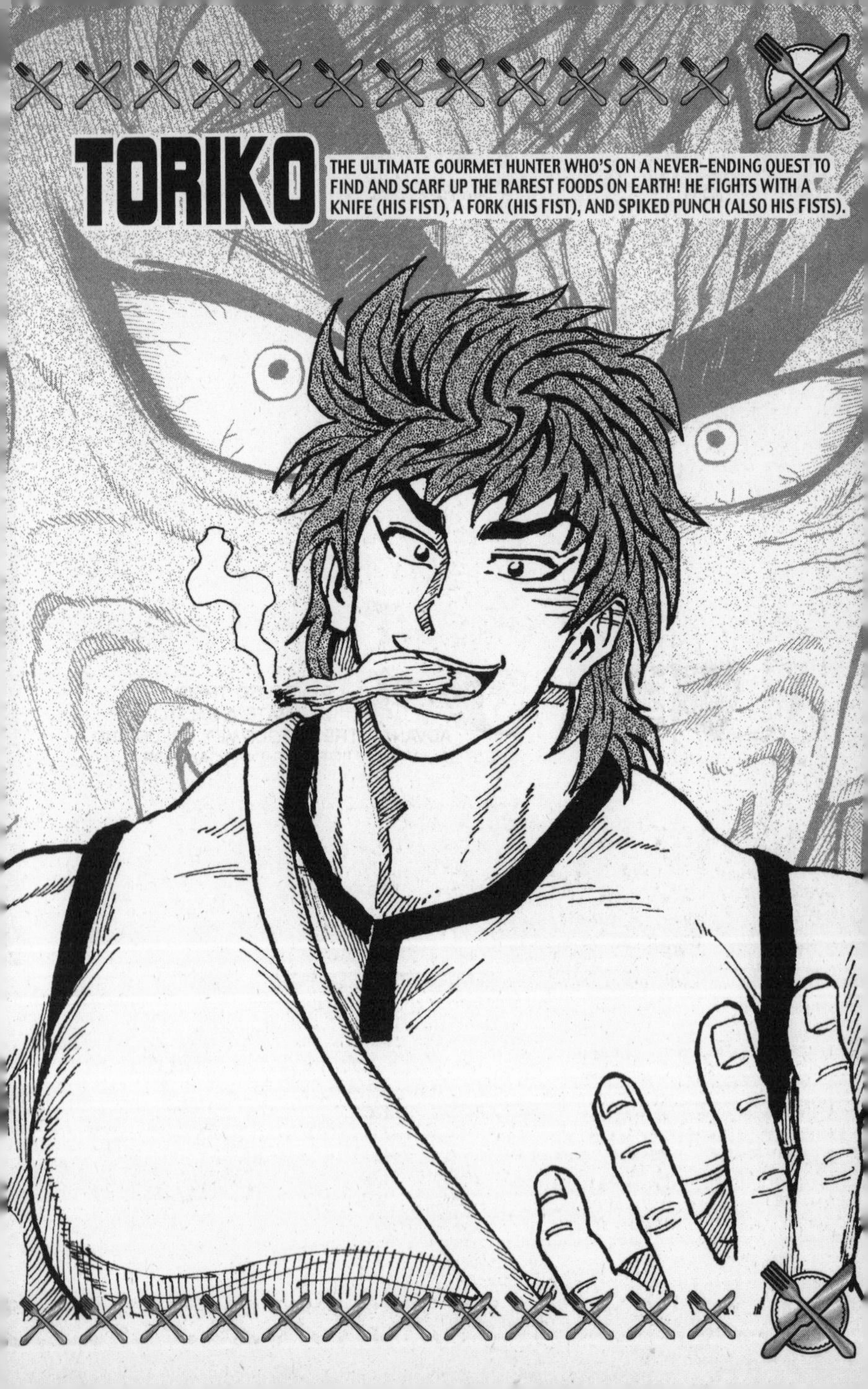
TORIKO
THE ULTIMATE GOURMET HUNTER WHO'S ON A NEVER-ENDING QUEST TO FIND AND SCARF UP THE RAREST FOODS ON EARTH! HE FIGHTS WITH A KNIFE (HIS FIST), A FORK (HIS FIST), AND SPIKED PUNCH (ALSO HIS FISTS).

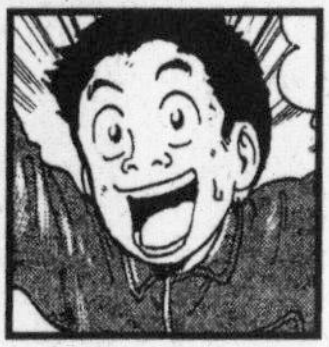

●KOMATSU
IGO HOTEL CHEF AND TORIKO'S #1 FAN.

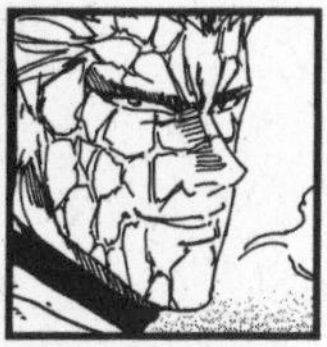

●MATCH
TRIPLE SLICIN' LIEUTENANT OF THE GOURMET MAFIA.

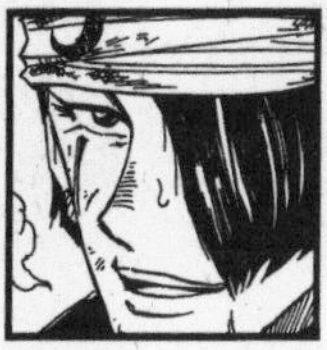

●TAKIMARU
A GOURMET KNIGHT, A GROUP OF GOURMET HUNTERS WHO ADHERE TO THE GOURMET FAITH.

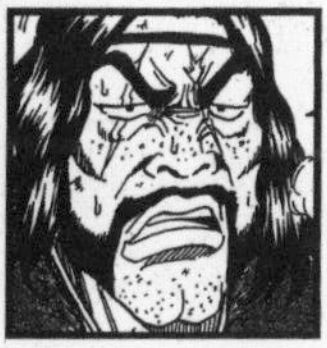

●ZONGEH
SELF-PROCLAIMED SUPER-AWESOME GOURMET HUNTER. LOOKS TOUGH, BUT IS PASSIONATE AND HAS LOYAL FOLLOWERS.

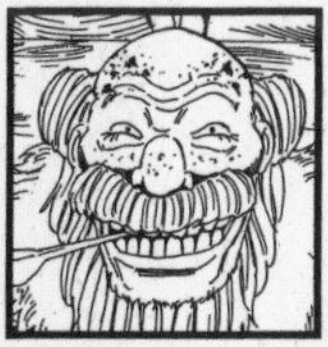

●COLONEL MOKKOI
PRESIDENT OF GOURMART, A COMPANY WITH AN ANNUAL TURNOVER OF TWENTY BILLION. SPONSOR OF THE QUEST FOR CENTURY SOUP.

WHAT'S FOR DINNER

IT'S THE AGE OF GOURMET! KOMATSU, THE HEAD CHEF AT THE HOTEL OWNED BY THE IGO (INTERNATIONAL GOURMET ORGANIZATION), BECAME FAST FRIENDS WITH THE LEGENDARY GOURMET HUNTER TORIKO WHILE GATOR HUNTING. NOW KOMATSU ACCOMPANIES TORIKO ON HIS LIFELONG QUEST TO CREATE THE PERFECT FULL-COURSE MEAL.

ONE DAY, HE AND TORIKO ENCOUNTERED A GT ROBOT, A MACHINE DISPATCHED BY THE IGO'S RIVAL ORGANIZATION, "GOURMET CORP." SENSING A FOUL PLOT AFOOT, THE IGO MADE AN EMERGENCY SUMMONS OF THE FOUR KINGS TO OPPOSE THEM. A BATTLE BROKE OUT OVER THE REGAL MAMMOTH'S "JEWEL MEAT," FROM WHICH TORIKO EMERGED VICTORIOUS AND WITH A FULL BELLY!

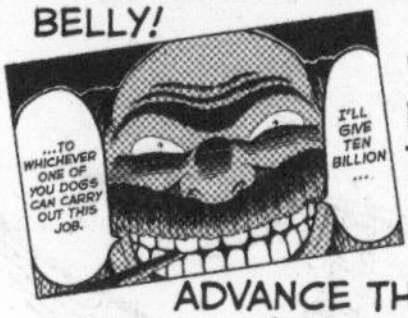

I'LL GIVE TEN BILLION...
...TO WHICHEVER ONE OF YOU DOGS CAN CARRY OUT THIS JOB.

WITH THE TASTE OF DEFEAT IN THEIR MOUTHS, THE GOURMET CORP. REVEALED THEIR ULTIMATE GOAL TO ADVANCE THEIR GOURMET CELLS AND EVENTUALLY ACQUIRE THE DELICACY OF DELICACIES: GOD! WITH AN ENRICHING NEW TARGET IN MIND, GOURMET CORP. JUMPED INTO ACTION...

MEANWHILE, AT THE BEHEST OF GOURMET LIVING LEGEND SETSUNO, TORIKO JOINED AN EXPEDITION LED BY GOURMET BILLIONAIRE COLONEL MOKKOI TO FIND THE CENTURY SOUP--A BIZARRE BREW THAT ONLY BUBBLES UP TO THE SURFACE ONCE EVERY HUNDRED YEARS. ALONG WITH A HORDE OF OTHER REWARD-HUNGRY GOURMET HUNTERS, TORIKO AND KOMATSU ARRIVED AT THE FROZEN CONTINENT OF ICE HELL. WHAT ICY TERRORS AWAIT?!

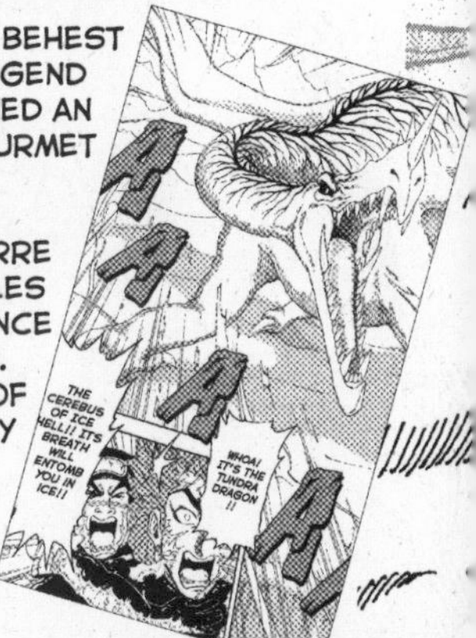

WHOA! IT'S THE TUNDRA DRAGON!!
THE CEREBUS OF ICE HELL!! ITS BREATH WILL ENTOMB YOU IN ICE!!

Contents

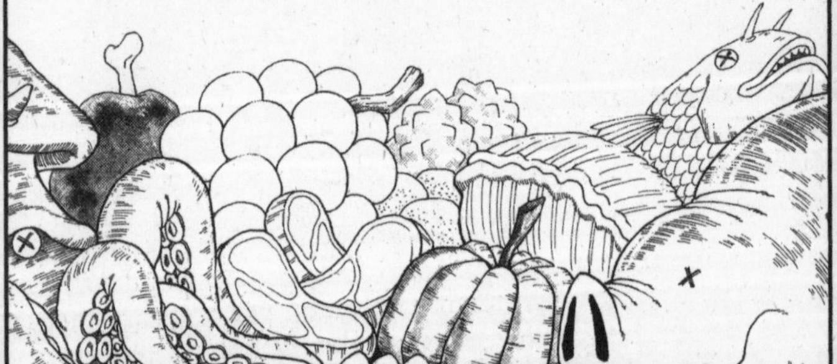

TORIKO

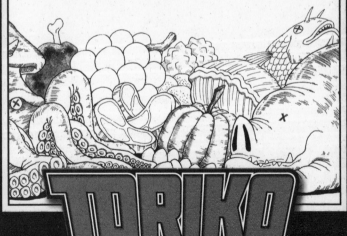

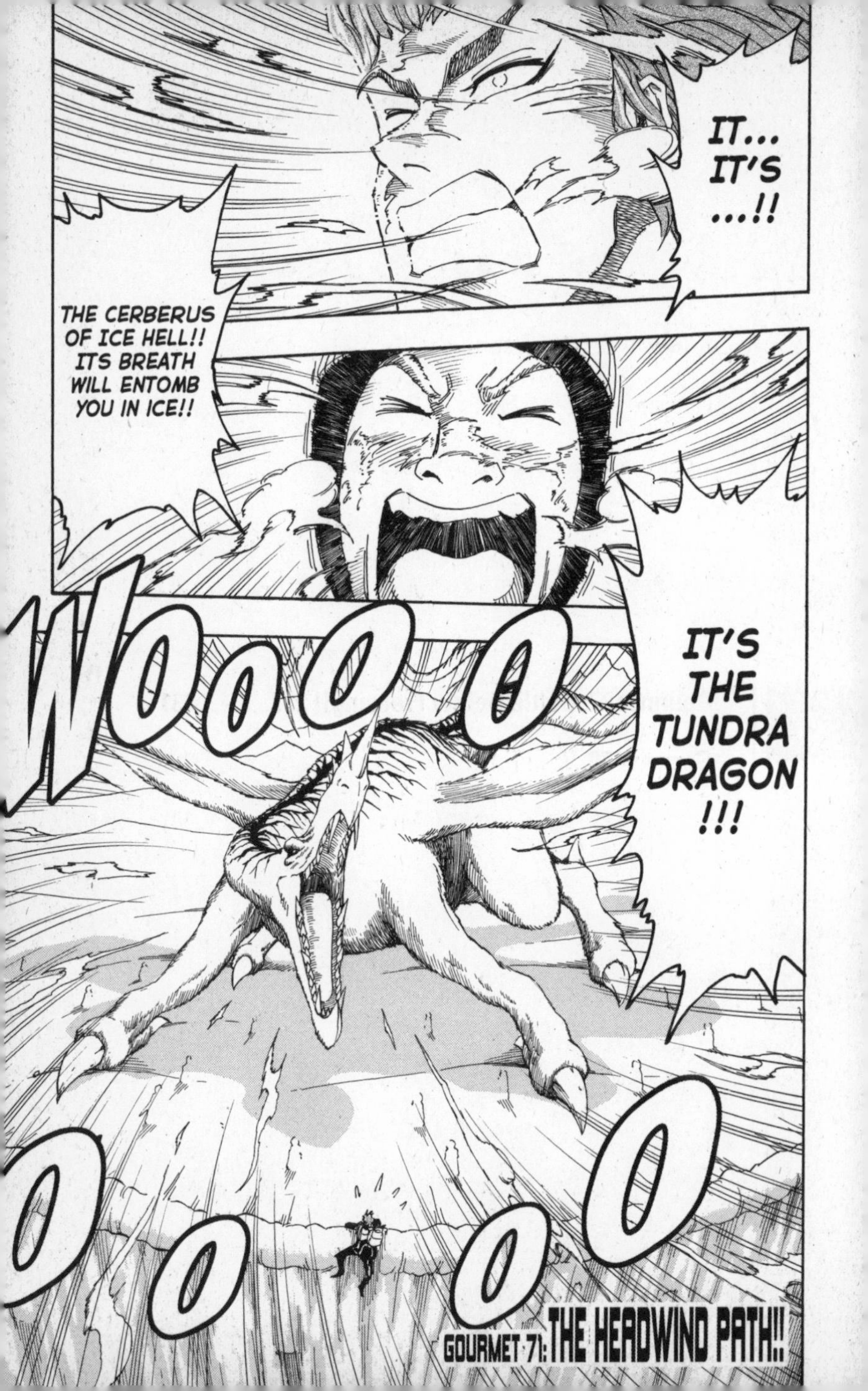
IT... IT'S ...!!
THE CERBERUS OF ICE HELL!! ITS BREATH WILL ENTOMB YOU IN ICE!!
IT'S THE TUNDRA DRAGON!!!
WOOOOO
OOOOOO
GOURMET 71: THE HEADWIND PATH!!

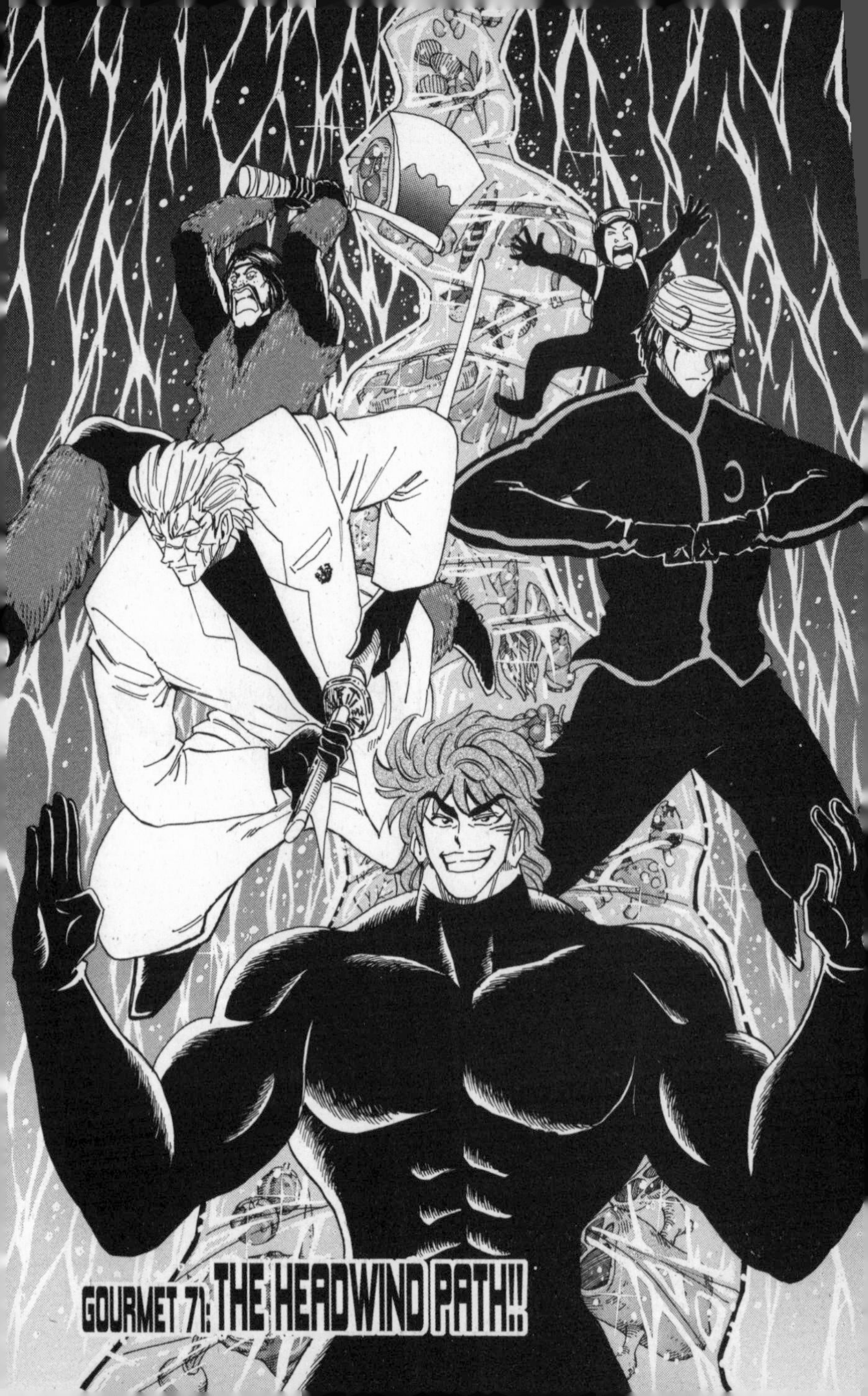
GOURMET 71: THE HEADWIND PATH!!

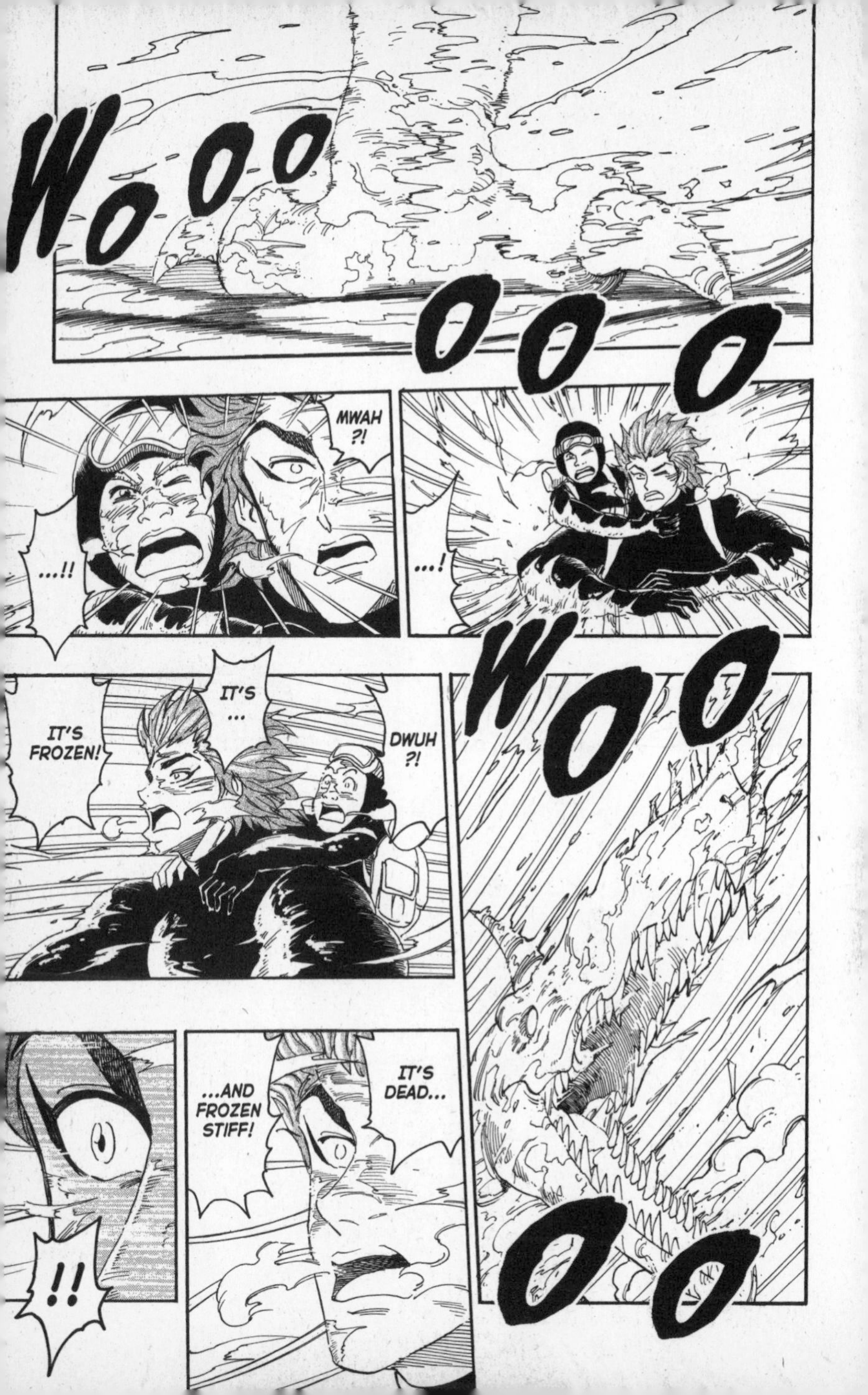
WOOOO
OOO
...!
MWAH ?!
...!!
WOOO
OO
DWUH ?!
IT'S ...
IT'S FROZEN!
IT'S DEAD...
...AND FROZEN STIFF!
!!

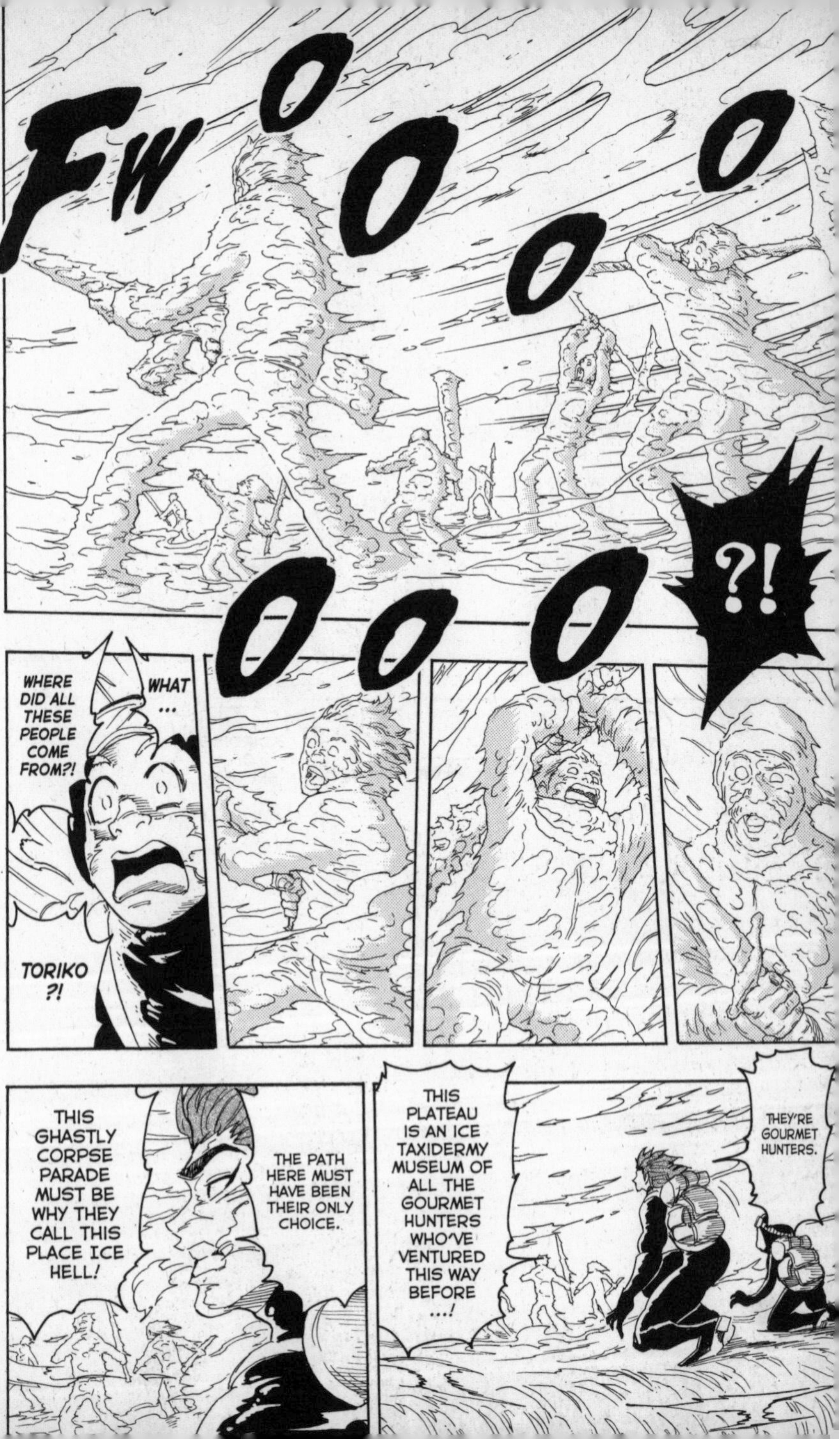
FWOOOOOOOOO
?!
WHAT ...
WHERE DID ALL THESE PEOPLE COME FROM?!
TORIKO ?!
THEY'RE GOURMET HUNTERS.
THIS PLATEAU IS AN ICE TAXIDERMY MUSEUM OF ALL THE GOURMET HUNTERS WHO'VE VENTURED THIS WAY BEFORE ...!
THE PATH HERE MUST HAVE BEEN THEIR ONLY CHOICE.
THIS GHASTLY CORPSE PARADE MUST BE WHY THEY CALL THIS PLACE ICE HELL!

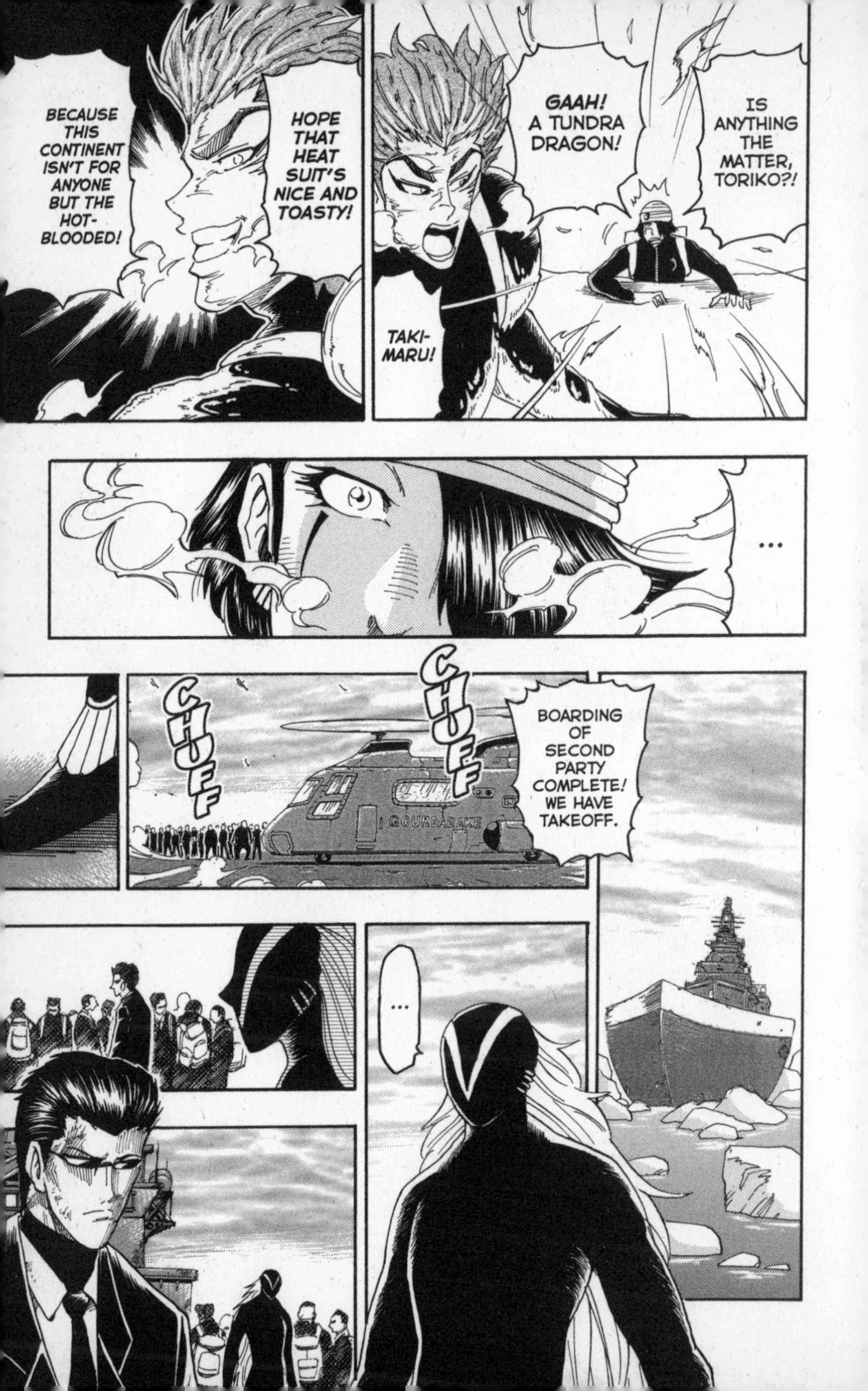
IS ANYTHING THE MATTER, TORIKO?!
GAAH! A TUNDRA DRAGON!
TAKI-MARU!
HOPE THAT HEAT SUIT'S NICE AND TOASTY!
BECAUSE THIS CONTINENT ISN'T FOR ANYONE BUT THE HOT-BLOODED!
...
BOARDING OF SECOND PARTY COMPLETE! WE HAVE TAKEOFF.
CHUFF
CHUFF
...

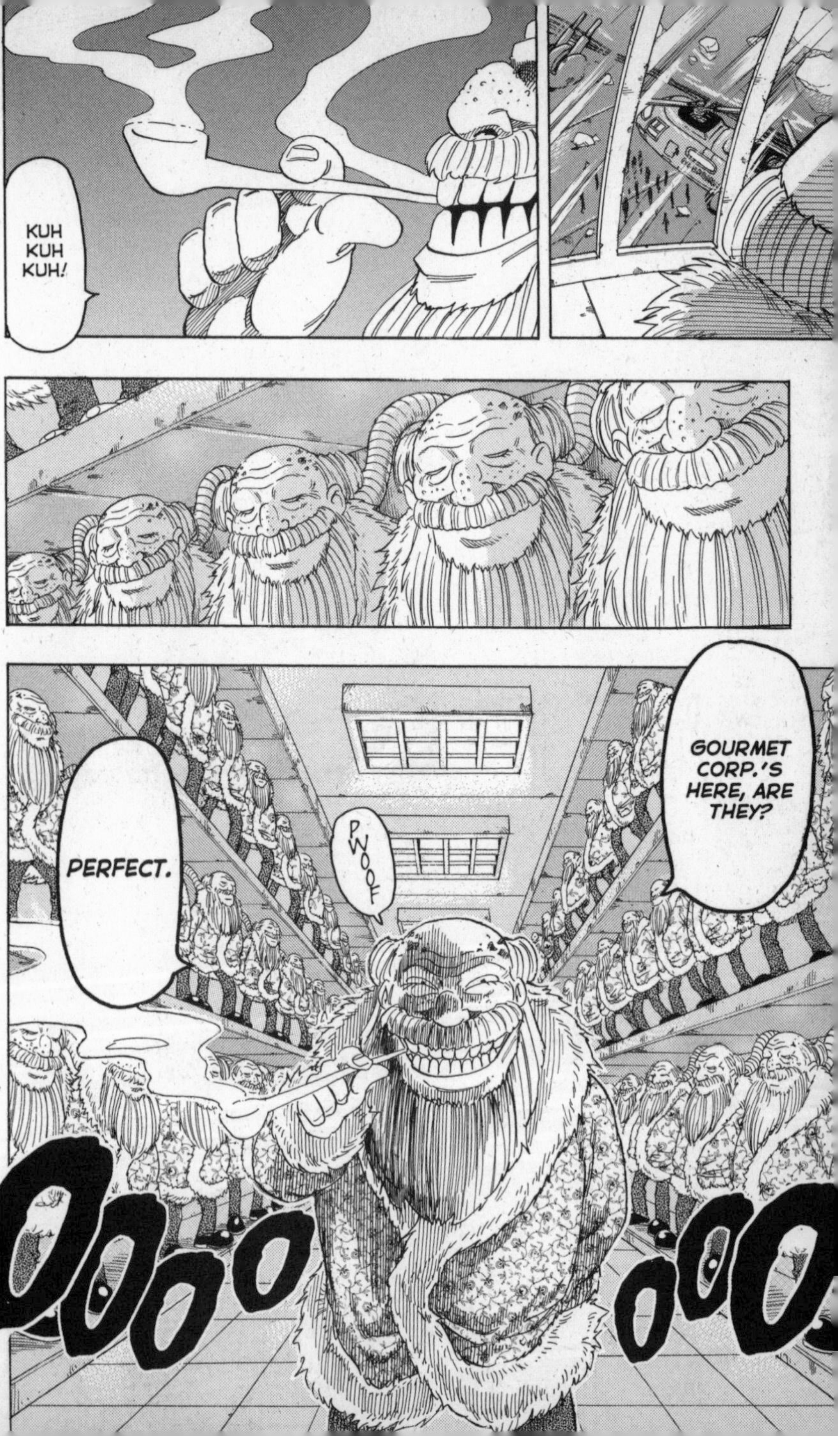
KUH KUH KUH!
GOURMET CORP.'S HERE, ARE THEY?
PWOOF
PERFECT.
OOOO
OOOOO

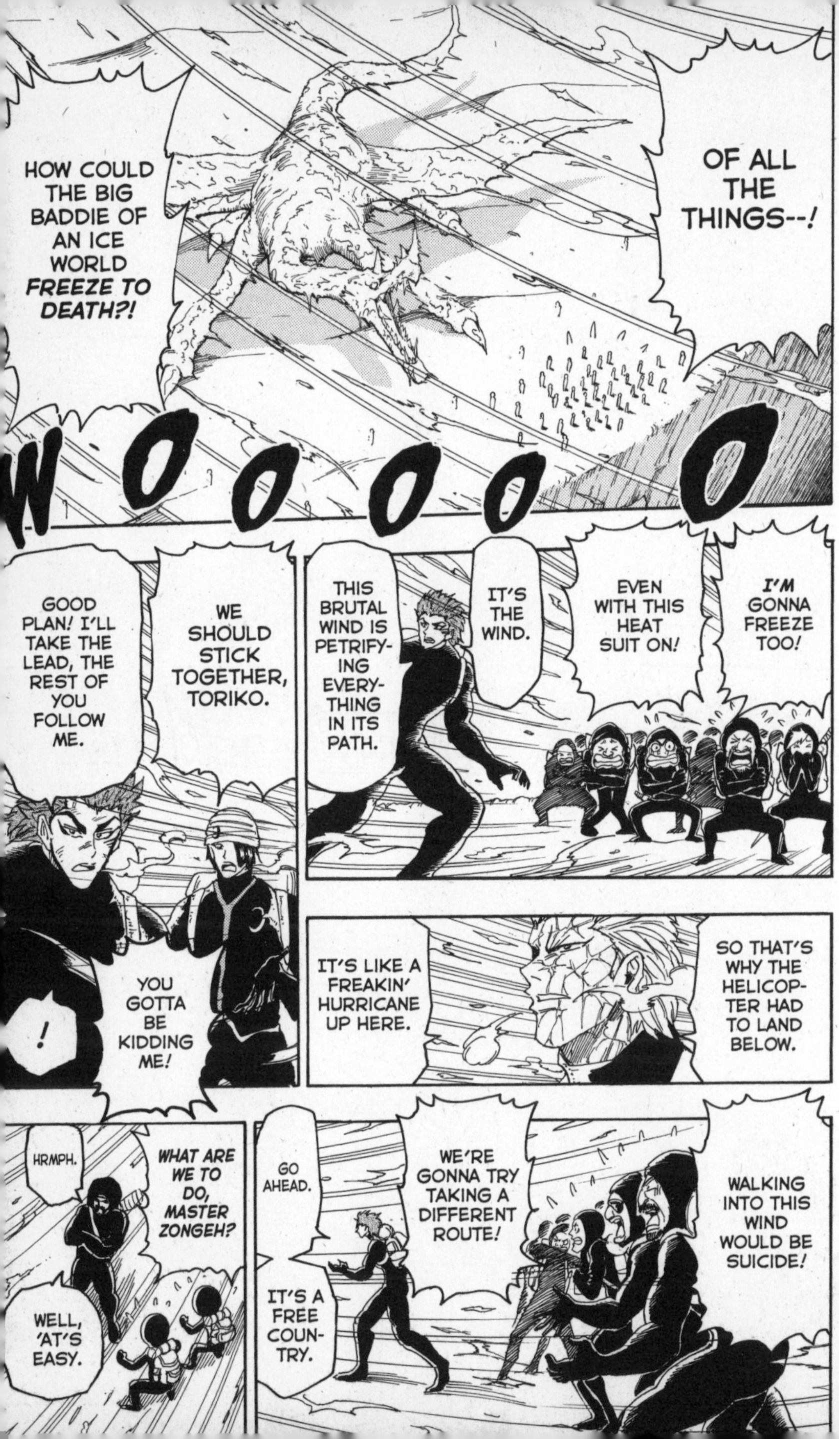
OF ALL THE THINGS--!
HOW COULD THE BIG BADDIE OF AN ICE WORLD *FREEZE TO DEATH?!*
WOOOOOO
I'M GONNA FREEZE TOO!
EVEN WITH THIS HEAT SUIT ON!
IT'S THE WIND.
THIS BRUTAL WIND IS PETRIFYING EVERYTHING IN ITS PATH.
SO THAT'S WHY THE HELICOPTER HAD TO LAND BELOW.
IT'S LIKE A FREAKIN' HURRICANE UP HERE.
WE SHOULD STICK TOGETHER, TORIKO.
GOOD PLAN! I'LL TAKE THE LEAD, THE REST OF YOU FOLLOW ME.
YOU GOTTA BE KIDDING ME!
!
WALKING INTO THIS WIND WOULD BE SUICIDE!
WE'RE GONNA TRY TAKING A DIFFERENT ROUTE!
GO AHEAD.
IT'S A FREE COUNTRY.
WHAT ARE WE TO DO, MASTER ZONGEH?
HRMPH.
WELL, 'AT'S EASY.

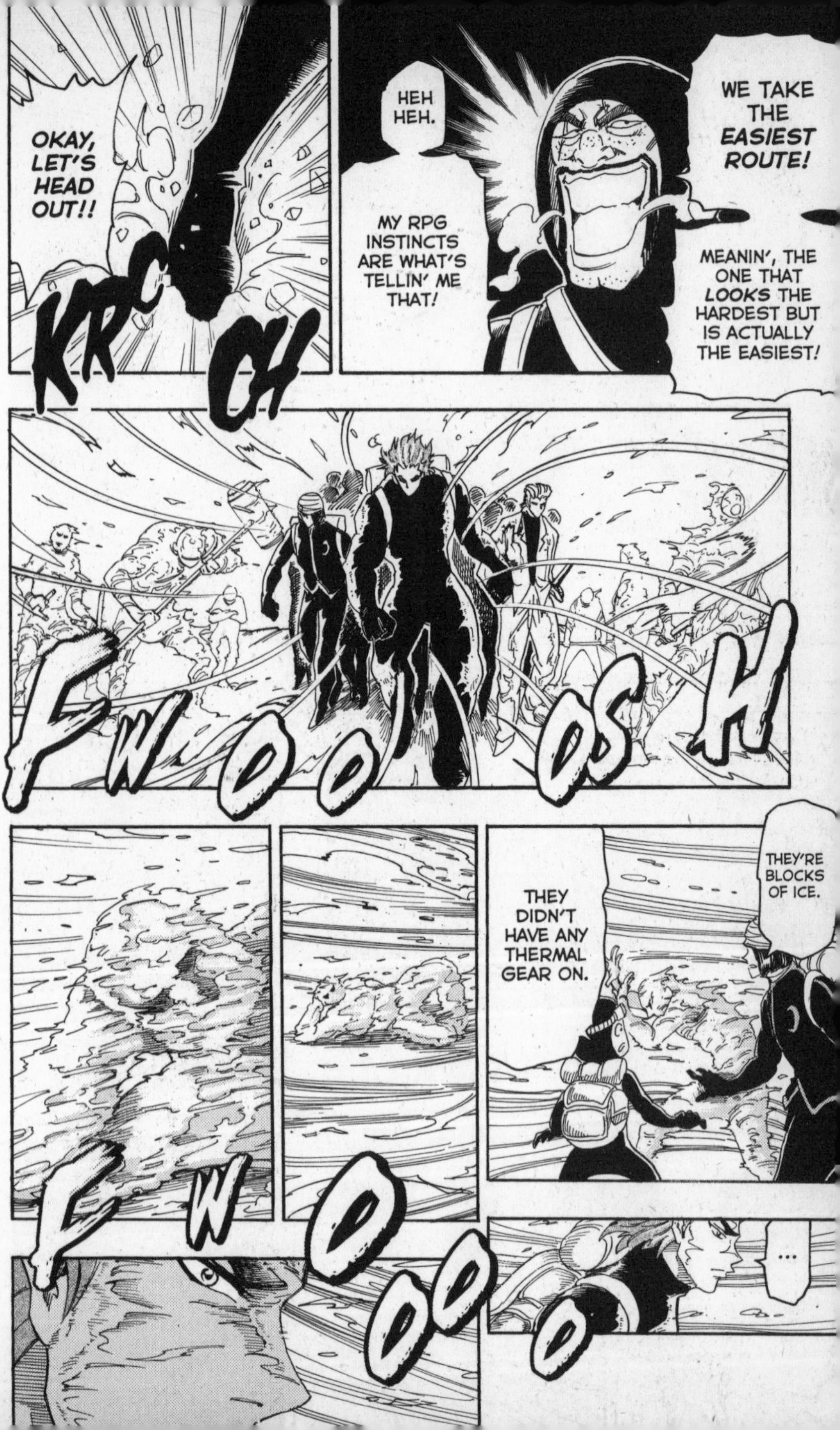
WE TAKE THE *EASIEST* ROUTE!
MEANIN', THE ONE THAT *LOOKS* THE HARDEST BUT IS ACTUALLY THE EASIEST!
HEH HEH.
MY RPG INSTINCTS ARE WHAT'S TELLIN' ME THAT!
OKAY, LET'S HEAD OUT!!
KRCH
FWOOOSH
THEY'RE BLOCKS OF ICE.
THEY DIDN'T HAVE ANY THERMAL GEAR ON.
...
FWOOOOO

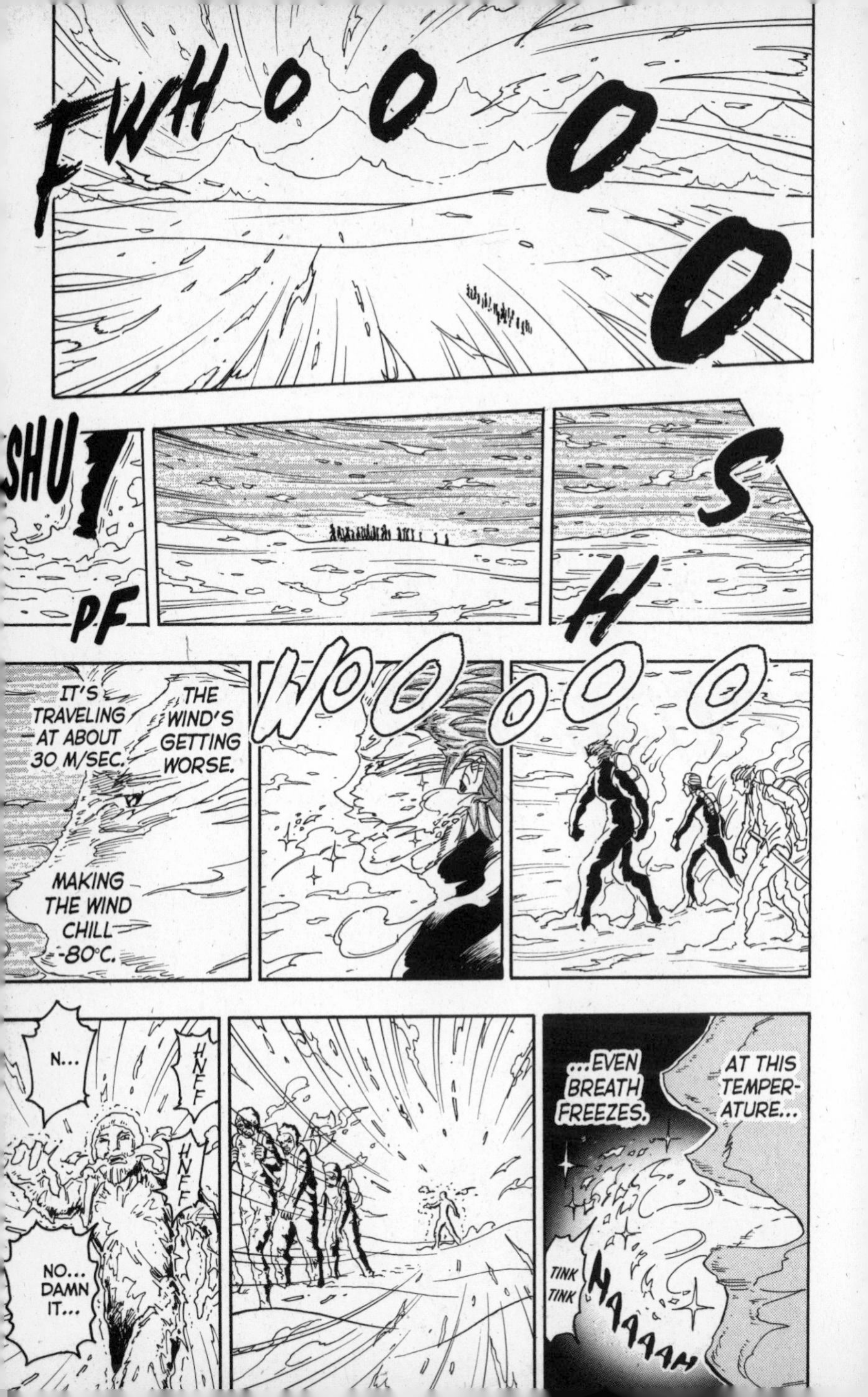
FWHOOOOO
SH
WOOOOOO
SHU
PF
THE WIND'S GETTING WORSE.
IT'S TRAVELING AT ABOUT 30 M/SEC.
MAKING THE WIND CHILL -80°C.
AT THIS TEMPER-ATURE...
...EVEN BREATH FREEZES.
TINK TINK
HAAAAAH
N...
HNFF
HNFF
NO... DAMN IT...

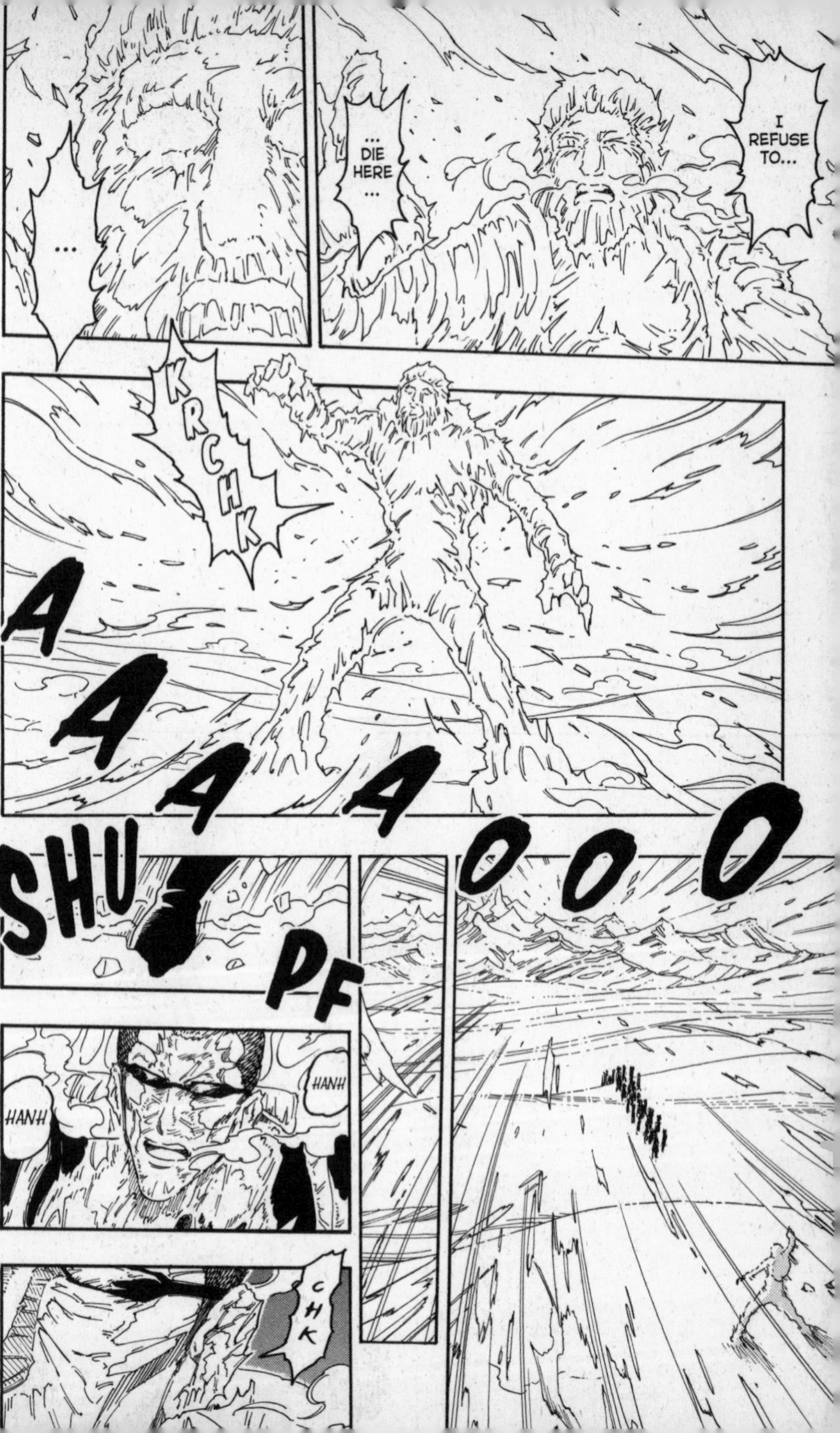
I REFUSE TO...
... DIE HERE ...
...
KRCHK
AAAAOOO
SHUPF
HANH
HANH
CHK

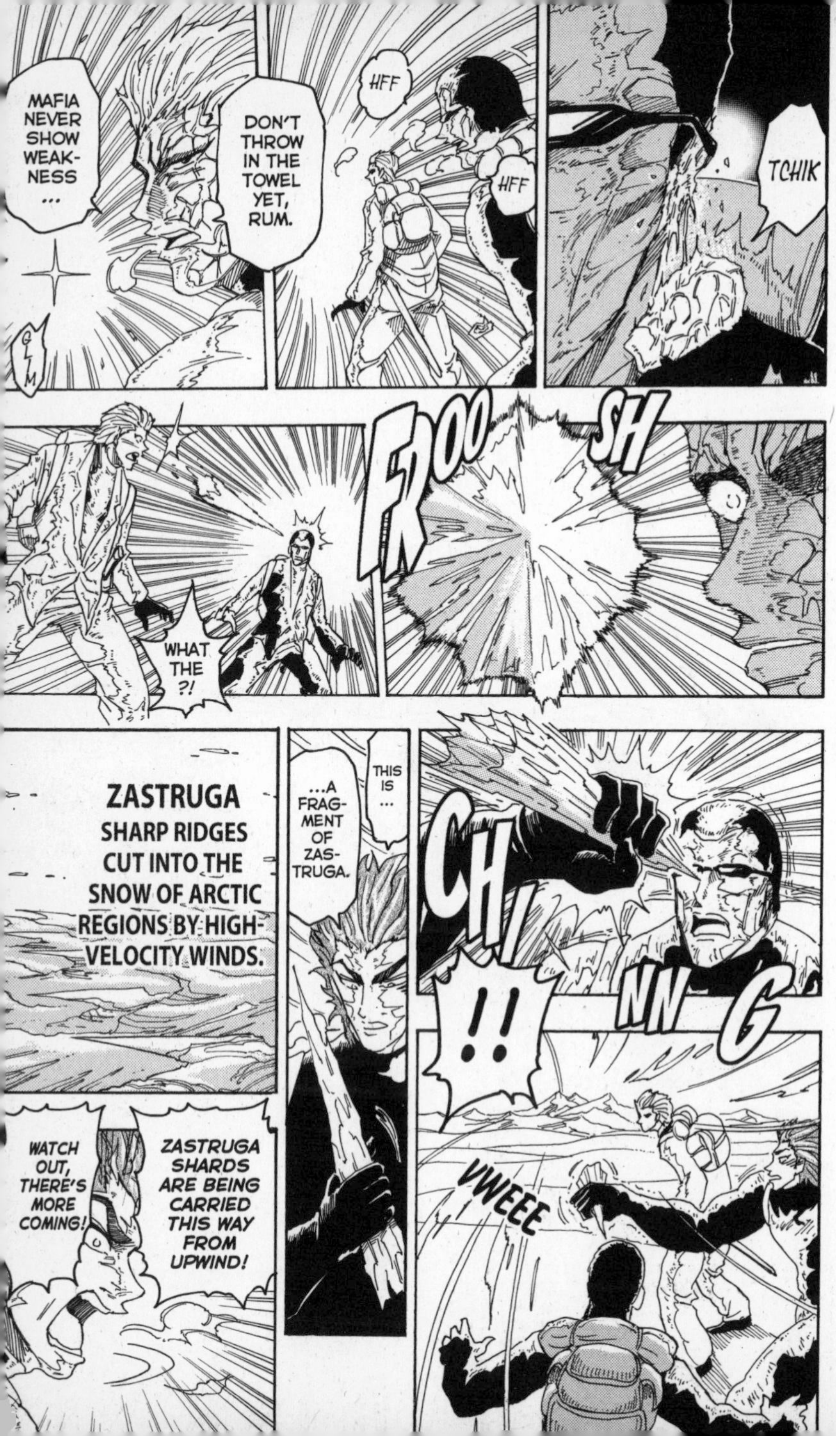
TCHIK
HFF
HFF
DON'T THROW IN THE TOWEL YET, RUM.
MAFIA NEVER SHOW WEAK-NESS ...
GLIM
FROOSH
WHAT THE ?!
CHINNG
!!
VWEEE
THIS IS ...
...A FRAG-MENT OF ZAS-TRUGA.
ZASTRUGA
SHARP RIDGES CUT INTO THE SNOW OF ARCTIC REGIONS BY HIGH-VELOCITY WINDS.
ZASTRUGA SHARDS ARE BEING CARRIED THIS WAY FROM UPWIND!
WATCH OUT, THERE'S MORE COMING!

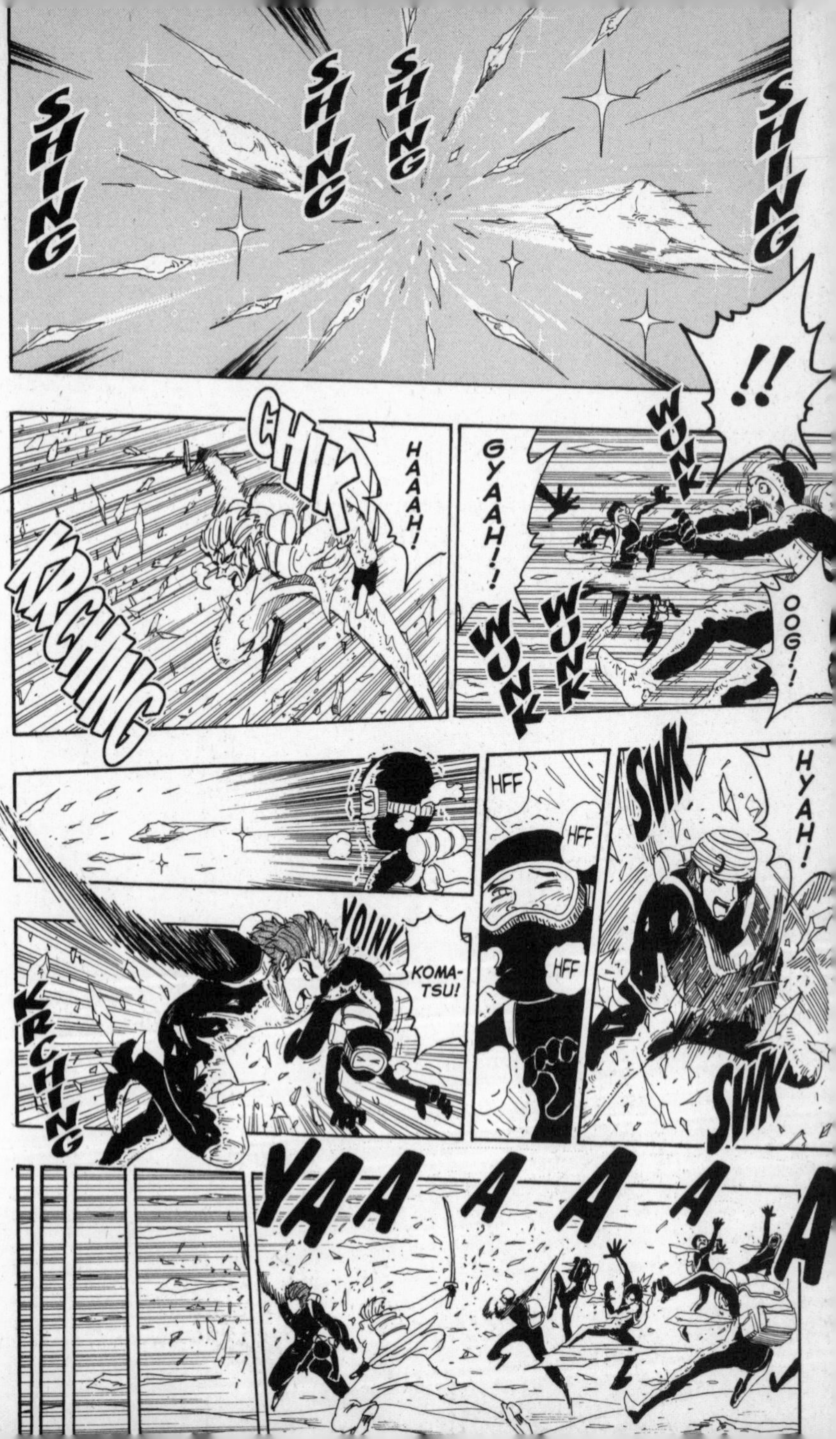
SHING
SHING
SHING
SHING
!!
WUNK
GYAAH!!
WUNK
WUNK
OOG!!
CHIK
HAAAAH!
KRCHING
HYAH!
SWK
SWK
HFF
HFF
HFF
YOINK
KOMA-TSU!
KRCHING
YAAAAAAAA

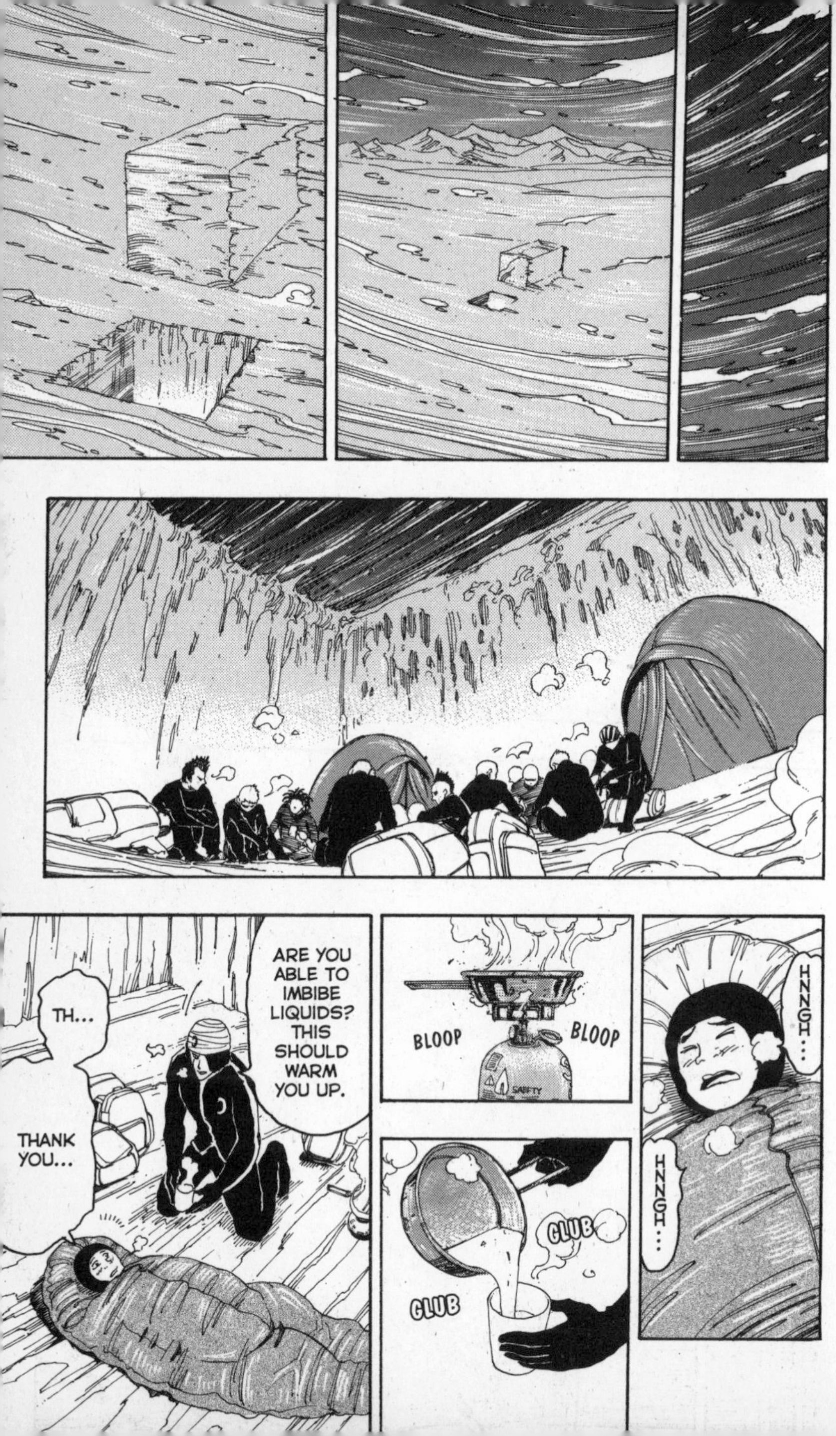
HNNGH...
HNNGH...
BLOOP
BLOOP
GLUB
GLUB
ARE YOU ABLE TO IMBIBE LIQUIDS? THIS SHOULD WARM YOU UP.
TH...
THANK YOU...

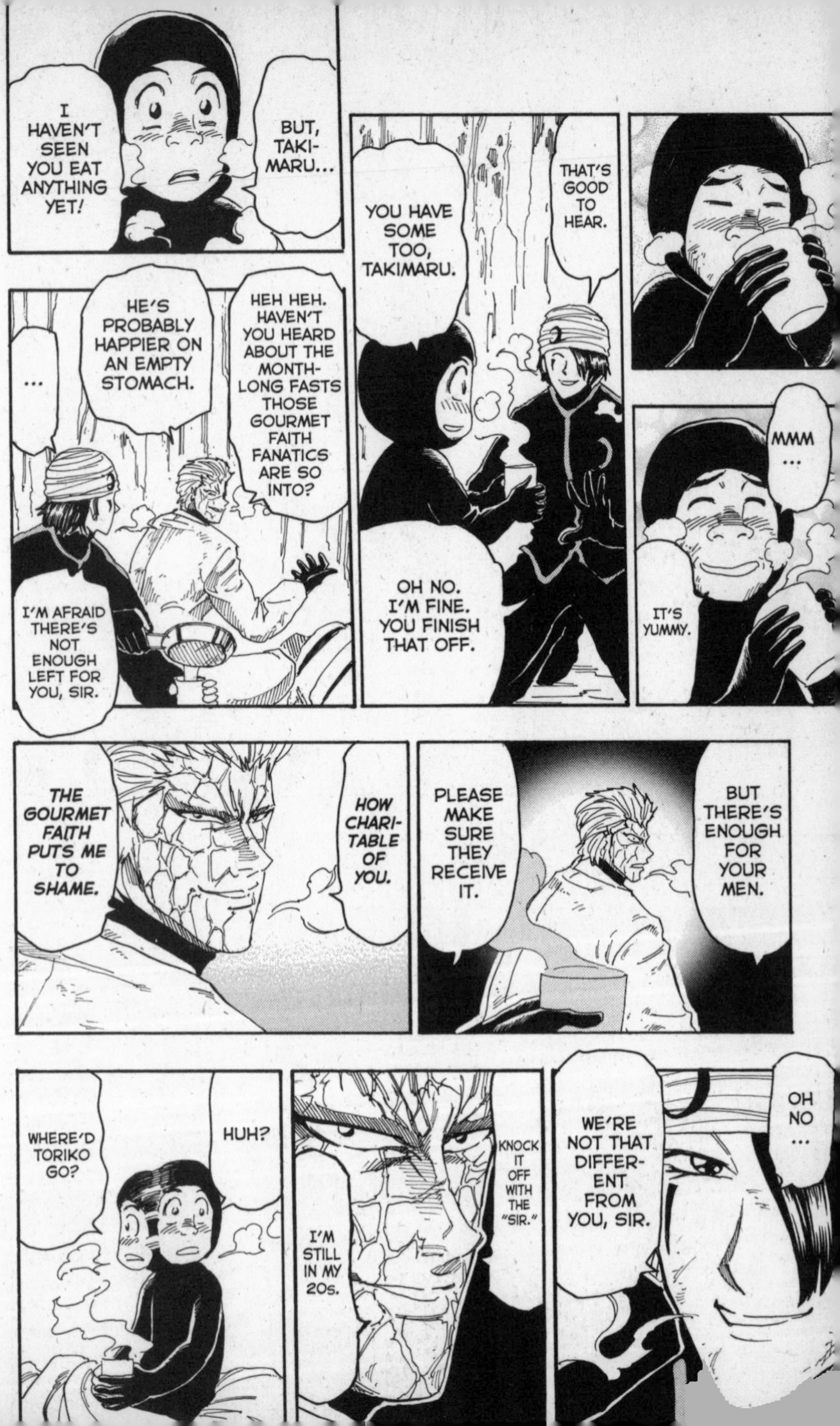
MMM...
IT'S YUMMY.
THAT'S GOOD TO HEAR.
YOU HAVE SOME TOO, TAKIMARU.
OH NO. I'M FINE. YOU FINISH THAT OFF.
BUT, TAKI-MARU...
I HAVEN'T SEEN YOU EAT ANYTHING YET!
HEH HEH. HAVEN'T YOU HEARD ABOUT THE MONTH-LONG FASTS THOSE GOURMET FAITH FANATICS ARE SO INTO?
HE'S PROBABLY HAPPIER ON AN EMPTY STOMACH.
...
I'M AFRAID THERE'S NOT ENOUGH LEFT FOR YOU, SIR.
BUT THERE'S ENOUGH FOR YOUR MEN.
PLEASE MAKE SURE THEY RECEIVE IT.
HOW CHARI-TABLE OF YOU.
THE GOURMET FAITH PUTS ME TO SHAME.
OH NO...
WE'RE NOT THAT DIFFER-ENT FROM YOU, SIR.
KNOCK IT OFF WITH THE "SIR."
I'M STILL IN MY 20s.
HUH?
WHERE'D TORIKO GO?

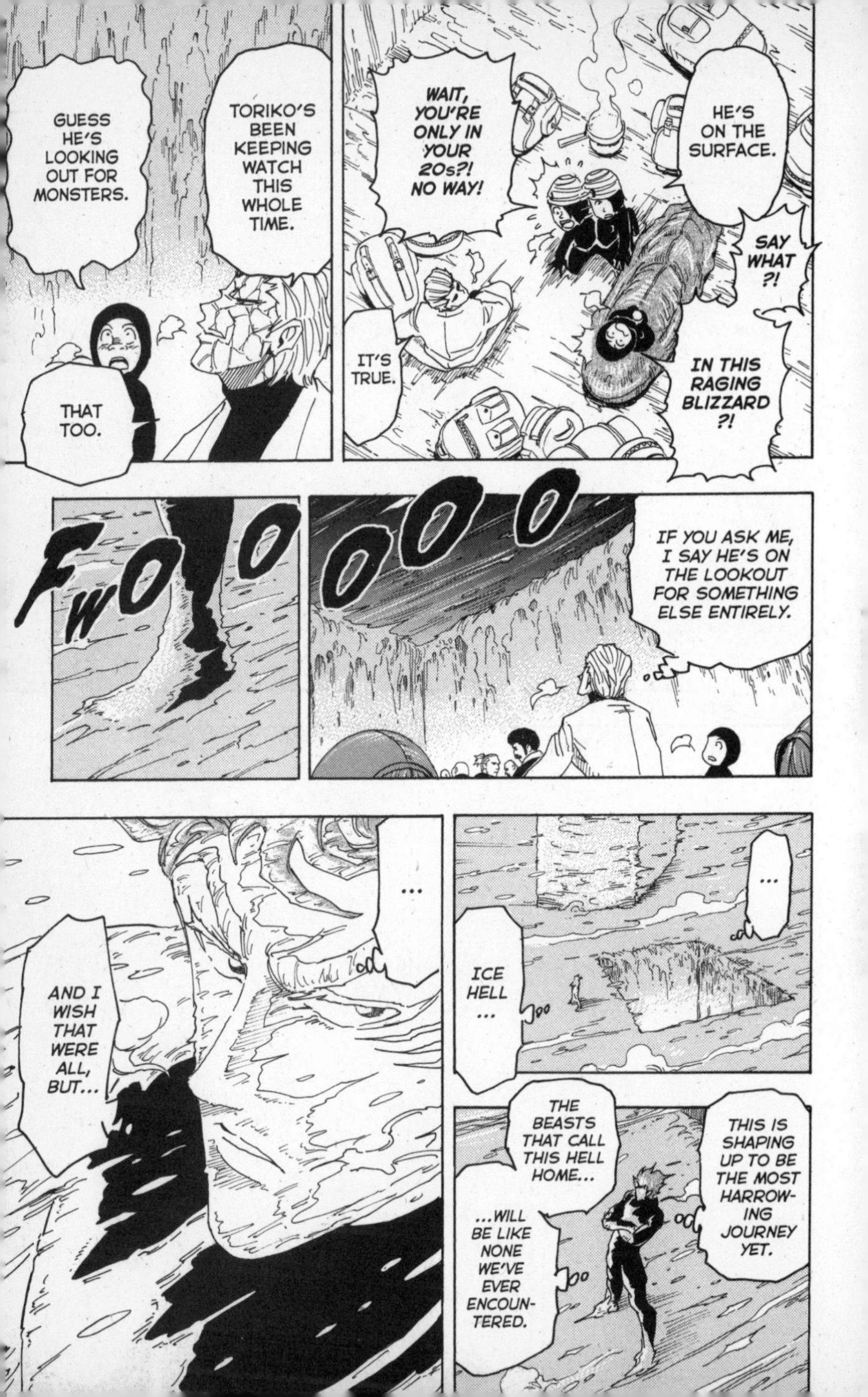
HE'S ON THE SURFACE.
WAIT, YOU'RE ONLY IN YOUR 20s?! NO WAY!
SAY WHAT?!
IN THIS RAGING BLIZZARD?!
IT'S TRUE.
TORIKO'S BEEN KEEPING WATCH THIS WHOLE TIME.
GUESS HE'S LOOKING OUT FOR MONSTERS.
THAT TOO.
IF YOU ASK ME, I SAY HE'S ON THE LOOKOUT FOR SOMETHING ELSE ENTIRELY.
FWOOOOOOO
...
ICE HELL...
THIS IS SHAPING UP TO BE THE MOST HARROWING JOURNEY YET.
THE BEASTS THAT CALL THIS HELL HOME...
...WILL BE LIKE NONE WE'VE EVER ENCOUNTERED.
...
AND I WISH THAT WERE ALL, BUT...

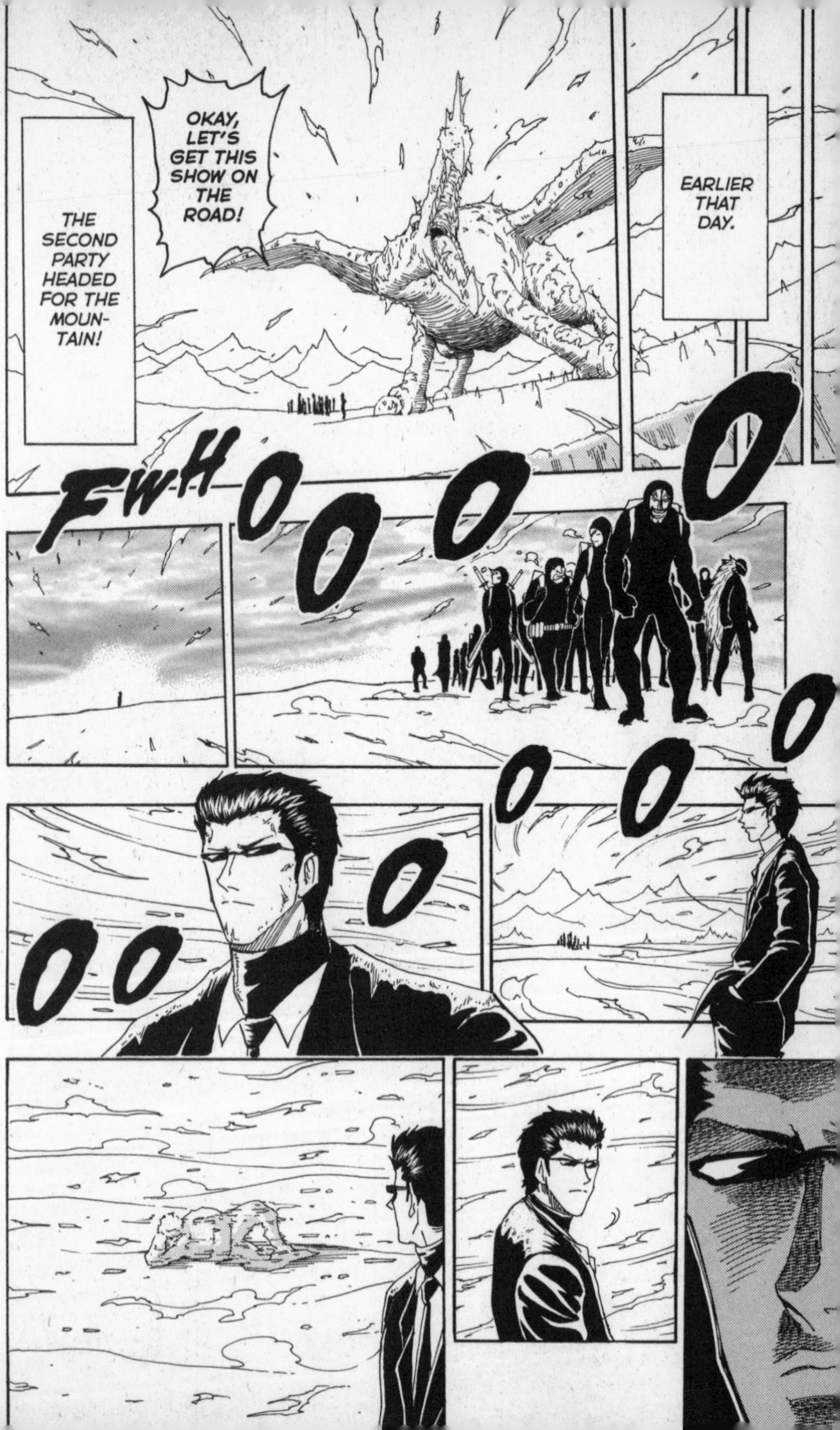
EARLIER THAT DAY.
OKAY, LET'S GET THIS SHOW ON THE ROAD!
THE SECOND PARTY HEADED FOR THE MOUN-TAIN!
FWHOOOOOOOOOOO

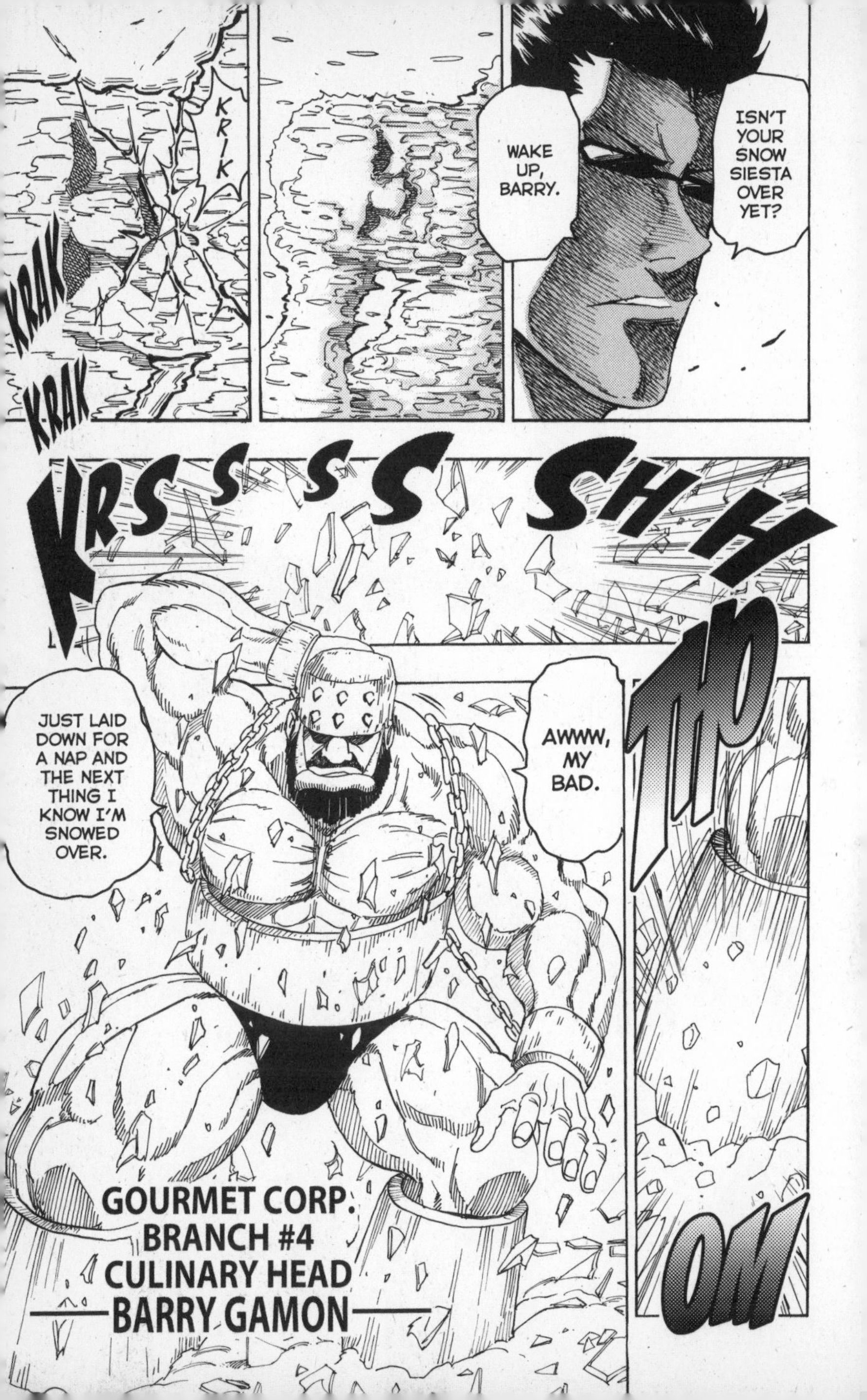
ISN'T YOUR SNOW SIESTA OVER YET?
WAKE UP, BARRY.
KRIK
KRAK
K-RAK
KRSSSSHH
THOOM
AWWW, MY BAD.
JUST LAID DOWN FOR A NAP AND THE NEXT THING I KNOW I'M SNOWED OVER.
GOURMET CORP. BRANCH #4 CULINARY HEAD
—BARRY GAMON—

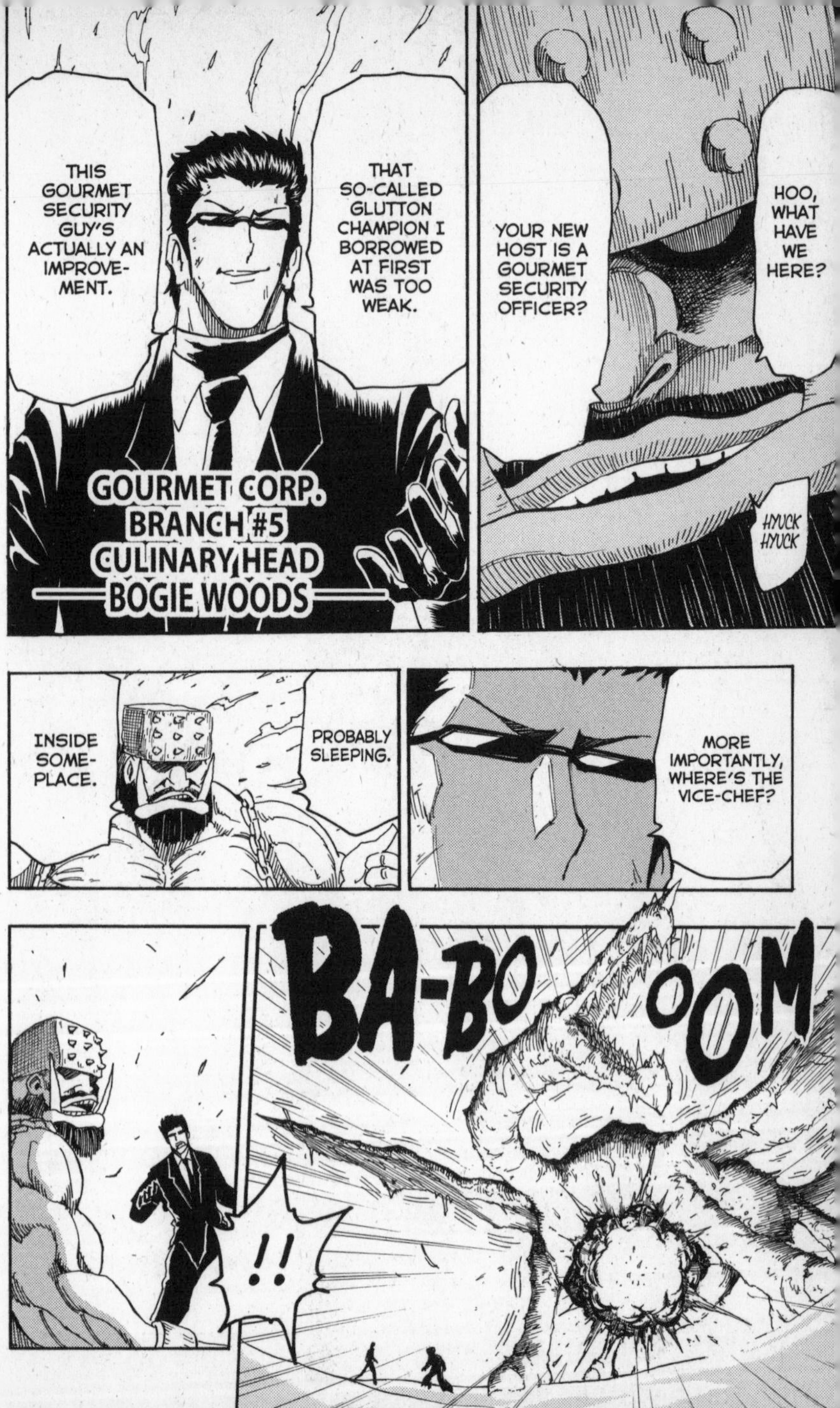
HOO, WHAT HAVE WE HERE?
YOUR NEW HOST IS A GOURMET SECURITY OFFICER?
HYUCK HYUCK
THAT SO-CALLED GLUTTON CHAMPION I BORROWED AT FIRST WAS TOO WEAK.
THIS GOURMET SECURITY GUY'S ACTUALLY AN IMPROVE-MENT.
GOURMET CORP. BRANCH #5 CULINARY HEAD
BOGIE WOODS
MORE IMPORTANTLY, WHERE'S THE VICE-CHEF?
PROBABLY SLEEPING.
INSIDE SOME-PLACE.
BA-BOOOM
!!

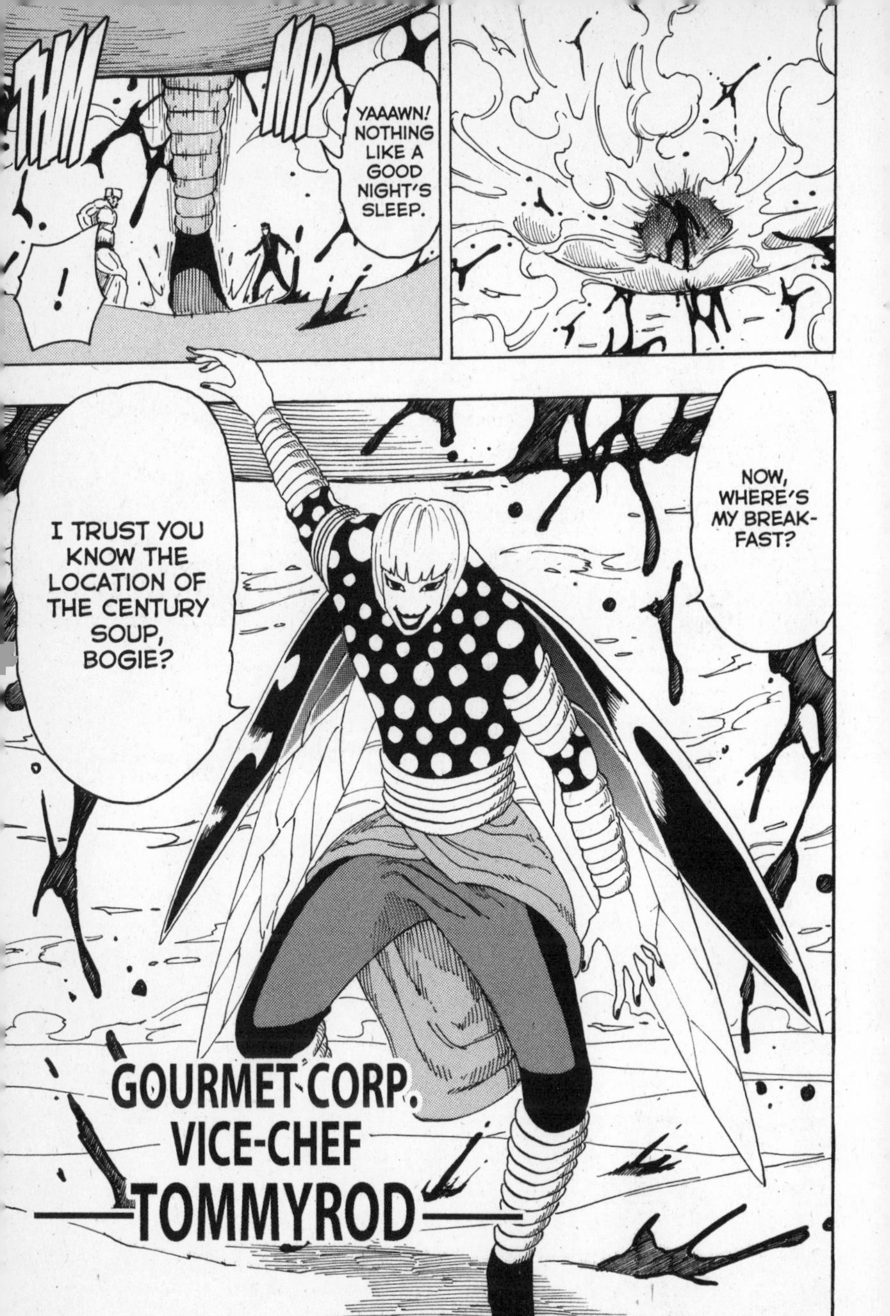
YAAAWN! NOTHING LIKE A GOOD NIGHT'S SLEEP.
!
NOW, WHERE'S MY BREAK-FAST?
I TRUST YOU KNOW THE LOCATION OF THE CENTURY SOUP, BOGIE?
GOURMET CORP. VICE-CHEF TOMMYROD

TORIKO

GOURMET CHECKLIST

Vol. 062
SNAIL SNAKE
(MOLLUSK)

CAPTURE LEVEL: 4

HABITAT: HOT, HUMID CLIMATES

LENGTH: 3.8 METERS

HEIGHT: 2.3 METERS

WEIGHT: 700 KG

PRICE: 100 G / 6,000 YEN

(BUT THEIR POISON MUST BE REMOVED.)

SNAIL SNAKE
(MOLLUSK)
CAPTURE LEVEL 4

SCALE

JUST ONE TOUCH FROM THIS SNAIL WILL SEND DEADLY POISON COURSING THROUGH YOUR BODY, SO NO ATTACKING IT WITH YOUR HANDS! THE SNAIL SNAKE ALSO DEFENDS ITSELF BY HIDING IN ITS SHELL, A PIECE OF ITS ANATOMY IT USES TO IMPRESS THE OPPOSITE SEX. THE CAPTURE LEVEL OF THESE SLIMY SERPENTS DEPENDS ON THE SPECIMEN'S SIZE, WITH THE ONE FOUND INSIDE THE REGAL MAMMOTH BEING A CAPTURE LEVEL 4. SNAIL SNAKES UP TO CAPTURE LEVEL 20 HAVE BEEN FOUND IN THE WILD!

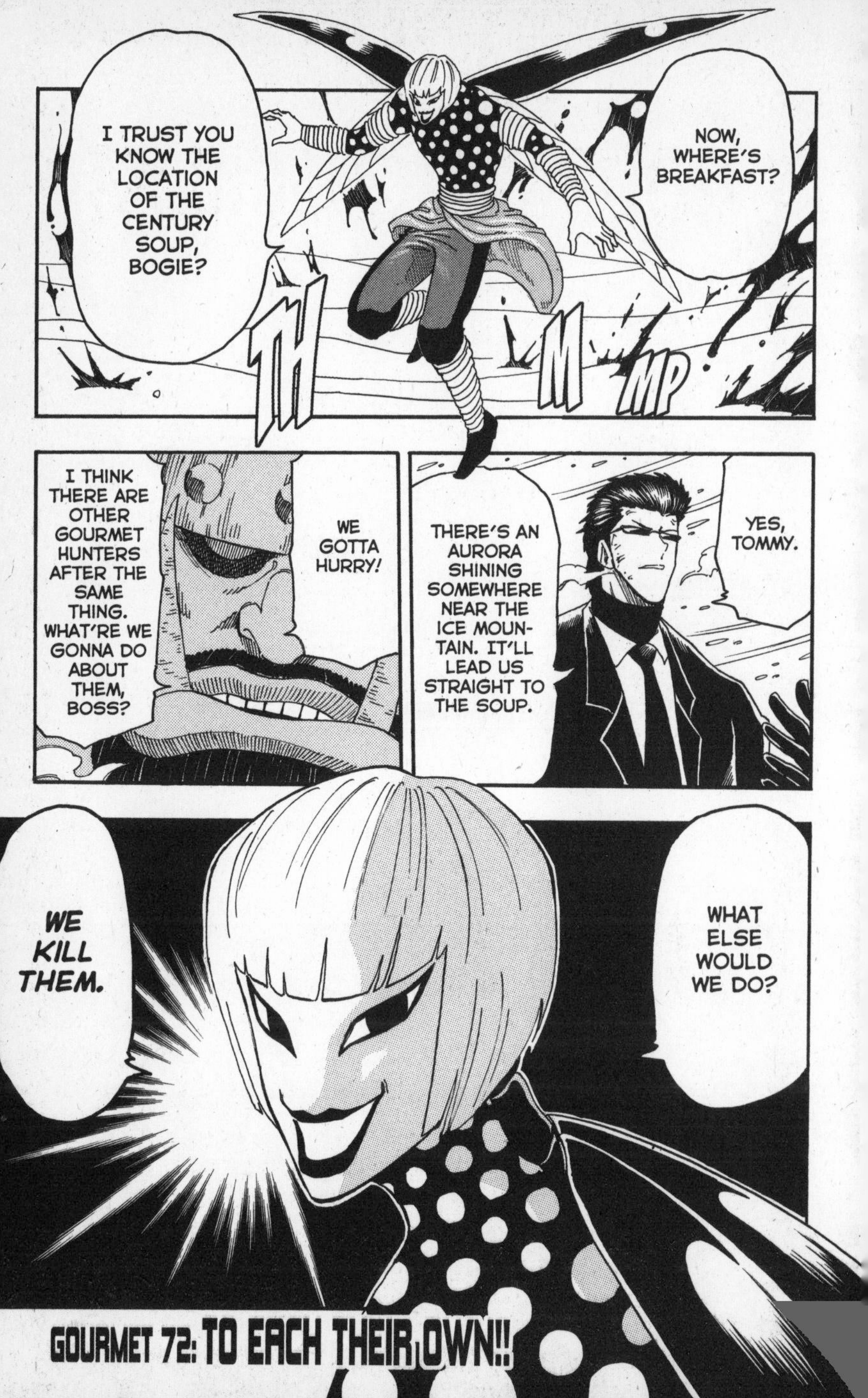
NOW, WHERE'S BREAKFAST?
I TRUST YOU KNOW THE LOCATION OF THE CENTURY SOUP, BOGIE?
THMMP
YES, TOMMY.
THERE'S AN AURORA SHINING SOMEWHERE NEAR THE ICE MOUNTAIN. IT'LL LEAD US STRAIGHT TO THE SOUP.
WE GOTTA HURRY!
I THINK THERE ARE OTHER GOURMET HUNTERS AFTER THE SAME THING. WHAT'RE WE GONNA DO ABOUT THEM, BOSS?
WHAT ELSE WOULD WE DO?
WE KILL THEM.

GOURMET 72: TO EACH THEIR OWN!!

GOURMET 72: TO EACH THEIR OWN!!

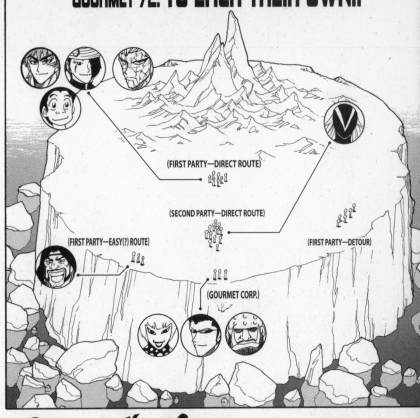

(FIRST PARTY—DIRECT ROUTE)

(SECOND PARTY—DIRECT ROUTE)

(FIRST PARTY—EASY(?) ROUTE)

(FIRST PARTY—DETOUR)

(GOURMET CORP.)

GNRRR

KRNZH

HOOO OO

HUFF

HUFF

HUFF

FIRST PARTY- DETOUR ROUTE

!!

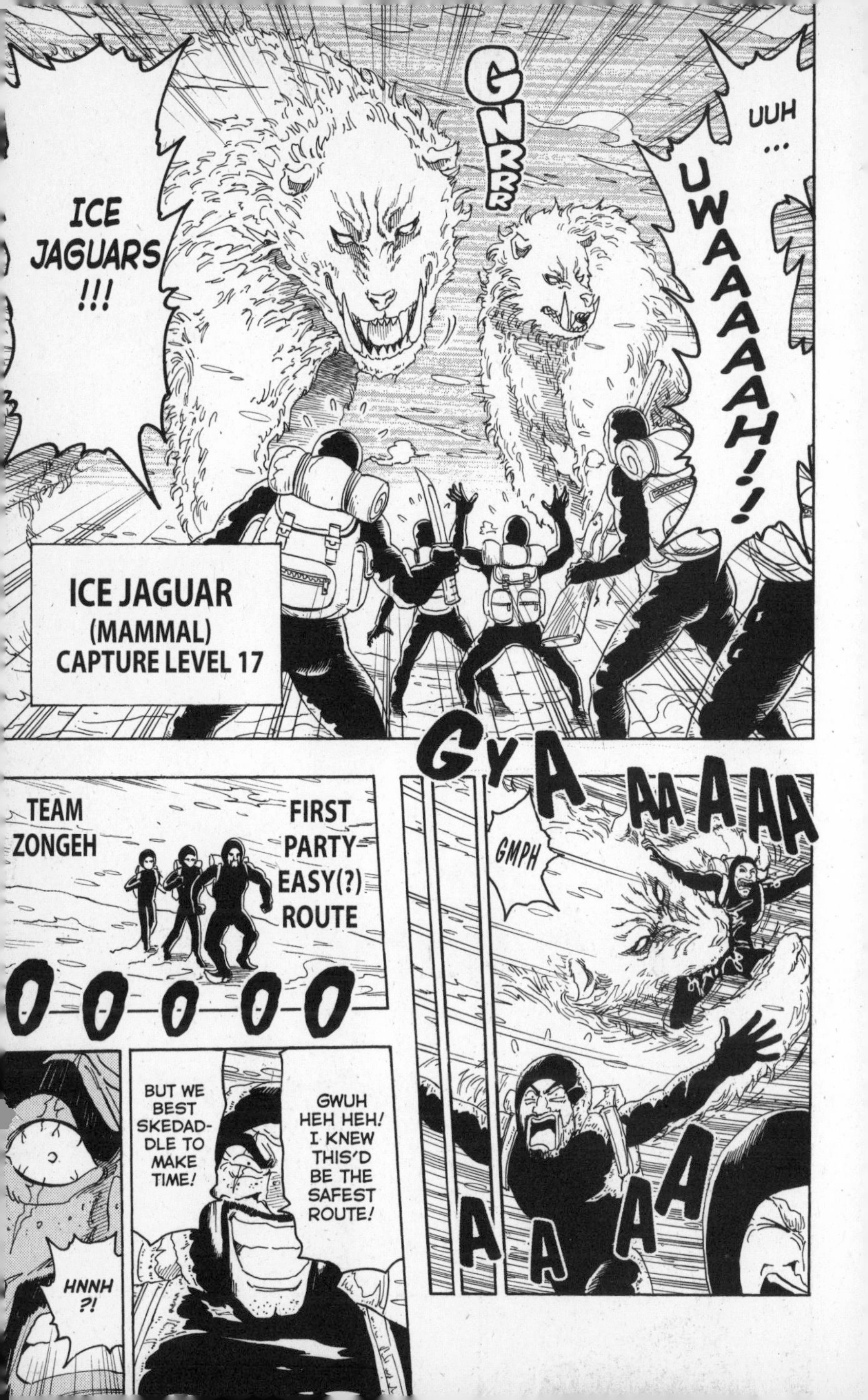
UUH ...
UWAAAAAH!!
GNRRR
ICE JAGUARS!!!
ICE JAGUAR
(MAMMAL)
CAPTURE LEVEL 17
GYAAAAAA
GMPH
AAAAA
FIRST PARTY EASY(?) ROUTE
TEAM ZONGEH
OOOOO
GWUH HEH HEH! I KNEW THIS'D BE THE SAFEST ROUTE!
BUT WE BEST SKEDADDLE TO MAKE TIME!
HNNH ?!

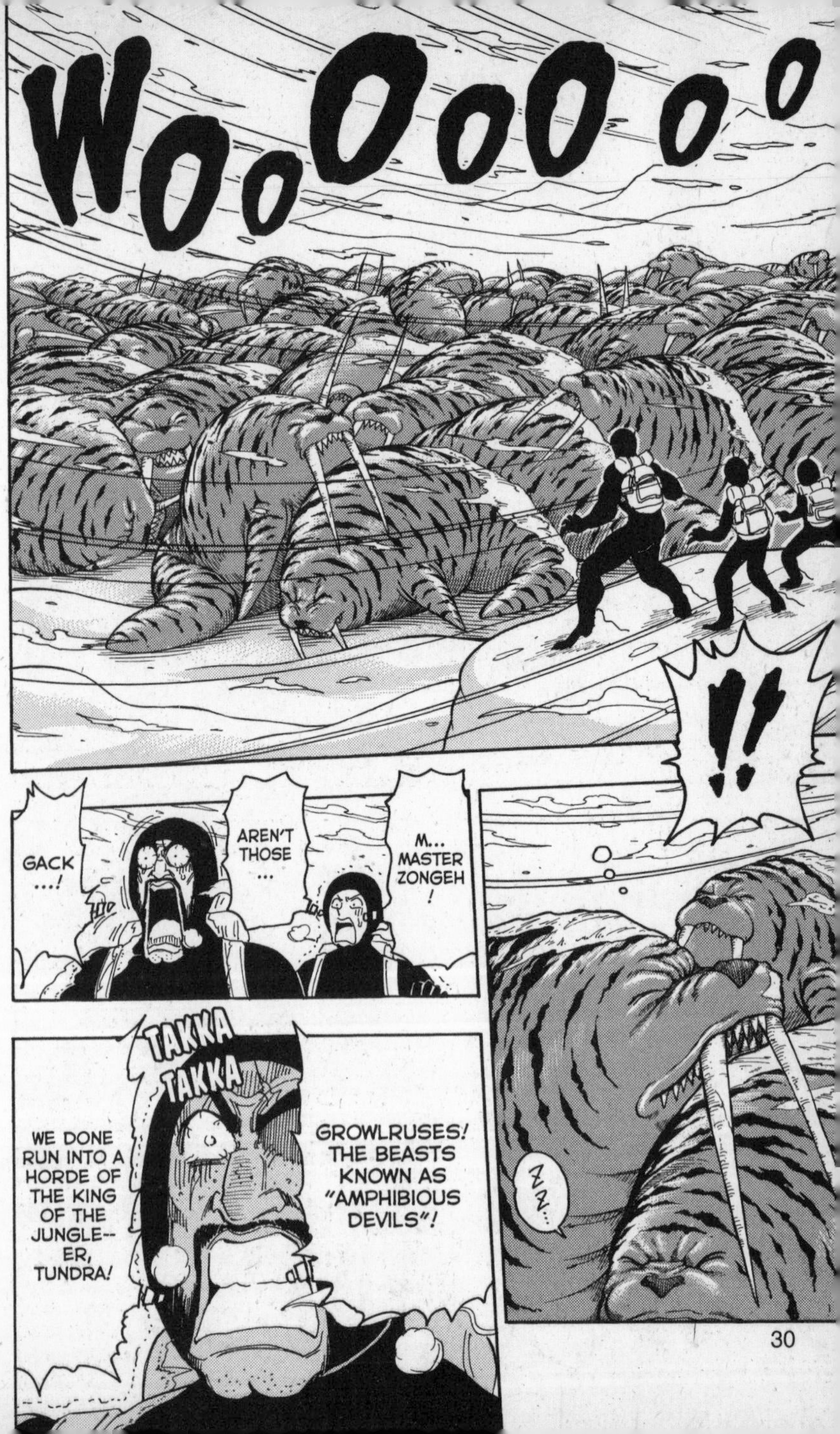
WOOOOOOO
!!
Z Z Z...
M... MASTER ZONGEH!
AREN'T THOSE...
GACK...!
TAKKA TAKKA
GROWLRUSES! THE BEASTS KNOWN AS "AMPHIBIOUS DEVILS"!
WE DONE RUN INTO A HORDE OF THE KING OF THE JUNGLE-- ER, TUNDRA!

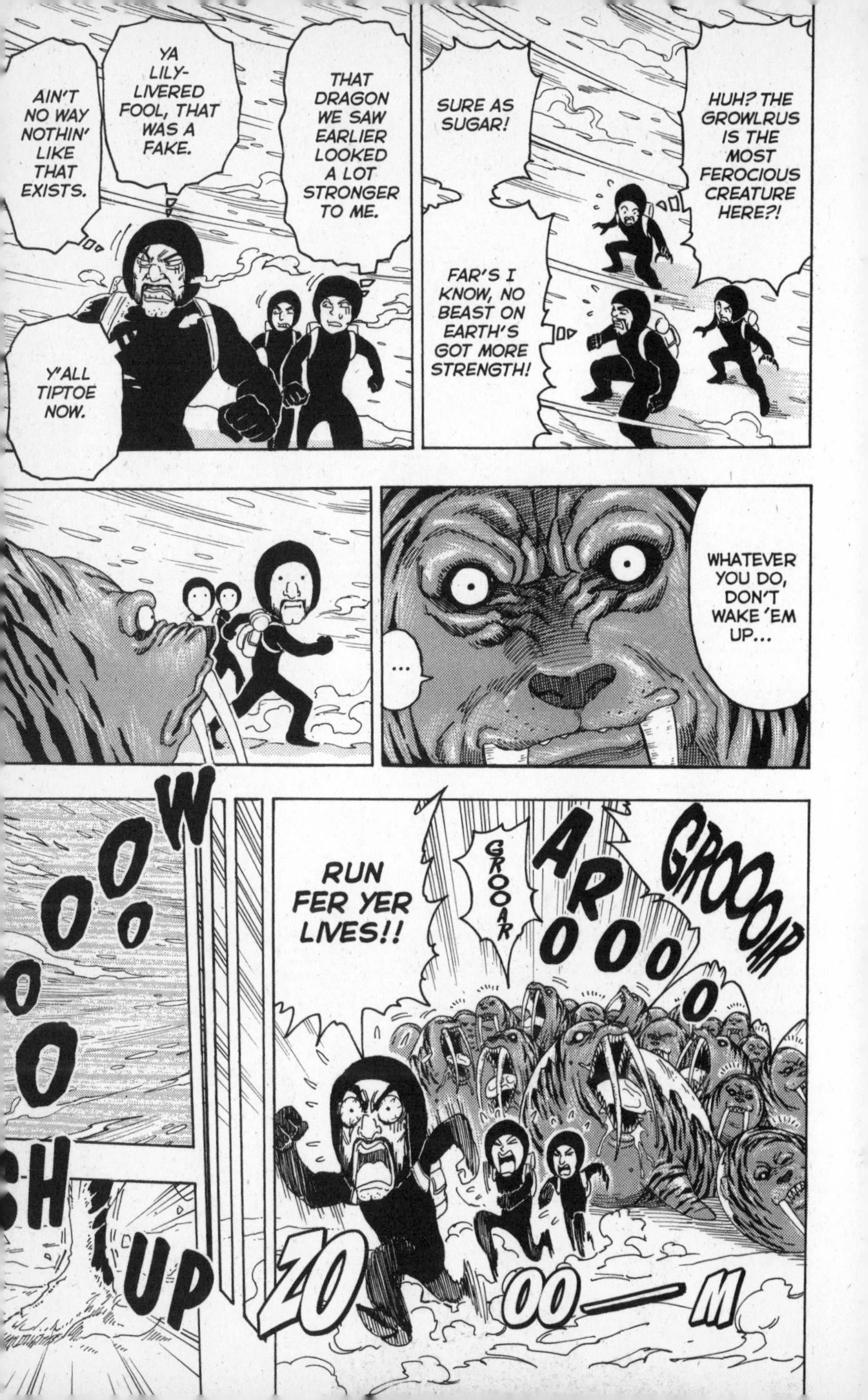
HUH? THE GROWLRUS IS THE MOST FEROCIOUS CREATURE HERE?!
SURE AS SUGAR!
FAR'S I KNOW, NO BEAST ON EARTH'S GOT MORE STRENGTH!
THAT DRAGON WE SAW EARLIER LOOKED A LOT STRONGER TO ME.
YA LILY-LIVERED FOOL, THAT WAS A FAKE.
AIN'T NO WAY NOTHIN' LIKE THAT EXISTS.
Y'ALL TIPTOE NOW.
WHATEVER YOU DO, DON'T WAKE 'EM UP...
...
GROOOOAR
AROOOO
GROOAR
RUN FER YER LIVES!!
ZOOO—M
WOOOOOOO
CH
UP

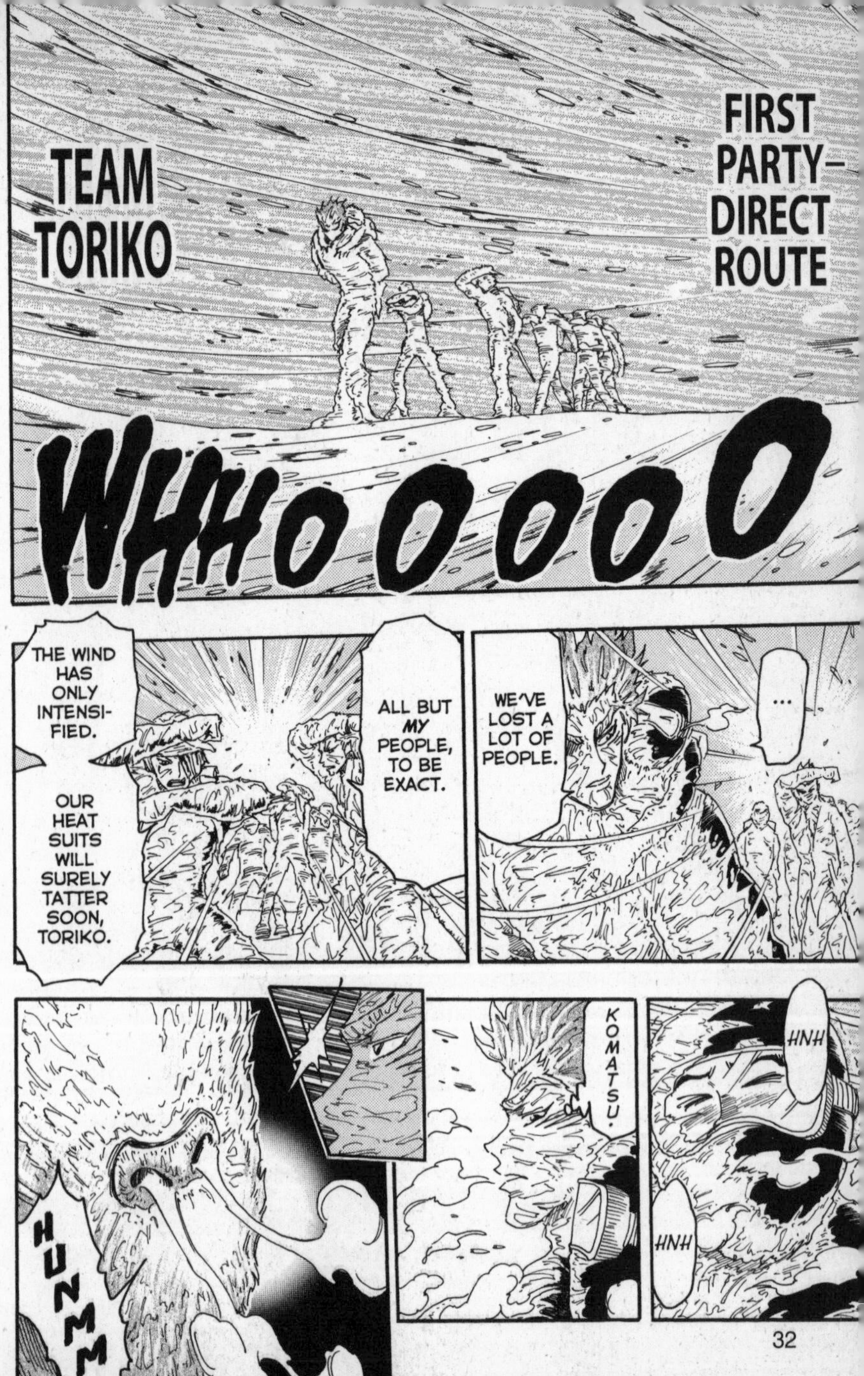
FIRST PARTY—DIRECT ROUTE
TEAM TORIKO
WHOOOOOO
...
WE'VE LOST A LOT OF PEOPLE.
ALL BUT *MY* PEOPLE, TO BE EXACT.
THE WIND HAS ONLY INTENSIFIED.
OUR HEAT SUITS WILL SURELY TATTER SOON, TORIKO.
HNH
HNH
KOMATSU.
HUNMM

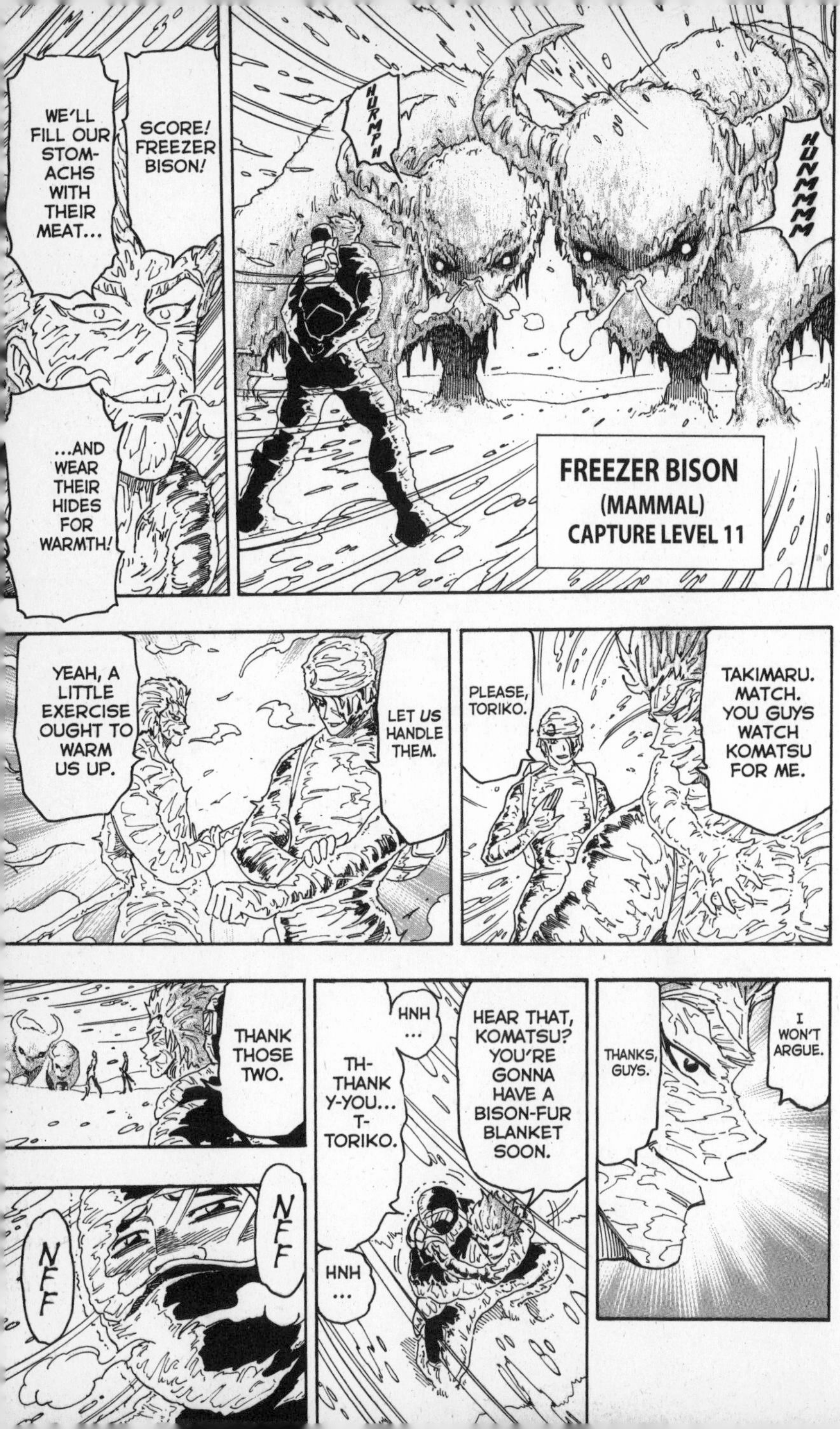
HURMPH
HUNMMMM
FREEZER BISON
(MAMMAL)
CAPTURE LEVEL 11
SCORE! FREEZER BISON!
WE'LL FILL OUR STOMACHS WITH THEIR MEAT...
...AND WEAR THEIR HIDES FOR WARMTH!
TAKIMARU. MATCH. YOU GUYS WATCH KOMATSU FOR ME.
PLEASE, TORIKO.
LET *US* HANDLE THEM.
YEAH, A LITTLE EXERCISE OUGHT TO WARM US UP.
I WON'T ARGUE.
THANKS, GUYS.
HEAR THAT, KOMATSU? YOU'RE GONNA HAVE A BISON-FUR BLANKET SOON.
HNH ...
TH-THANK Y-YOU... T-TORIKO.
HNH ...
THANK THOSE TWO.
NFF
NFF

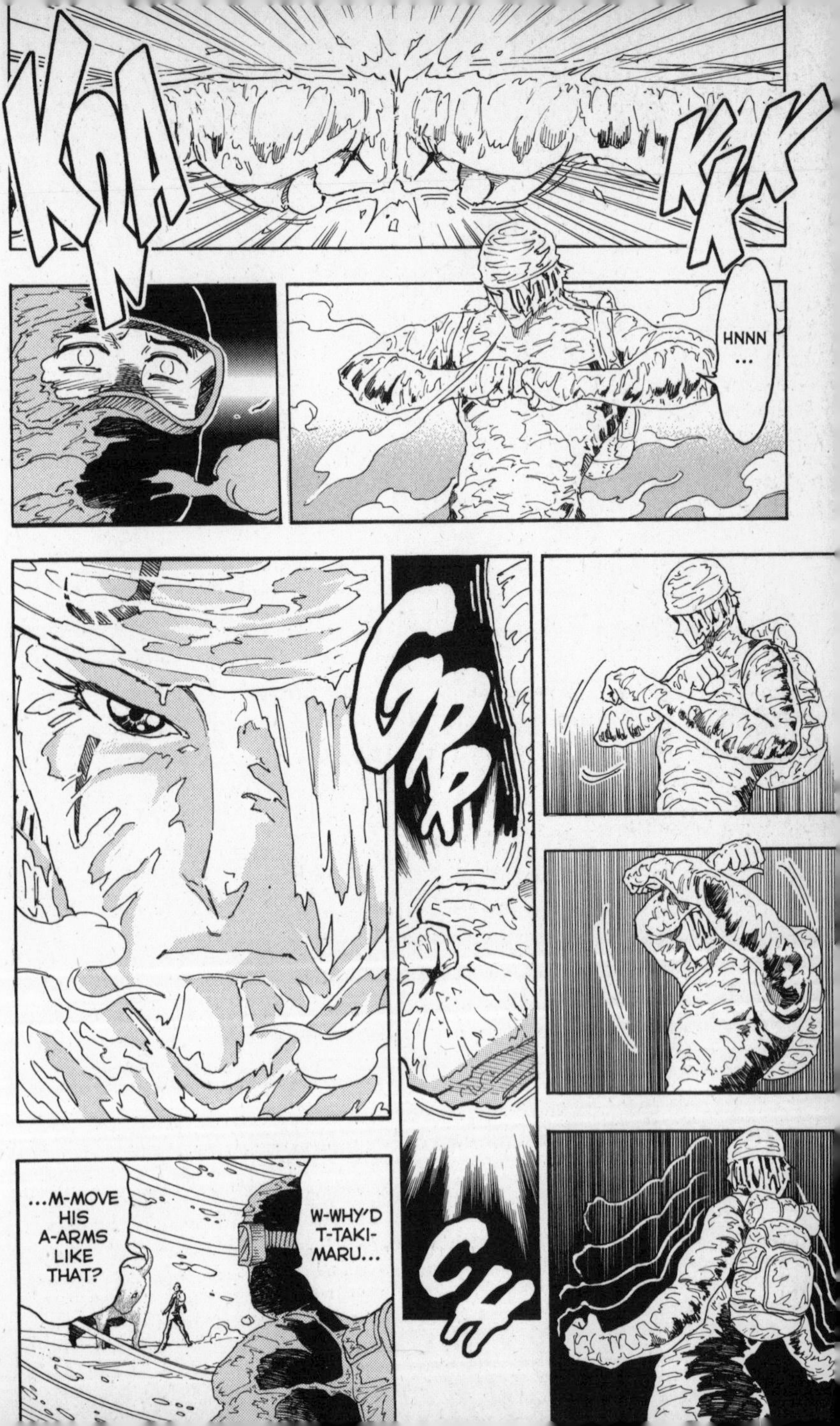
HNNN ...
W-WHY'D T-TAKI-MARU...
...M-MOVE HIS A-ARMS LIKE THAT?

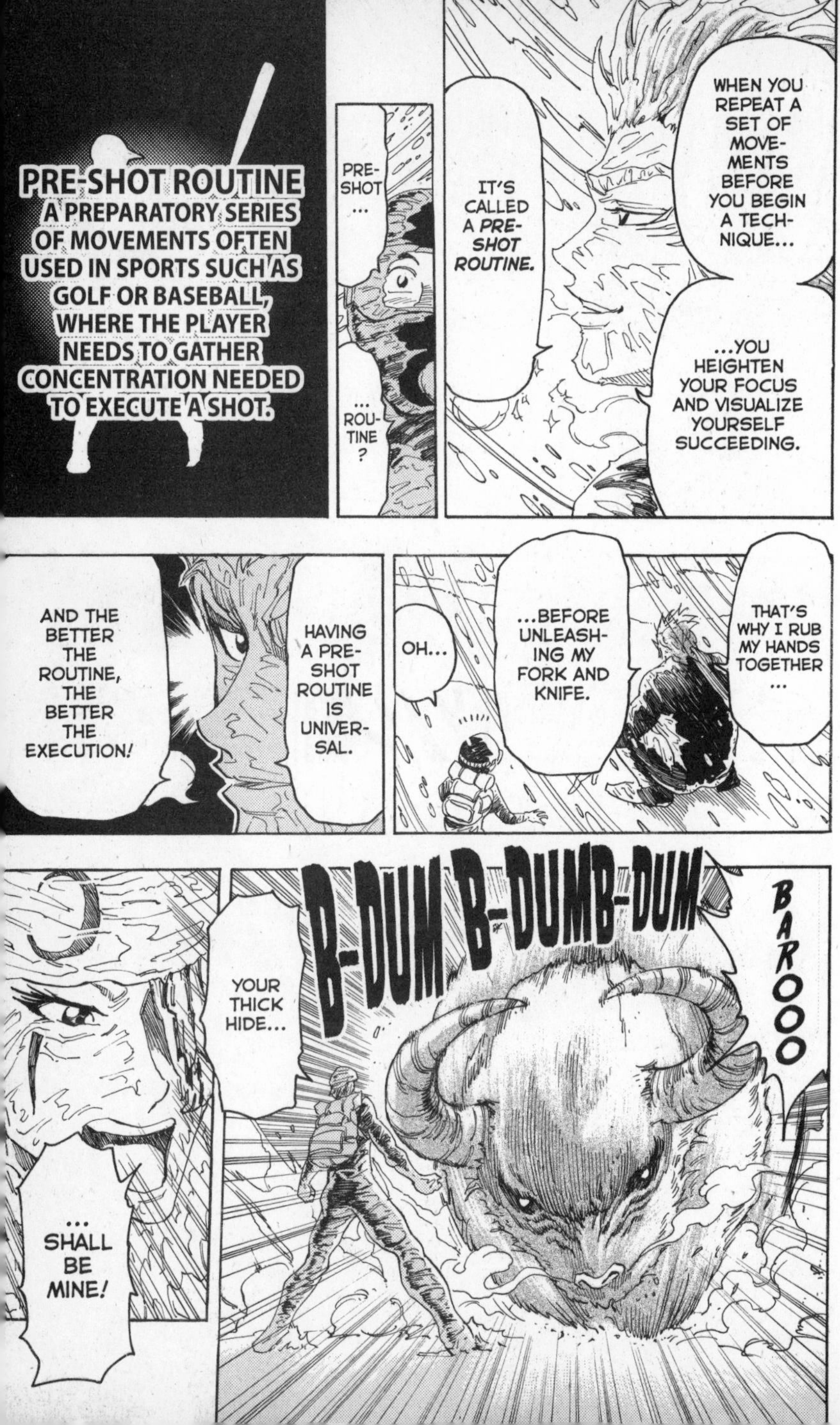
WHEN YOU REPEAT A SET OF MOVEMENTS BEFORE YOU BEGIN A TECHNIQUE...
...YOU HEIGHTEN YOUR FOCUS AND VISUALIZE YOURSELF SUCCEEDING.
IT'S CALLED A *PRE-SHOT ROUTINE.*
PRE-SHOT...
...ROUTINE?
PRE-SHOT ROUTINE
A PREPARATORY SERIES OF MOVEMENTS OFTEN USED IN SPORTS SUCH AS GOLF OR BASEBALL, WHERE THE PLAYER NEEDS TO GATHER CONCENTRATION NEEDED TO EXECUTE A SHOT.
THAT'S WHY I RUB MY HANDS TOGETHER...
...BEFORE UNLEASHING MY FORK AND KNIFE.
OH...
HAVING A PRE-SHOT ROUTINE IS UNIVERSAL.
AND THE BETTER THE ROUTINE, THE BETTER THE EXECUTION!
B-DUM B-DUMB-DUM
BAROOOO
YOUR THICK HIDE...
...SHALL BE MINE!

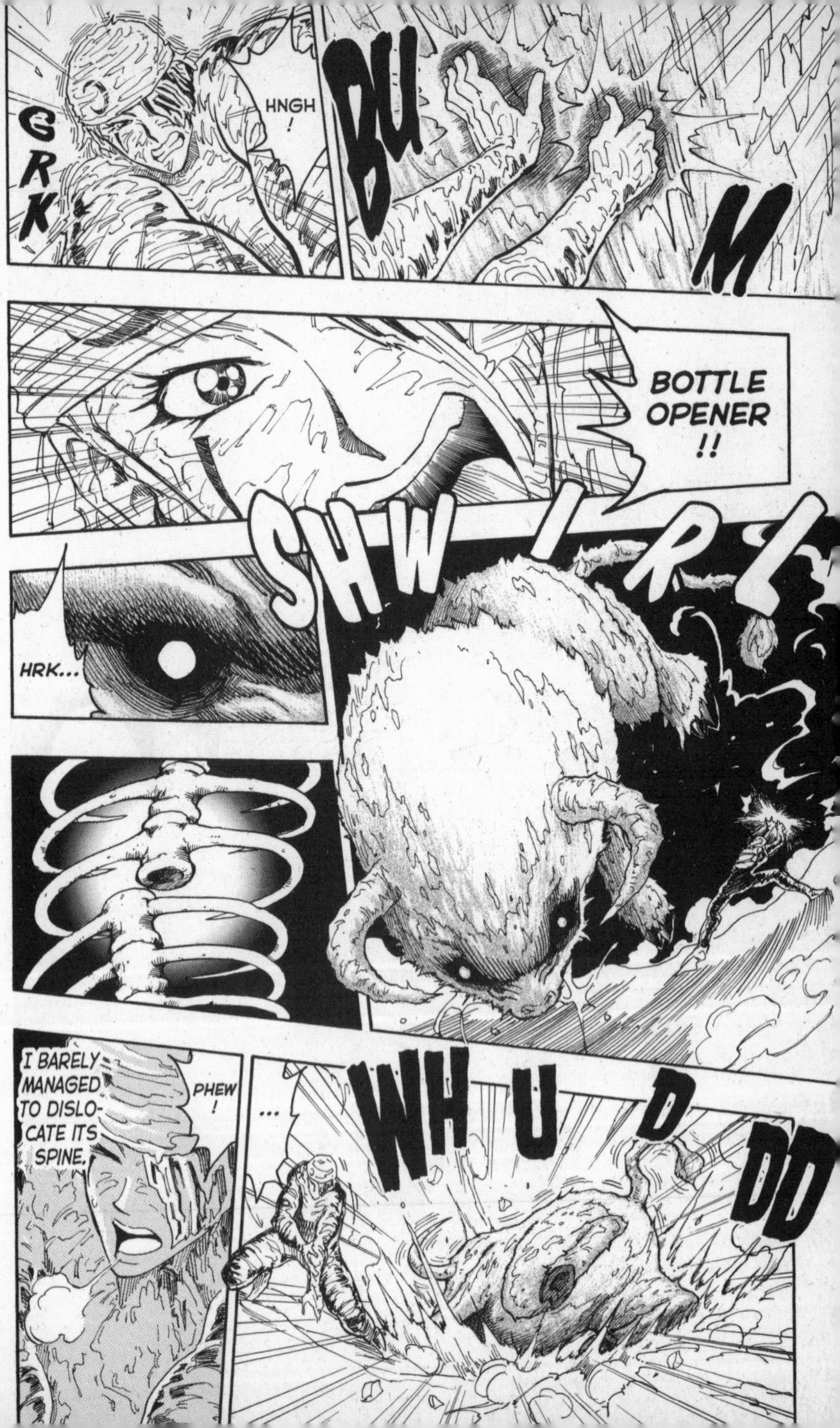
BUM
HNGH!
GRK
BOTTLE OPENER!!
SHWIRL
HRK...
WHUDDD
...
PHEW!
I BARELY MANAGED TO DISLOCATE ITS SPINE.

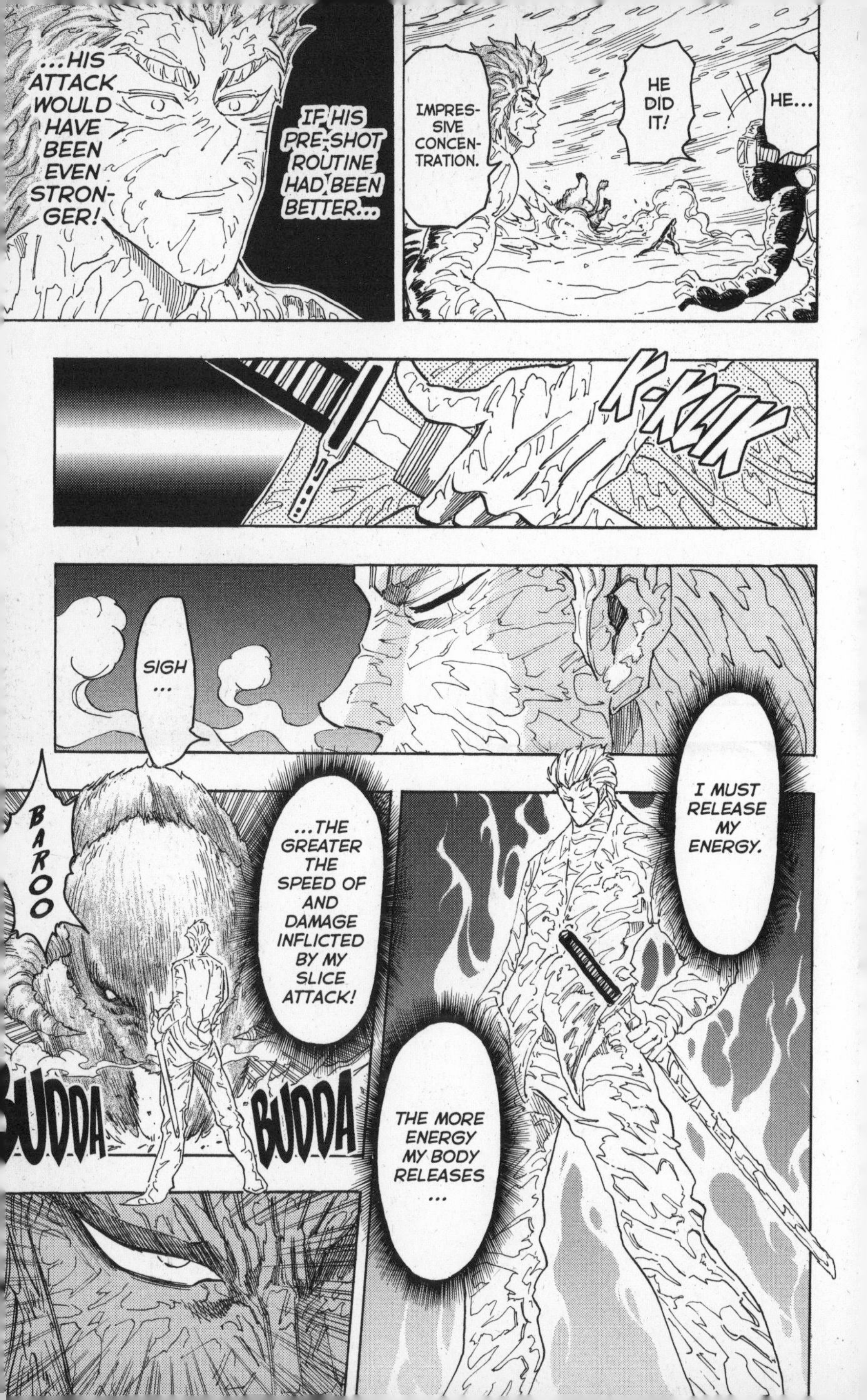
HE...
HE DID IT!
IMPRESSIVE CONCENTRATION.
IF HIS PRE-SHOT ROUTINE HAD BEEN BETTER...
...HIS ATTACK WOULD HAVE BEEN EVEN STRONGER!
K-KLIK
SIGH...
I MUST RELEASE MY ENERGY.
THE MORE ENERGY MY BODY RELEASES...
...THE GREATER THE SPEED OF AND DAMAGE INFLICTED BY MY SLICE ATTACK!
BAROO
BUDDA
BUDDA

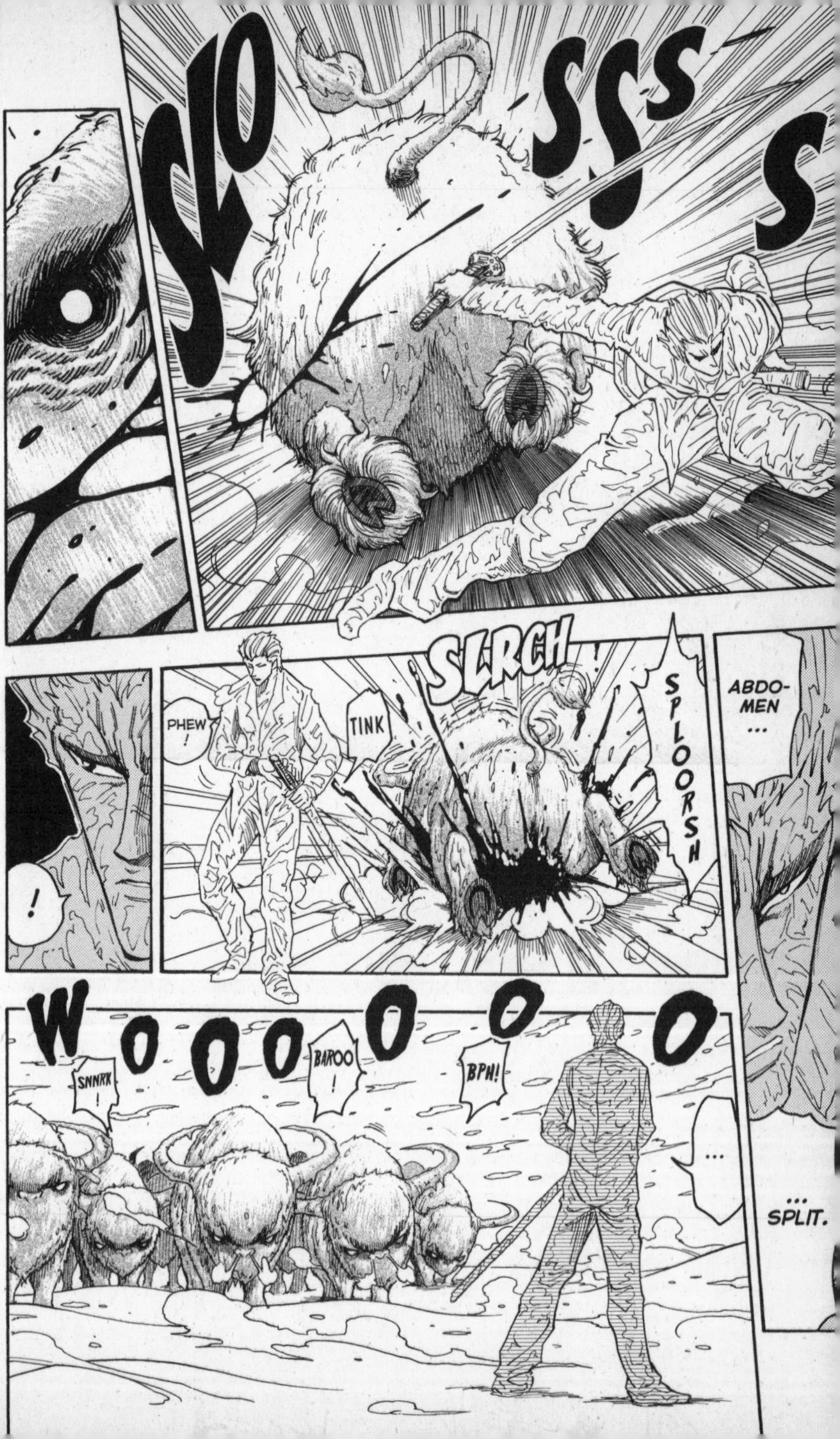
SCLOSSS-S
ABDO-MEN...
...SPLIT.
SLRCH
SPLOORSH
TINK
PHEW!
!
WOOOOOOO
...
BPH!
BAROO!
SNNRK!

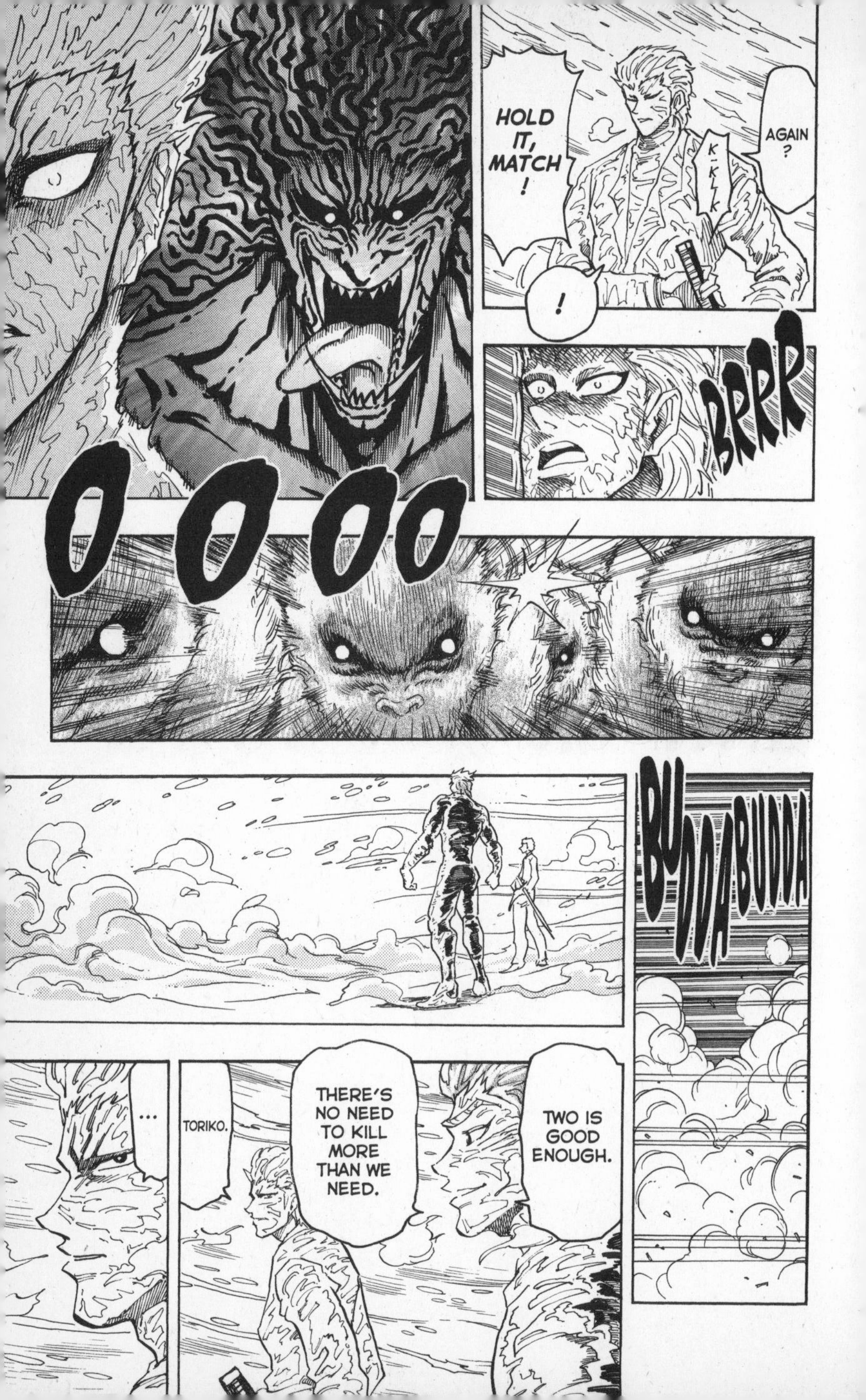
AGAIN?
K-K-K
HOLD IT, MATCH!
!
BRRR
OOOO
BUDDABUDDA
TWO IS GOOD ENOUGH.
THERE'S NO NEED TO KILL MORE THAN WE NEED.
TORIKO.
...

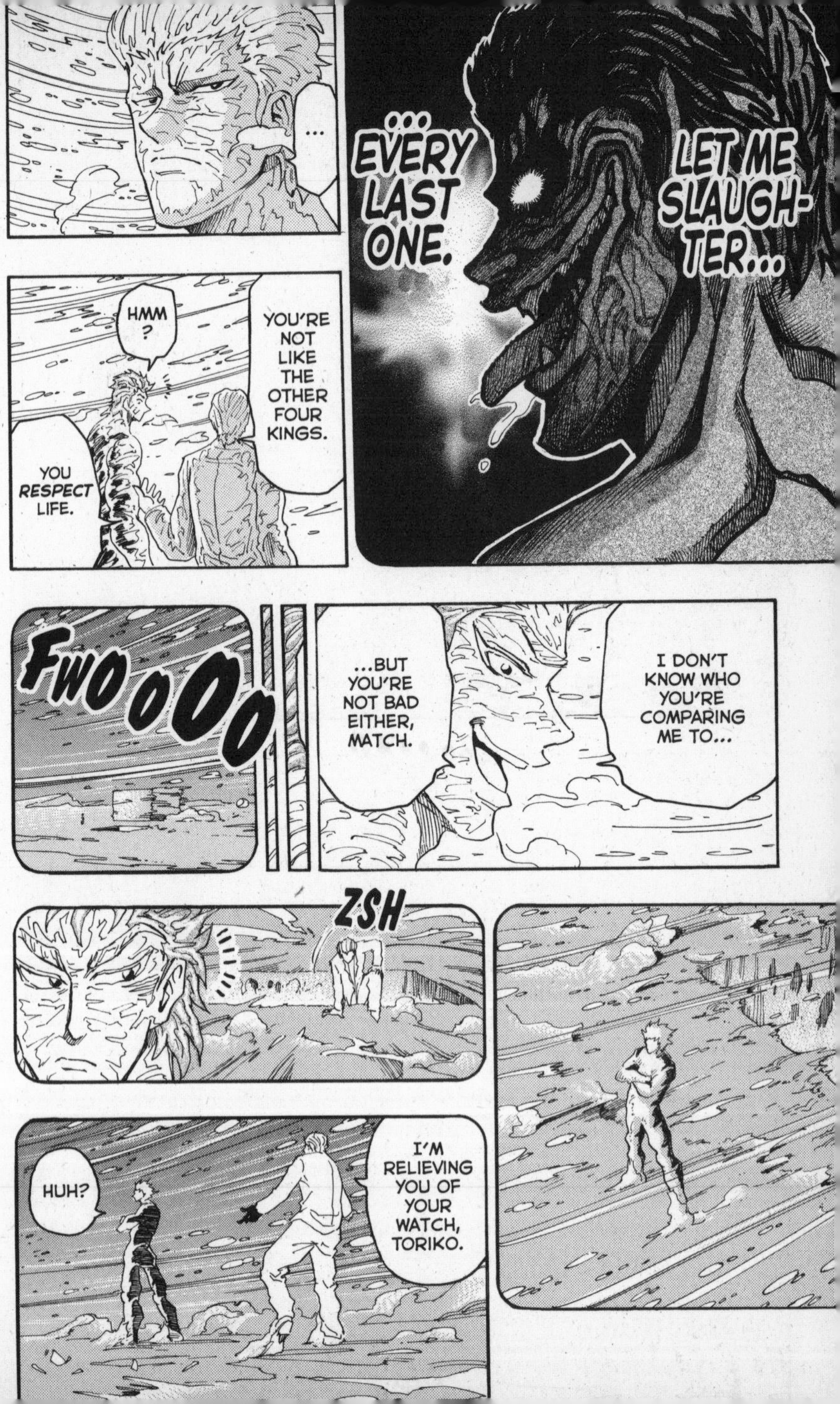
LET ME SLAUGHTER...
...EVERY LAST ONE.
...
YOU'RE NOT LIKE THE OTHER FOUR KINGS.
HMM?
YOU RESPECT LIFE.
I DON'T KNOW WHO YOU'RE COMPARING ME TO...
...BUT YOU'RE NOT BAD EITHER, MATCH.
FWOOOOO
ZSH
I'M RELIEVING YOU OF YOUR WATCH, TORIKO.
HUH?

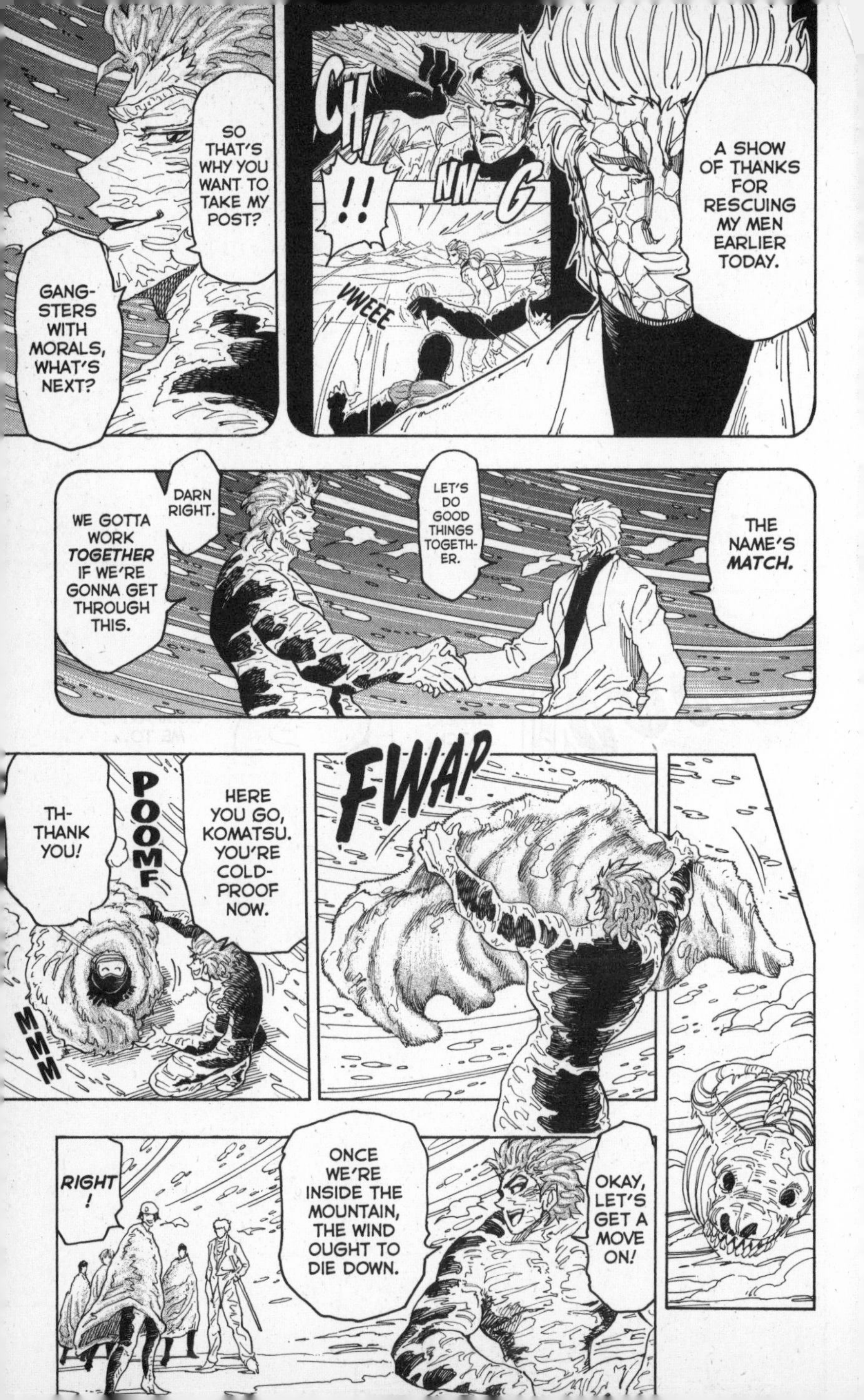
A SHOW OF THANKS FOR RESCUING MY MEN EARLIER TODAY.
CHINNG
!!
VWEEE
SO THAT'S WHY YOU WANT TO TAKE MY POST?
GANG-STERS WITH MORALS, WHAT'S NEXT?
THE NAME'S *MATCH.*
LET'S DO GOOD THINGS TOGETH-ER.
DARN RIGHT.
WE GOTTA WORK *TOGETHER* IF WE'RE GONNA GET THROUGH THIS.
FWAP
HERE YOU GO, KOMATSU. YOU'RE COLD-PROOF NOW.
POOMF
TH-THANK YOU!
MMM
OKAY, LET'S GET A MOVE ON!
ONCE WE'RE INSIDE THE MOUNTAIN, THE WIND OUGHT TO DIE DOWN.
RIGHT!

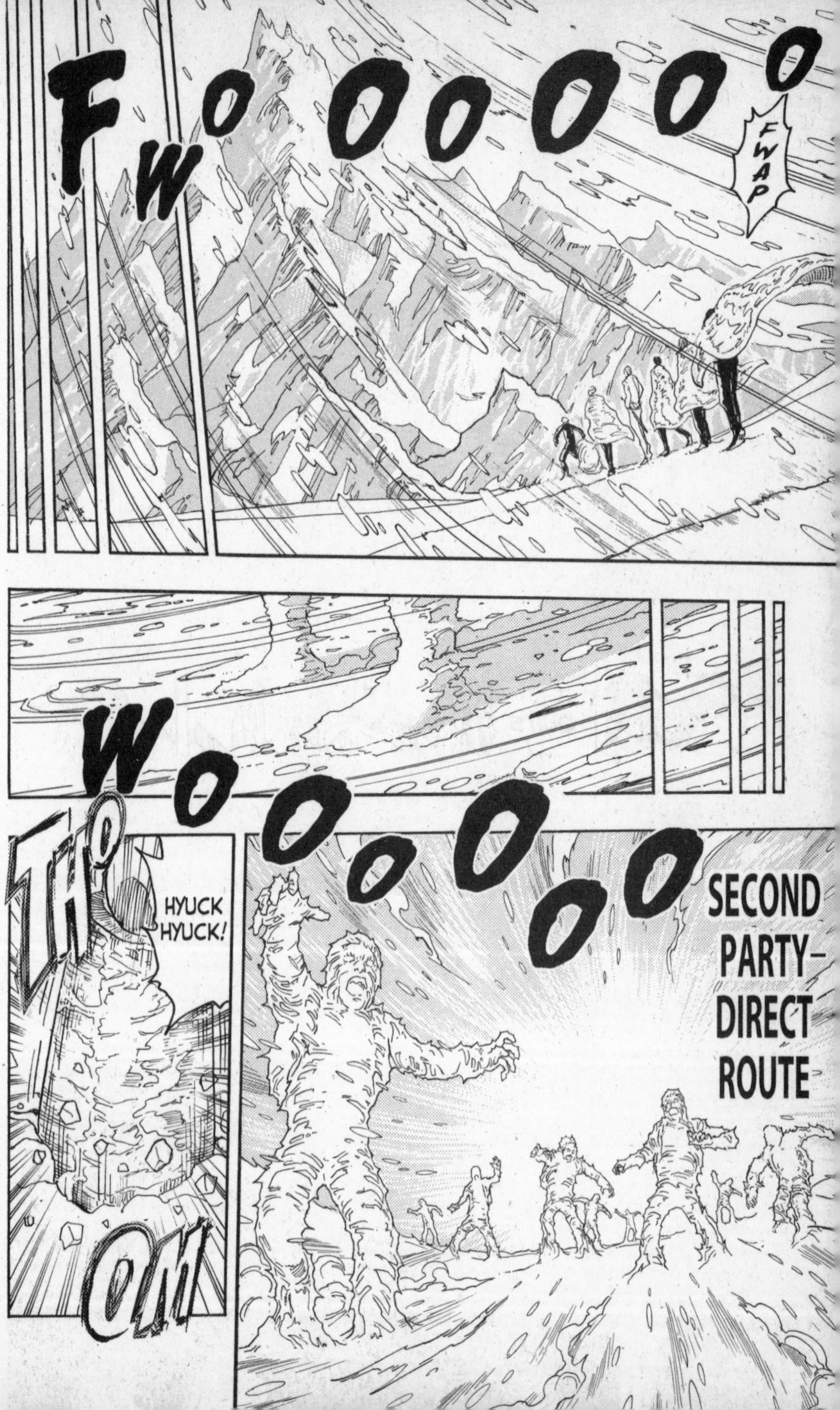
FWOOOOOO
FWAP
WOOOOOOOOO
SECOND PARTY—DIRECT ROUTE
THOOM
HYUCK HYUCK!

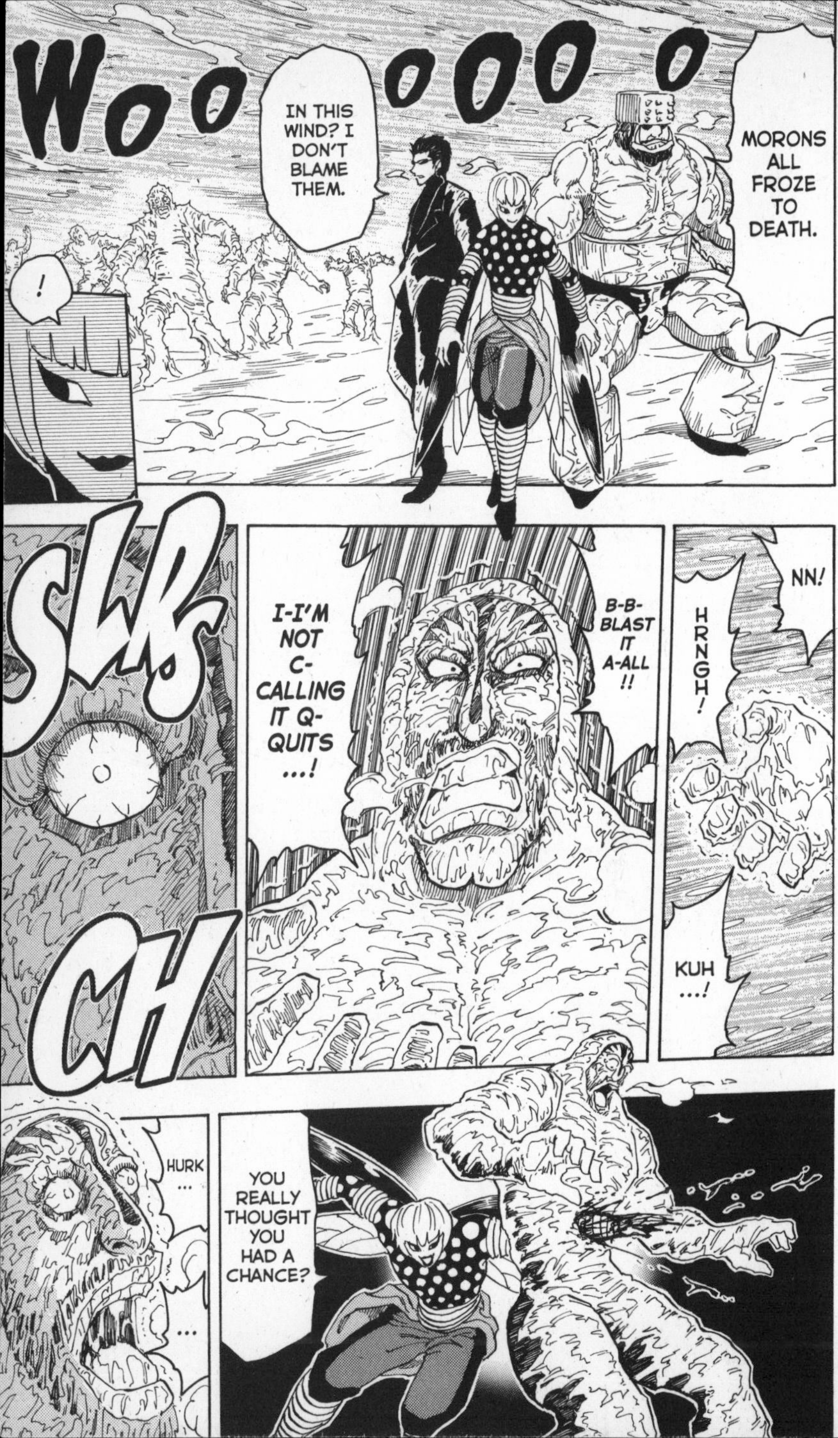
MORONS ALL FROZE TO DEATH.
IN THIS WIND? I DON'T BLAME THEM.
WOOOOOOO
!
NN!
HRNGH!
KUH ...!
B-B-BLAST IT A-ALL !!
I-I'M NOT C-CALLING IT Q-QUITS ...!
SLRSCH
YOU REALLY THOUGHT YOU HAD A CHANCE?
HURK ...
...

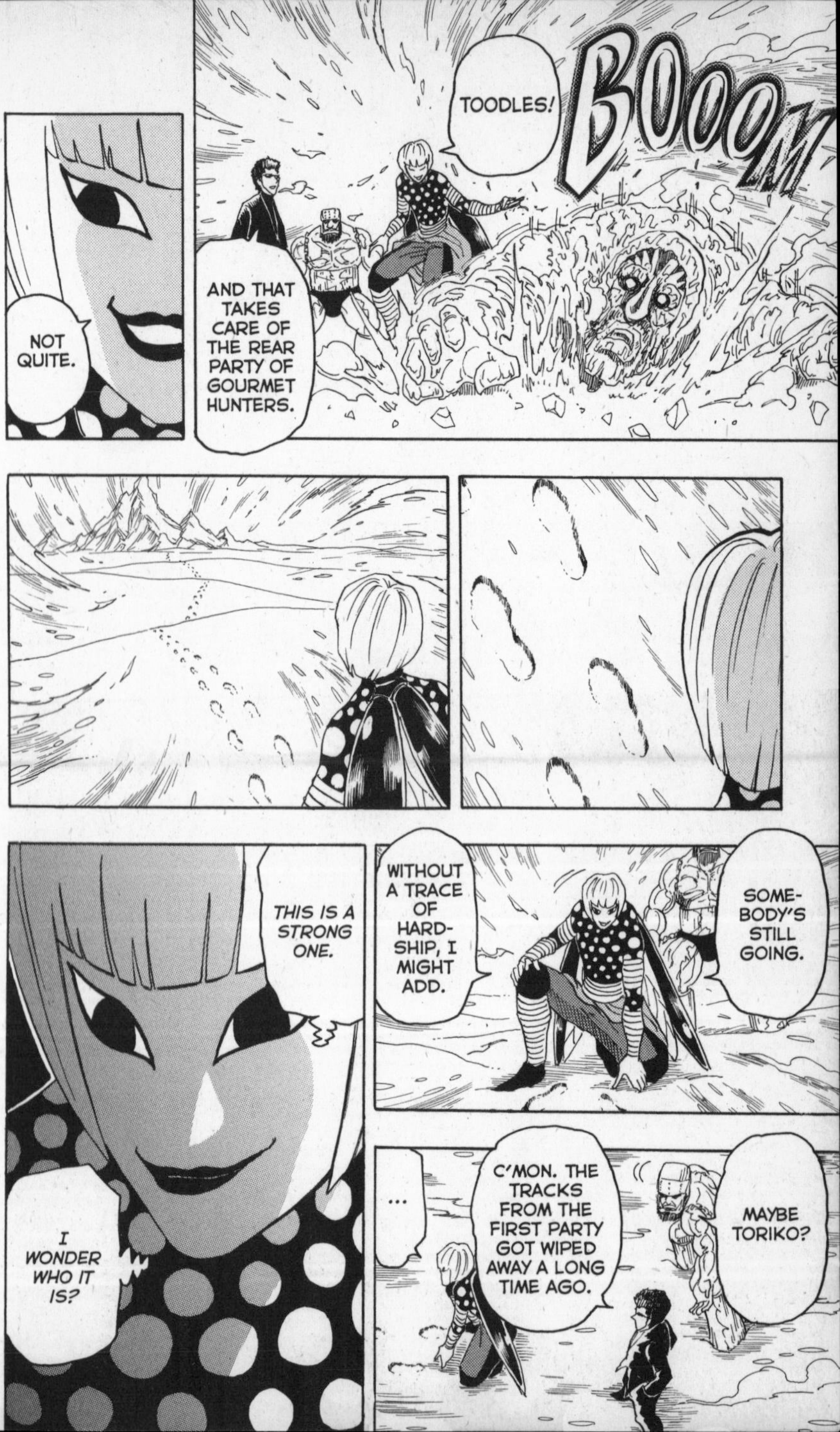
TOODLES!
BOOOOM
AND THAT TAKES CARE OF THE REAR PARTY OF GOURMET HUNTERS.
NOT QUITE.
SOME-BODY'S STILL GOING.
WITHOUT A TRACE OF HARD-SHIP, I MIGHT ADD.
MAYBE TORIKO?
C'MON. THE TRACKS FROM THE FIRST PARTY GOT WIPED AWAY A LONG TIME AGO.
...
THIS IS A STRONG ONE.
I WONDER WHO IT IS?

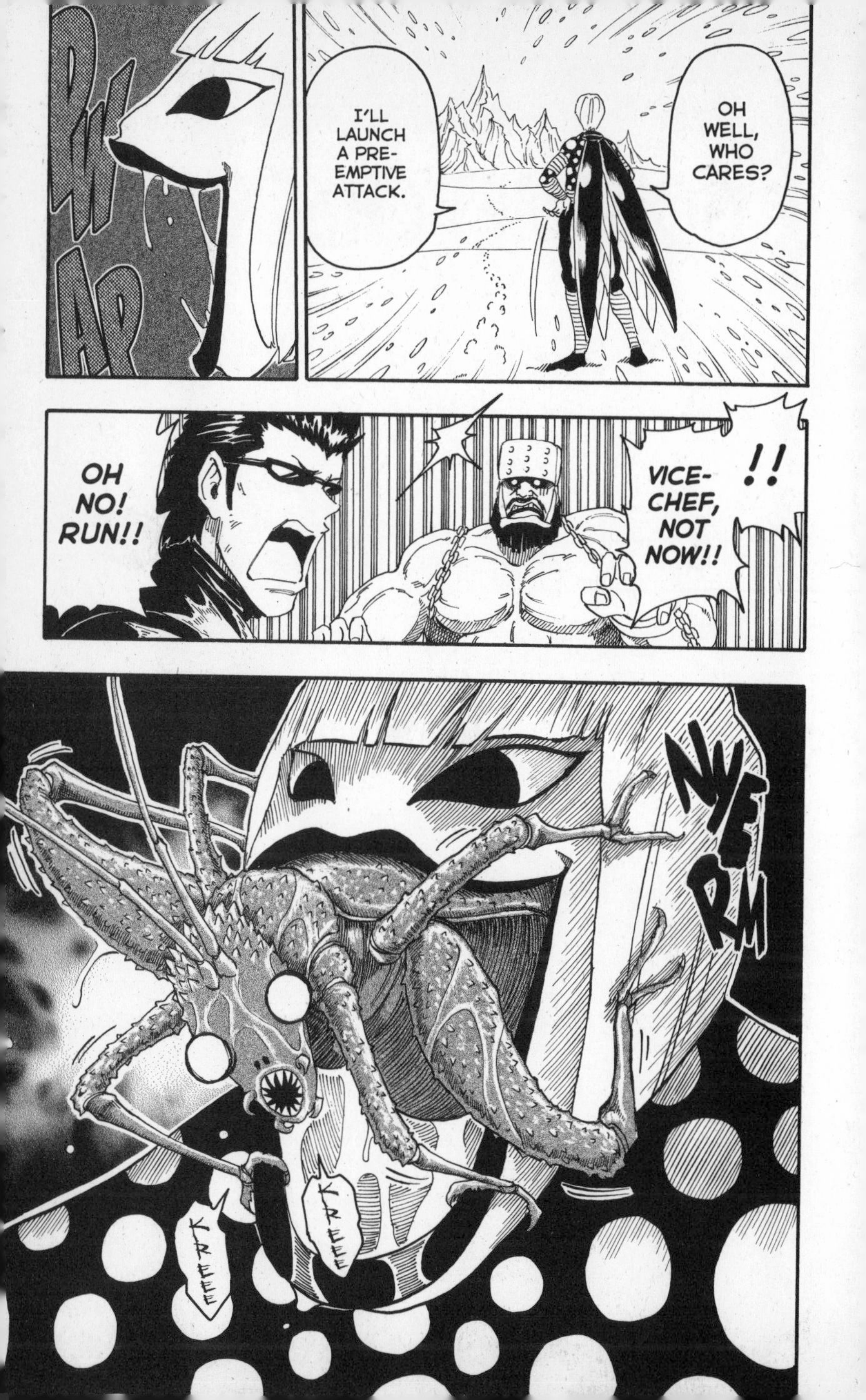
OH WELL, WHO CARES?
I'LL LAUNCH A PRE-EMPTIVE ATTACK.
BWAP
!!
VICE-CHEF, NOT NOW!!
OH NO! RUN!!
NYERM
KREEE
KREEE

TORIKO

GOURMET CHECKLIST

Vol. 063

REGAL MAMMOTH

(MAMMAL)

CAPTURE LEVEL: 48

HABITAT: REGAL ISLE (ACCORDING TO RUMOR, SOME LIVE IN THE WILD)

LENGTH: 1,500 METERS

HEIGHT: 1,000 METERS

WEIGHT: APPROX. 50,000,000 KG

PRICE: 100 G / 5,000,000 YEN (JEWEL MEAT); 100 G / 150,000 YEN (NORMAL MEAT)

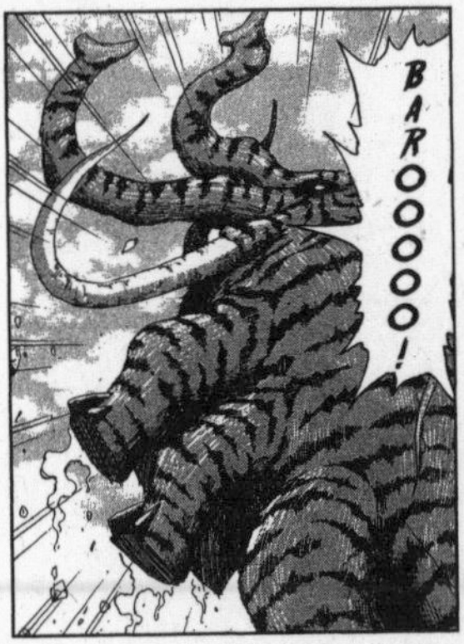
BAROOOOOO!

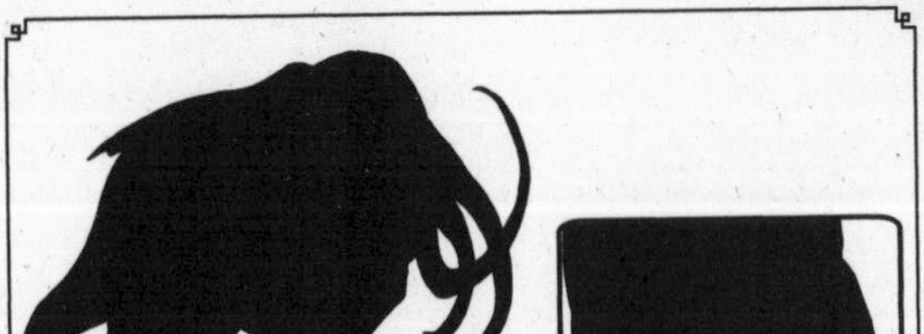

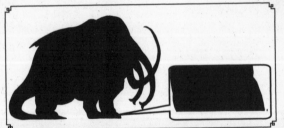

SCALE

AN ANCIENT SPECIES OF MAMMOTH THAT GROWS MIND-BOGGLINGLY FAST, REACHING A LENGTH OF 50 METERS JUST A FEW WEEKS AFTER BEING BORN (AND IT'S ROUGHLY 10 METERS AT BIRTH). THE SPECIES IS NOT PROLIFIC, BUT A REGAL MAMMOTH CAN LIVE UP TO 500 YEARS, DURING WHICH IT NEVER STOPS GROWING. THE MAMMOTH'S CAPTURE LEVEL IS PROPORTIONATE TO ITS SIZE. EACH CONTAINS WITHIN ITS BODY "JEWEL MEAT"--A CHUNK OF FLESH THAT COMBINES FLAVORS FROM EVERY OTHER CUT OF MEAT IN ITS BODY. HOWEVER, THE LOCATION OF SAID JEWEL MEAT DIFFERS FROM ONE MAMMOTH TO ANOTHER, MAKING IT VERY HARD TO FIND. THIS LUXURY FOOD HAS BEEN HIGHLY VALUED THROUGHOUT HUMAN HISTORY. IN ANCIENT TIMES IT WAS THE CENTERPIECE OF GRAND FEASTS, AND THEY SAY THAT BECAUSE OF ITS JEWEL-LIKE GLITTER, IT COULD DOUBLE AS A WEDDING RING. IN ORDER TO WIN OVER A WOMAN, A MAN WOULD PRESENT JEWEL MEAT TO HER TO PROVE HIS STRENGTH. EVEN NOW, IT IS A JEWEL THAT ONLY THE BRAVEST AND STRONGEST CAN PROCURE.

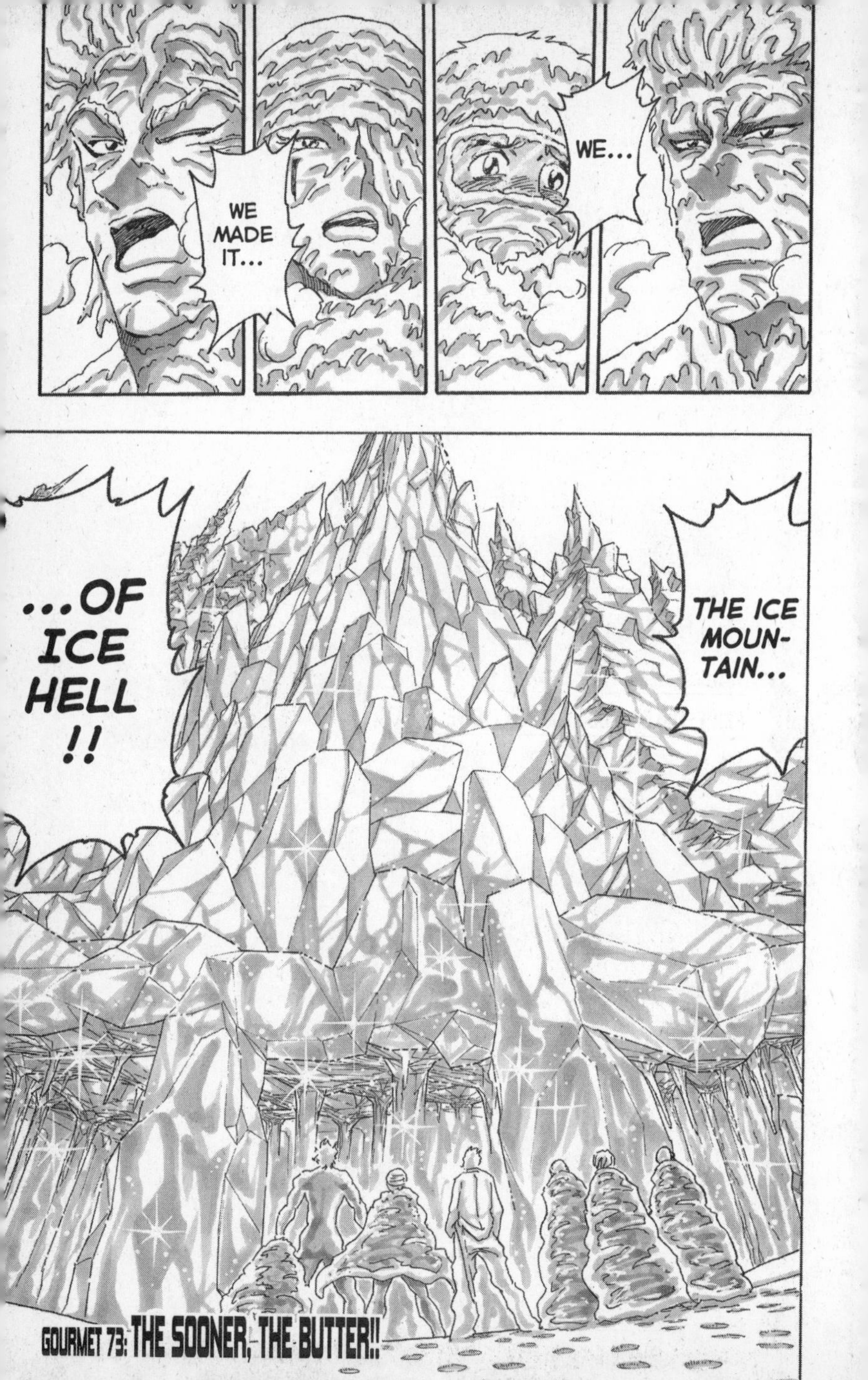
WE...
WE MADE IT...
THE ICE MOUN-TAIN...
...OF ICE HELL!!
GOURMET 73: THE SOONER, THE BUTTER!!

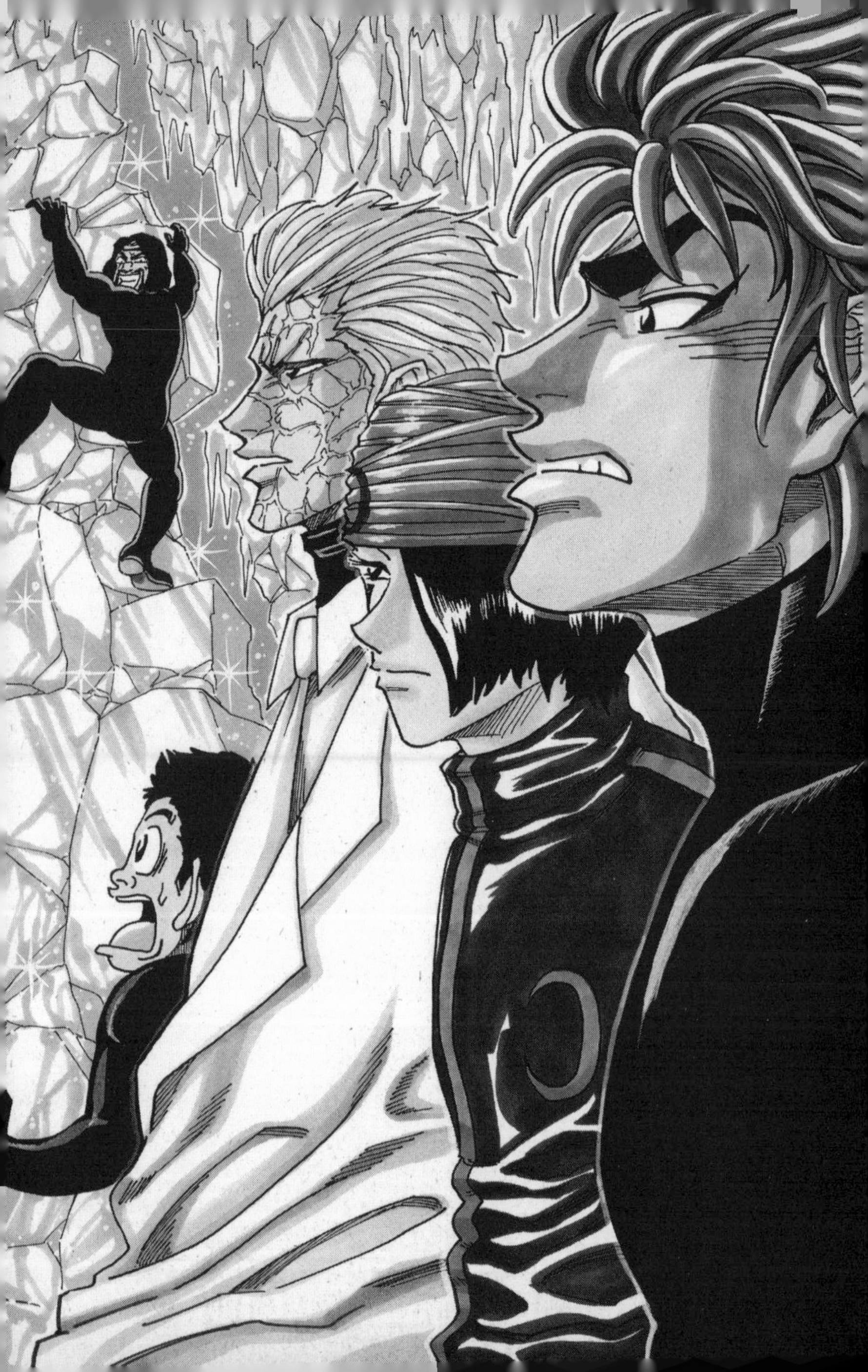

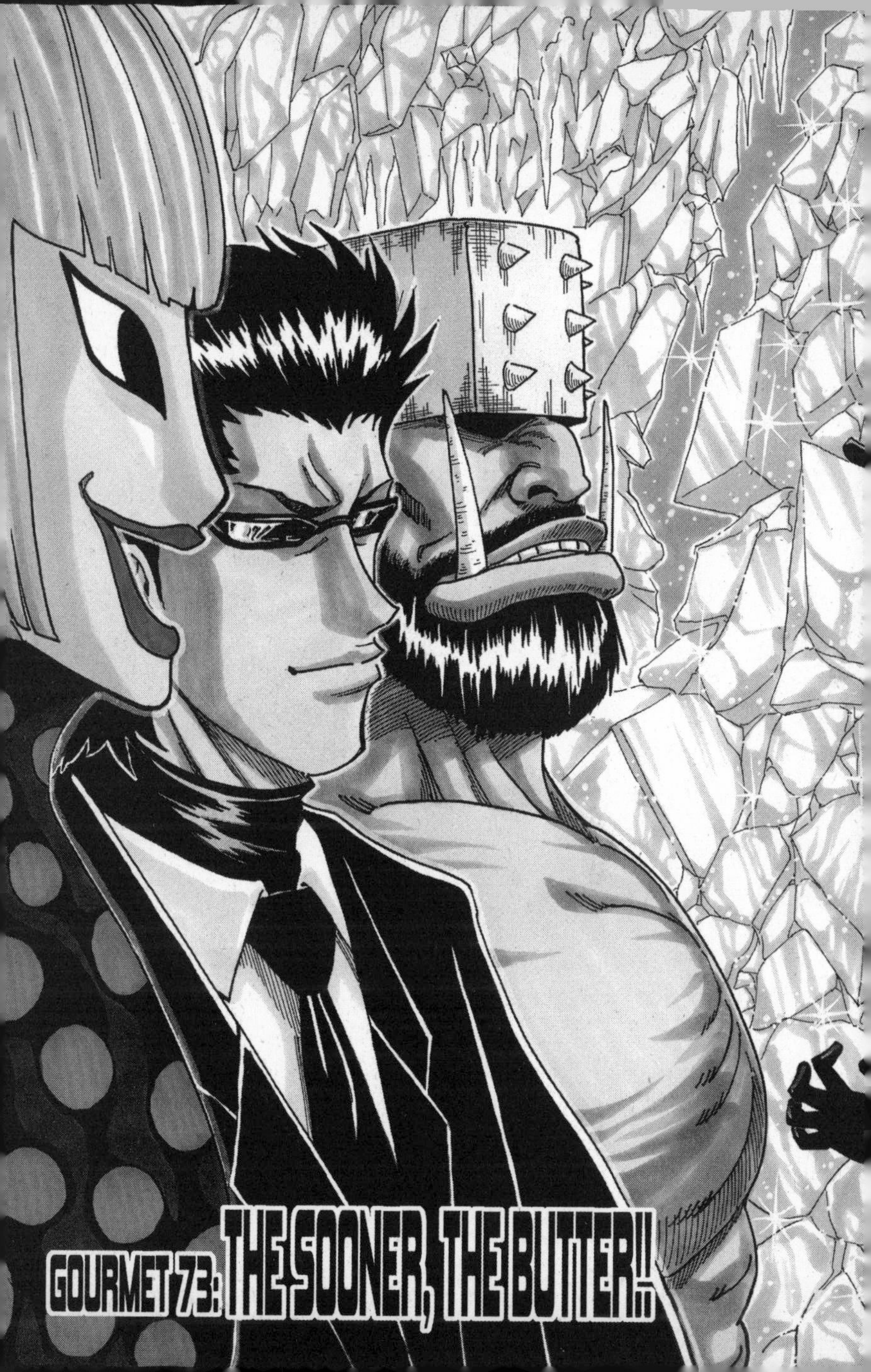
GOURMET 73: THE SOONER, THE BUTTER!!

TORIKO

GOURMET CHECKLIST

Vol. 064
MEGA OCTOPUS
(MOLLUSK)

CAPTURE LEVEL: 25

HABITAT: LAND AND WATER

LENGTH: ---

HEIGHT: 18 METERS

WEIGHT: 12 TONS

PRICE: 100 G / 1,200 YEN

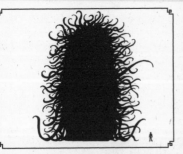

SCALE

A MOLLUSK SPORTING TENS OF THOUSANDS OF ELASTIC TENTACLES. MEGA OCTOPI
TYPICALLY LIVE UNDER THE SHELTER OF ROCKS IN THE SEA AND USE THEIR MANY
APPENDAGES TO SURPRISE AND CAPTURE THEIR PREY. THEY ALSO HAVE RESPIRATORY
ORGANS ENABLING THEM TO LIVE ON LAND, WHERE THEY HUNT BY MIMICKING
OTHER ORGANISMS AND LYING IN WAIT. THE MEGA OCTOPUS THAT SUNNY BATTLED
WAS MIMICKING ONE OF THE REGAL MAMMOTH'S INTERNAL ORGANS WHEN IT WAS
CAPTURED BY CEDRE AND FORCED TO BATTLE (NORMALLY, THEY ARE NOT SO VIOLENT
AND AGGRESSIVE). MEGA OCTOPI TASTE UNIQUE AND FLAVORFUL, AND WITH ONE
TENTACLE YIELDING ROUGHLY 300 OCTOPUS DUMPLINGS, JUST ONE MEGA OCTOPUS
COULD SUPPLY A MAJOR RESTAURANT CHAIN FOR A YEAR.

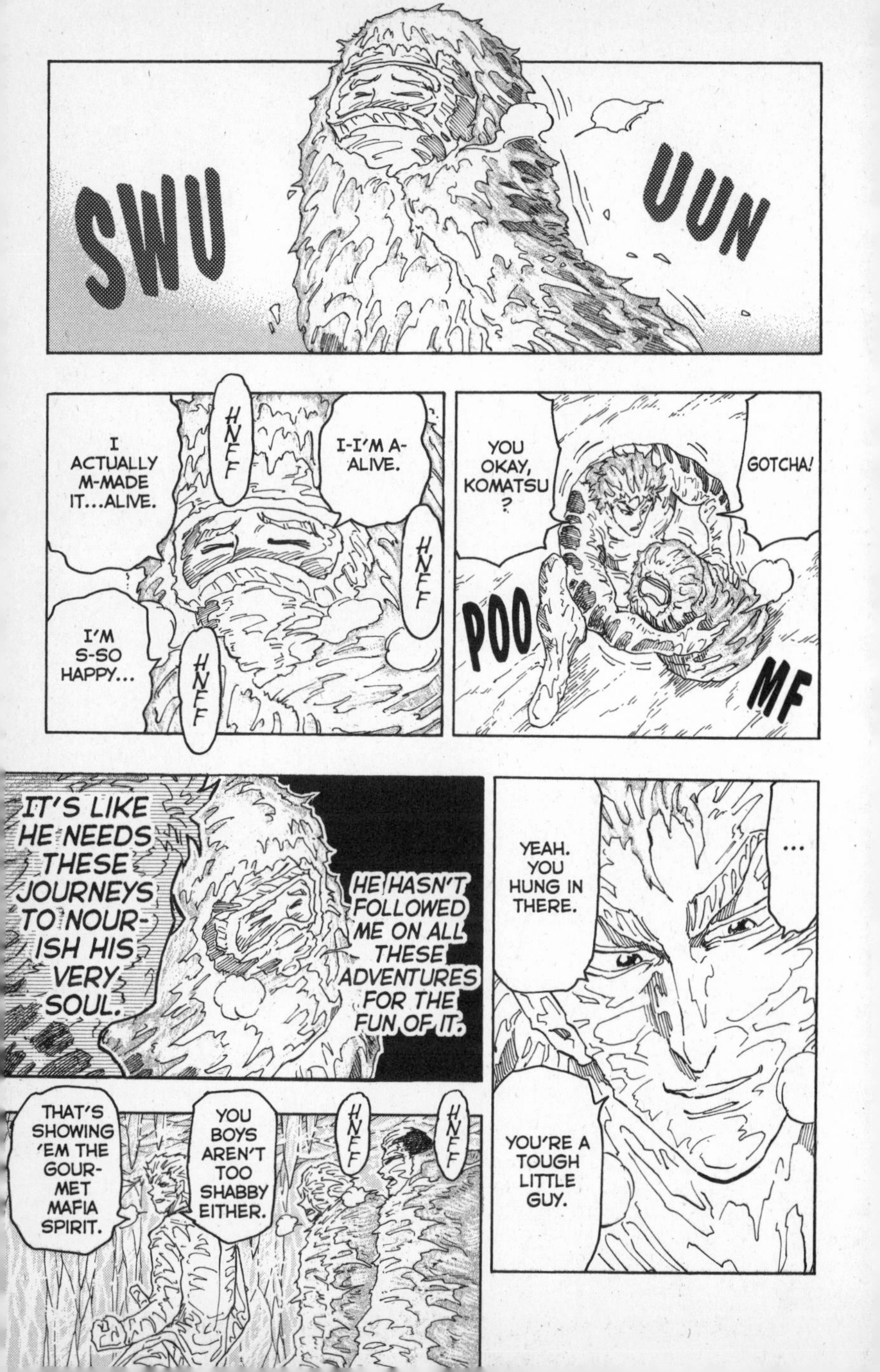
SWU
UUN
GOTCHA!
YOU OKAY, KOMATSU?
POOMF
I-I'M A-ALIVE.
HNFF
I ACTUALLY M-MADE IT...ALIVE.
HNFF
I'M S-SO HAPPY...
HNFF
...
YEAH. YOU HUNG IN THERE.
YOU'RE A TOUGH LITTLE GUY.
HE HASN'T FOLLOWED ME ON ALL THESE ADVENTURES FOR THE FUN OF IT.
IT'S LIKE HE NEEDS THESE JOURNEYS TO NOURISH HIS VERY SOUL.
HNFF
HNFF
YOU BOYS AREN'T TOO SHABBY EITHER.
THAT'S SHOWING 'EM THE GOURMET MAFIA SPIRIT.

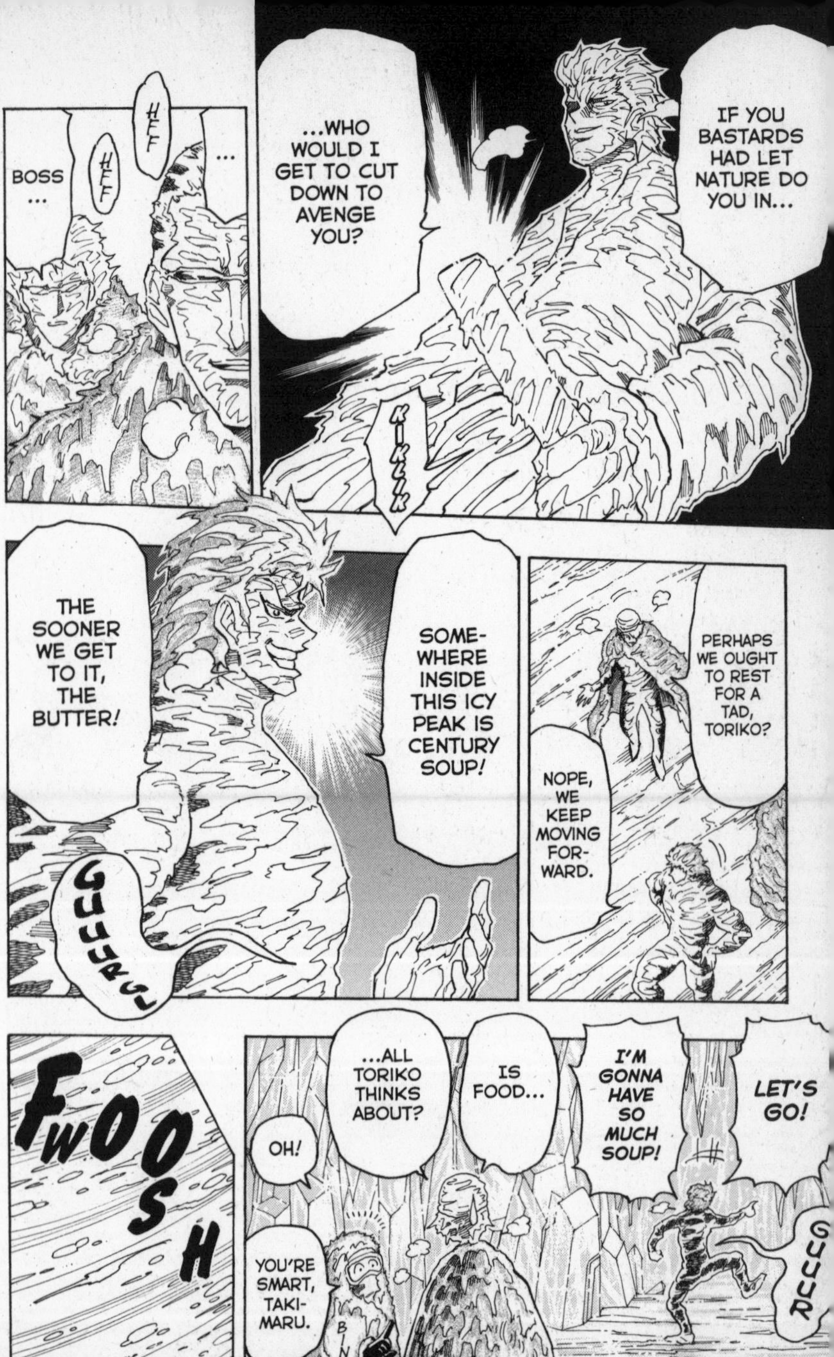
IF YOU BASTARDS HAD LET NATURE DO YOU IN...
...WHO WOULD I GET TO CUT DOWN TO AVENGE YOU?
KIKLIK
...
HEFF
HEFF
BOSS ...
PERHAPS WE OUGHT TO REST FOR A TAD, TORIKO?
NOPE, WE KEEP MOVING FOR-WARD.
SOME-WHERE INSIDE THIS ICY PEAK IS CENTURY SOUP!
THE SOONER WE GET TO IT, THE BUTTER!
GUUURGL
LET'S GO!
GUUUR
I'M GONNA HAVE SO MUCH SOUP!
IS FOOD...
...ALL TORIKO THINKS ABOUT?
OH!
YOU'RE SMART, TAKI-MARU.
BINGO!
FWOOSH

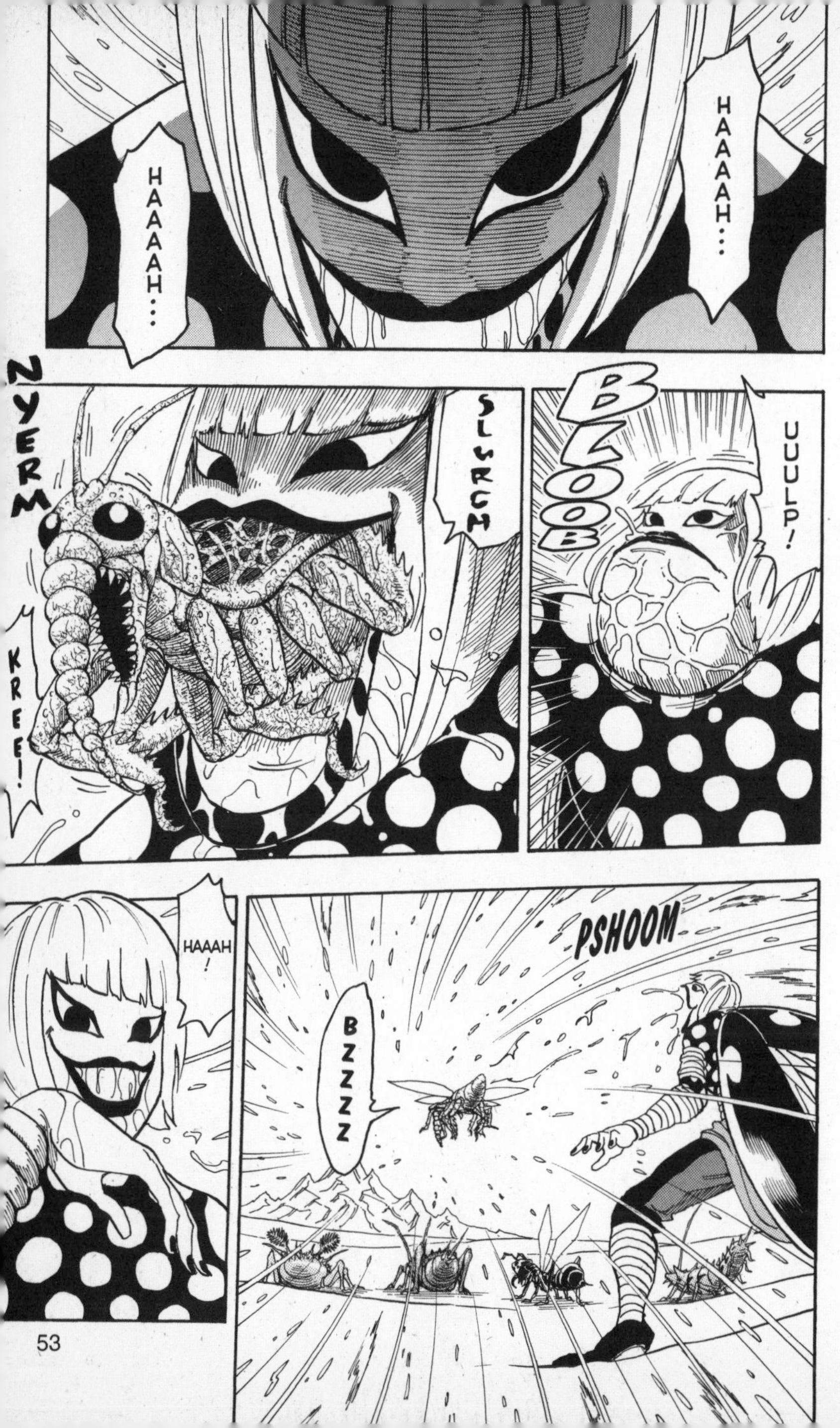
HAAAAAH...
HAAAAAH...
BLOOB
UUULP!
SLURCH
NYERM
KREE!
PSHOOM
BZZZZ
HAAAH!

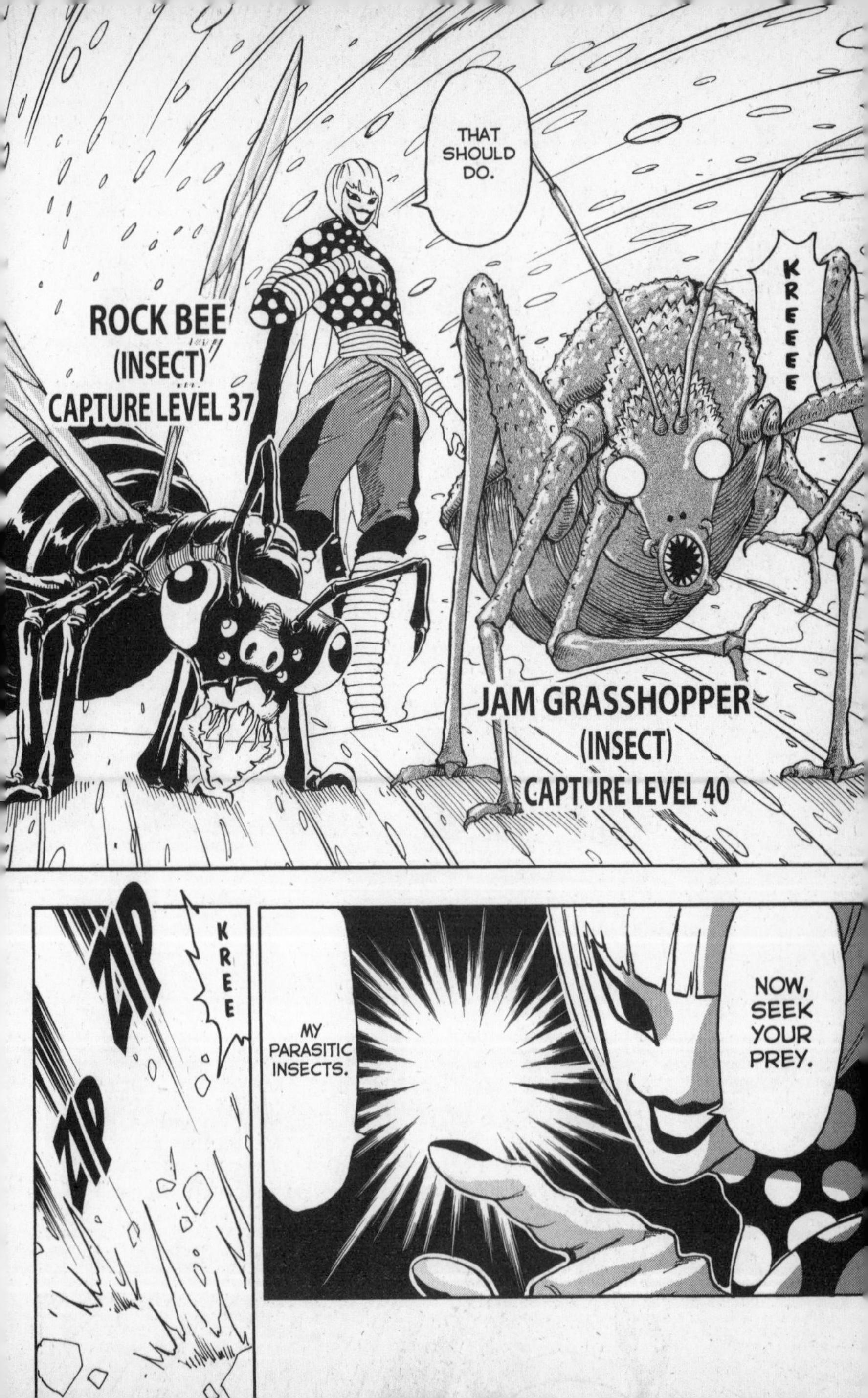
THAT SHOULD DO.
KREEEE
ROCK BEE
(INSECT)
CAPTURE LEVEL 37
JAM GRASSHOPPER
(INSECT)
CAPTURE LEVEL 40
NOW, SEEK YOUR PREY.
MY PARASITIC INSECTS.
KREE
ZIP
ZIP

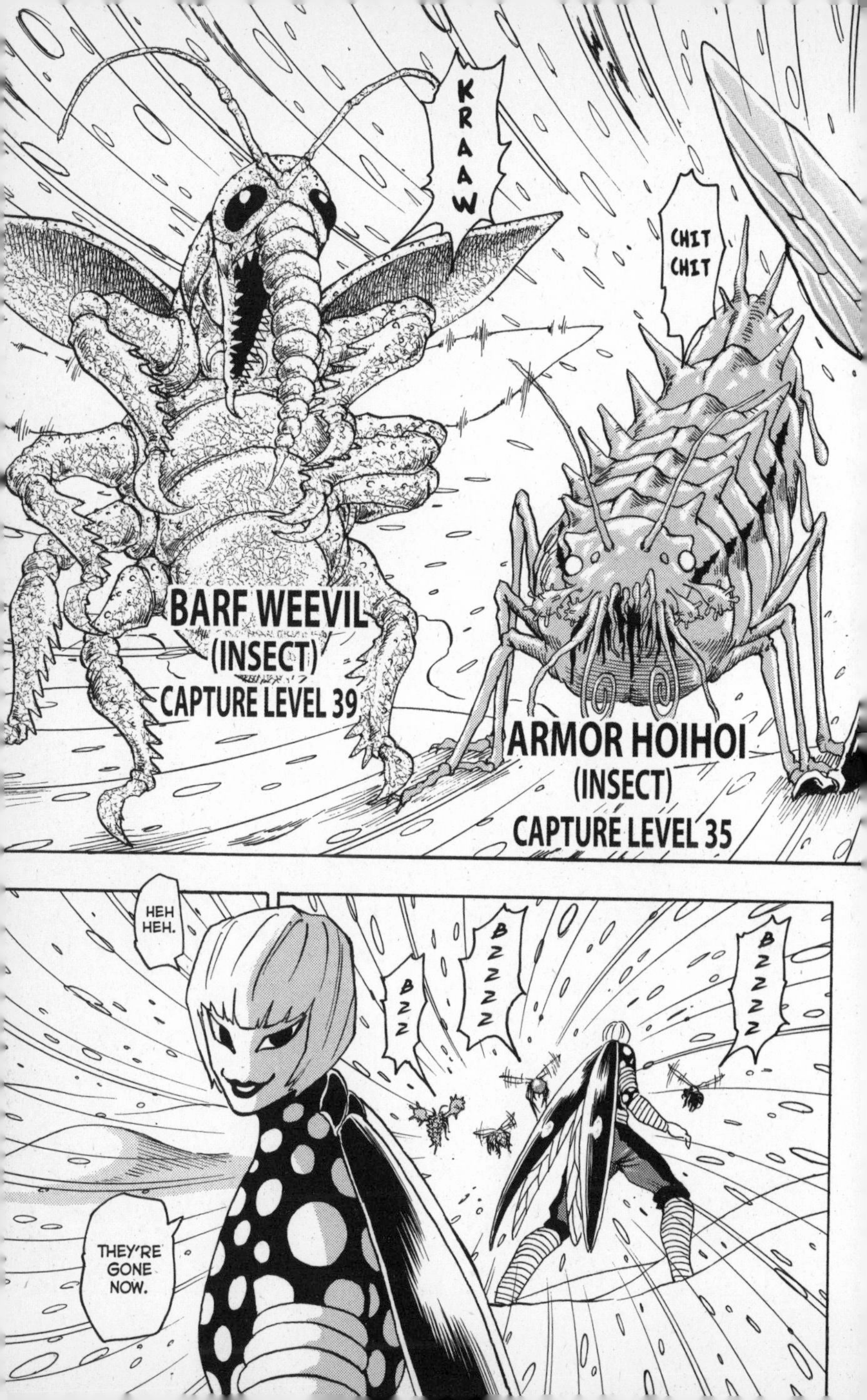
KRAAW
CHIT CHIT
BARF WEEVIL
(INSECT)
CAPTURE LEVEL 39
ARMOR HOIHOI
(INSECT)
CAPTURE LEVEL 35
BZZZZ
BZZZZ
BZZ
HEH HEH.
THEY'RE GONE NOW.

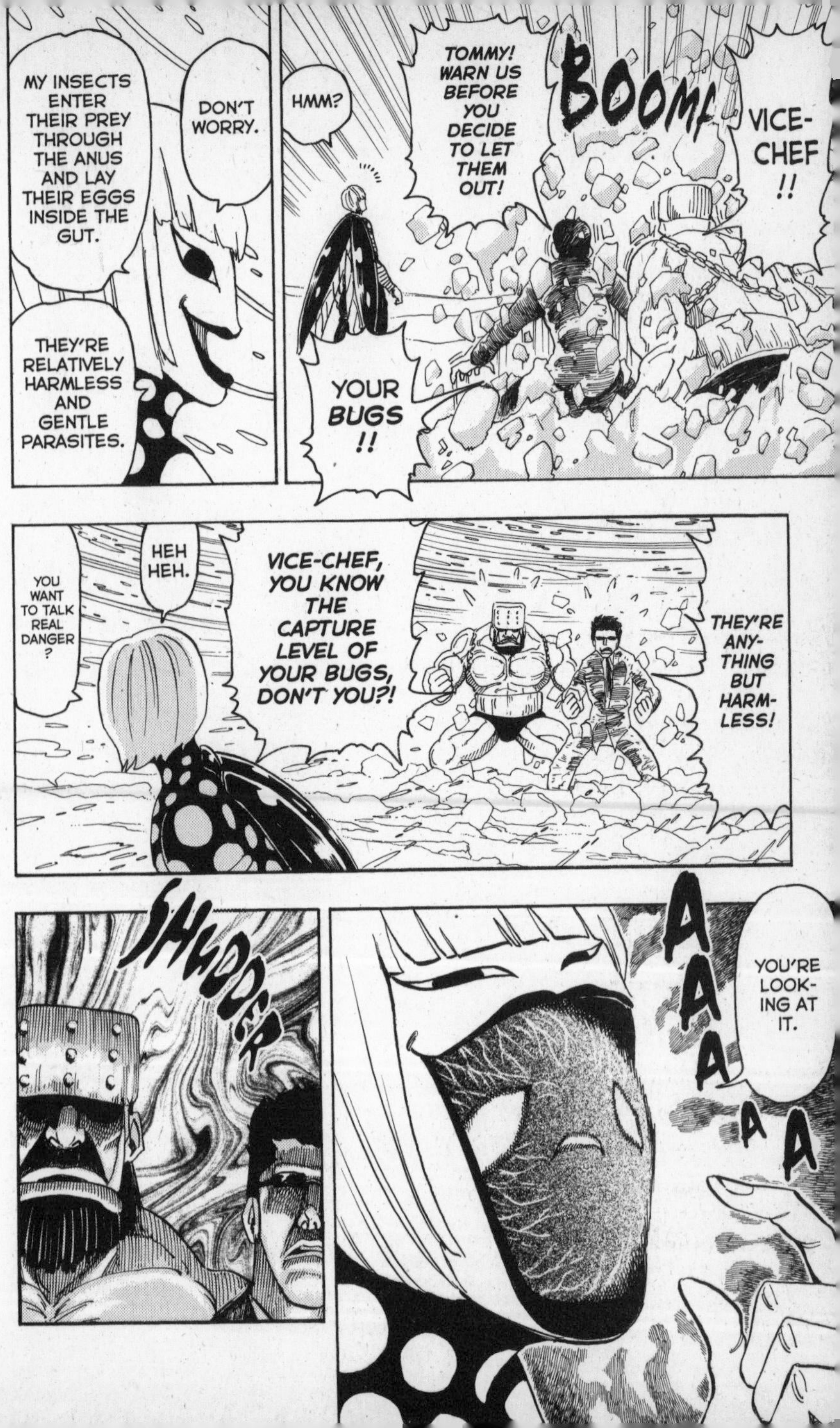
VICE-CHEF !!
BOOM
TOMMY! WARN US BEFORE YOU DECIDE TO LET THEM OUT!
HMM?
YOUR BUGS !!
DON'T WORRY.
MY INSECTS ENTER THEIR PREY THROUGH THE ANUS AND LAY THEIR EGGS INSIDE THE GUT.
THEY'RE RELATIVELY HARMLESS AND GENTLE PARASITES.
THEY'RE ANY-THING BUT HARM-LESS!
VICE-CHEF, YOU KNOW THE CAPTURE LEVEL OF YOUR BUGS, DON'T YOU?!
HEH HEH.
YOU WANT TO TALK REAL DANGER?
YOU'RE LOOK-ING AT IT.
AAAAAA
SHUDDER

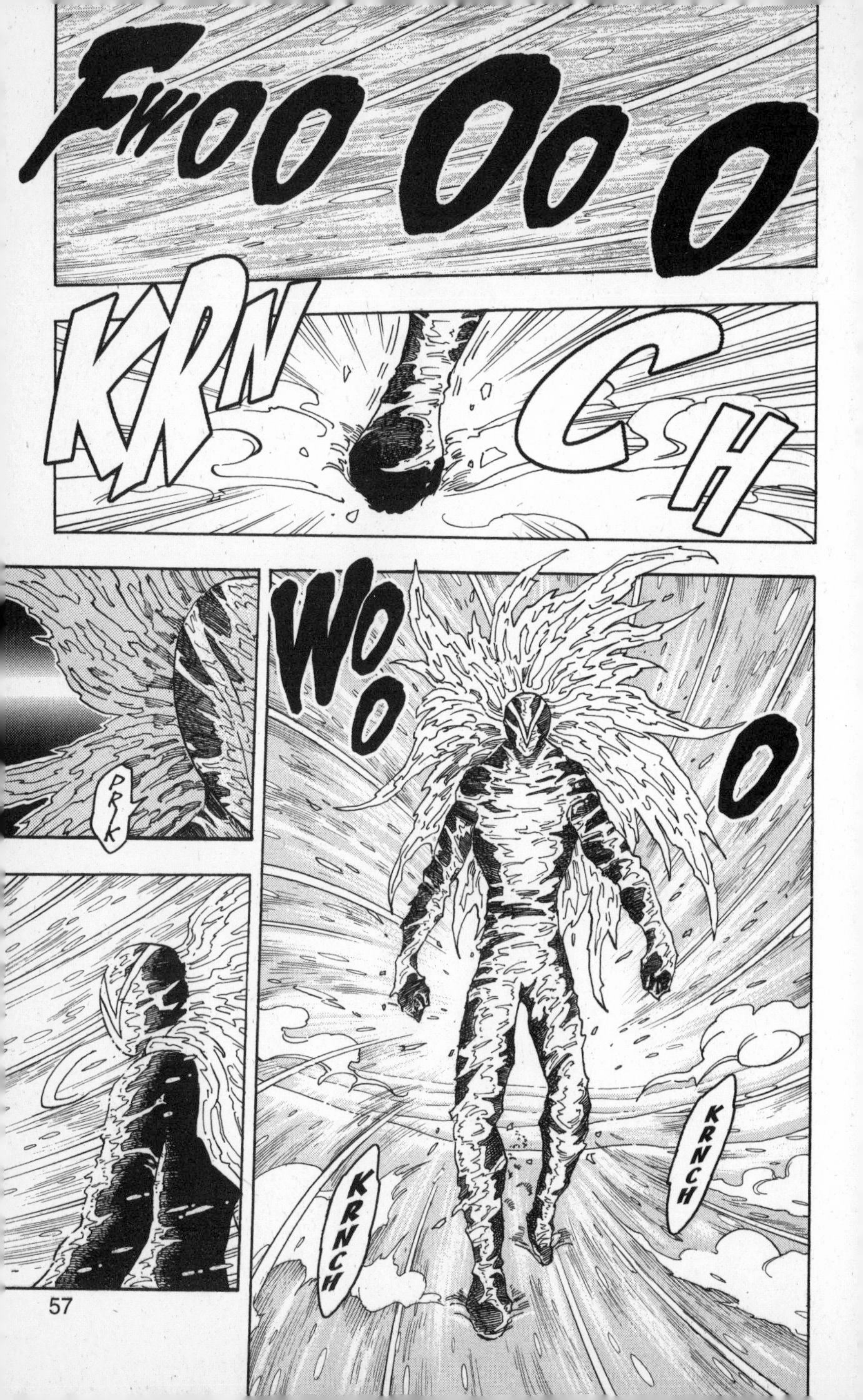
FWOOOOOO
KRNCH
WOOOO
KRNCH
KRNCH
PRIK

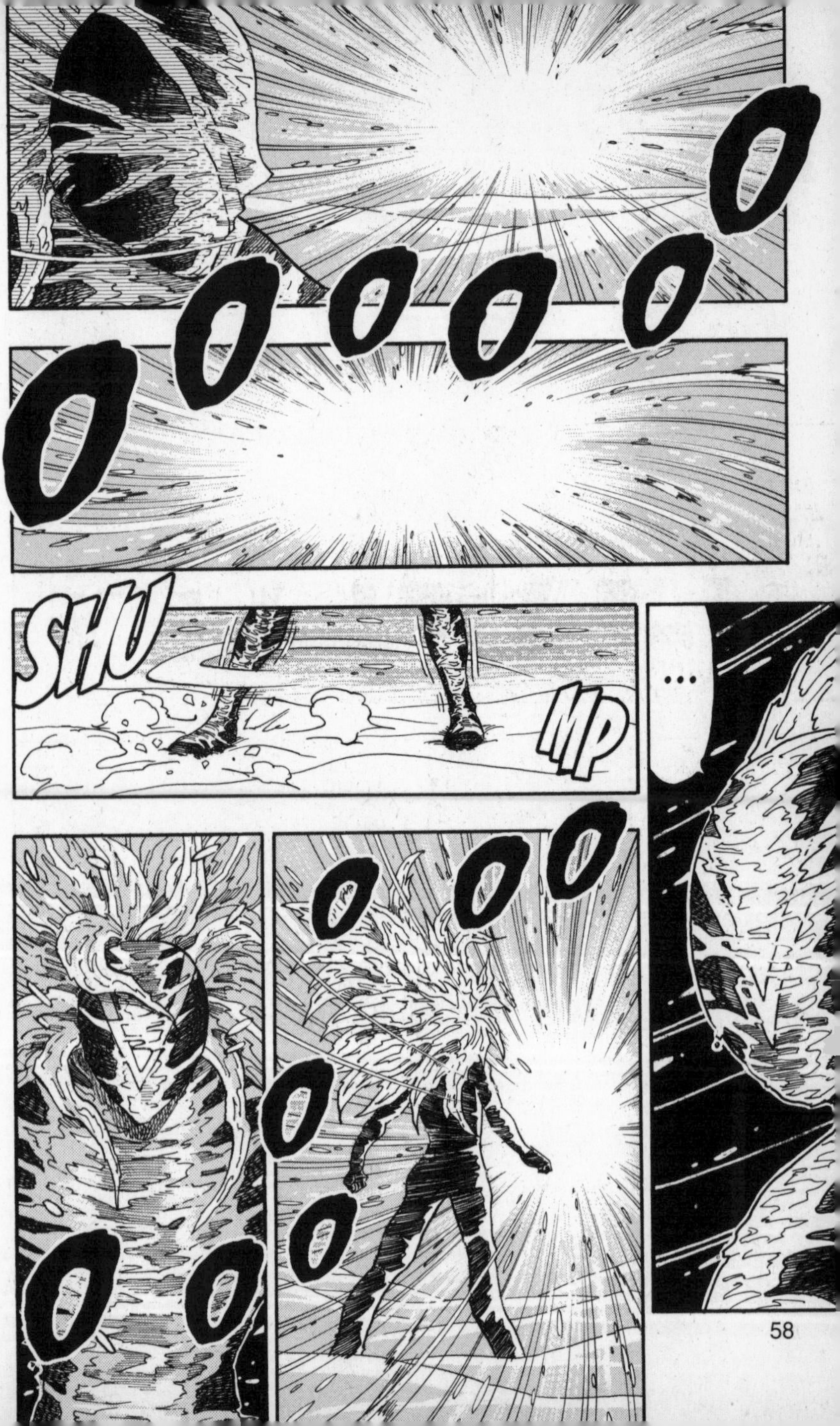
OOOOOO
...
SHU
MP
OOO
OO
OO

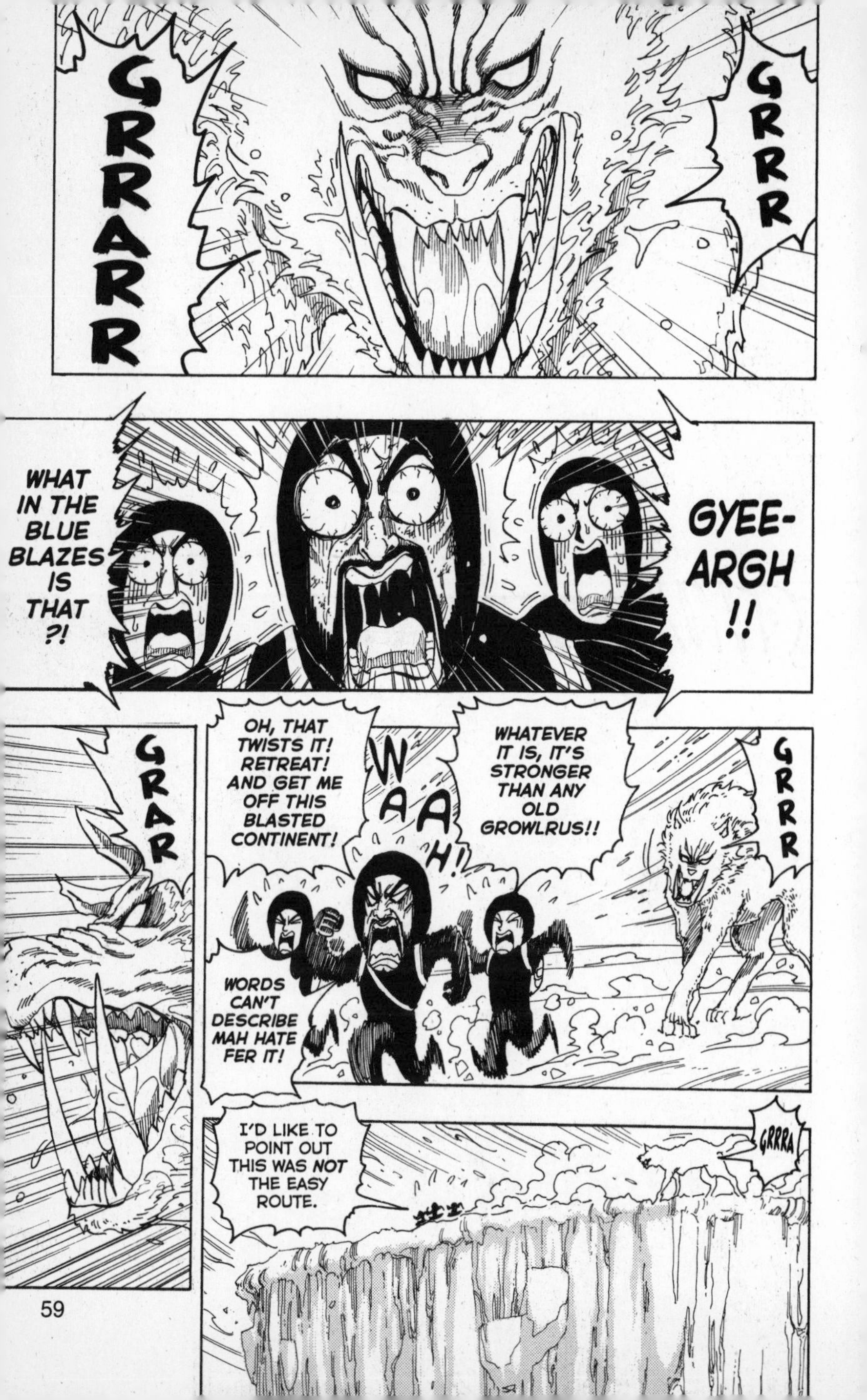
GRRR
GRRARR
GYEE-ARGH!!
WHAT IN THE BLUE BLAZES IS THAT?!
GRRR
WHATEVER IT IS, IT'S STRONGER THAN ANY OLD GROWLRUS!!
WAAAH!
OH, THAT TWISTS IT! RETREAT! AND GET ME OFF THIS BLASTED CONTINENT!
WORDS CAN'T DESCRIBE MAH HATE FER IT!
GRRRA
I'D LIKE TO POINT OUT THIS WAS *NOT* THE EASY ROUTE.
GRAR

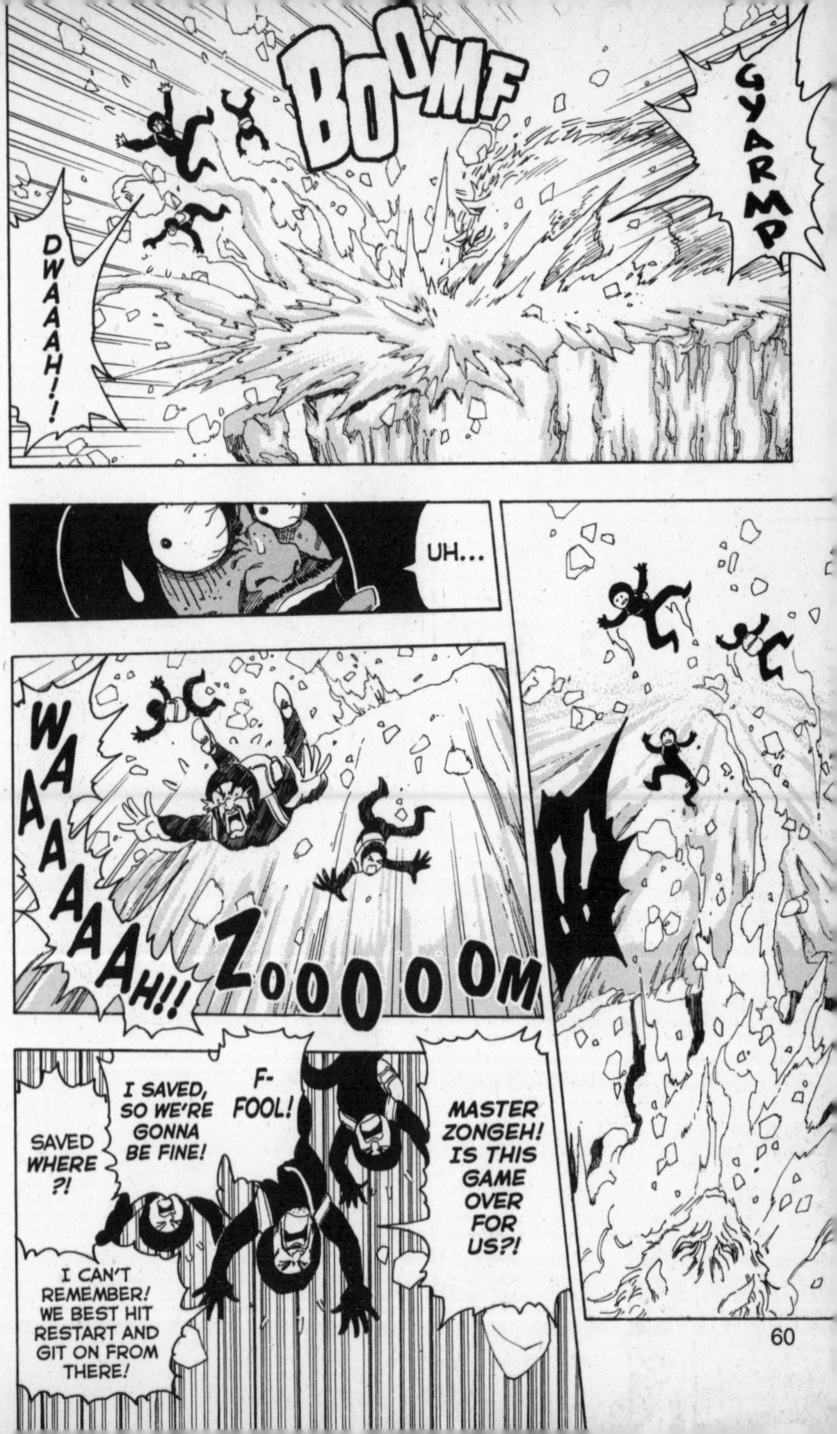
GYARMP
BOOMF
DWAAAAH!!
UH...
WAAAAAAAH!!
ZOOOOOM
MASTER ZONGEH! IS THIS GAME OVER FOR US?!
F-FOOL!
I SAVED, SO WE'RE GONNA BE FINE!
SAVED WHERE?!
I CAN'T REMEMBER! WE BEST HIT RESTART AND GIT ON FROM THERE!

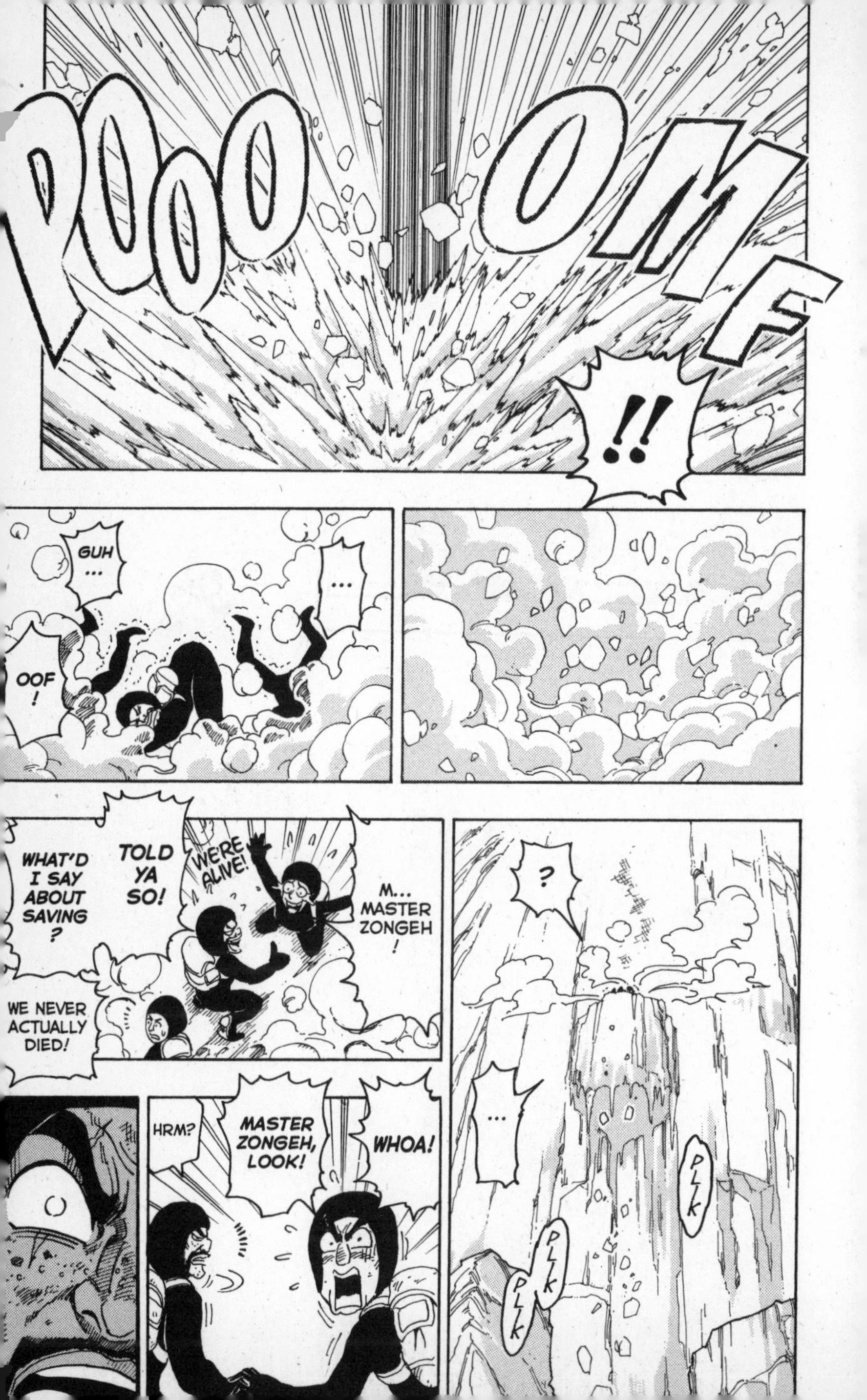
POOOOOMF
!!
...
GUH ...
OOF !
?
...
PLIK
PLIK
PLIK
M... MASTER ZONGEH !
WE'RE ALIVE!
TOLD YA SO!
WHAT'D I SAY ABOUT SAVING ?
WE NEVER ACTUALLY DIED!
WHOA!
MASTER ZONGEH, LOOK!
HRM?

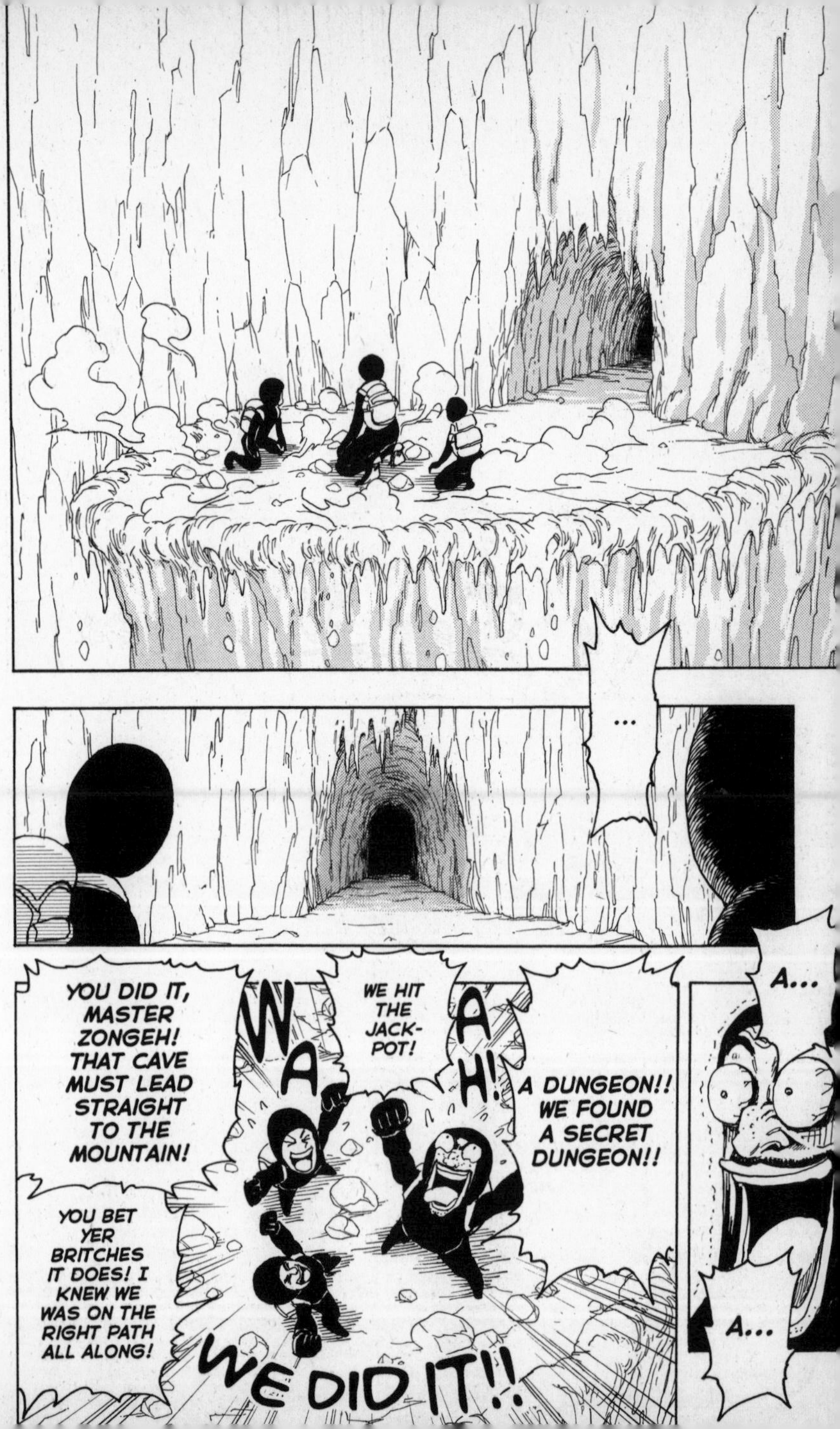
...
A...
A...
WAAH!
WE HIT THE JACKPOT!
A DUNGEON!! WE FOUND A SECRET DUNGEON!!
YOU DID IT, MASTER ZONGEH! THAT CAVE MUST LEAD STRAIGHT TO THE MOUNTAIN!
YOU BET YER BRITCHES IT DOES! I KNEW WE WAS ON THE RIGHT PATH ALL ALONG!
WE DID IT!!

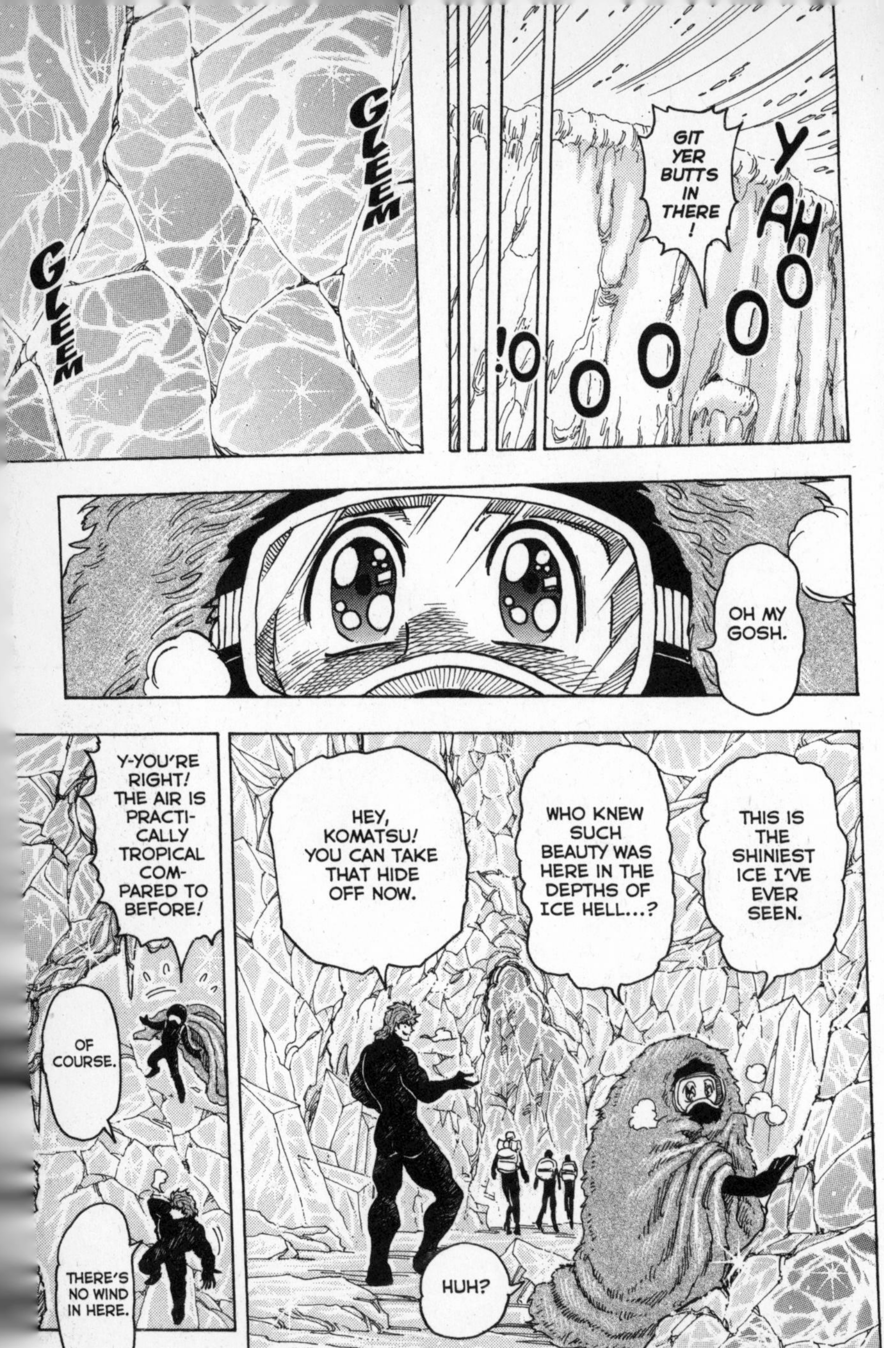
GIT YER BUTTS IN THERE!
YAHOOOOOOO!
GLEEM
GLEEM
OH MY GOSH.
THIS IS THE SHINIEST ICE I'VE EVER SEEN.
WHO KNEW SUCH BEAUTY WAS HERE IN THE DEPTHS OF ICE HELL...?
HEY, KOMATSU! YOU CAN TAKE THAT HIDE OFF NOW.
HUH?
Y-YOU'RE RIGHT! THE AIR IS PRACTI-CALLY TROPICAL COM-PARED TO BEFORE!
OF COURSE.
THERE'S NO WIND IN HERE.

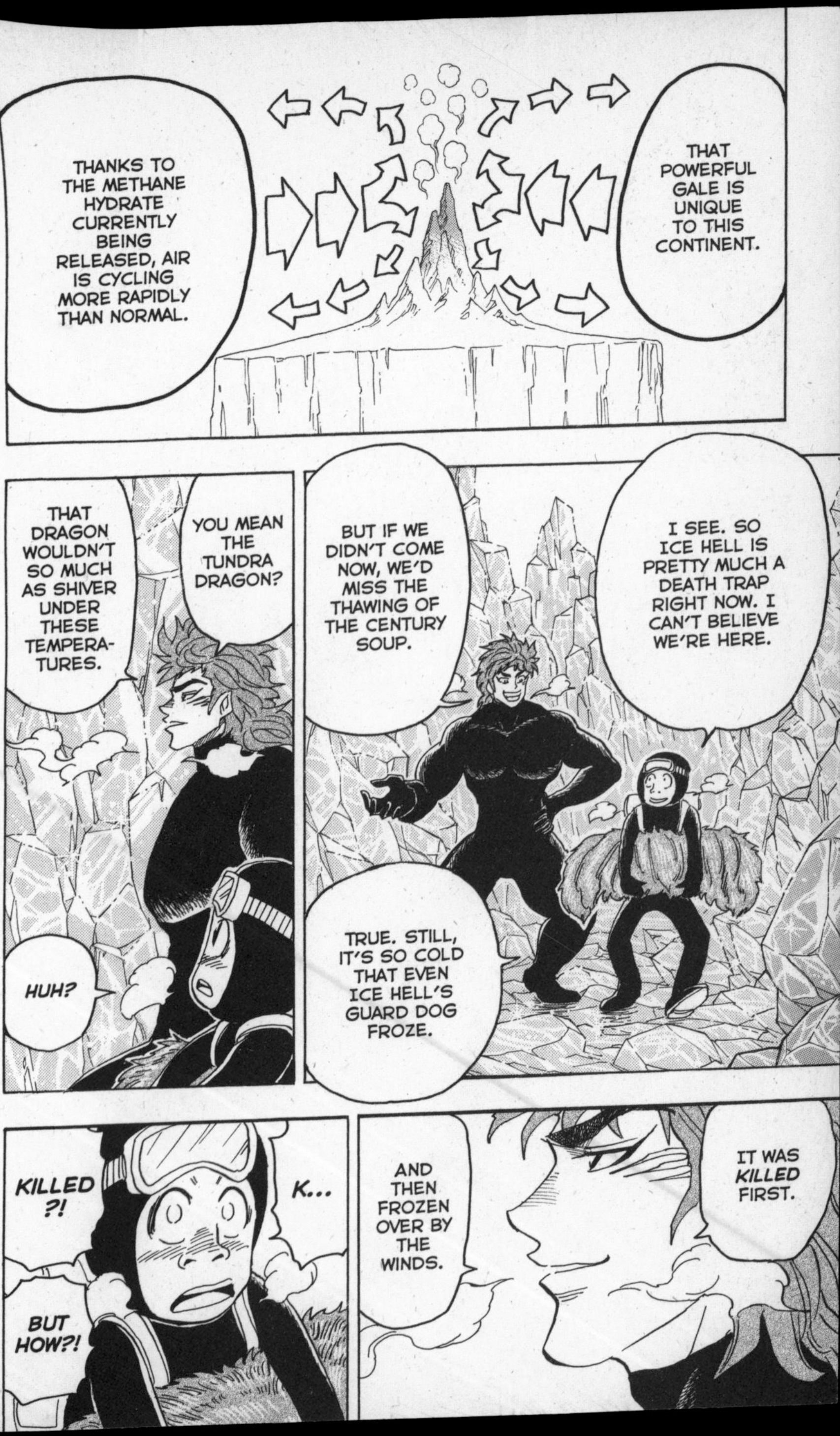
THAT POWERFUL GALE IS UNIQUE TO THIS CONTINENT.
THANKS TO THE METHANE HYDRATE CURRENTLY BEING RELEASED, AIR IS CYCLING MORE RAPIDLY THAN NORMAL.
I SEE. SO ICE HELL IS PRETTY MUCH A DEATH TRAP RIGHT NOW. I CAN'T BELIEVE WE'RE HERE.
BUT IF WE DIDN'T COME NOW, WE'D MISS THE THAWING OF THE CENTURY SOUP.
TRUE. STILL, IT'S SO COLD THAT EVEN ICE HELL'S GUARD DOG FROZE.
YOU MEAN THE TUNDRA DRAGON?
THAT DRAGON WOULDN'T SO MUCH AS SHIVER UNDER THESE TEMPERA-TURES.
HUH?
IT WAS KILLED FIRST.
AND THEN FROZEN OVER BY THE WINDS.
K...
KILLED?!
BUT HOW?!

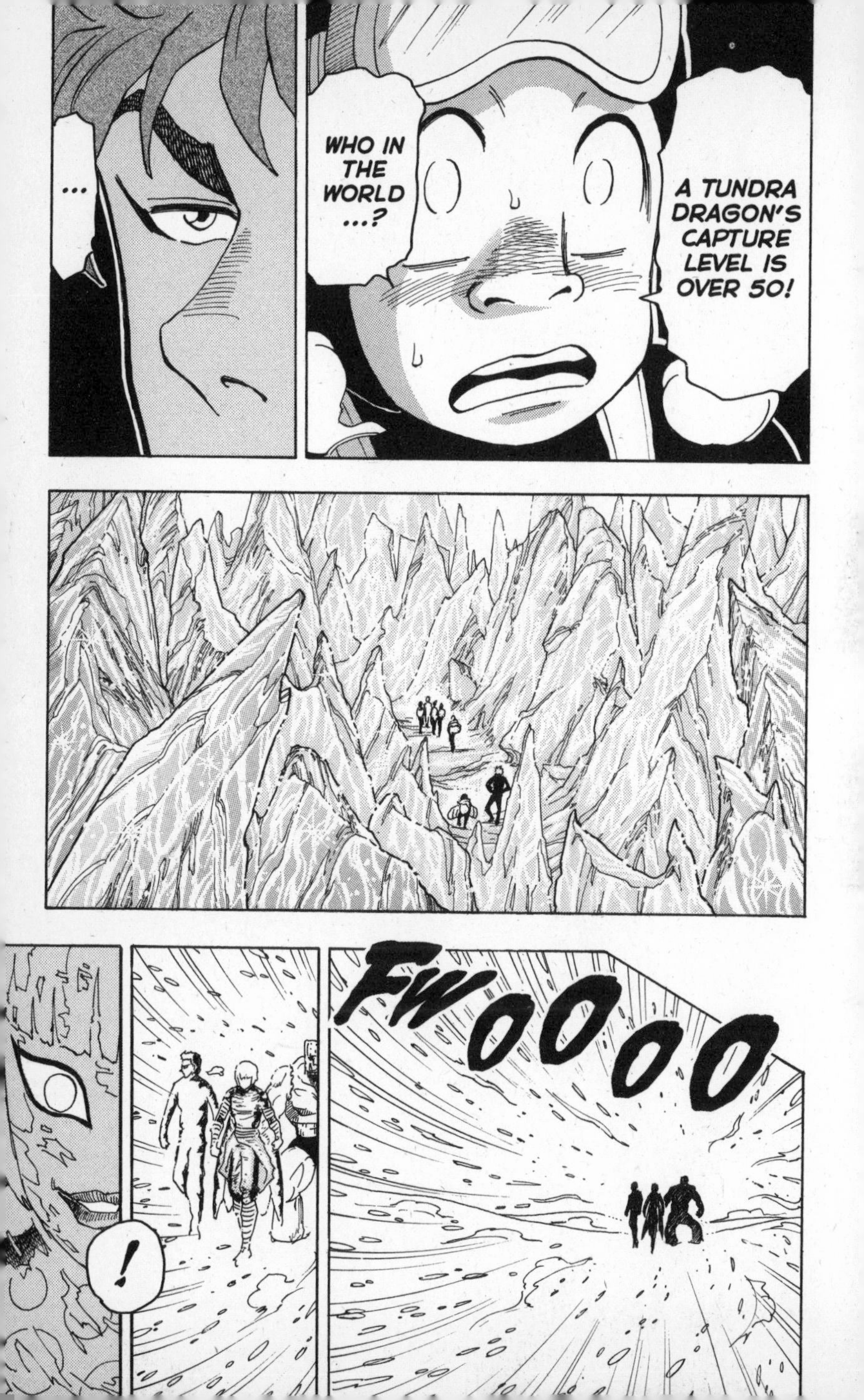
A TUNDRA DRAGON'S CAPTURE LEVEL IS OVER 50!
WHO IN THE WORLD ...?
...
FWOOOO
!

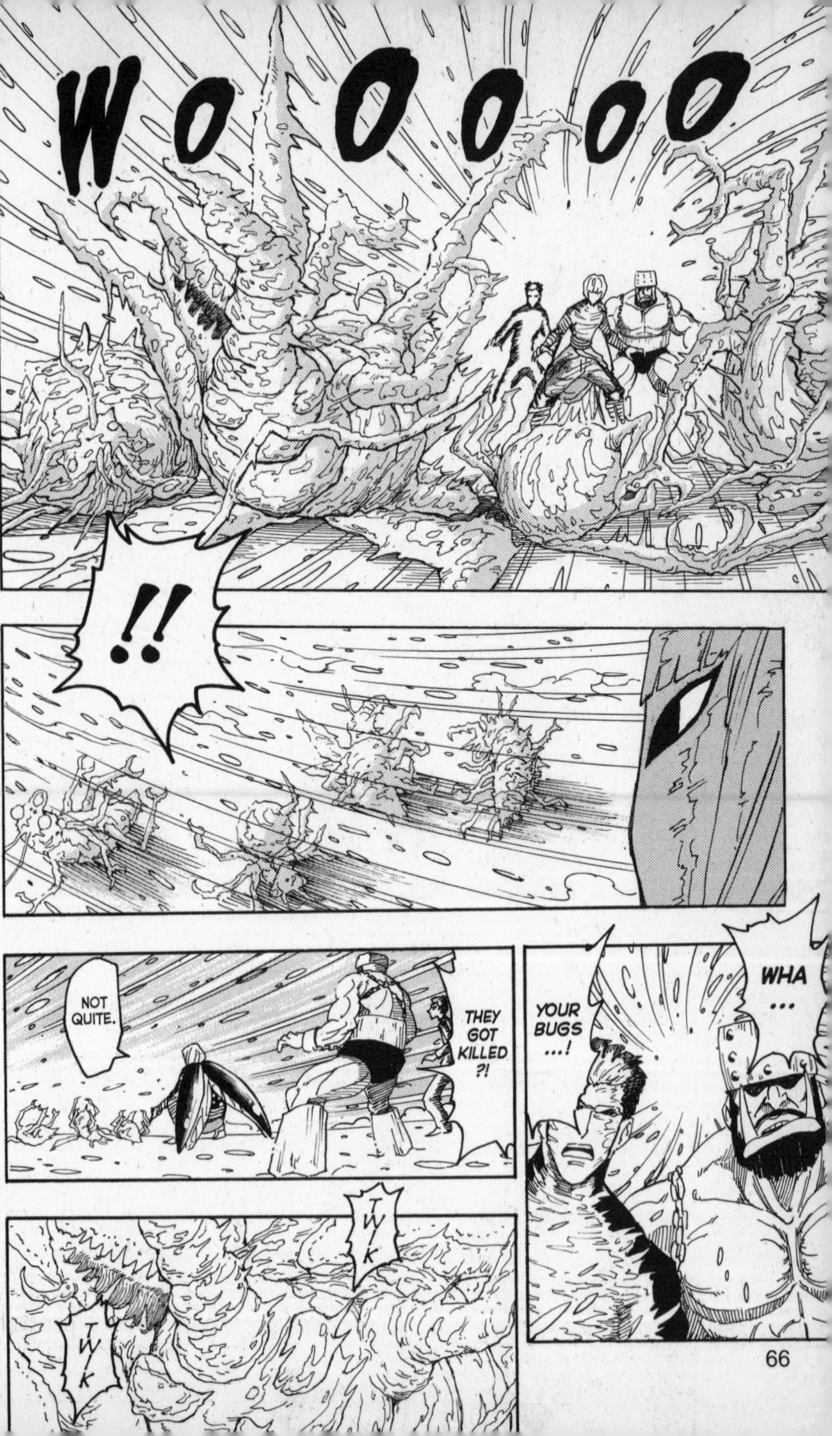
WOOOOOO
!!
WHA ...
YOUR BUGS ...!
THEY GOT KILLED ?!
NOT QUITE.
TWIK
TWIK

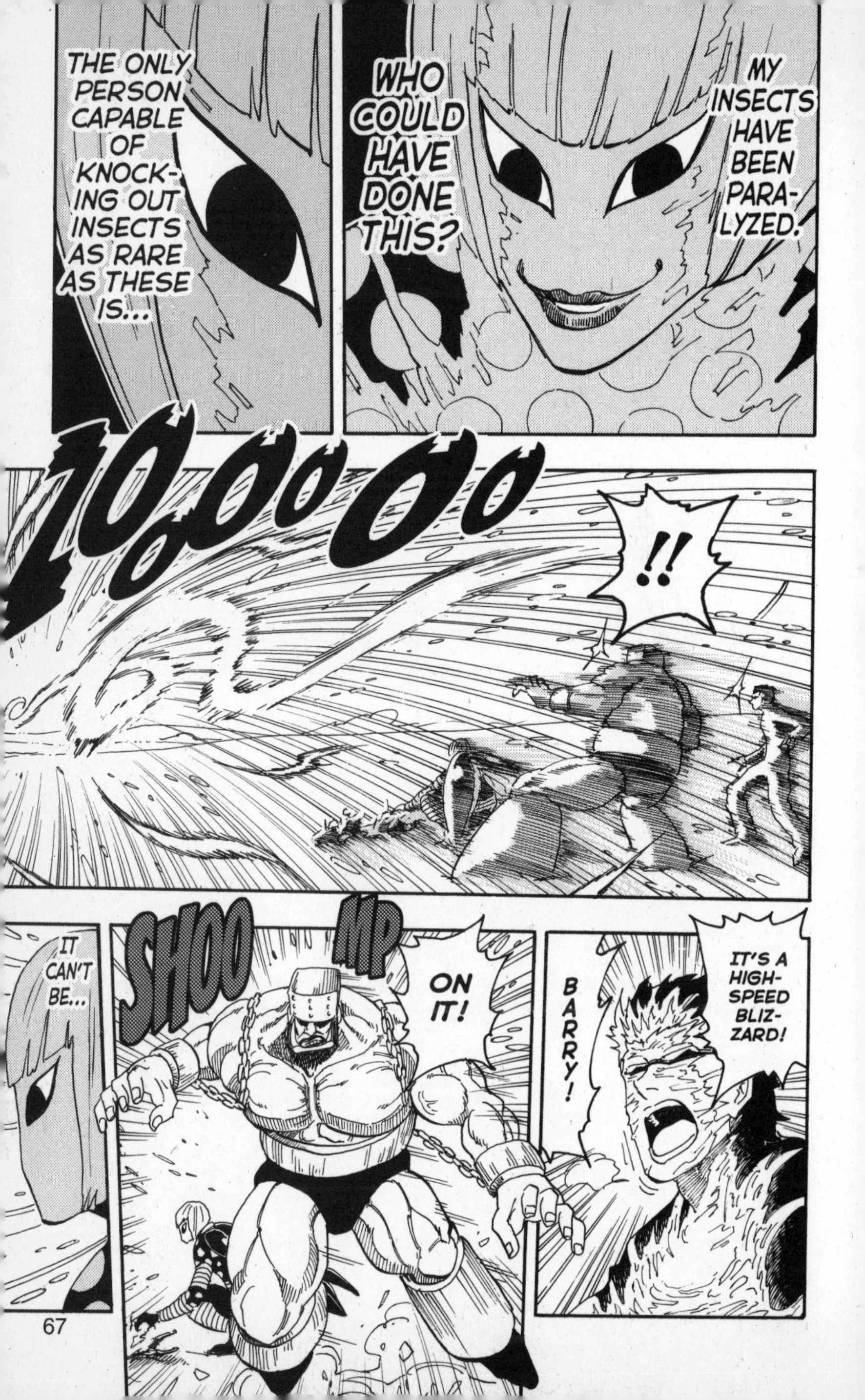
MY INSECTS HAVE BEEN PARALYZED.
WHO COULD HAVE DONE THIS?
THE ONLY PERSON CAPABLE OF KNOCKING OUT INSECTS AS RARE AS THESE IS...
!!
ZOOOOOO
IT'S A HIGH-SPEED BLIZZARD!
BARRY!
ON IT!
SHOOMP
IT CAN'T BE...

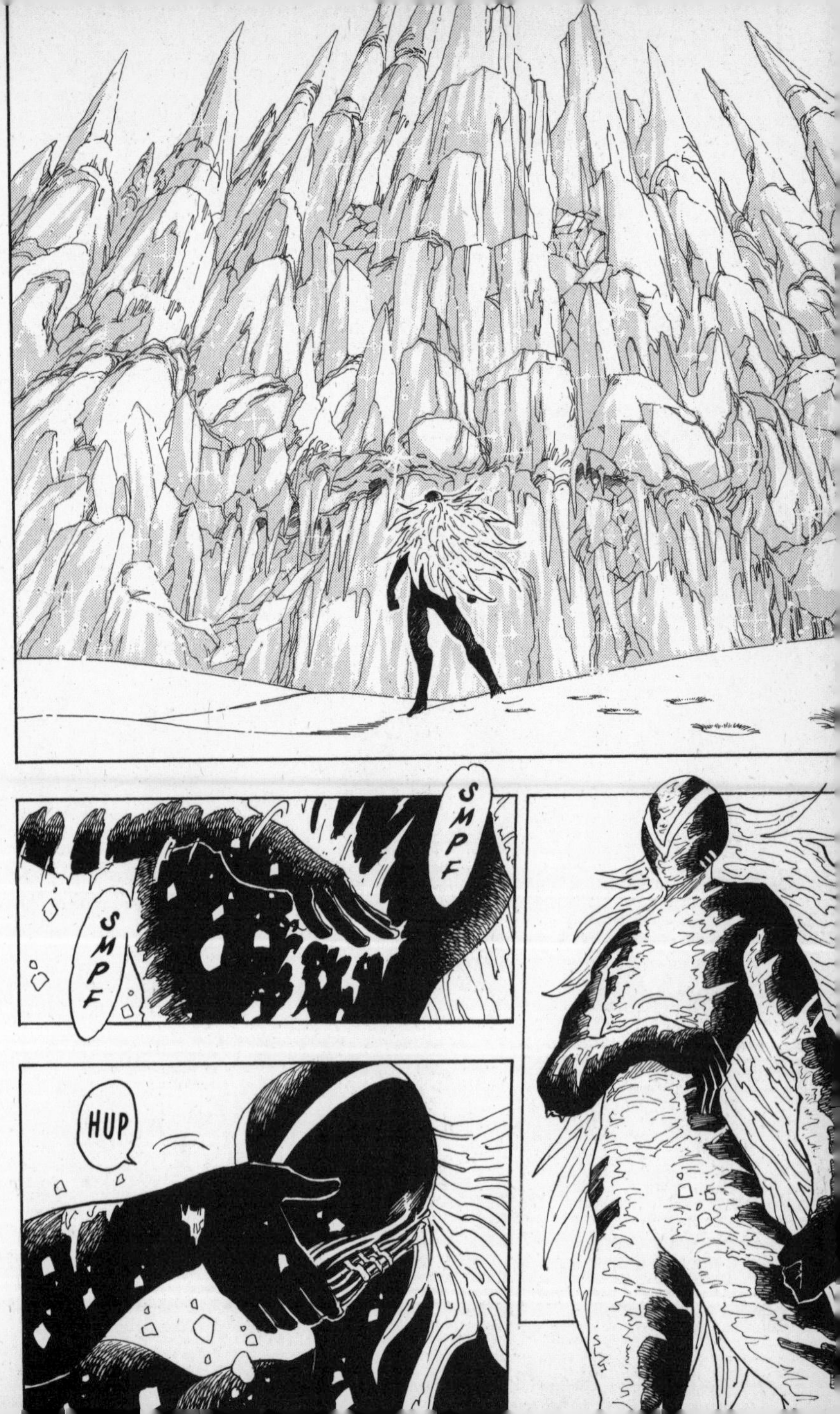
SMPF
SMPF
HUP

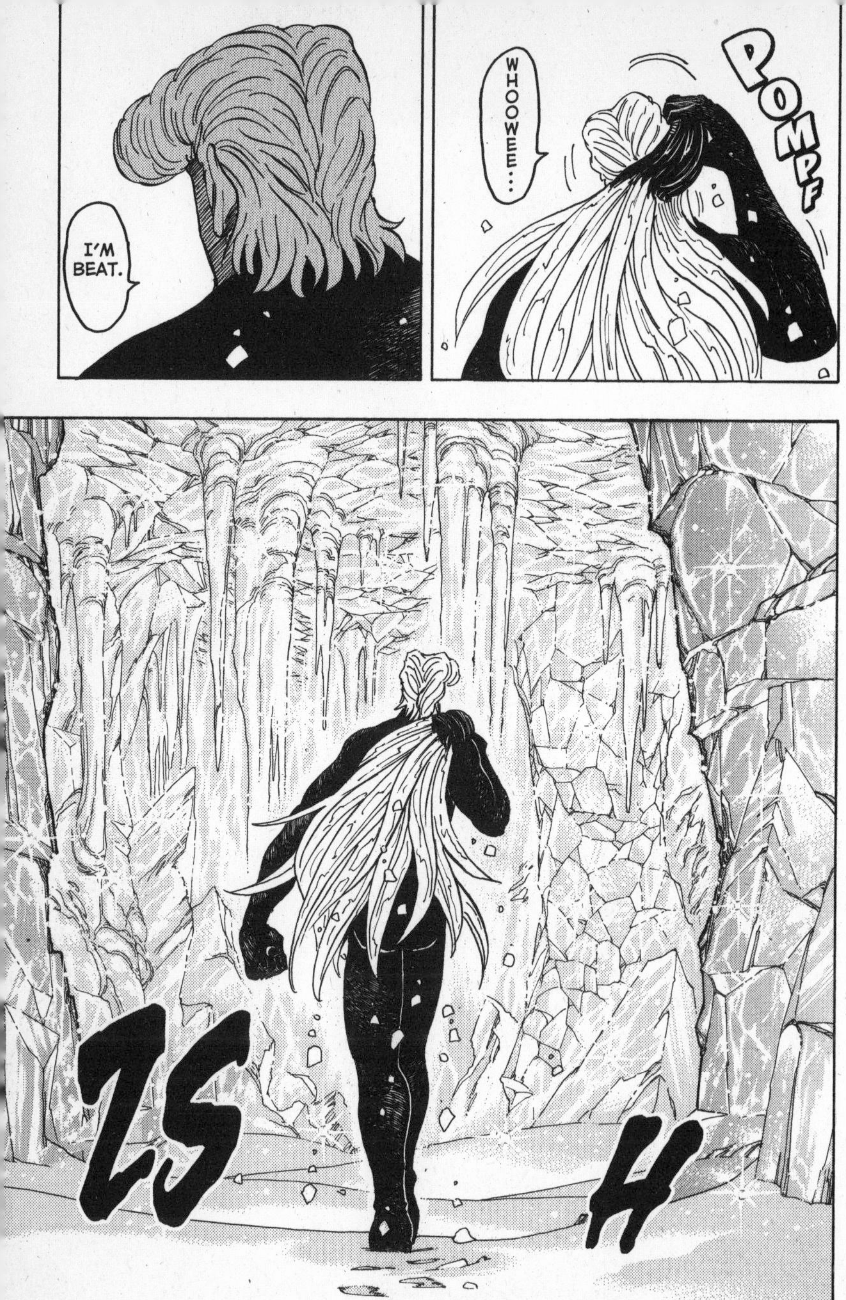
WHOOWEE...
POMPF
I'M BEAT.
ZS
H

TORIKO

GOURMET CHECKLIST

Vol. 065

GOURMET JELLYFISH

(UNKNOWN)

CAPTURE LEVEL: UNKNOWN

HABITAT: DEEP OCEAN

LENGTH: UNKNOWN

HEIGHT: UNKNOWN

WEIGHT: UNKNOWN

PRICE: UNKNOWN

SCALE

LONG AGO, A LEGENDARY GOURMET HUNTER NAMED ACACIA, CALLED THE "GOURMET GOD," DISCOVERED MIRACLE CELLS WITHIN THIS JELLYFISH. HE NAMED THEM GOURMET CELLS. HE NOTICED THAT CREATURES WHO ATE GOURMET JELLYFISH WOULD INCREASE IN FLAVOR; ADDITIONALLY, THE MORE HIGH-QUALITY FOODS THOSE CREATURES SUBSEQUENTLY CONSUMED, THE STRONGER THE REGENERATIVE PROPERTIES AND LIFE PROCESSES OF THEIR GOURMET CELLS. NOW, BOTH THE IGO AND OTHER LEGAL (AND ILLEGAL) ORGANIZATIONS ARE RESEARCHING THESE GOURMET CELLS, BUT THE RESULTS OF SAID RESEARCH ARE SHROUDED IN MYSTERY.

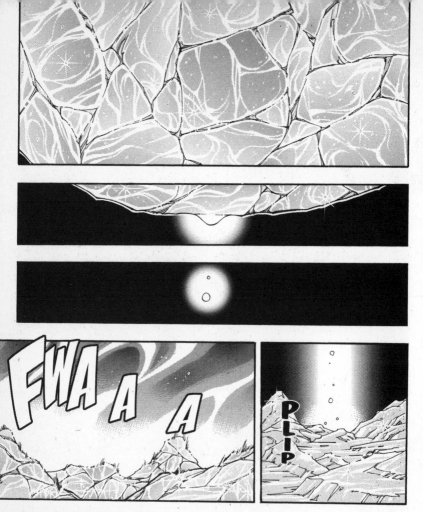

GOURMET 74: A CAUSE FOR ADVENTURE!!

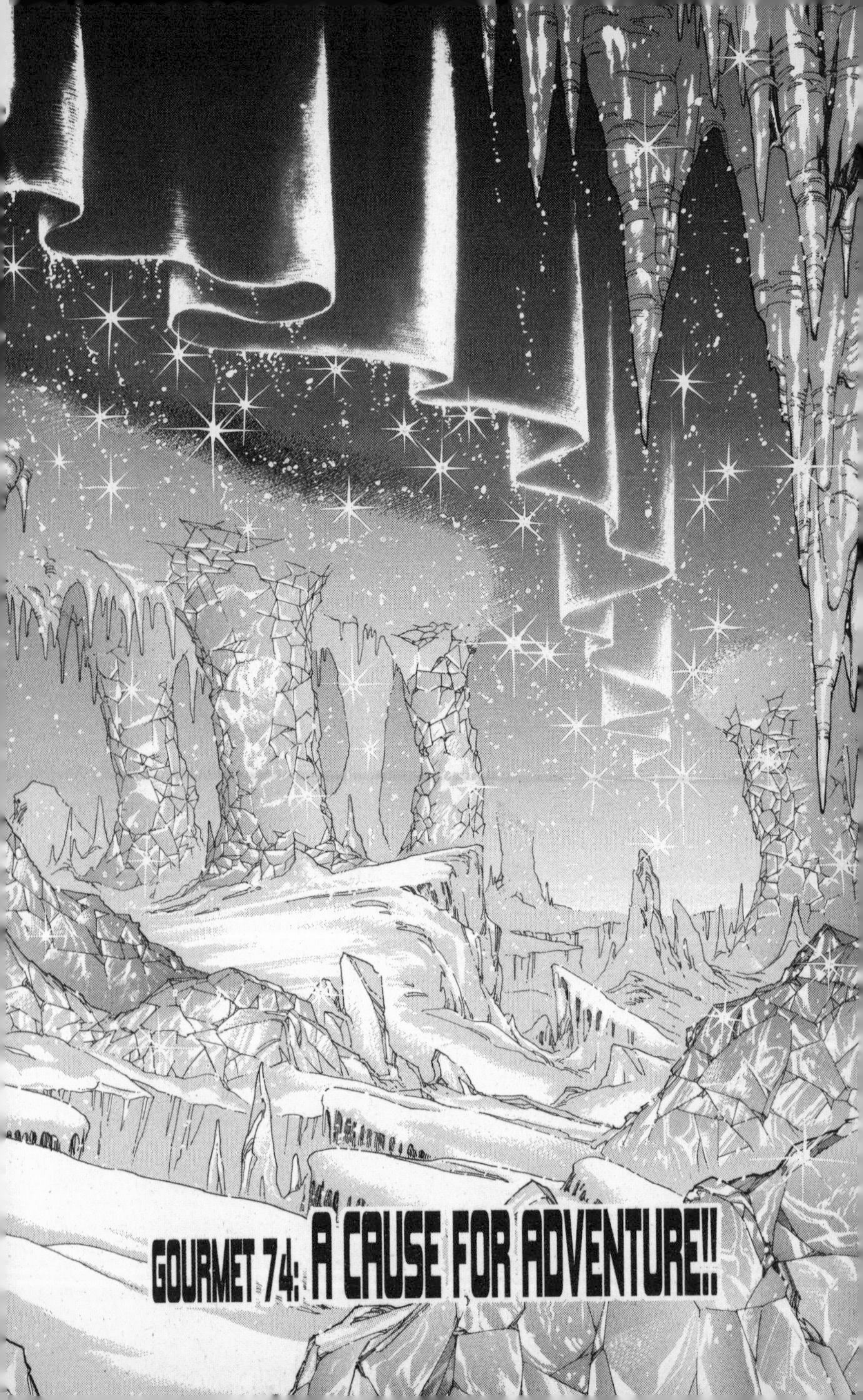
GOURMET 74: A CAUSE FOR ADVENTURE!!

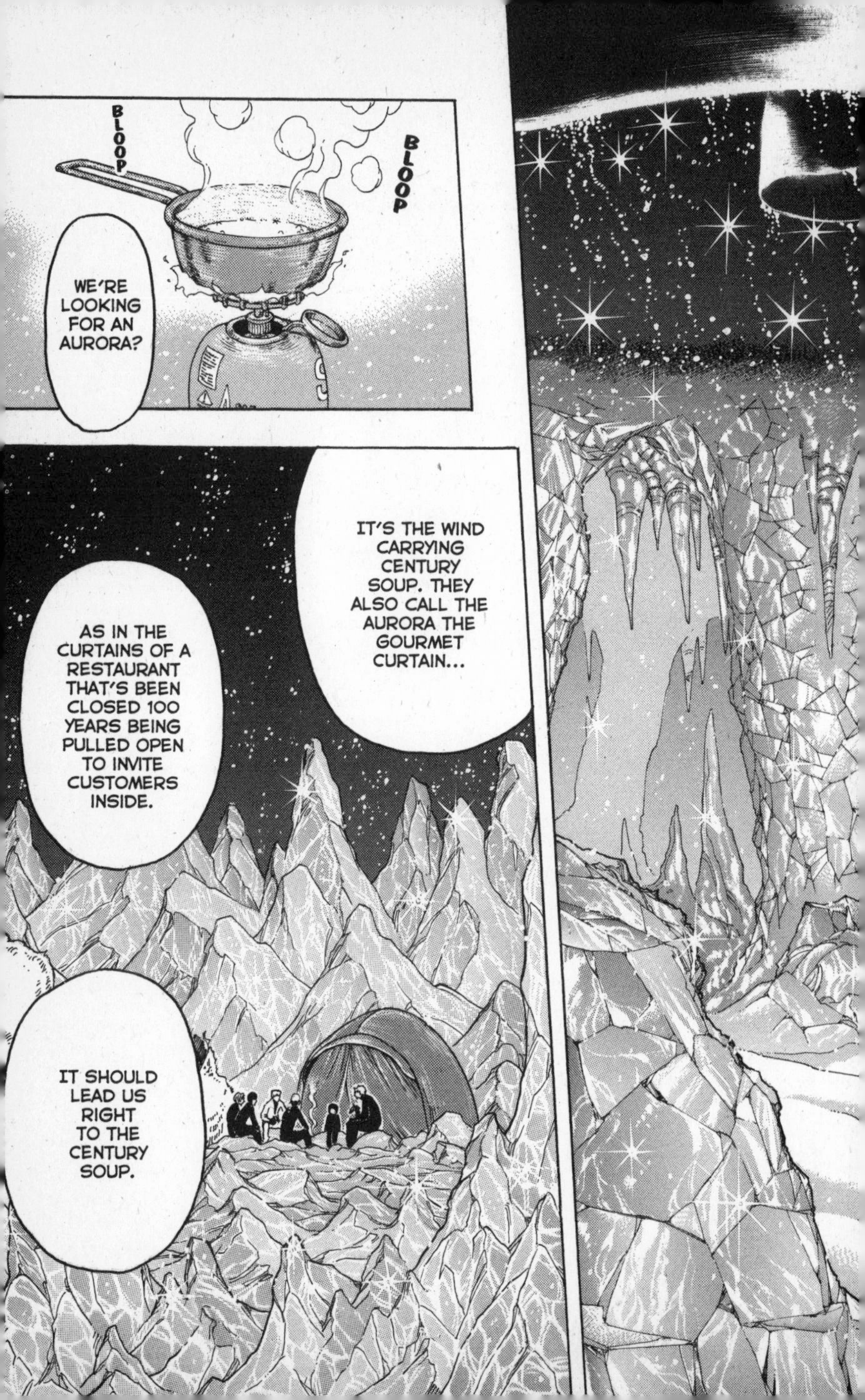
BLOOP
BLOOP
WE'RE LOOKING FOR AN AURORA?
IT'S THE WIND CARRYING CENTURY SOUP. THEY ALSO CALL THE AURORA THE GOURMET CURTAIN...
AS IN THE CURTAINS OF A RESTAURANT THAT'S BEEN CLOSED 100 YEARS BEING PULLED OPEN TO INVITE CUSTOMERS INSIDE.
IT SHOULD LEAD US RIGHT TO THE CENTURY SOUP.

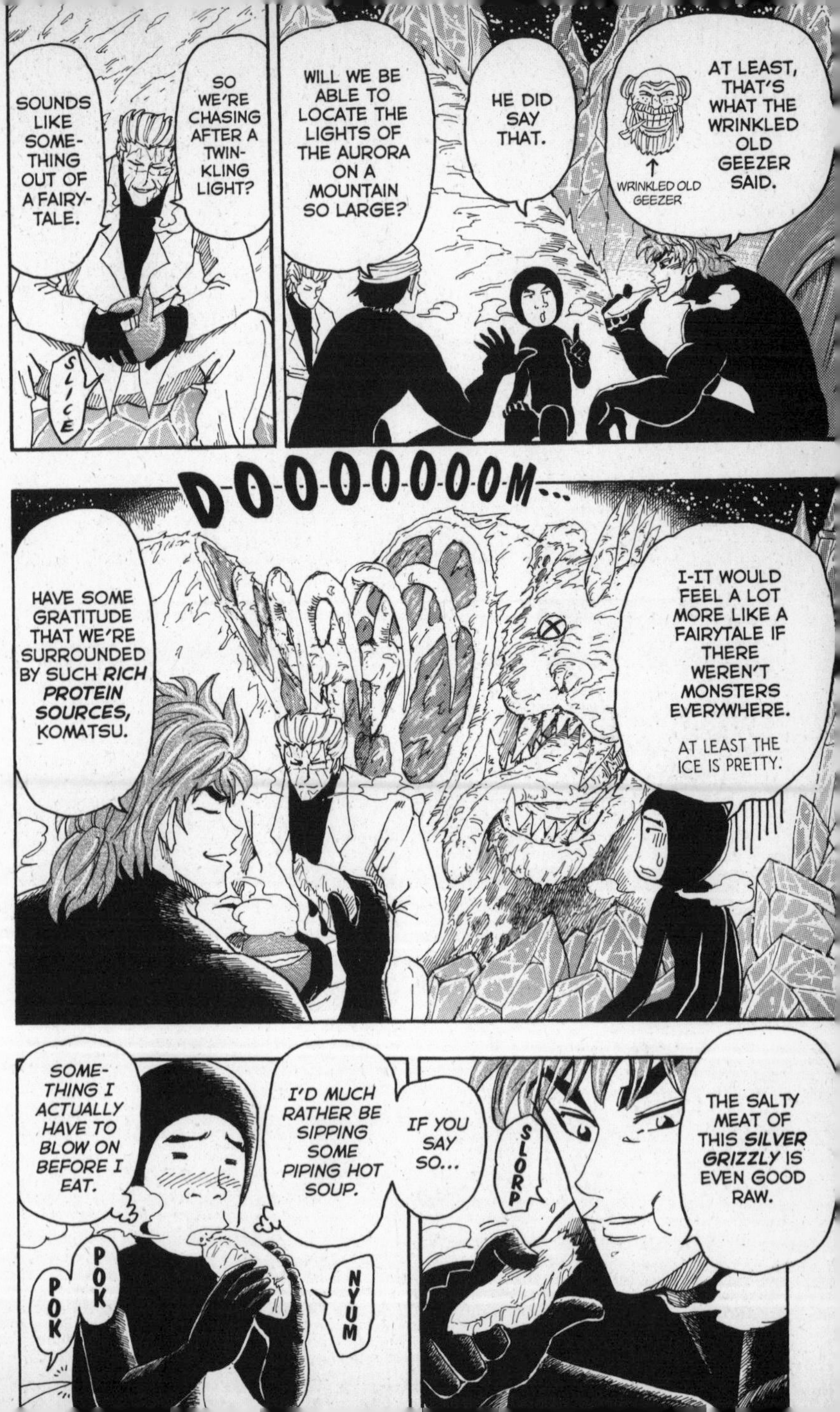
AT LEAST, THAT'S WHAT THE WRINKLED OLD GEEZER SAID.
WRINKLED OLD GEEZER
HE DID SAY THAT.
WILL WE BE ABLE TO LOCATE THE LIGHTS OF THE AURORA ON A MOUNTAIN SO LARGE?
SO WE'RE CHASING AFTER A TWIN-KLING LIGHT?
SOUNDS LIKE SOME-THING OUT OF A FAIRY-TALE.
SLICE
D-O-O-O-O-O-O-M...
I-IT WOULD FEEL A LOT MORE LIKE A FAIRYTALE IF THERE WEREN'T MONSTERS EVERYWHERE.
AT LEAST THE ICE IS PRETTY.
HAVE SOME GRATITUDE THAT WE'RE SURROUNDED BY SUCH *RICH PROTEIN SOURCES*, KOMATSU.
THE SALTY MEAT OF THIS *SILVER GRIZZLY* IS EVEN GOOD RAW.
SLORP
IF YOU SAY SO...
I'D MUCH RATHER BE SIPPING SOME PIPING HOT SOUP.
SOME-THING I ACTUALLY HAVE TO BLOW ON BEFORE I EAT.
NYUM
POK
POK

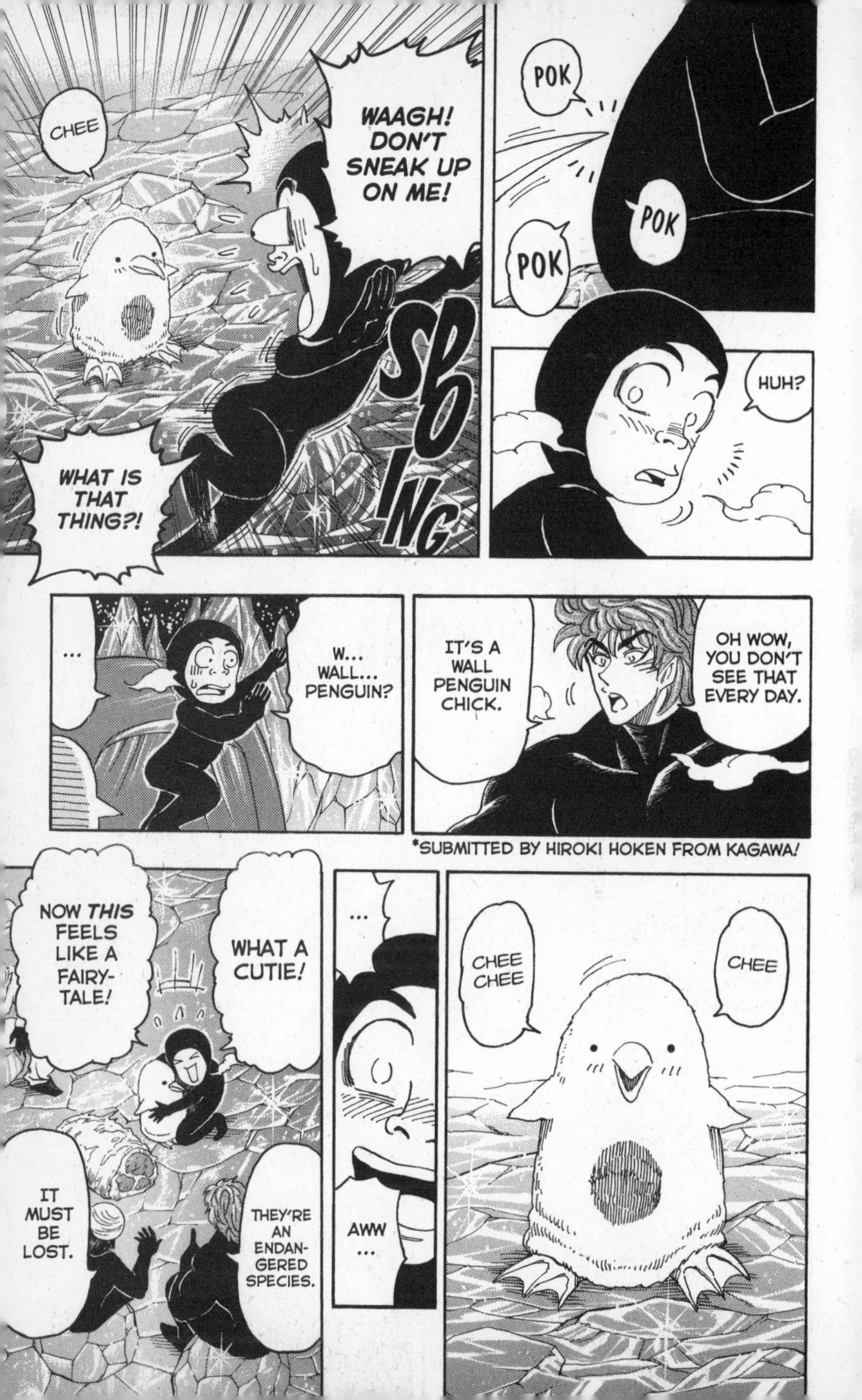
POK
POK
POK
HUH?
WAAGH! DON'T SNEAK UP ON ME!
CHEE
SBOING
WHAT IS THAT THING?!
OH WOW, YOU DON'T SEE THAT EVERY DAY.
IT'S A WALL PENGUIN CHICK.
W... WALL... PENGUIN?
...
*SUBMITTED BY HIROKI HOKEN FROM KAGAWA!
CHEE
CHEE CHEE
...
AWW ...
WHAT A CUTIE!
NOW THIS FEELS LIKE A FAIRY-TALE!
THEY'RE AN ENDANGERED SPECIES.
IT MUST BE LOST.

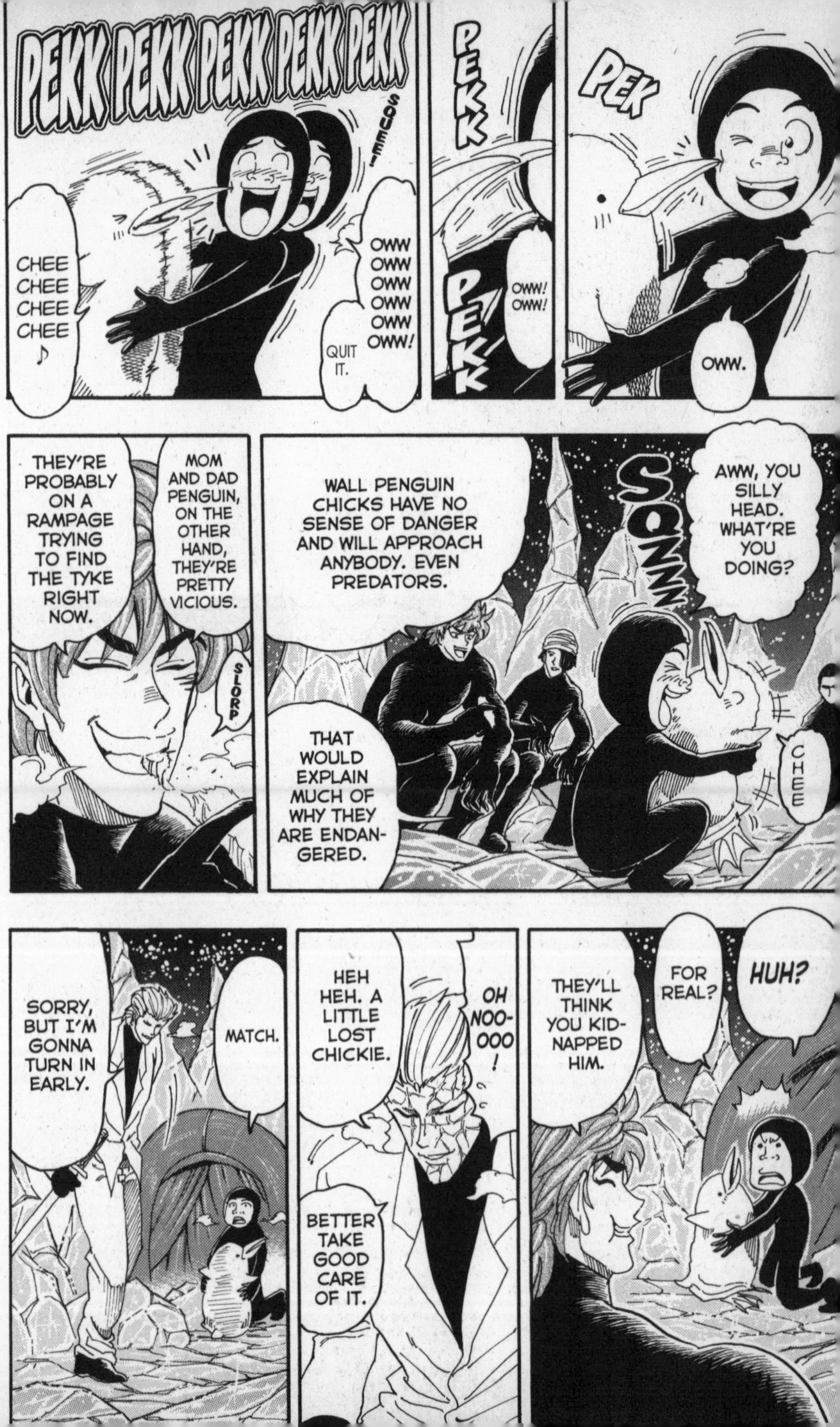
PEK
OWW.
PEKK
OWW! OWW!
PEKK
SQUEE!
PEKK PEKK PEKK PEKK PEKK
OWW OWW OWW OWW OWW OWW!
QUIT IT.
CHEE CHEE CHEE CHEE ♪
AWW, YOU SILLY HEAD. WHAT'RE YOU DOING?
SQNNN
WALL PENGUIN CHICKS HAVE NO SENSE OF DANGER AND WILL APPROACH ANYBODY. EVEN PREDATORS.
CHEE
THAT WOULD EXPLAIN MUCH OF WHY THEY ARE ENDANGERED.
MOM AND DAD PENGUIN, ON THE OTHER HAND, THEY'RE PRETTY VICIOUS.
THEY'RE PROBABLY ON A RAMPAGE TRYING TO FIND THE TYKE RIGHT NOW.
SLORP
HUH?
FOR REAL?
THEY'LL THINK YOU KIDNAPPED HIM.
OH NOOOOO!
HEH HEH. A LITTLE LOST CHICKIE.
BETTER TAKE GOOD CARE OF IT.
MATCH.
SORRY, BUT I'M GONNA TURN IN EARLY.

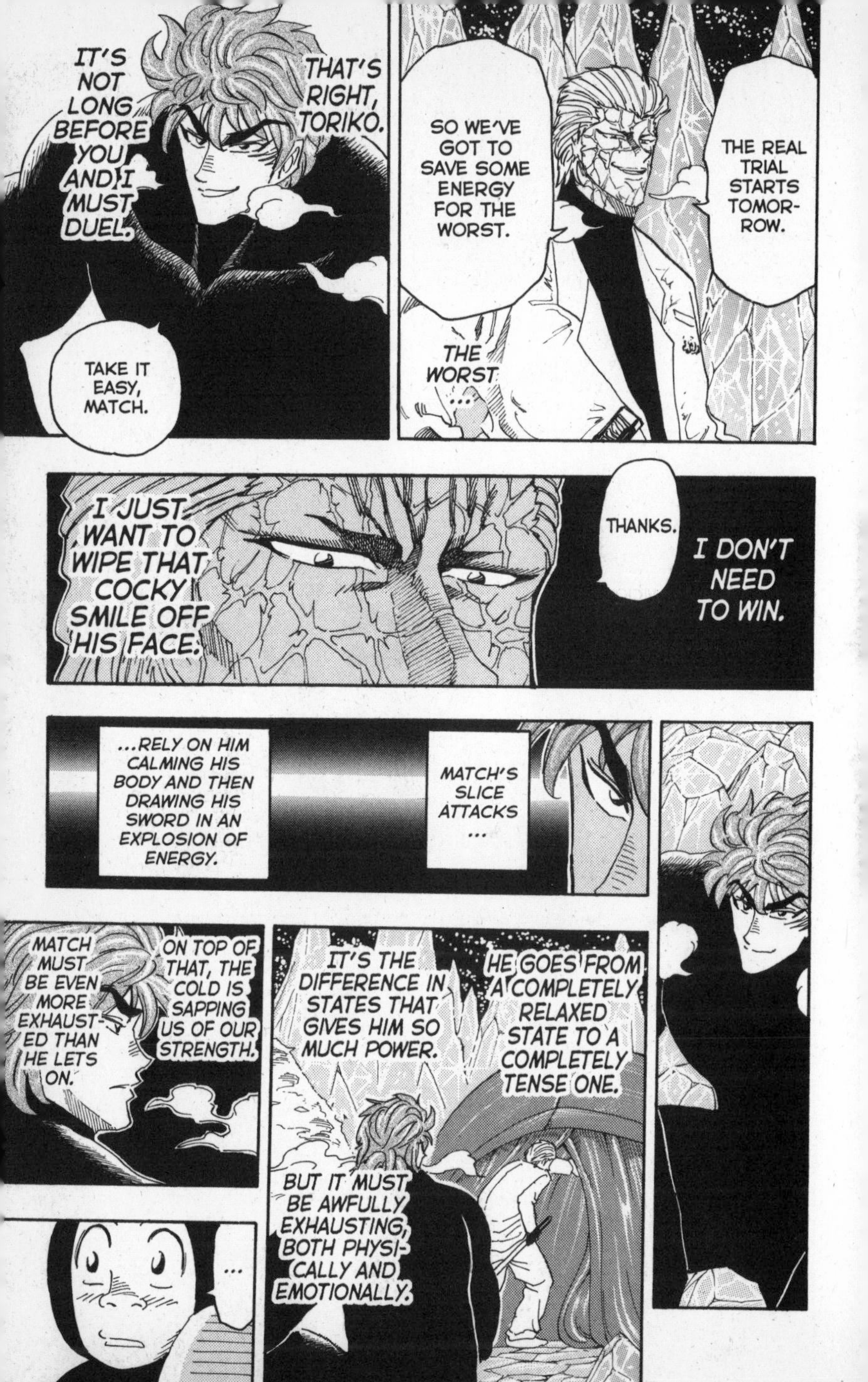
THE REAL TRIAL STARTS TOMORROW.
SO WE'VE GOT TO SAVE SOME ENERGY FOR THE WORST.
THE WORST...
THAT'S RIGHT, TORIKO.
IT'S NOT LONG BEFORE YOU AND I MUST DUEL.
TAKE IT EASY, MATCH.
THANKS.
I DON'T NEED TO WIN.
I JUST WANT TO WIPE THAT COCKY SMILE OFF HIS FACE.
MATCH'S SLICE ATTACKS ...
...RELY ON HIM CALMING HIS BODY AND THEN DRAWING HIS SWORD IN AN EXPLOSION OF ENERGY.
HE GOES FROM A COMPLETELY RELAXED STATE TO A COMPLETELY TENSE ONE.
IT'S THE DIFFERENCE IN STATES THAT GIVES HIM SO MUCH POWER.
BUT IT MUST BE AWFULLY EXHAUSTING, BOTH PHYSICALLY AND EMOTIONALLY.
ON TOP OF THAT, THE COLD IS SAPPING US OF OUR STRENGTH.
MATCH MUST BE EVEN MORE EXHAUSTED THAN HE LETS ON.
...

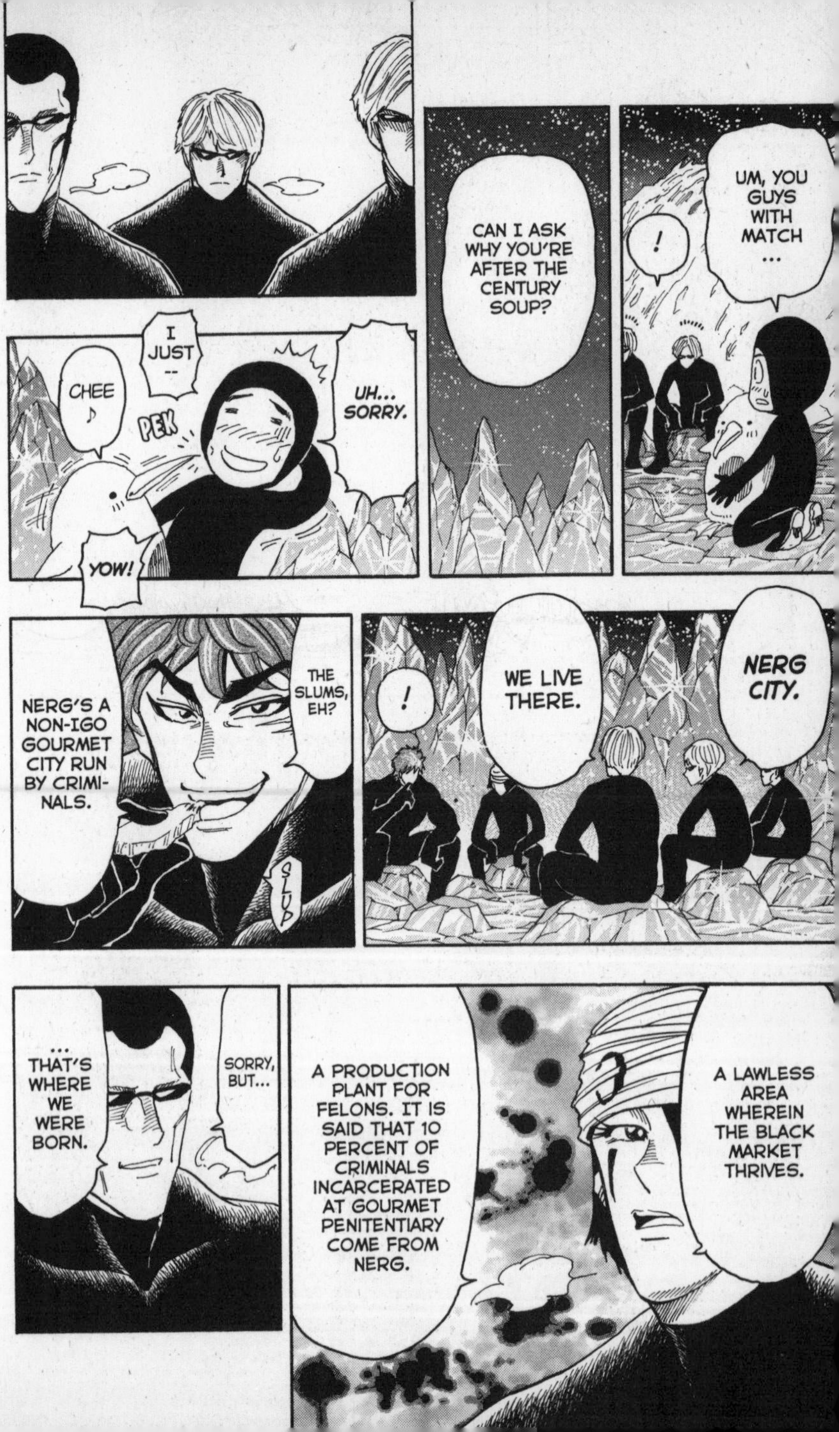
UM, YOU GUYS WITH MATCH ...
!
CAN I ASK WHY YOU'RE AFTER THE CENTURY SOUP?
UH... SORRY.
I JUST --
CHEE ♪
PEK
YOW!
NERG CITY.
WE LIVE THERE.
!
THE SLUMS, EH?
NERG'S A NON-IGO GOURMET CITY RUN BY CRIMINALS.
SLUP
A LAWLESS AREA WHEREIN THE BLACK MARKET THRIVES.
A PRODUCTION PLANT FOR FELONS. IT IS SAID THAT 10 PERCENT OF CRIMINALS INCARCERATED AT GOURMET PENITENTIARY COME FROM NERG.
SORRY, BUT...
... THAT'S WHERE WE WERE BORN.

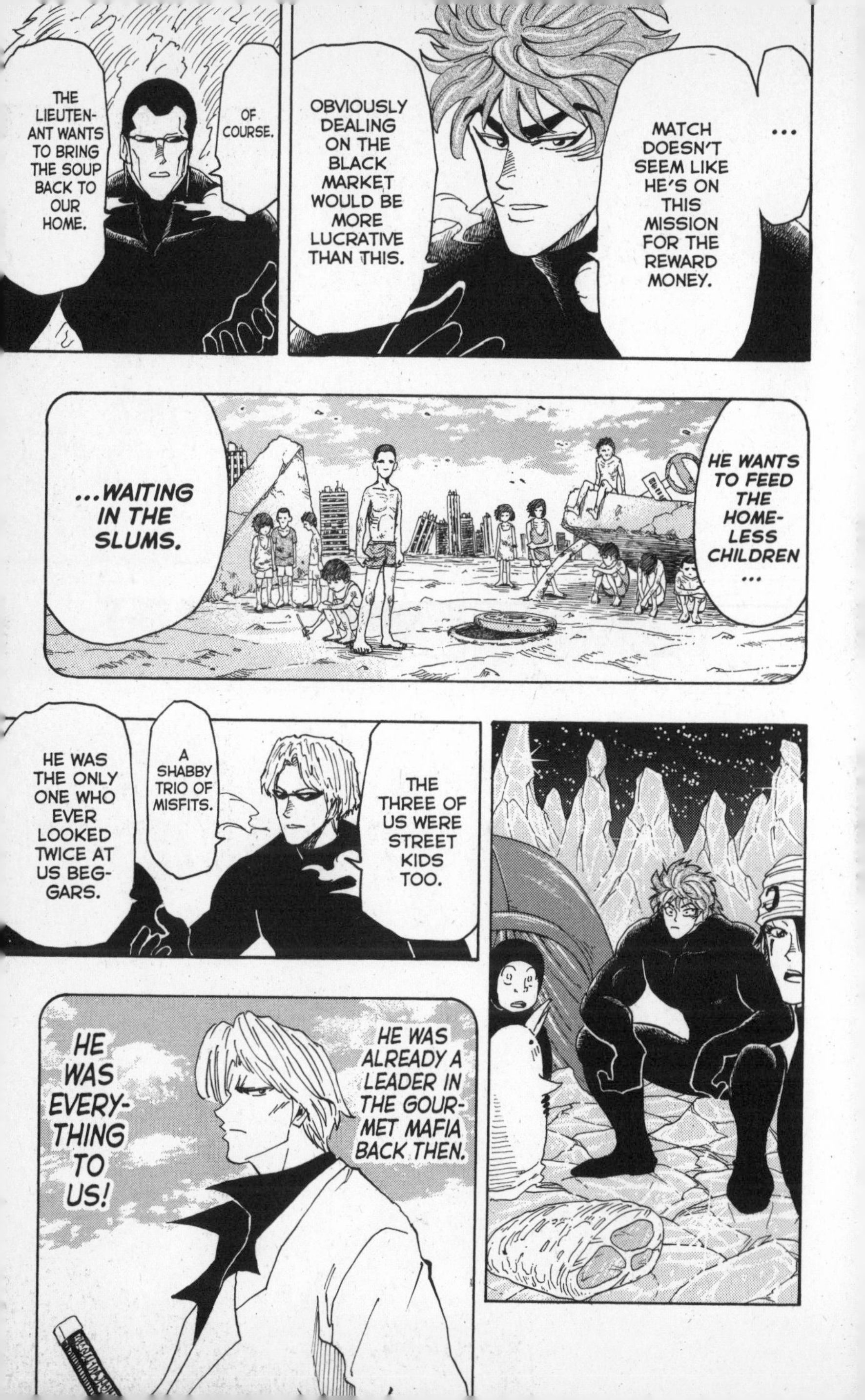
...
MATCH DOESN'T SEEM LIKE HE'S ON THIS MISSION FOR THE REWARD MONEY.
OBVIOUSLY DEALING ON THE BLACK MARKET WOULD BE MORE LUCRATIVE THAN THIS.
OF COURSE.
THE LIEUTENANT WANTS TO BRING THE SOUP BACK TO OUR HOME.
HE WANTS TO FEED THE HOMELESS CHILDREN...
...WAITING IN THE SLUMS.
THE THREE OF US WERE STREET KIDS TOO.
A SHABBY TRIO OF MISFITS.
HE WAS THE ONLY ONE WHO EVER LOOKED TWICE AT US BEGGARS.
HE WAS ALREADY A LEADER IN THE GOURMET MAFIA BACK THEN.
HE WAS EVERYTHING TO US!

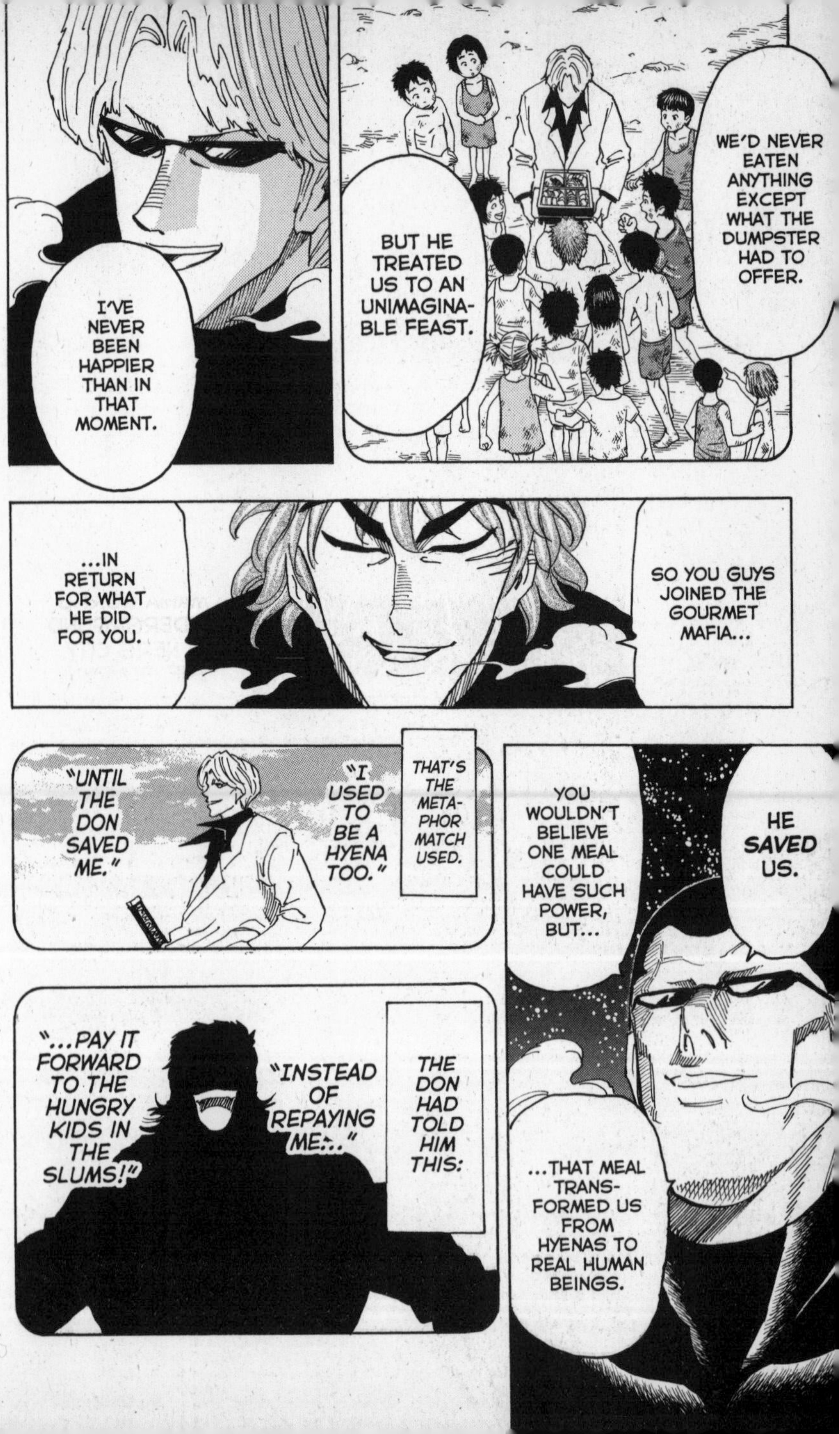
WE'D NEVER EATEN ANYTHING EXCEPT WHAT THE DUMPSTER HAD TO OFFER.
BUT HE TREATED US TO AN UNIMAGINABLE FEAST.
I'VE NEVER BEEN HAPPIER THAN IN THAT MOMENT.
SO YOU GUYS JOINED THE GOURMET MAFIA...
...IN RETURN FOR WHAT HE DID FOR YOU.
HE *SAVED* US.
YOU WOULDN'T BELIEVE ONE MEAL COULD HAVE SUCH POWER, BUT...
...THAT MEAL TRANSFORMED US FROM HYENAS TO REAL HUMAN BEINGS.
THAT'S THE METAPHOR MATCH USED.
"I USED TO BE A HYENA TOO."
"UNTIL THE DON SAVED ME."
THE DON HAD TOLD HIM THIS:
"INSTEAD OF REPAYING ME..."
"...PAY IT FORWARD TO THE HUNGRY KIDS IN THE SLUMS!"

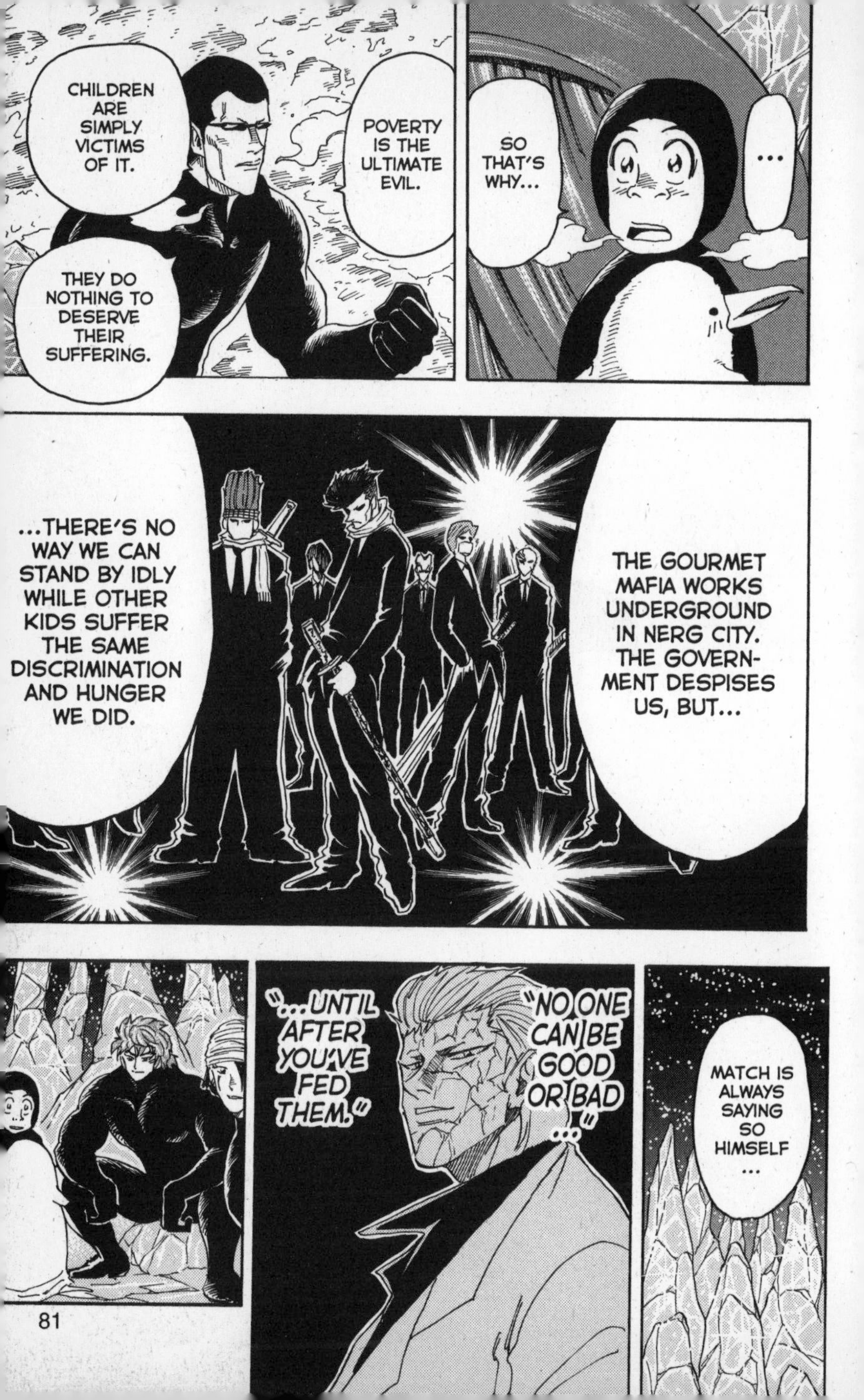
...
SO THAT'S WHY...
POVERTY IS THE ULTIMATE EVIL.
CHILDREN ARE SIMPLY VICTIMS OF IT.
THEY DO NOTHING TO DESERVE THEIR SUFFERING.
THE GOURMET MAFIA WORKS UNDERGROUND IN NERG CITY. THE GOVERN-MENT DESPISES US, BUT...
...THERE'S NO WAY WE CAN STAND BY IDLY WHILE OTHER KIDS SUFFER THE SAME DISCRIMINATION AND HUNGER WE DID.
MATCH IS ALWAYS SAYING SO HIMSELF ...
"NO ONE CAN BE GOOD OR BAD"...
"...UNTIL AFTER YOU'VE FED THEM."

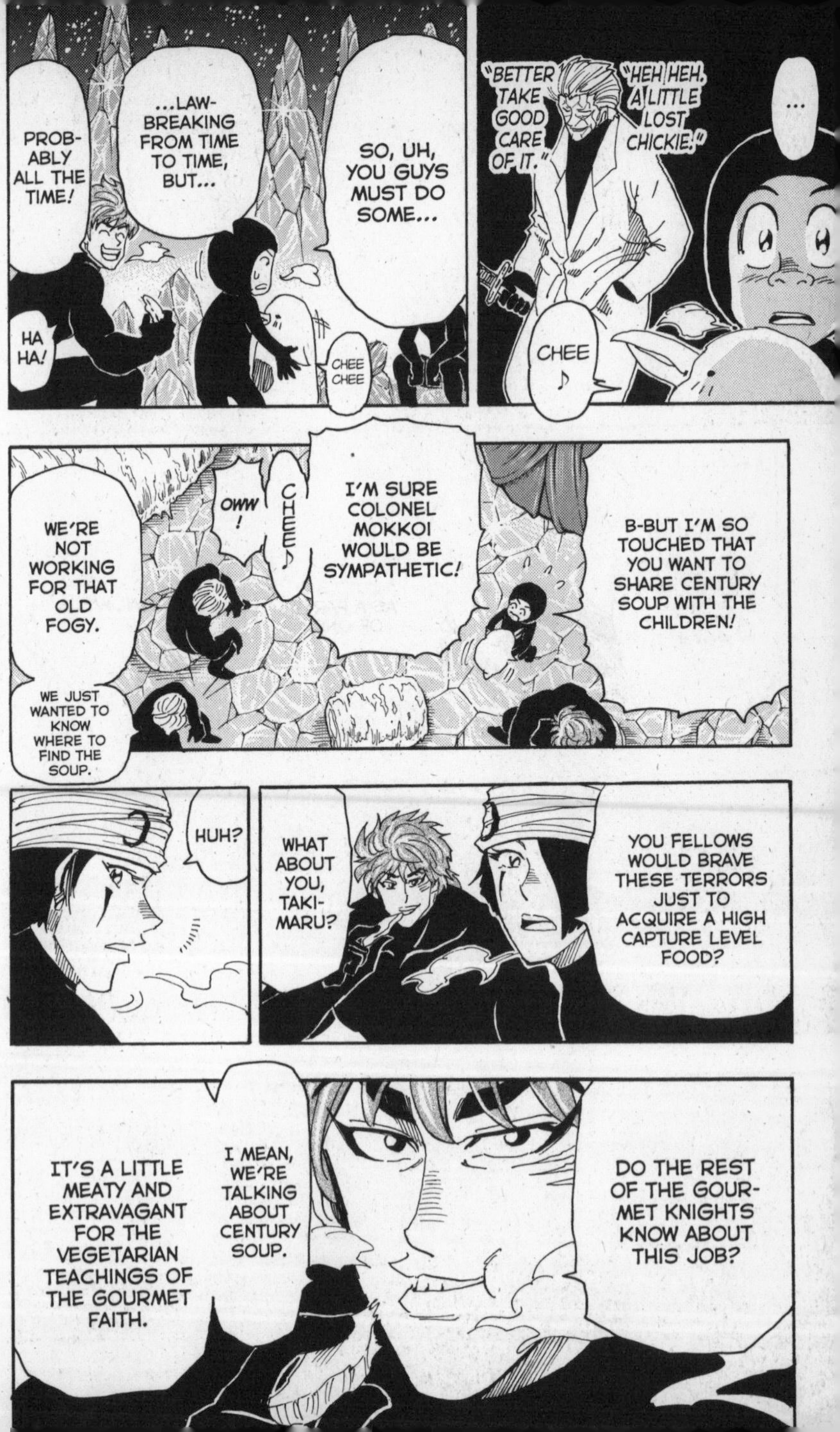
...
"HEH HEH, A LITTLE LOST CHICKIE."
"BETTER TAKE GOOD CARE OF IT."
CHEE ♪
SO, UH, YOU GUYS MUST DO SOME...
...LAW-BREAKING FROM TIME TO TIME, BUT...
PROB-ABLY ALL THE TIME!
HA HA!
CHEE CHEE
B-BUT I'M SO TOUCHED THAT YOU WANT TO SHARE CENTURY SOUP WITH THE CHILDREN!
I'M SURE COLONEL MOKKOI WOULD BE SYMPATHETIC!
CHEE♪
OWW!
WE'RE NOT WORKING FOR THAT OLD FOGY.
WE JUST WANTED TO KNOW WHERE TO FIND THE SOUP.
YOU FELLOWS WOULD BRAVE THESE TERRORS JUST TO ACQUIRE A HIGH CAPTURE LEVEL FOOD?
WHAT ABOUT YOU, TAKI-MARU?
HUH?
DO THE REST OF THE GOUR-MET KNIGHTS KNOW ABOUT THIS JOB?
I MEAN, WE'RE TALKING ABOUT CENTURY SOUP.
IT'S A LITTLE MEATY AND EXTRAVAGANT FOR THE VEGETARIAN TEACHINGS OF THE GOURMET FAITH.

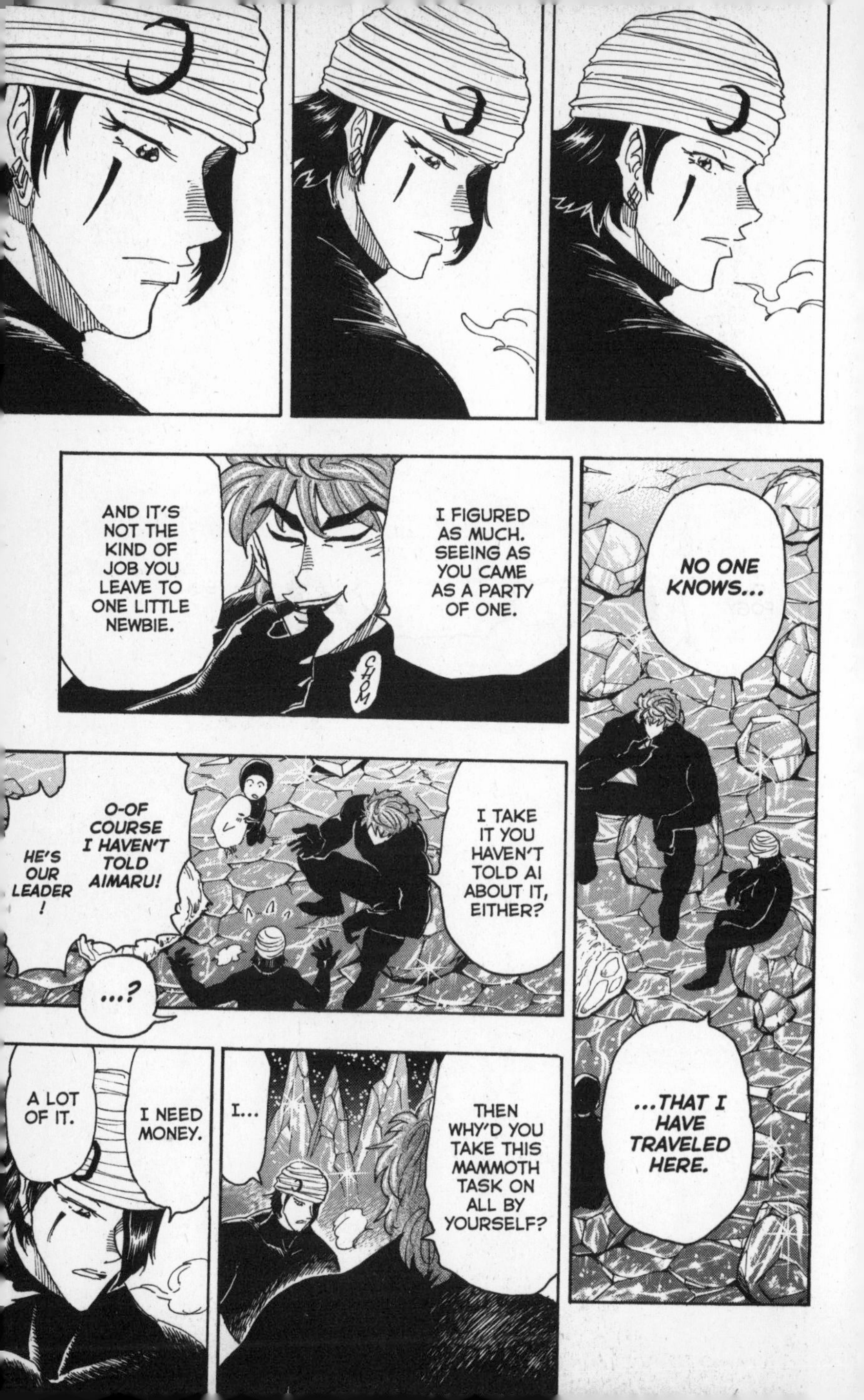
NO ONE KNOWS...
...THAT I HAVE TRAVELED HERE.
I FIGURED AS MUCH. SEEING AS YOU CAME AS A PARTY OF ONE.
AND IT'S NOT THE KIND OF JOB YOU LEAVE TO ONE LITTLE NEWBIE.
CHOM
I TAKE IT YOU HAVEN'T TOLD AI ABOUT IT, EITHER?
...?
O-OF COURSE I HAVEN'T TOLD AIMARU!
HE'S OUR LEADER!
THEN WHY'D YOU TAKE THIS MAMMOTH TASK ON ALL BY YOURSELF?
I...
I NEED MONEY.
A LOT OF IT.

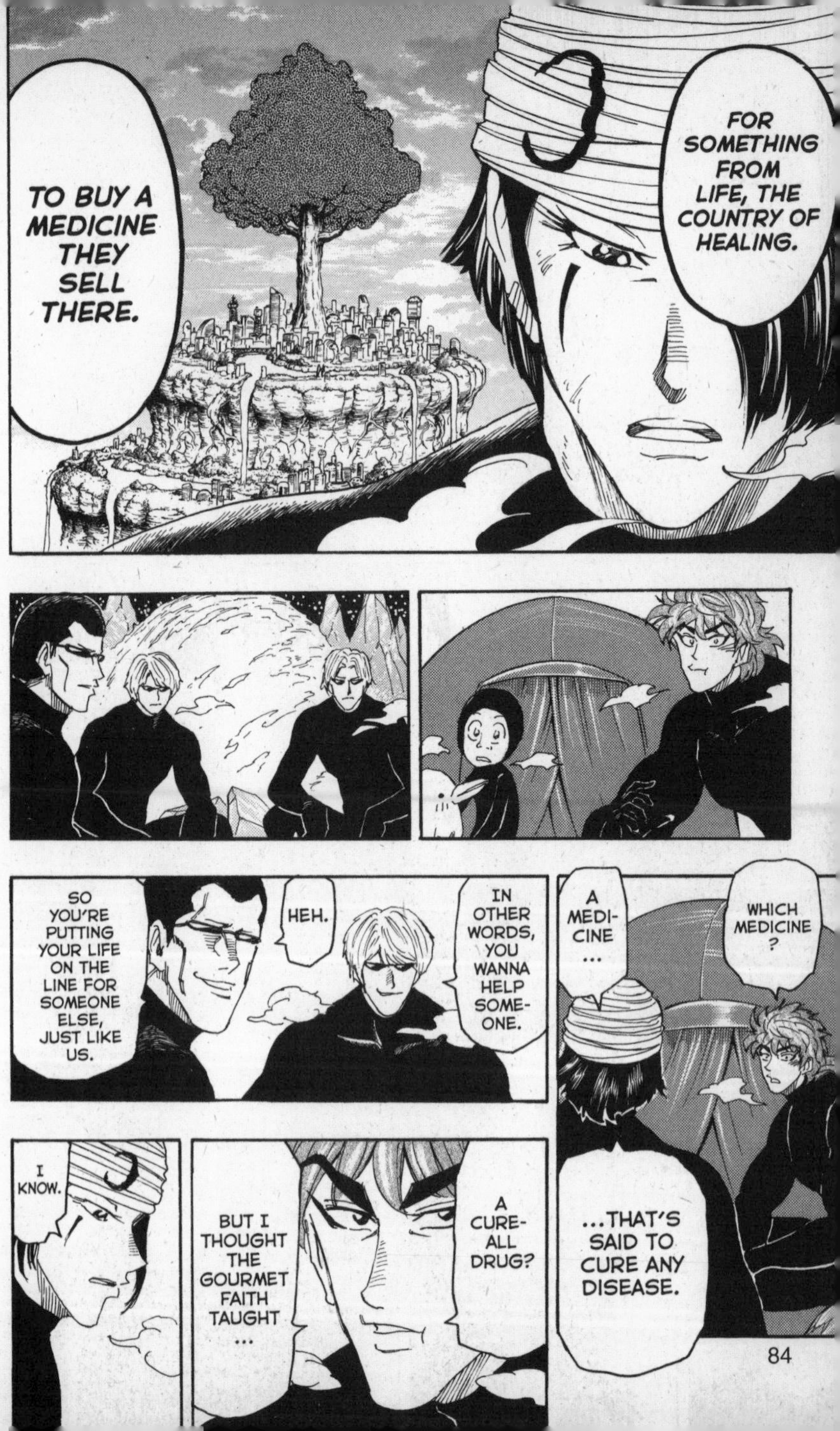
FOR SOMETHING FROM LIFE, THE COUNTRY OF HEALING.
TO BUY A MEDICINE THEY SELL THERE.
WHICH MEDICINE ?
A MEDICINE ...
...THAT'S SAID TO CURE ANY DISEASE.
IN OTHER WORDS, YOU WANNA HELP SOMEONE.
HEH.
SO YOU'RE PUTTING YOUR LIFE ON THE LINE FOR SOMEONE ELSE, JUST LIKE US.
A CURE-ALL DRUG?
BUT I THOUGHT THE GOURMET FAITH TAUGHT ...
I KNOW.

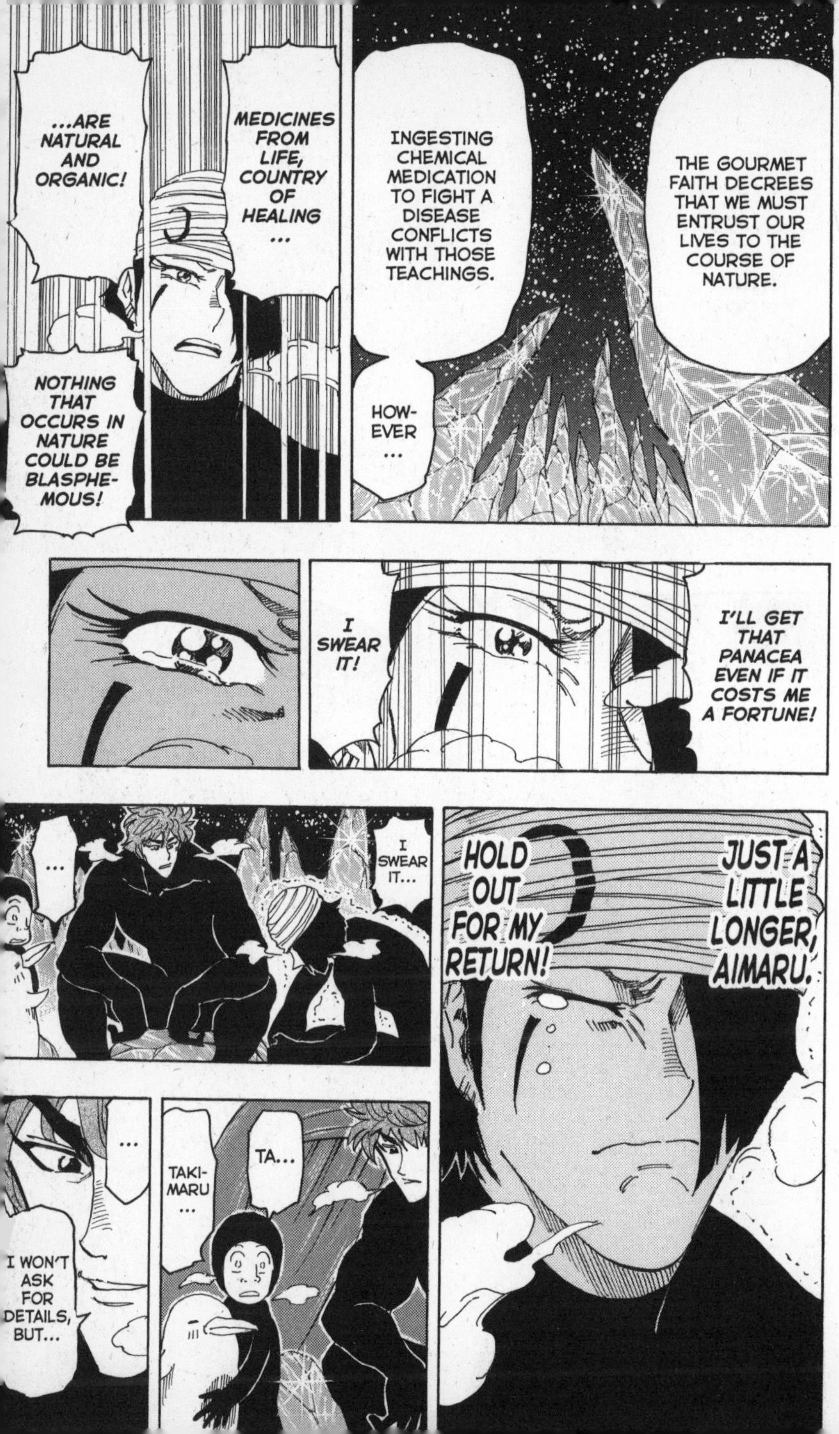

THE GOURMET FAITH DECREES THAT WE MUST ENTRUST OUR LIVES TO THE COURSE OF NATURE.
INGESTING CHEMICAL MEDICATION TO FIGHT A DISEASE CONFLICTS WITH THOSE TEACHINGS.
HOW-EVER...
MEDICINES FROM LIFE, COUNTRY OF HEALING...
...ARE NATURAL AND ORGANIC!
NOTHING THAT OCCURS IN NATURE COULD BE BLASPHE-MOUS!
I'LL GET THAT PANACEA EVEN IF IT COSTS ME A FORTUNE!
I SWEAR IT!
JUST A LITTLE LONGER, AIMARU.
HOLD OUT FOR MY RETURN!
I SWEAR IT...
...
TA...
TAKI-MARU...
...
I WON'T ASK FOR DETAILS, BUT...

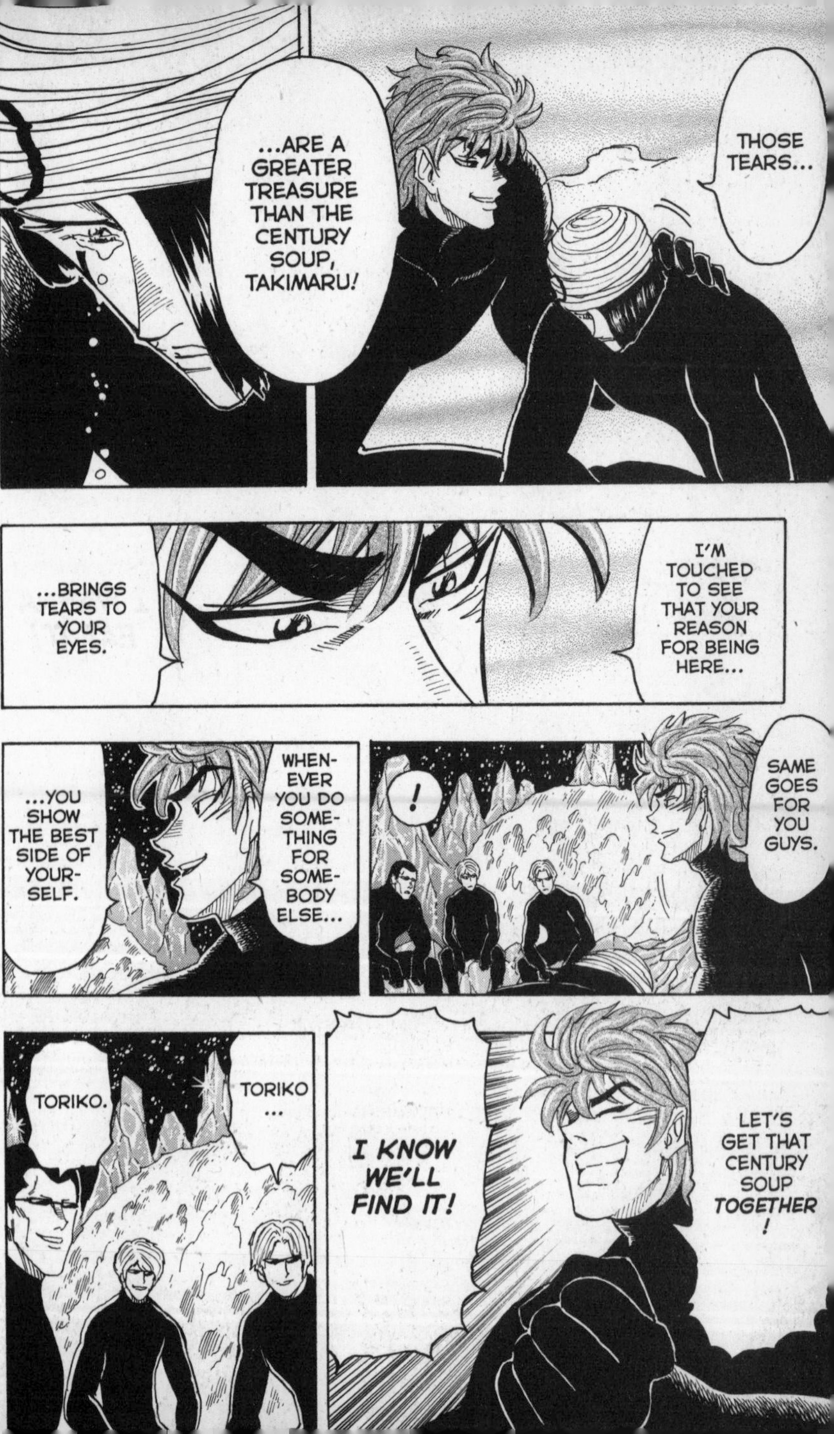
THOSE TEARS...
...ARE A GREATER TREASURE THAN THE CENTURY SOUP, TAKIMARU!
I'M TOUCHED TO SEE THAT YOUR REASON FOR BEING HERE...
...BRINGS TEARS TO YOUR EYES.
SAME GOES FOR YOU GUYS.
!
WHEN-EVER YOU DO SOME-THING FOR SOME-BODY ELSE...
...YOU SHOW THE BEST SIDE OF YOUR-SELF.
LET'S GET THAT CENTURY SOUP *TOGETHER*!
I KNOW WE'LL FIND IT!
TORIKO...
TORIKO.

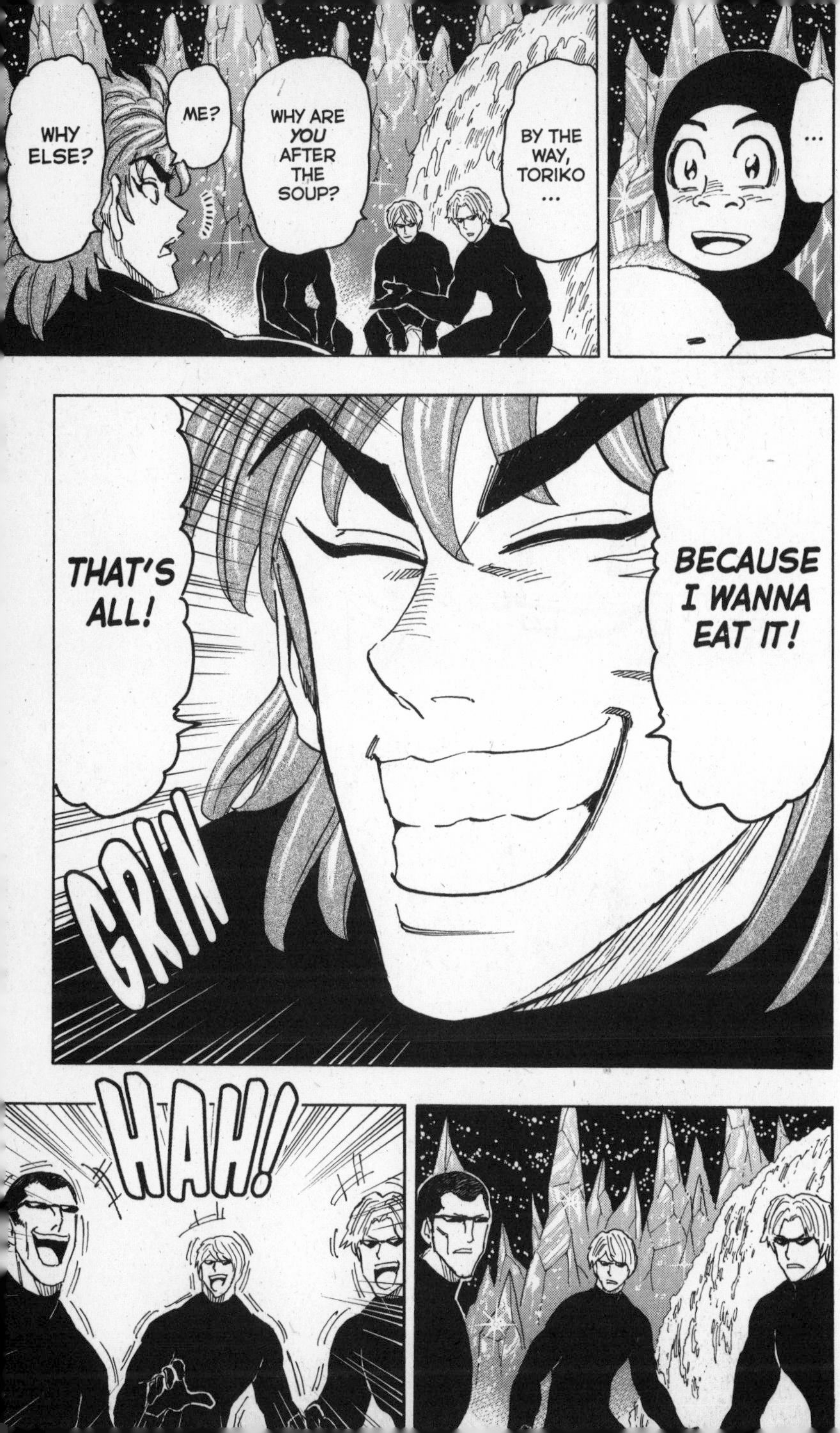
...
BY THE WAY, TORIKO ...
WHY ARE YOU AFTER THE SOUP?
ME?
WHY ELSE?
BECAUSE I WANNA EAT IT!
THAT'S ALL!
GRIN
HAH!

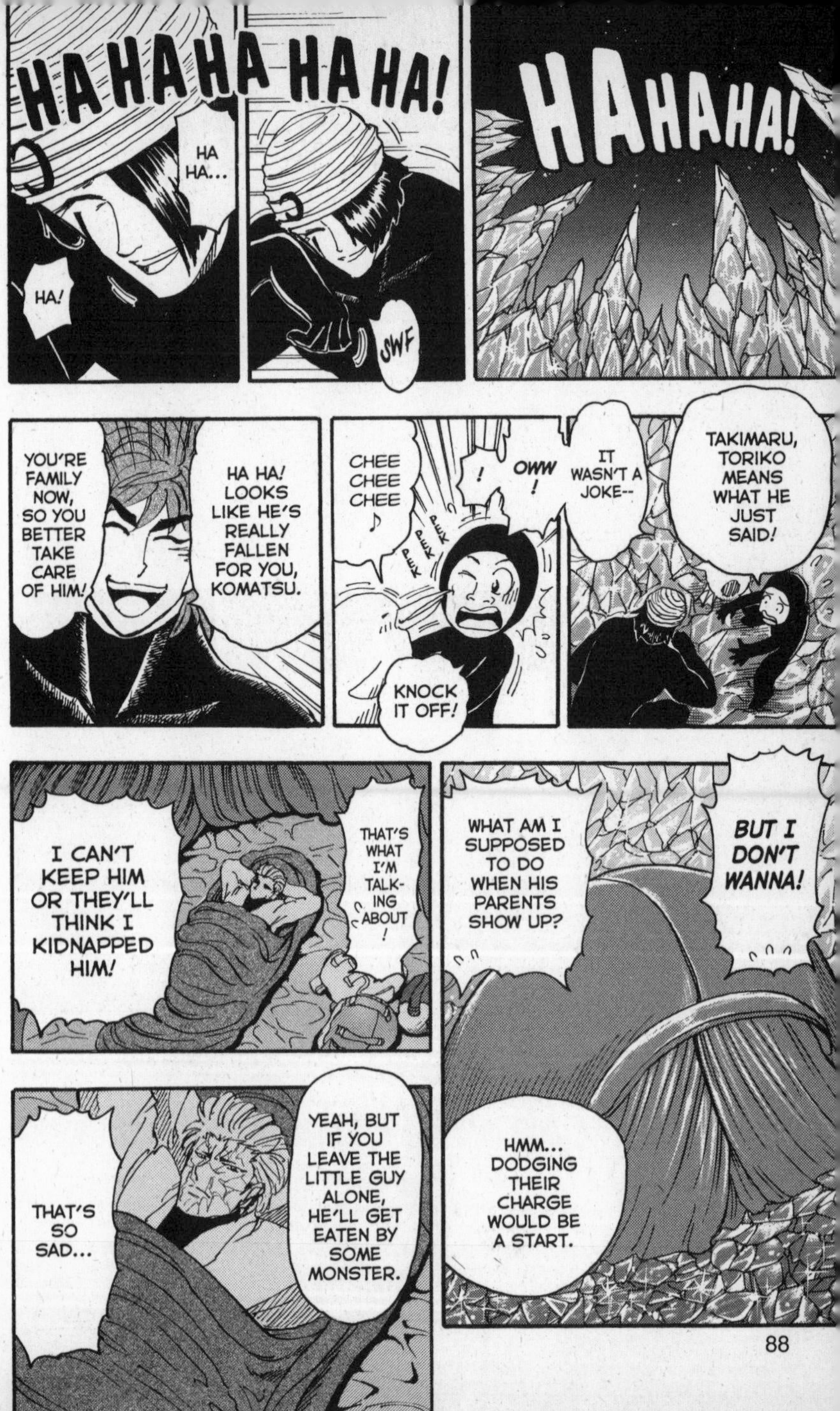
HAHAHA!
HA HA HA HA HA HA!
HA HA...
SWF
HA!
TAKIMARU, TORIKO MEANS WHAT HE JUST SAID!
IT WASN'T A JOKE--
OWW!
!
CHEE CHEE CHEE ♪
KNOCK IT OFF!
HA HA! LOOKS LIKE HE'S REALLY FALLEN FOR YOU, KOMATSU.
YOU'RE FAMILY NOW, SO YOU BETTER TAKE CARE OF HIM!
BUT I DON'T WANNA!
WHAT AM I SUPPOSED TO DO WHEN HIS PARENTS SHOW UP?
HMM... DODGING THEIR CHARGE WOULD BE A START.
THAT'S WHAT I'M TALKING ABOUT!
I CAN'T KEEP HIM OR THEY'LL THINK I KIDNAPPED HIM!
YEAH, BUT IF YOU LEAVE THE LITTLE GUY ALONE, HE'LL GET EATEN BY SOME MONSTER.
THAT'S SO SAD...

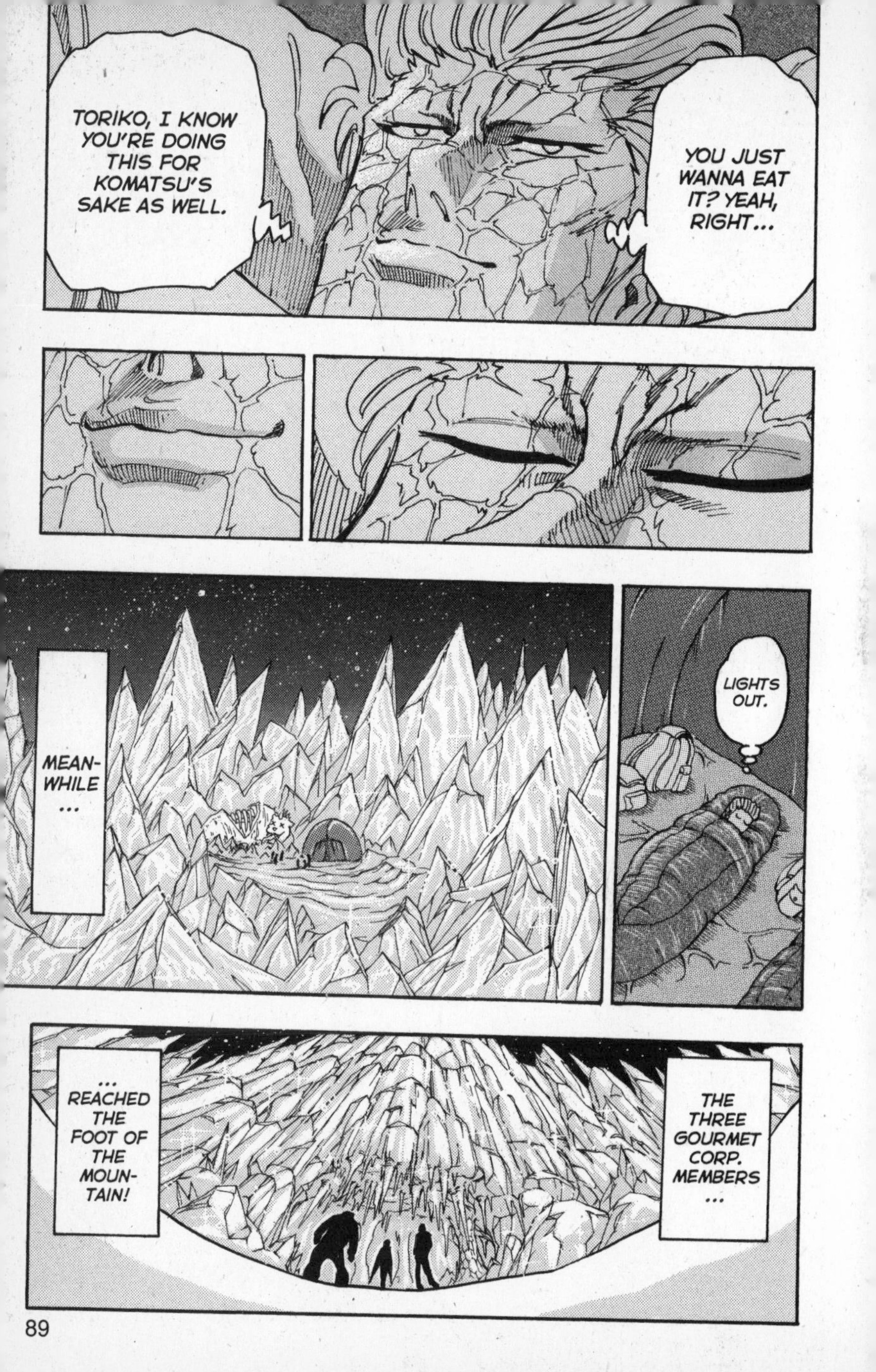
YOU JUST WANNA EAT IT? YEAH, RIGHT...
TORIKO, I KNOW YOU'RE DOING THIS FOR KOMATSU'S SAKE AS WELL.
LIGHTS OUT.
MEAN-WHILE ...
THE THREE GOURMET CORP. MEMBERS ...
... REACHED THE FOOT OF THE MOUN-TAIN!

TORIKO

GOURMET CHECKLIST

Vol. 066
GUARANA EEL
(FISH)

CAPTURE LEVEL: 16

HABITAT: RIVERS

LENGTH: 6 METERS

HEIGHT: ---

WEIGHT: 700 KG

PRICE: 100 G / 12,000 YEN

YEP.

MIGHT THAT BE GUARANA EEL PICKLED IN SHOCHU LIQUOR?

SCALE

THESE EELS LAY THEIR EGGS IN THE DEEP OCEAN, WHERE THEY WILL HATCH AND THE YOUNG EELS WILL LIVE. UPON REACHING MATURITY, THEY TRAVEL INTO RIVERS. AS THE NAME WOULD INDICATE, THESE EELS ARE RICH IN CAFFEINE AND TANNIN, MAKING THEM LIVING ENERGY DRINKS! WHEN STEEPED IN HIGHLY ALCOHOLIC SHOCHU, GUARANA EEL TASTES SIMILAR TO TIGER TESTICLES AND AMPS UP THE BODY'S BLOOD CIRCULATION AND PERSPIRATION PRODUCTION. IT'S ALSO A POPULAR TREAT ON THE SUMMERTIME GRILL.

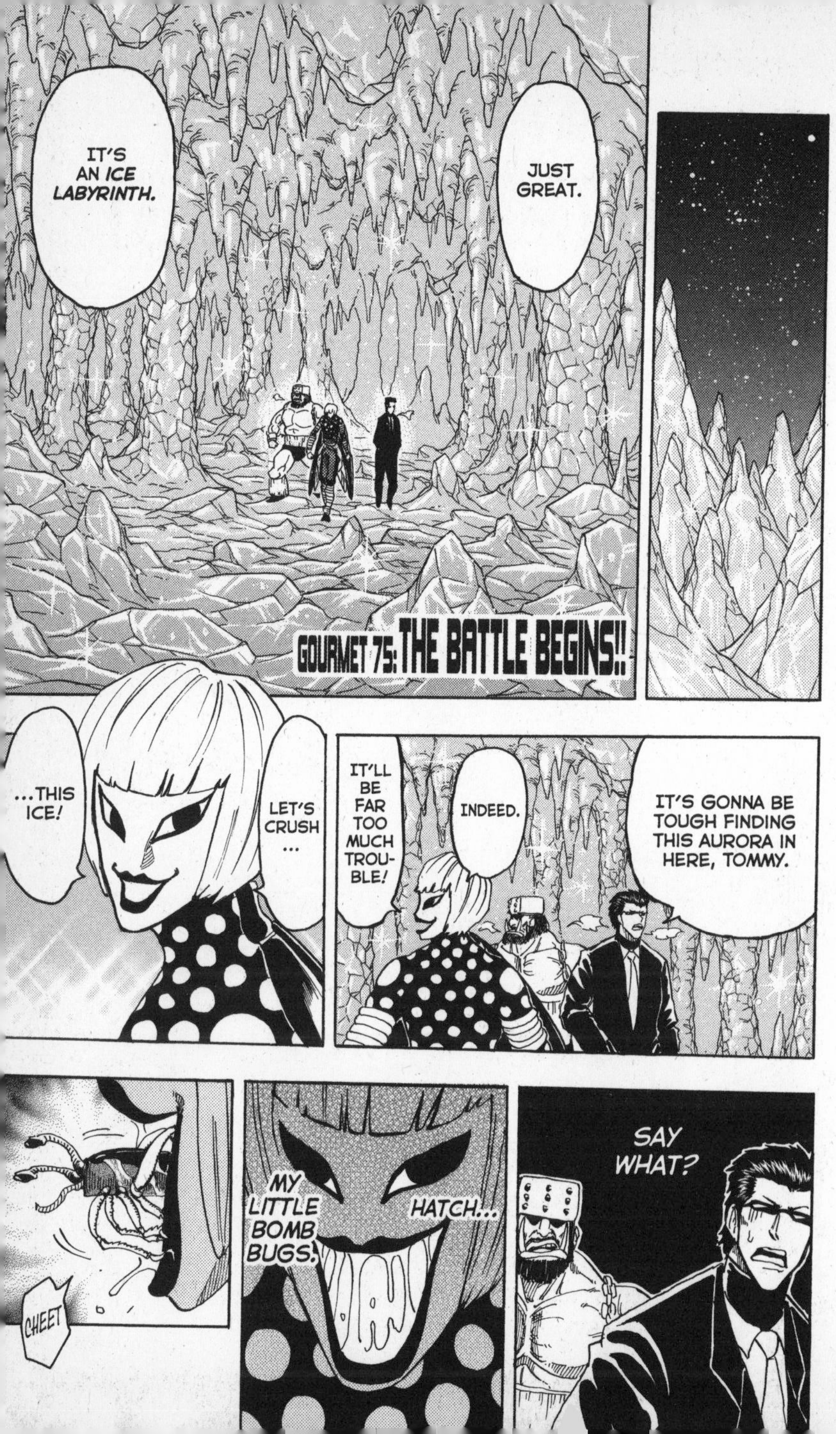
JUST GREAT.
IT'S AN ICE LABYRINTH.
GOURMET 75: THE BATTLE BEGINS!!
IT'S GONNA BE TOUGH FINDING THIS AURORA IN HERE, TOMMY.
INDEED.
IT'LL BE FAR TOO MUCH TROUBLE!
LET'S CRUSH ...
...THIS ICE!
SAY WHAT?
HATCH...
MY LITTLE BOMB BUGS.
CHEET

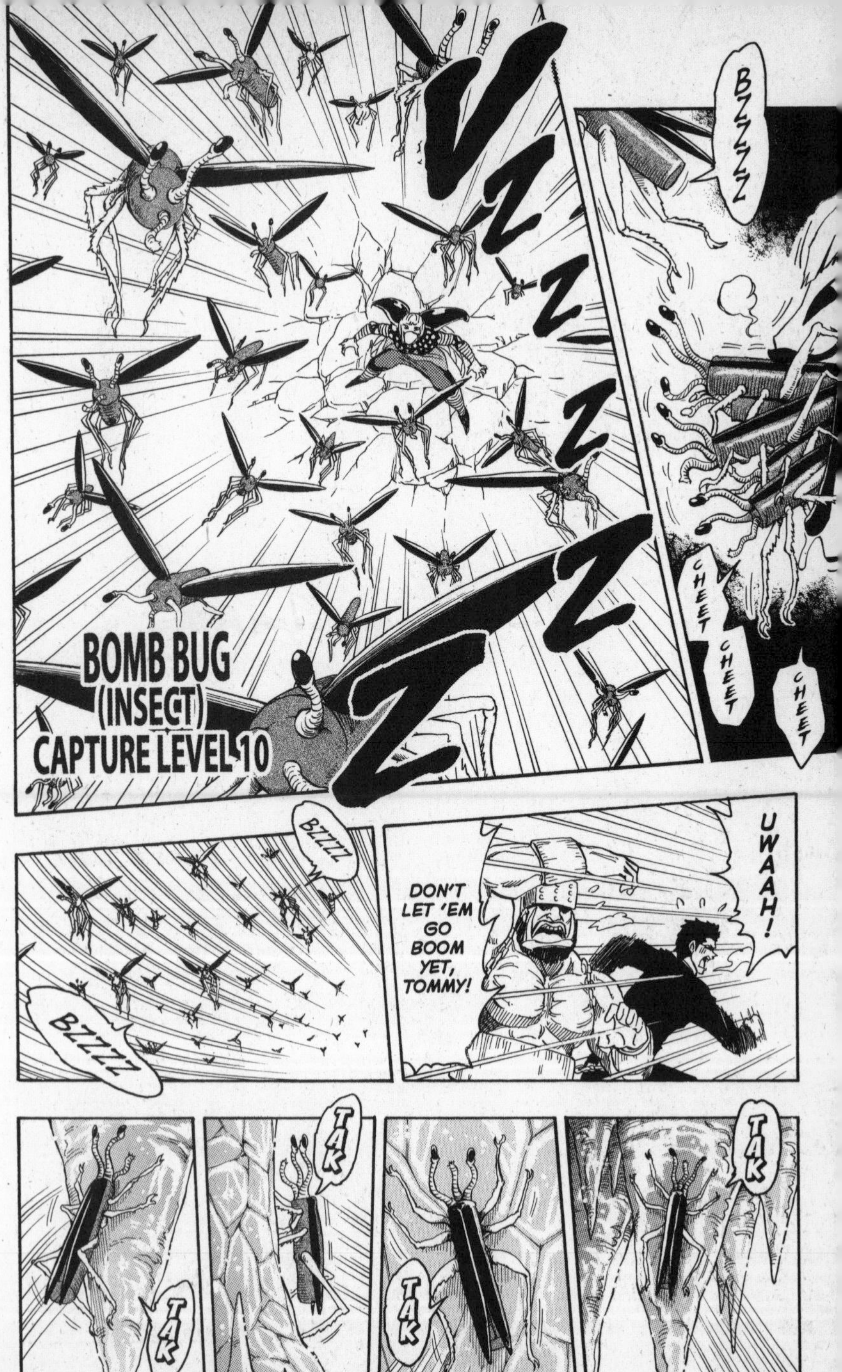
BZZZZZ
CHEET
CHEET
CHEET
BOMB BUG (INSECT) CAPTURE LEVEL 10
UWAAAH!
DON'T LET 'EM GO BOOM YET, TOMMY!
BZZZZZ
BZZZZZ
TAK
TAK
TAK
TAK

COME FORTH...
SPARK CRICKET!
KRCHA
KRCHA
KRCHA
SPARK CRICKET (INSECT) CAPTURE LEVEL 25
GLOOP
VVVVV...!
SWITCH...
...ON!
CHK

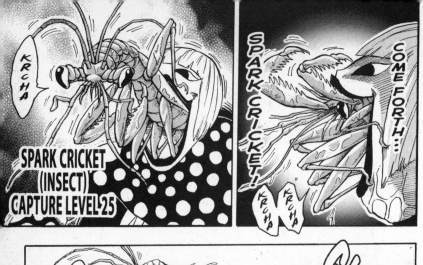

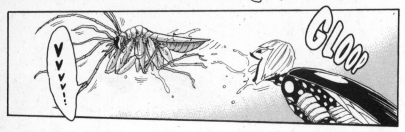

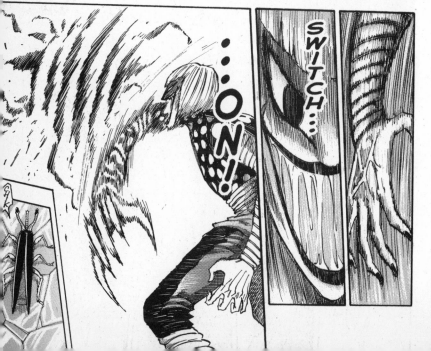

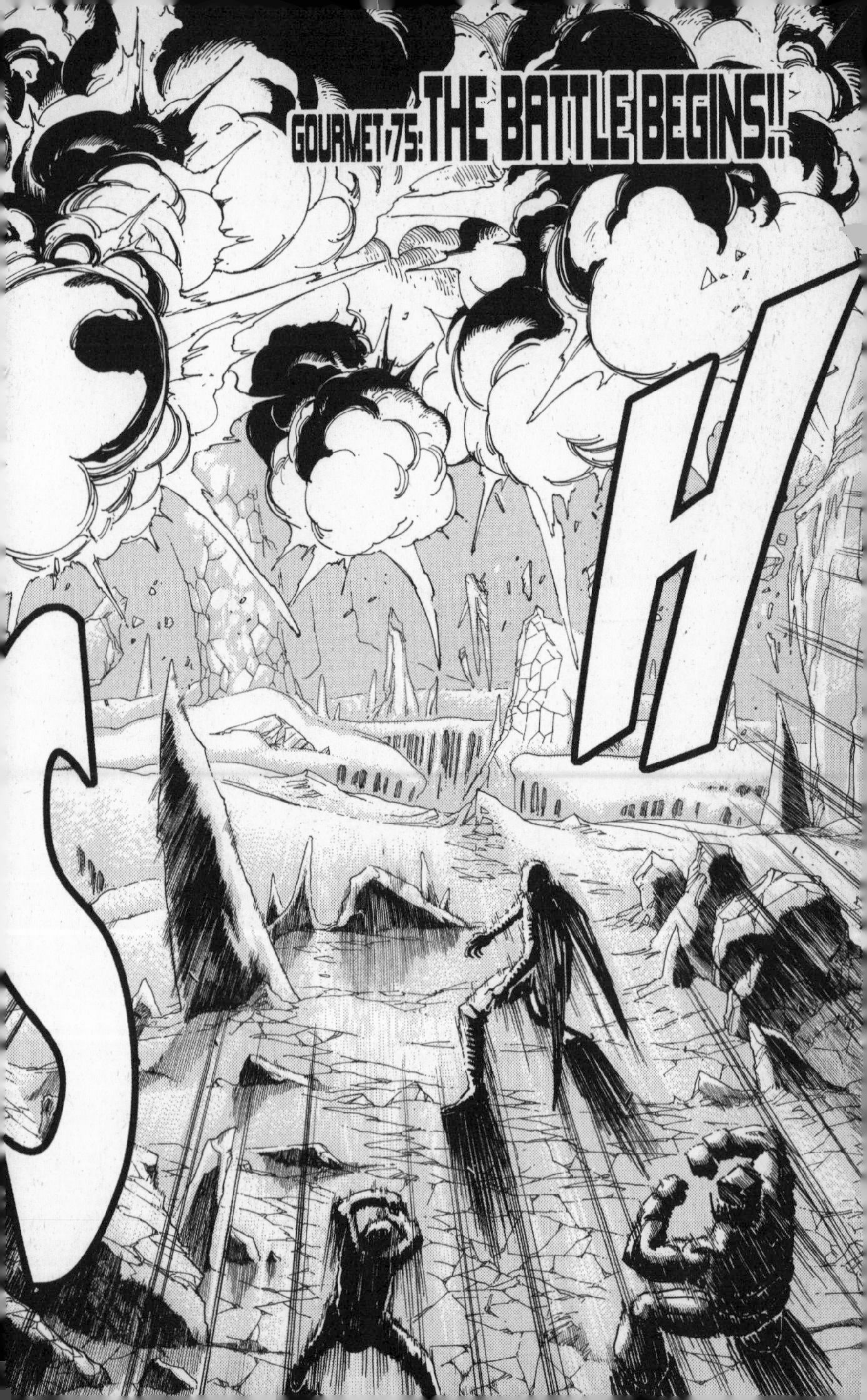
GOURMET 75: THE BATTLE BEGINS!!
SH

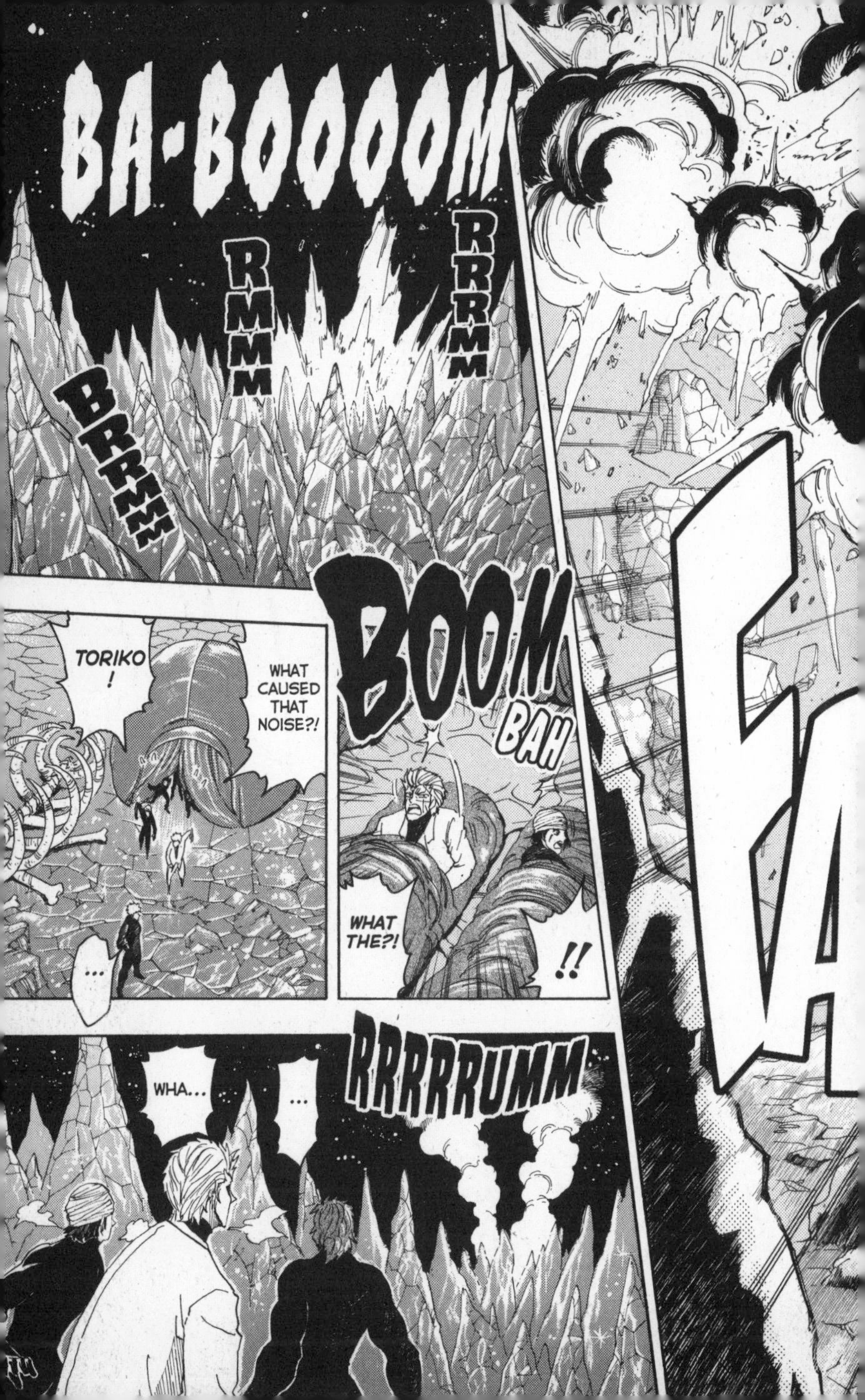
BA-BOOOOM
RRRRMM
RMMM
BRRRMMM
BOOM
BAH
!!
WHAT THE?!
WHAT CAUSED THAT NOISE?!
TORIKO!
...
RRRRRUMM
...
WHA...

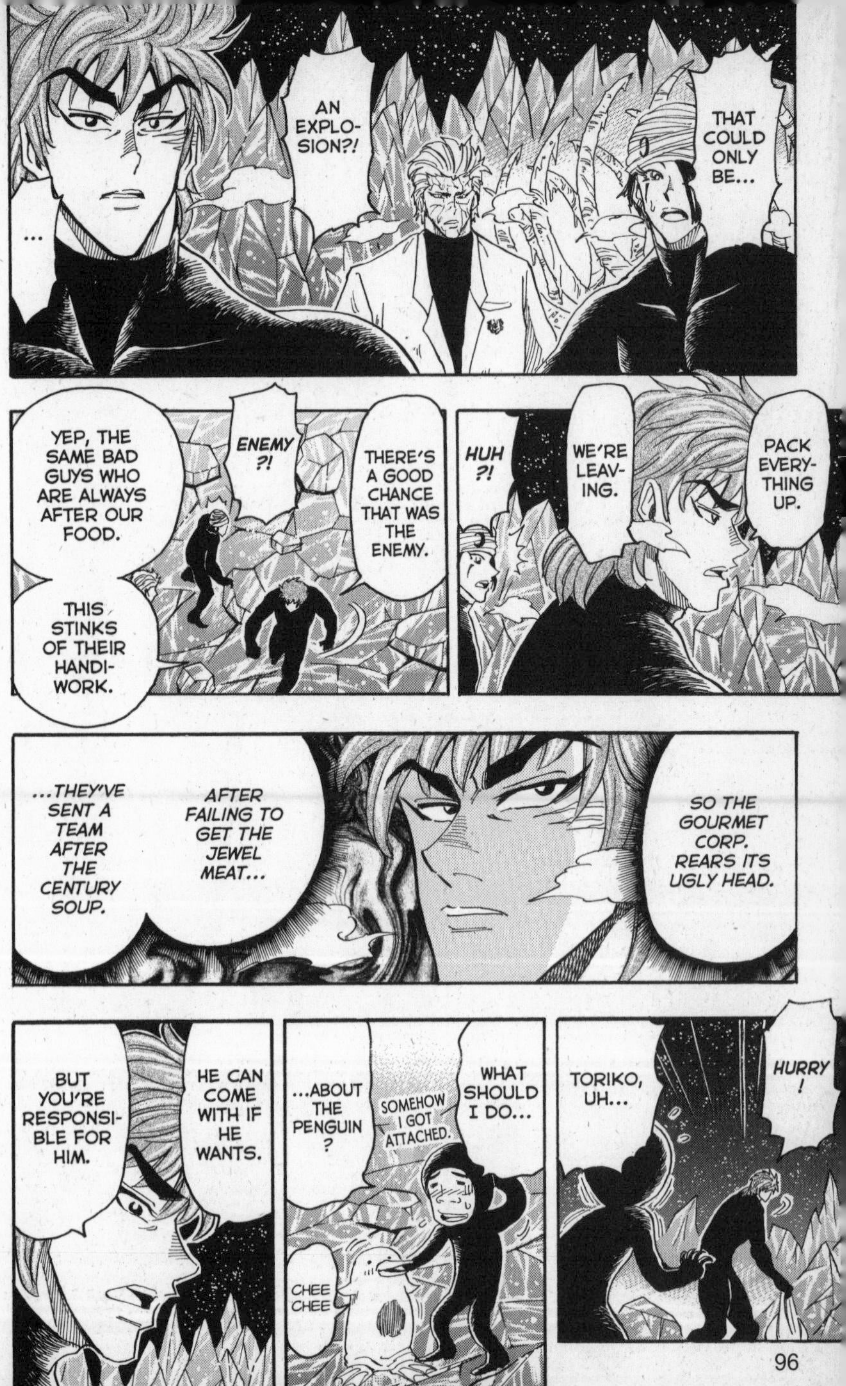
THAT COULD ONLY BE...
AN EXPLOSION?!
...
PACK EVERYTHING UP.
WE'RE LEAVING.
HUH ?!
THERE'S A GOOD CHANCE THAT WAS THE ENEMY.
ENEMY ?!
YEP, THE SAME BAD GUYS WHO ARE ALWAYS AFTER OUR FOOD.
THIS STINKS OF THEIR HANDIWORK.
SO THE GOURMET CORP. REARS ITS UGLY HEAD.
AFTER FAILING TO GET THE JEWEL MEAT...
...THEY'VE SENT A TEAM AFTER THE CENTURY SOUP.
HURRY!
TORIKO, UH...
WHAT SHOULD I DO...
...ABOUT THE PENGUIN?
SOMEHOW I GOT ATTACHED.
CHEE CHEE
HE CAN COME WITH IF HE WANTS.
BUT YOU'RE RESPONSIBLE FOR HIM.

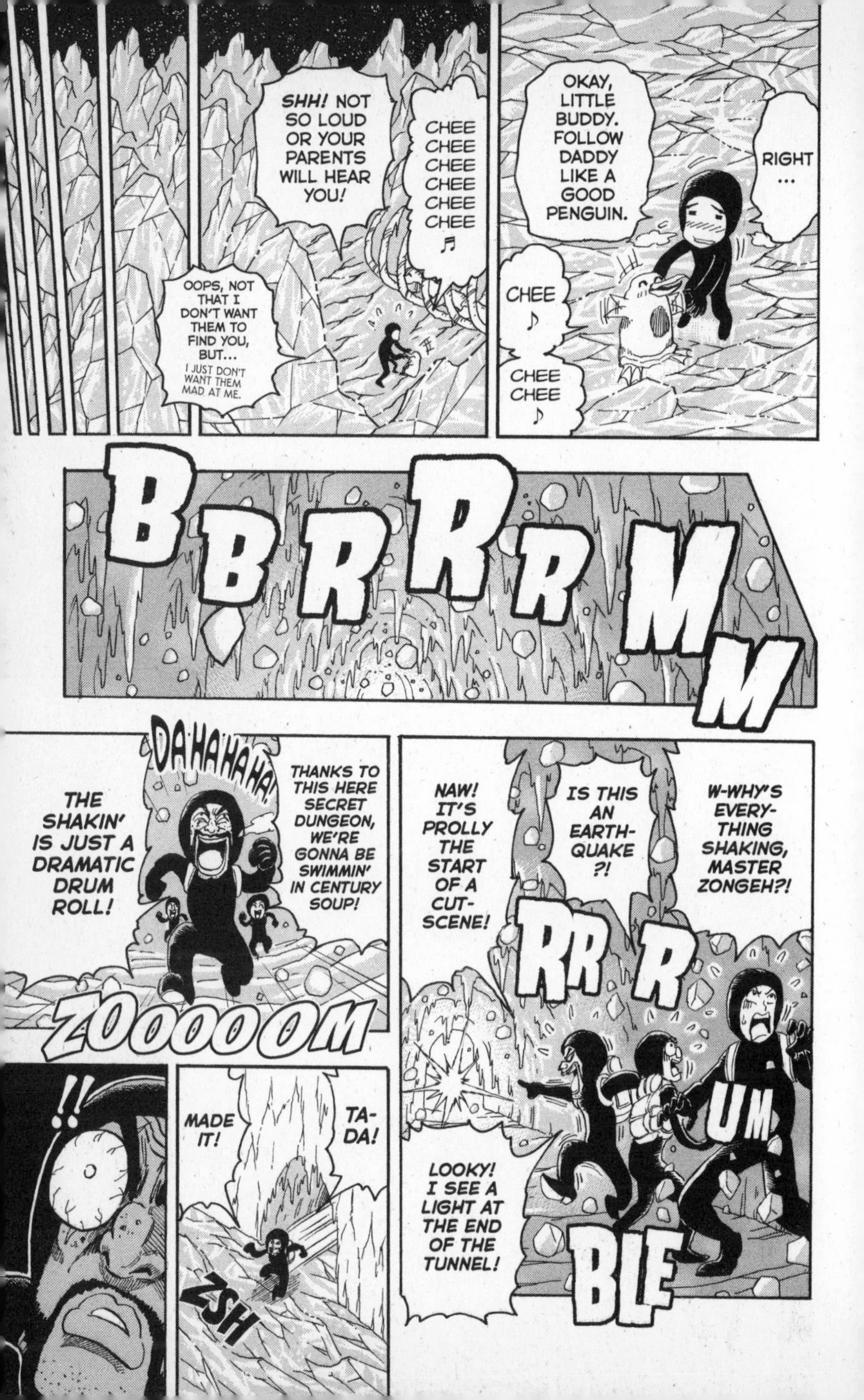
RIGHT ...
OKAY, LITTLE BUDDY. FOLLOW DADDY LIKE A GOOD PENGUIN.
CHEE ♪
CHEE CHEE ♪
CHEE CHEE CHEE CHEE CHEE CHEE ♬
SHH! NOT SO LOUD OR YOUR PARENTS WILL HEAR YOU!
OOPS, NOT THAT I DON'T WANT THEM TO FIND YOU, BUT...
I JUST DON'T WANT THEM MAD AT ME.
BBRRRRMMM
W-WHY'S EVERY-THING SHAKING, MASTER ZONGEH?!
IS THIS AN EARTH-QUAKE?!
NAW! IT'S PROLLY THE START OF A CUT-SCENE!
RRR
RUMBLE
LOOKY! I SEE A LIGHT AT THE END OF THE TUNNEL!
THANKS TO THIS HERE SECRET DUNGEON, WE'RE GONNA BE SWIMMIN' IN CENTURY SOUP!
DAHAHAHAHA!
THE SHAKIN' IS JUST A DRAMATIC DRUM ROLL!
ZOOOOOM
TA-DA!
MADE IT!
ZSH
!!

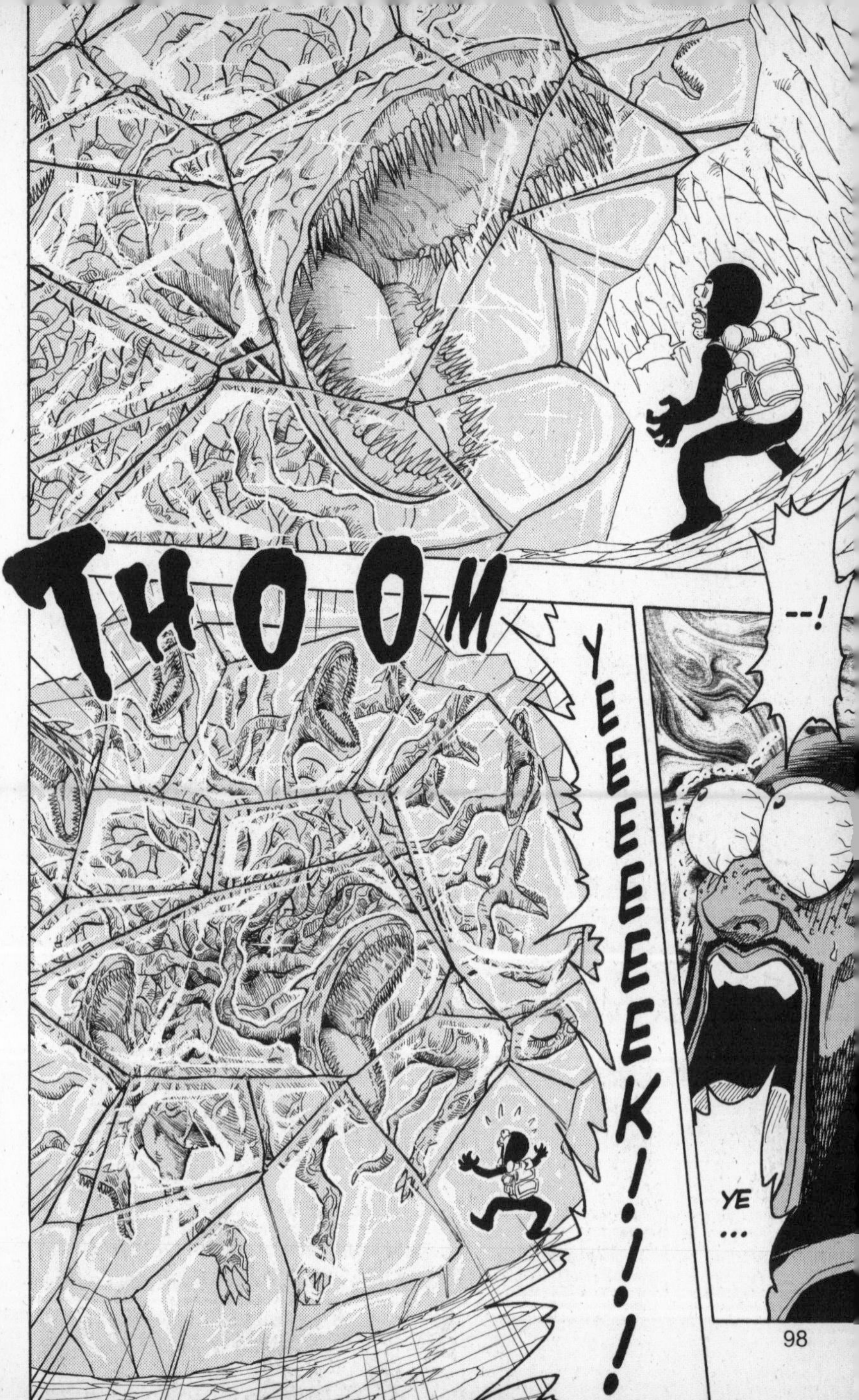
THOOM
--!
YE ...
YEEEEEEEK!!!

WHAT IS THAT THING?!

DWA....

IT'S...

IT'S...

HWA...

WAAARGH!

GYAAAAH!

WE FOUND THE FINAL BOSS!!

...THE FINAL BOSS!

...?

...

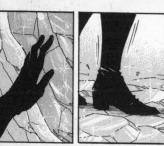

KACHK

HUSH, YOU.

ZZS

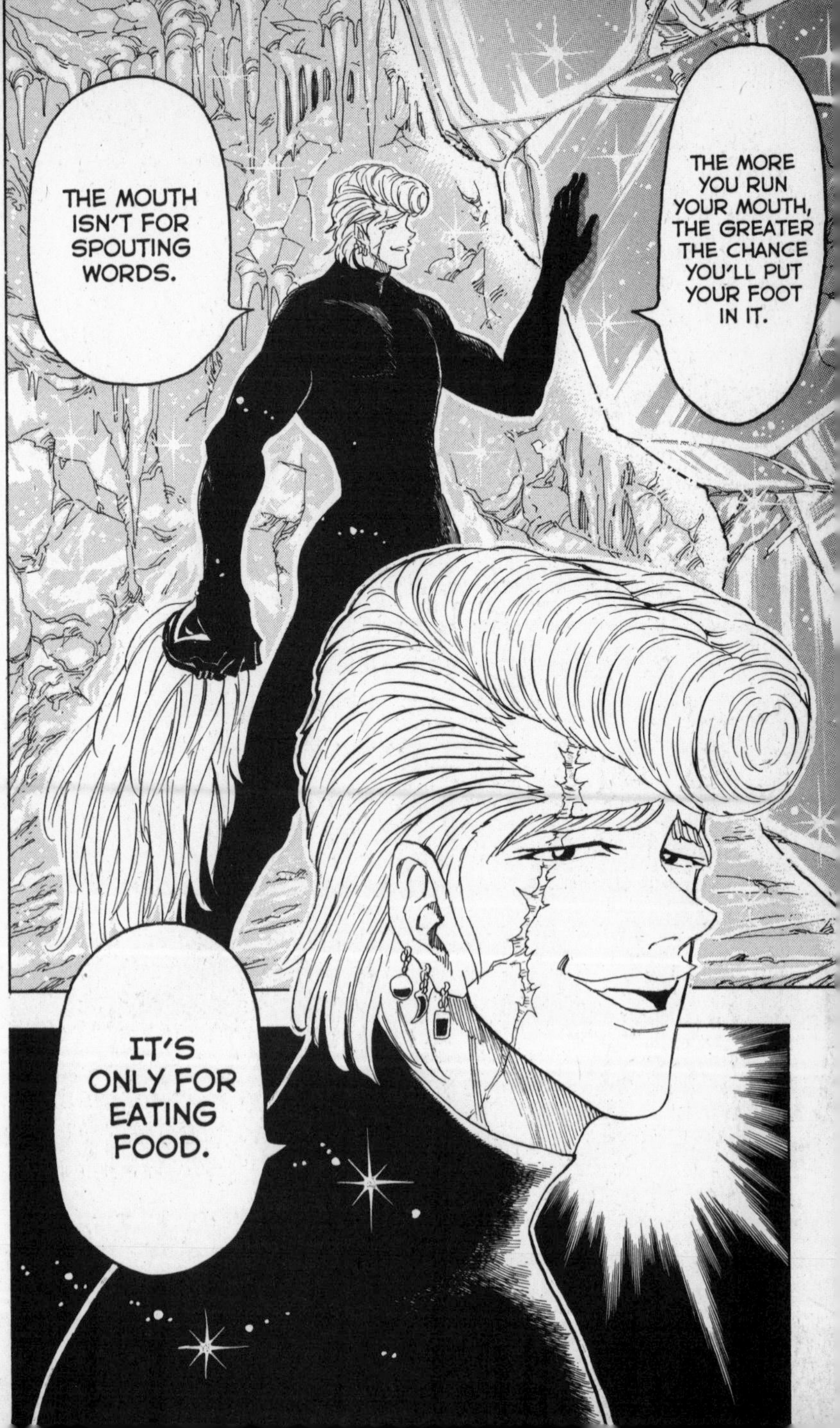
THE MORE YOU RUN YOUR MOUTH, THE GREATER THE CHANCE YOU'LL PUT YOUR FOOT IN IT.
THE MOUTH ISN'T FOR SPOUTING WORDS.
IT'S ONLY FOR EATING FOOD.

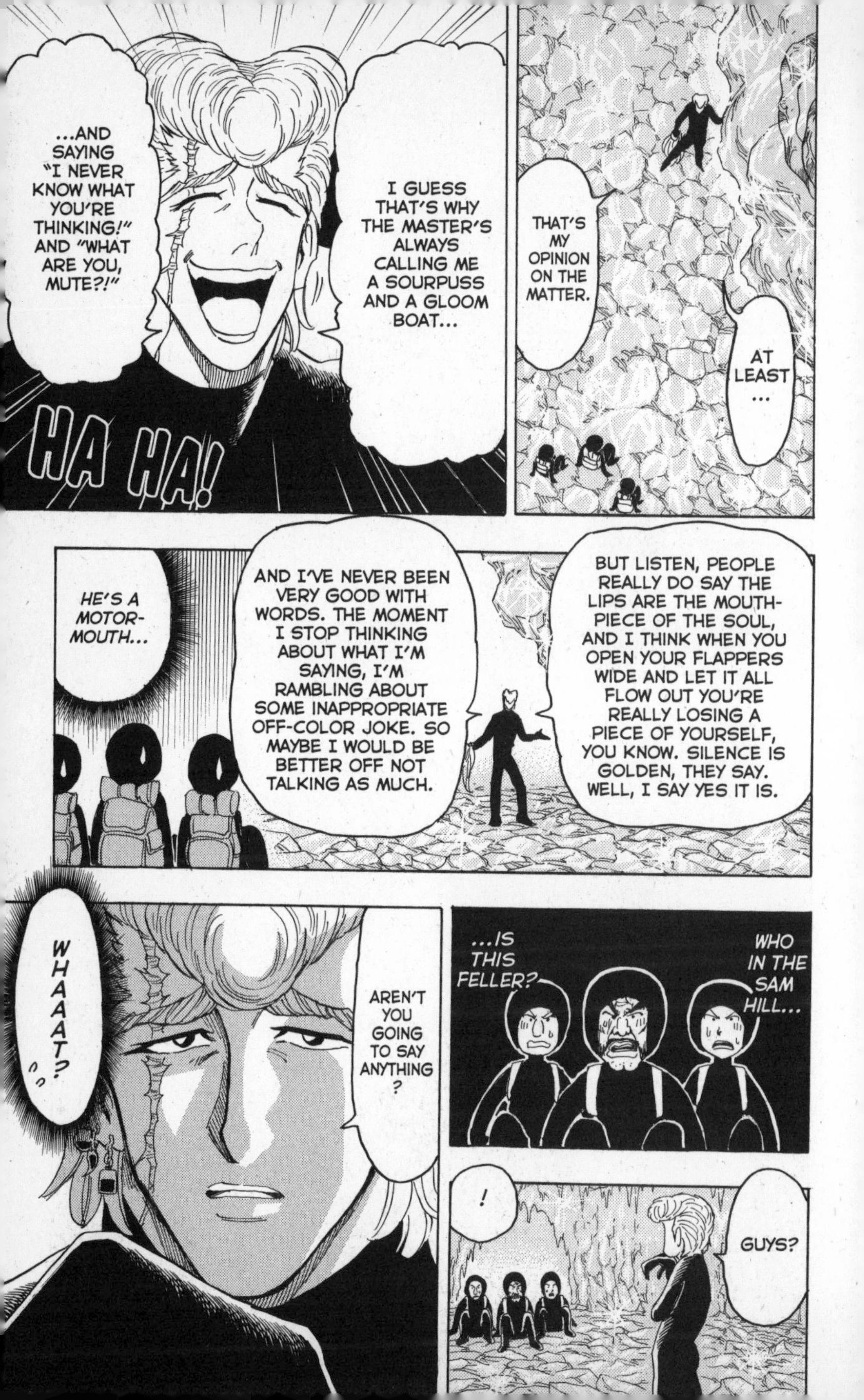
AT LEAST...
THAT'S MY OPINION ON THE MATTER.
I GUESS THAT'S WHY THE MASTER'S ALWAYS CALLING ME A SOURPUSS AND A GLOOM BOAT...
...AND SAYING "I NEVER KNOW WHAT YOU'RE THINKING!" AND "WHAT ARE YOU, MUTE?!"
HA HA!
BUT LISTEN, PEOPLE REALLY DO SAY THE LIPS ARE THE MOUTH-PIECE OF THE SOUL, AND I THINK WHEN YOU OPEN YOUR FLAPPERS WIDE AND LET IT ALL FLOW OUT YOU'RE REALLY LOSING A PIECE OF YOURSELF, YOU KNOW. SILENCE IS GOLDEN, THEY SAY. WELL, I SAY YES IT IS.
AND I'VE NEVER BEEN VERY GOOD WITH WORDS. THE MOMENT I STOP THINKING ABOUT WHAT I'M SAYING, I'M RAMBLING ABOUT SOME INAPPROPRIATE OFF-COLOR JOKE. SO MAYBE I WOULD BE BETTER OFF NOT TALKING AS MUCH.
HE'S A MOTOR-MOUTH...
WHO IN THE SAM HILL...
...IS THIS FELLER?
GUYS?
!
AREN'T YOU GOING TO SAY ANYTHING?
WHAAAT?!

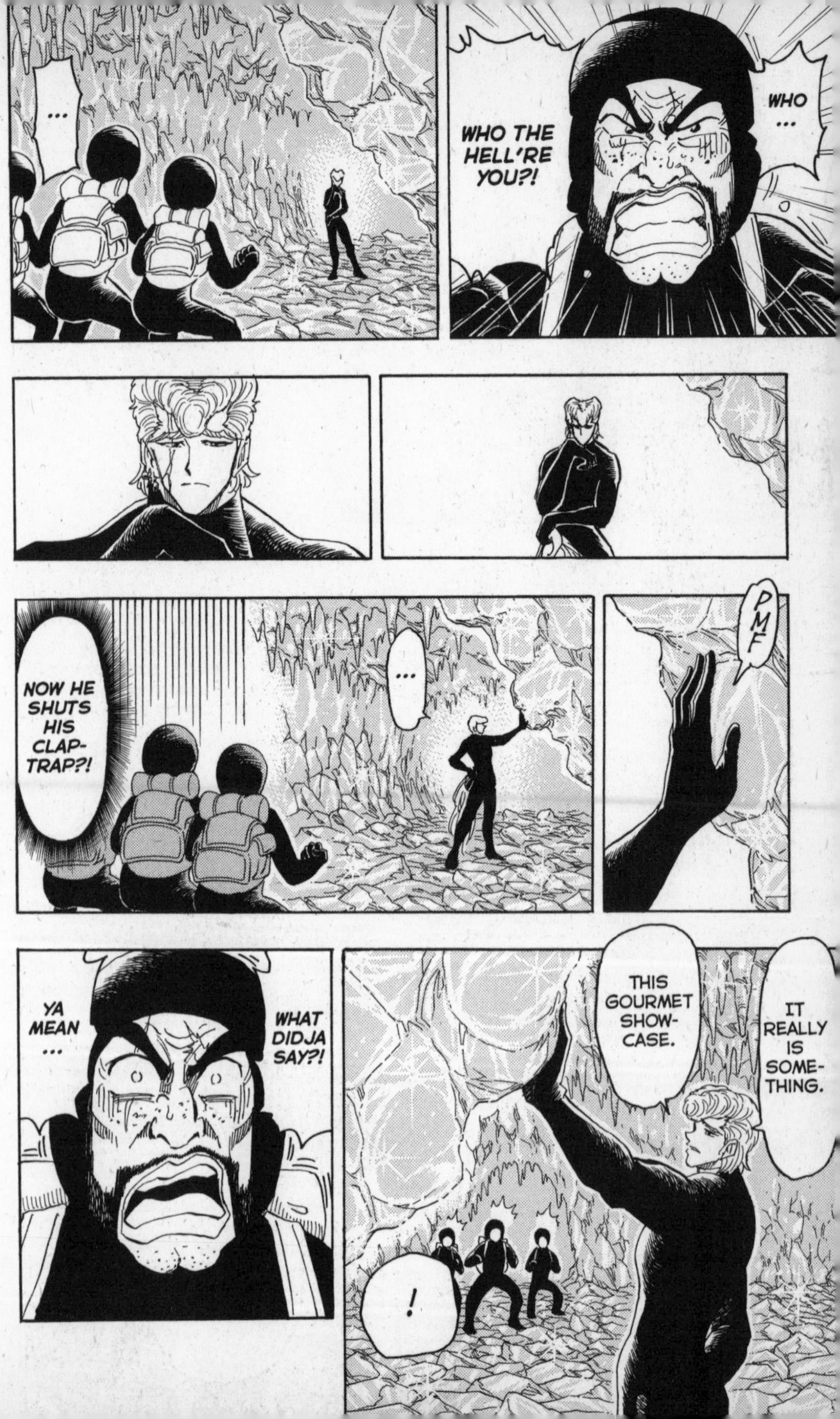
WHO ...
WHO THE HELL'RE YOU?!
...
PMF
...
NOW HE SHUTS HIS CLAP-TRAP?!
IT REALLY IS SOME-THING.
THIS GOURMET SHOW-CASE.
!
WHAT DIDJA SAY?!
YA MEAN ...

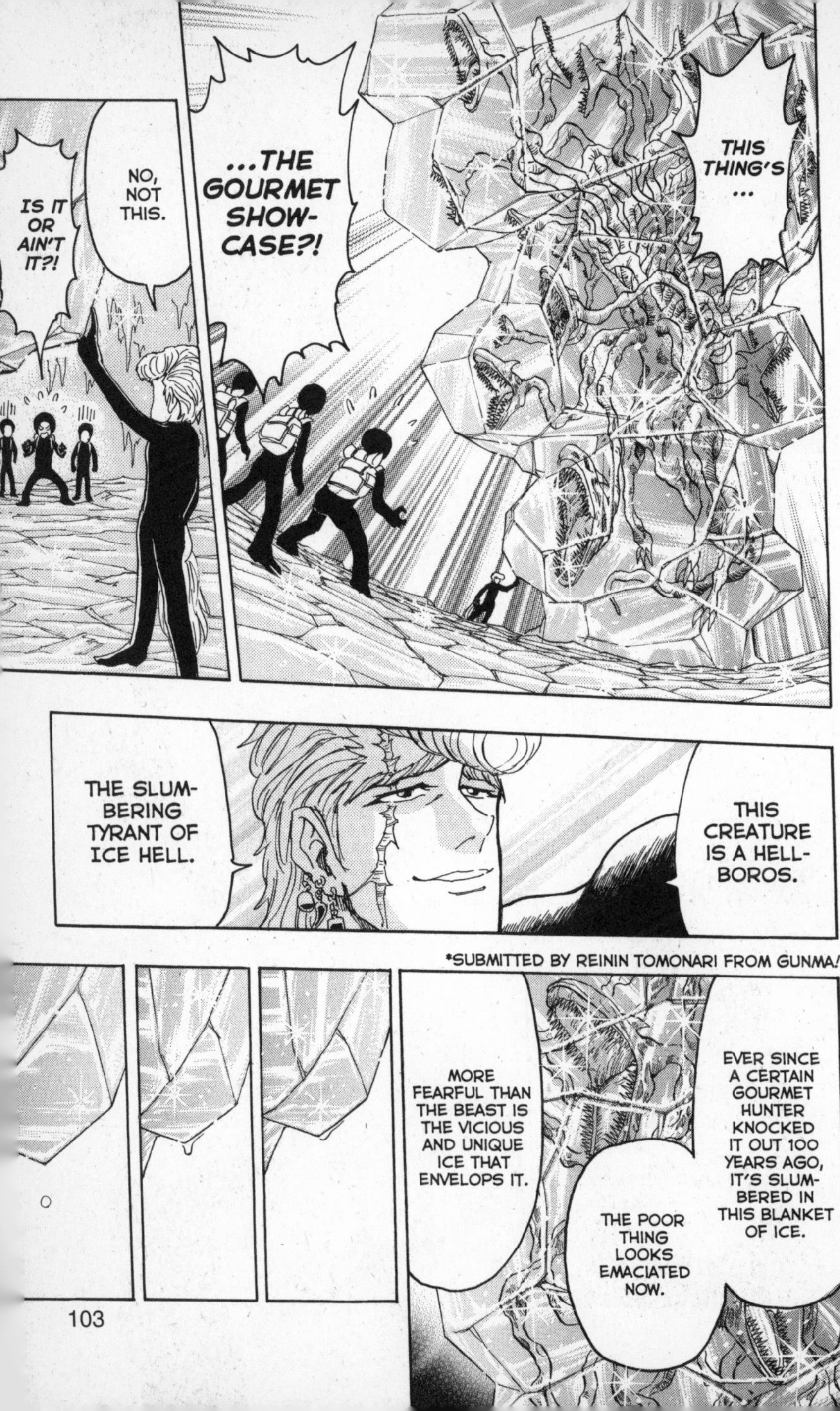
THIS THING'S...
...THE GOURMET SHOWCASE?!
NO, NOT THIS.
IS IT OR AIN'T IT?!
THIS CREATURE IS A HELLBOROS.
THE SLUMBERING TYRANT OF ICE HELL.
*SUBMITTED BY REININ TOMONARI FROM GUNMA!
EVER SINCE A CERTAIN GOURMET HUNTER KNOCKED IT OUT 100 YEARS AGO, IT'S SLUMBERED IN THIS BLANKET OF ICE.
MORE FEARFUL THAN THE BEAST IS THE VICIOUS AND UNIQUE ICE THAT ENVELOPS IT.
THE POOR THING LOOKS EMACIATED NOW.

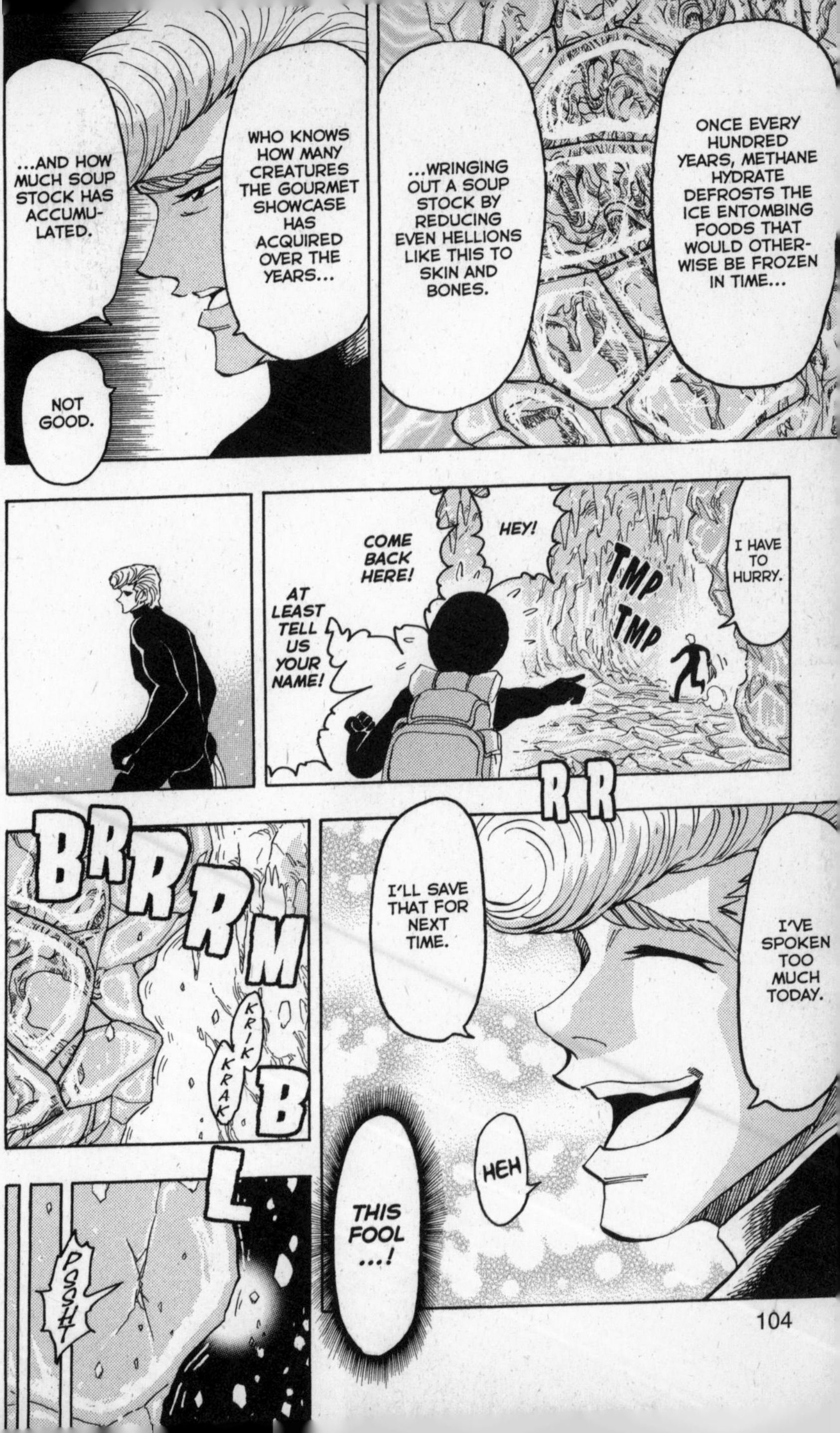
ONCE EVERY HUNDRED YEARS, METHANE HYDRATE DEFROSTS THE ICE ENTOMBING FOODS THAT WOULD OTHERWISE BE FROZEN IN TIME...
...WRINGING OUT A SOUP STOCK BY REDUCING EVEN HELLIONS LIKE THIS TO SKIN AND BONES.
WHO KNOWS HOW MANY CREATURES THE GOURMET SHOWCASE HAS ACQUIRED OVER THE YEARS...
...AND HOW MUCH SOUP STOCK HAS ACCUMULATED.
NOT GOOD.
I HAVE TO HURRY.
TMP TMP
HEY!
COME BACK HERE!
AT LEAST TELL US YOUR NAME!
R R
I'VE SPOKEN TOO MUCH TODAY.
I'LL SAVE THAT FOR NEXT TIME.
HEH
THIS FOOL ...!
BRRRRMBL
KRIK KRAK
PSSHT

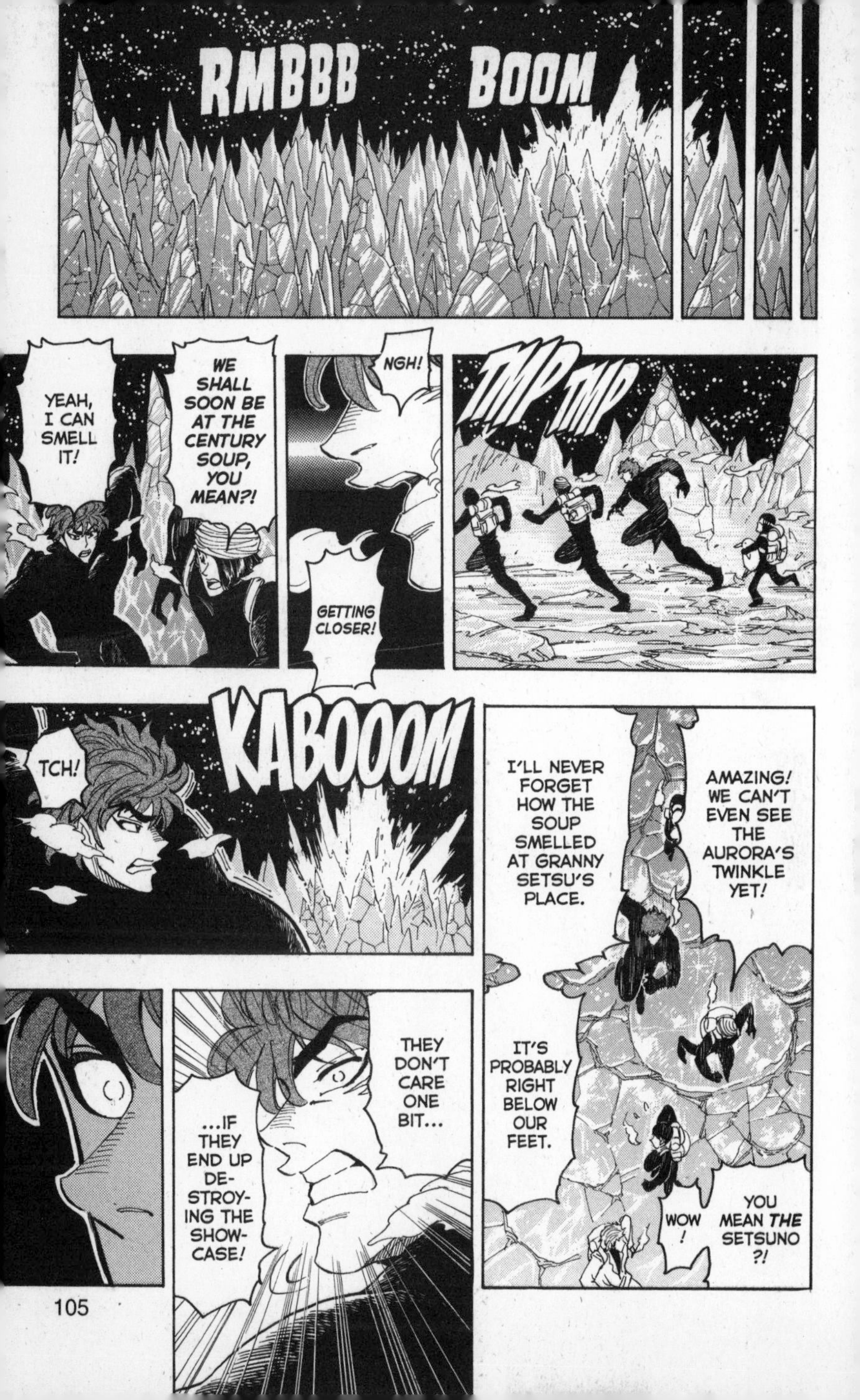
BOOM
RMBBB
TMP TMP
NGH!
GETTING CLOSER!
WE SHALL SOON BE AT THE CENTURY SOUP, YOU MEAN?!
YEAH, I CAN SMELL IT!
AMAZING! WE CAN'T EVEN SEE THE AURORA'S TWINKLE YET!
I'LL NEVER FORGET HOW THE SOUP SMELLED AT GRANNY SETSU'S PLACE.
IT'S PROBABLY RIGHT BELOW OUR FEET.
YOU MEAN *THE* SETSUNO?!
WOW!
KABOOOM
TCH!
THEY DON'T CARE ONE BIT...
...IF THEY END UP DE-STROY-ING THE SHOW-CASE!

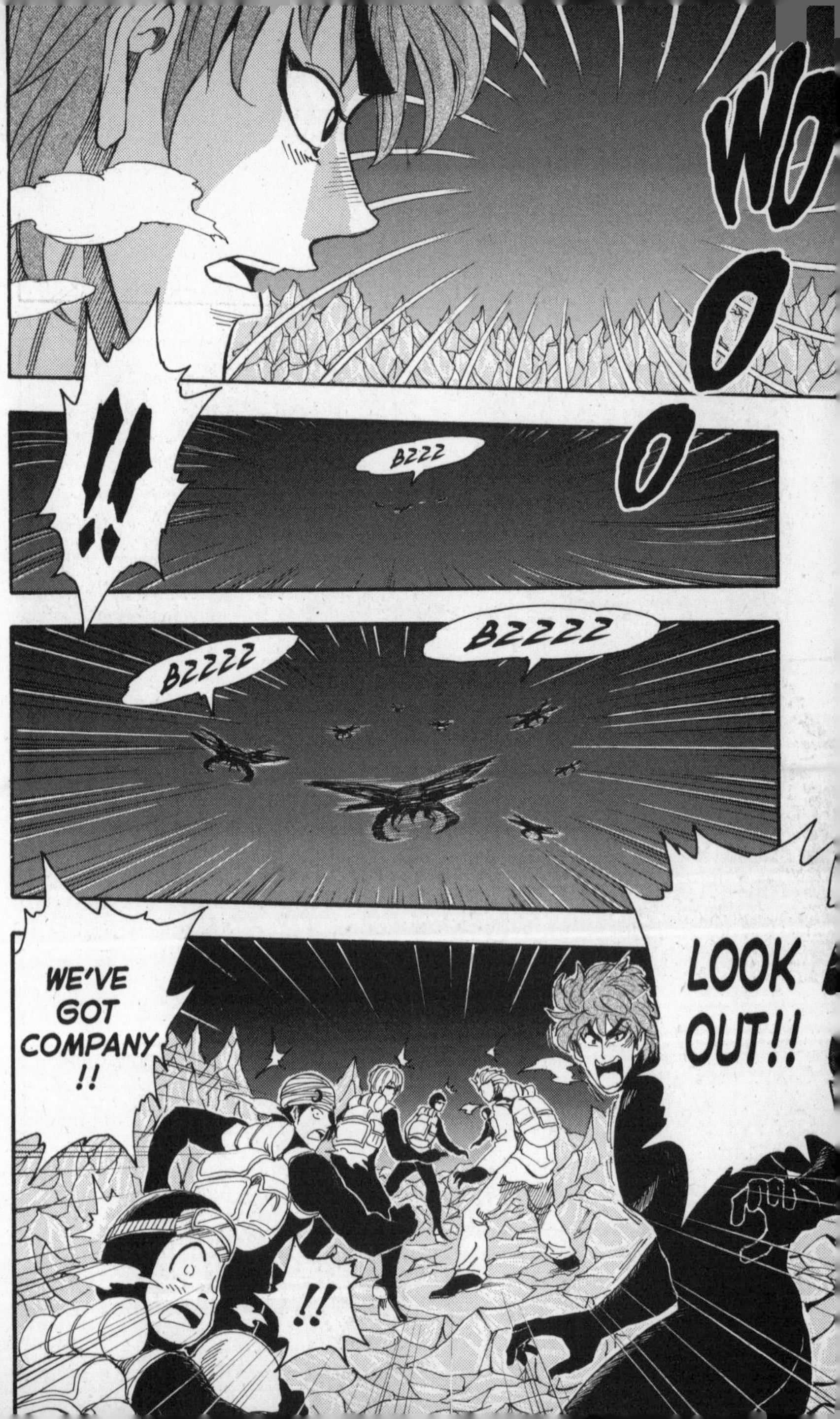
WOOO
!!
BZZZ
BZZZZZ
BZZZZ
LOOK OUT!!
WE'VE GOT COMPANY!!
!!

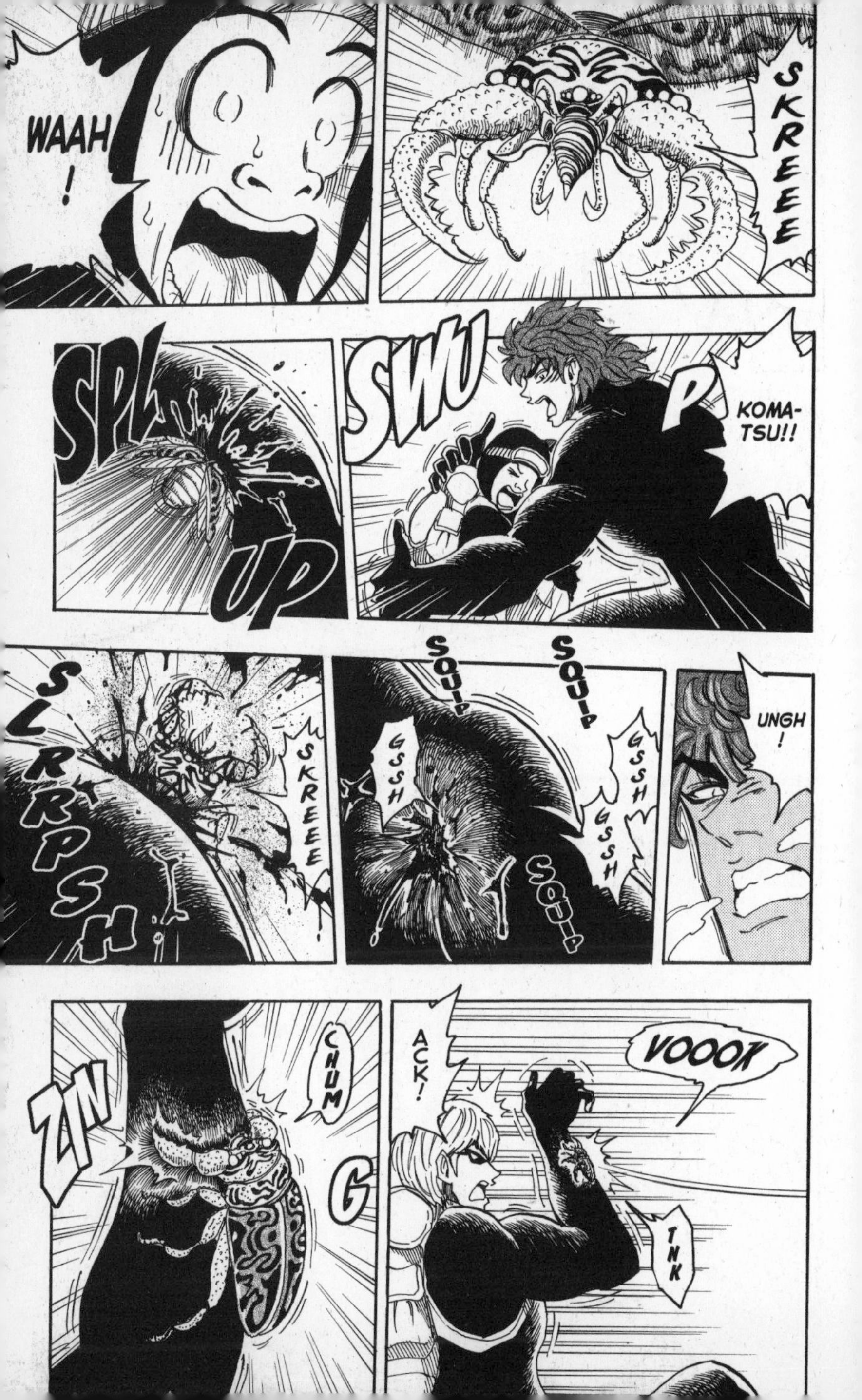
SKREEE
WAAH!
SWU
P
KOMA-TSU!!
SPL
UP
UNGH!
SQUIP
SQUIP
GSSH
GSSH
GSSH
SQUIP
SKREEE
SLRRPSH
VOOOK
ACK!
TNK
CHUM
ZIN
G

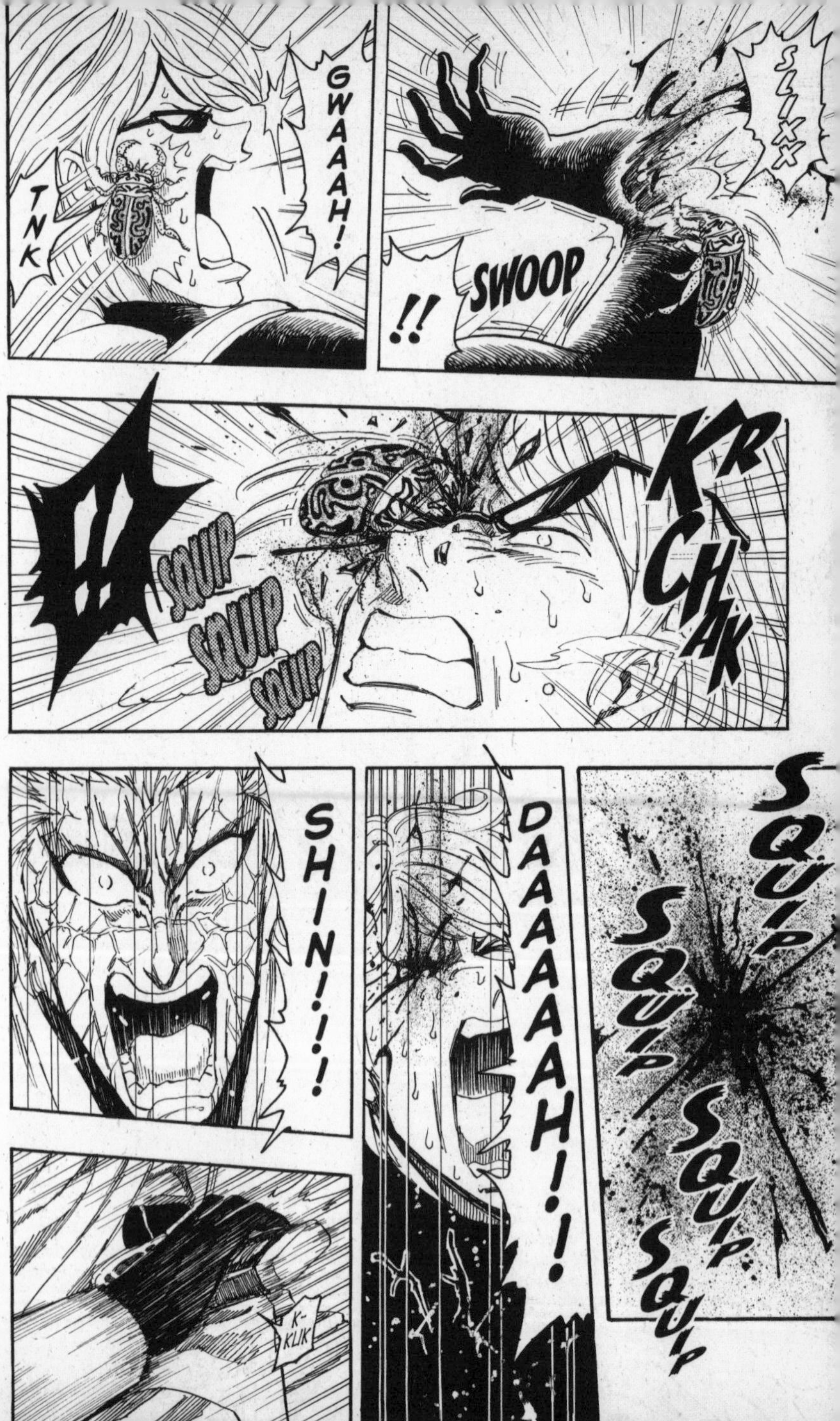
SLIXX
SWOOP
!!
GWAAAAH!
TNK
KRCHAK
SQUIP SQUIP SQUIP SQUIP
!!
SQUIP SQUIP SQUIP SQUIP SQUIP SQUIP
DAAAAAAAAH!!!!
SHINI!!!!
K-KLIK

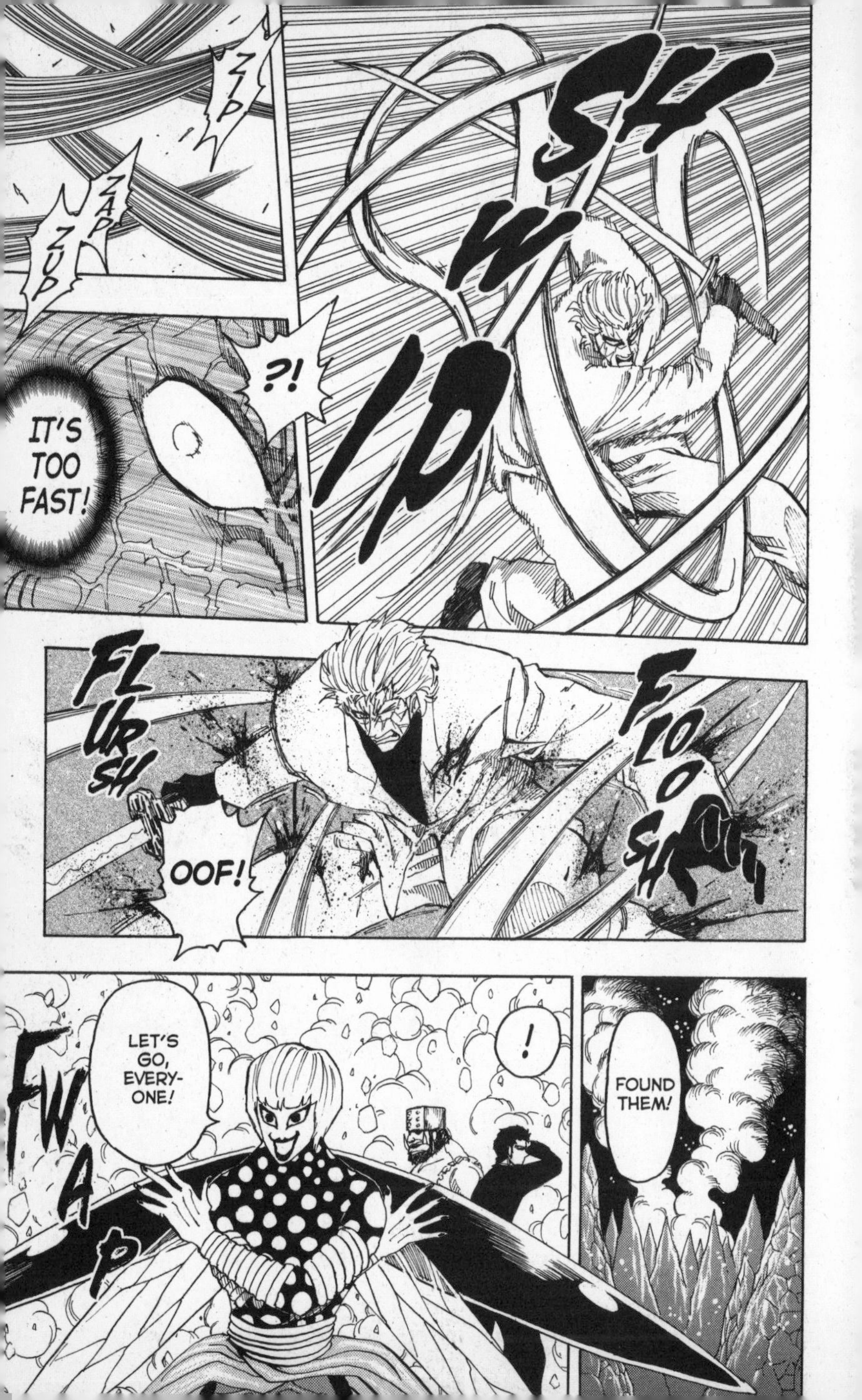
SHWIP
ZIP
ZAP
ZUP
?!
IT'S TOO FAST!
FLOOSH
FLURSH
OOF!
FOUND THEM!
!
LET'S GO, EVERY-ONE!
FWAP

TORIKO

GOURMET CHECKLIST

Vol. 067

WHITE APPLE
(FRUIT)

CAPTURE LEVEL: LESS THAN 1 (DOMESTICATED)

HABITAT: FERTILE SOILS

LENGTH: 20 CM (FRUIT)

HEIGHT: ---

WEIGHT: 1 KG

PRICE: 1,500 YEN PER APPLE

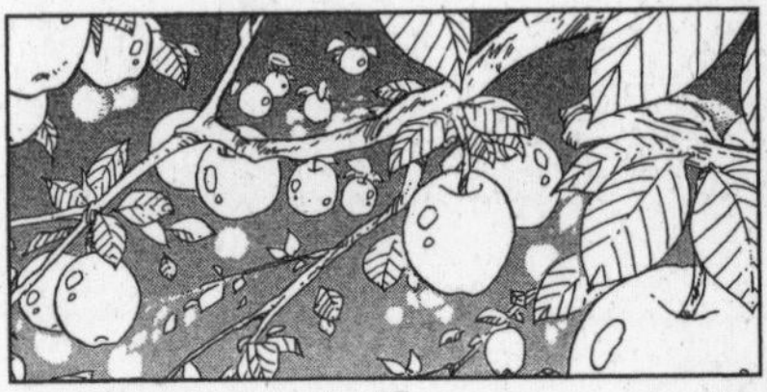

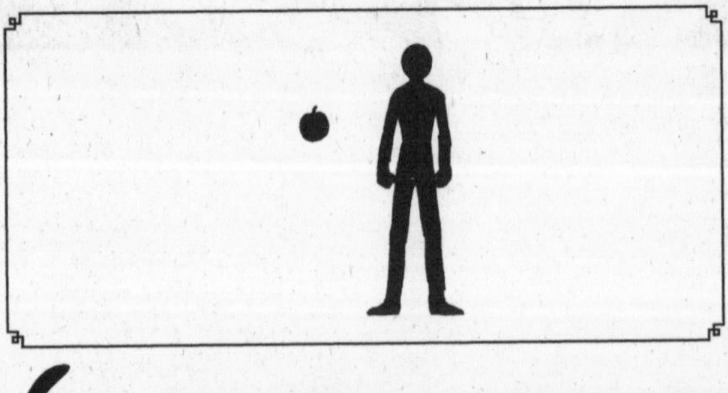

SCALE

THE FRUIT OF A FLOWERING DECIDUOUS TREE THAT BLOSSOMS IN LATE SPRING. WITH A HIGHER SUGAR CONTENT THAN NORMAL APPLES, IT'S THE PERFECT INGREDIENT FOR JUICING AND COCKTAILS. WHITE APPLES ARE ALSO VERY PREVALENT IN CONFECTIONS, WITH WHITE APPLE PIE BEING PARTICULARLY POPULAR WITH GIRLS.

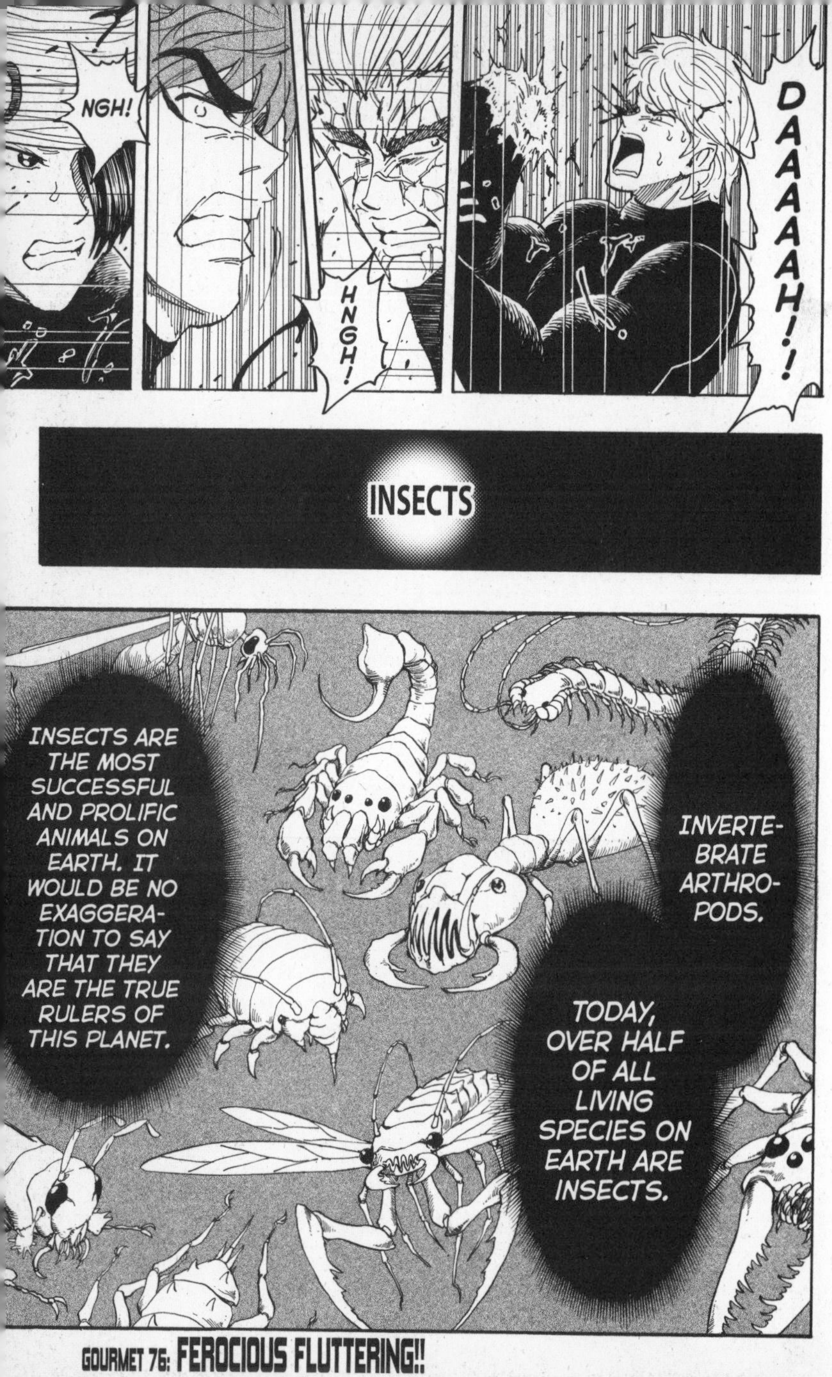
DAAAAAH!!
HNGH!
NGH!
INSECTS
INVERTE-BRATE ARTHROPODS.
INSECTS ARE THE MOST SUCCESSFUL AND PROLIFIC ANIMALS ON EARTH. IT WOULD BE NO EXAGGERA-TION TO SAY THAT THEY ARE THE TRUE RULERS OF THIS PLANET.
TODAY, OVER HALF OF ALL LIVING SPECIES ON EARTH ARE INSECTS.

GOURMET 76: FEROCIOUS FLUTTERING!!

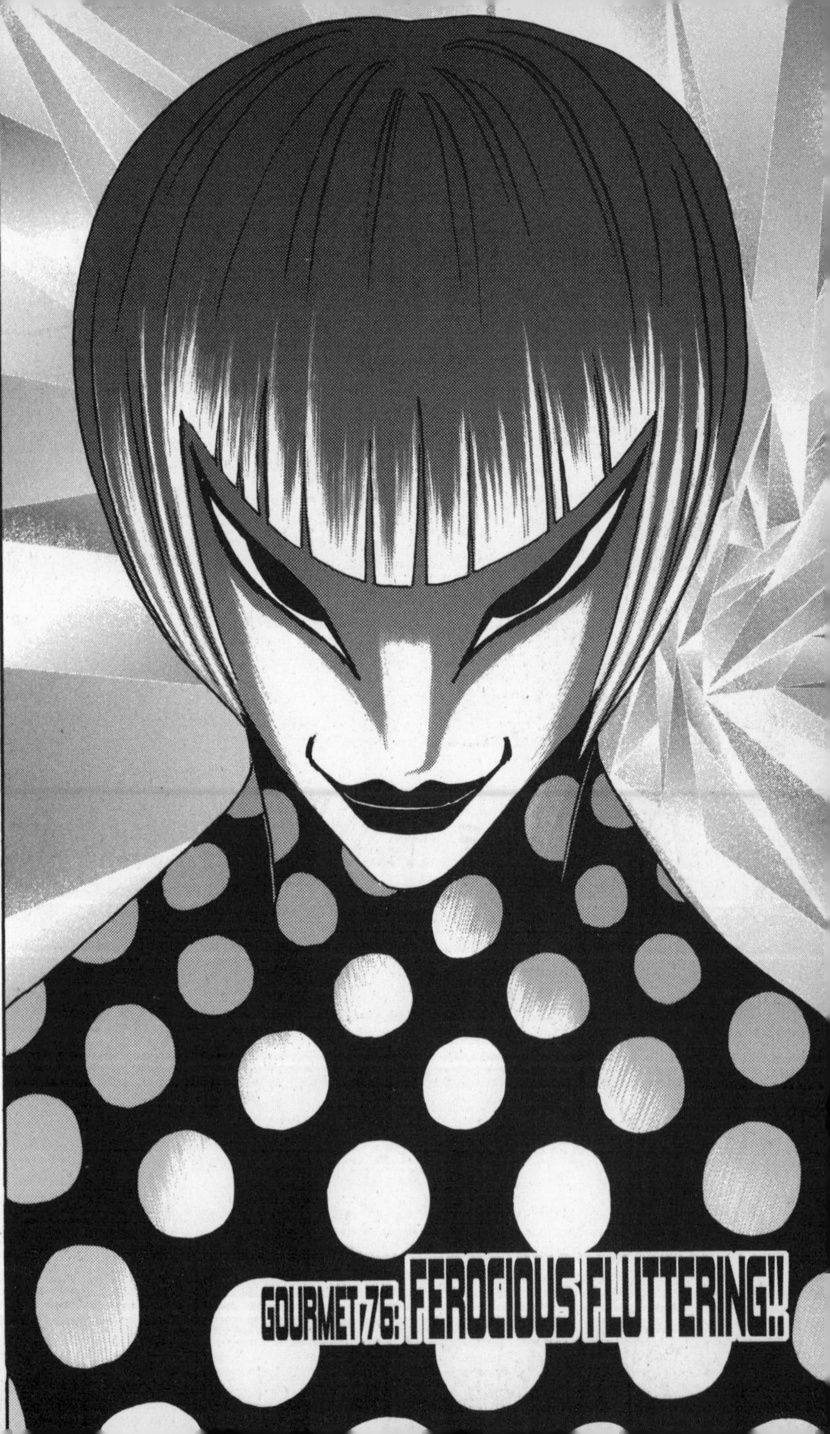
GOURMET 76: FEROCIOUS FLUTTERING!!

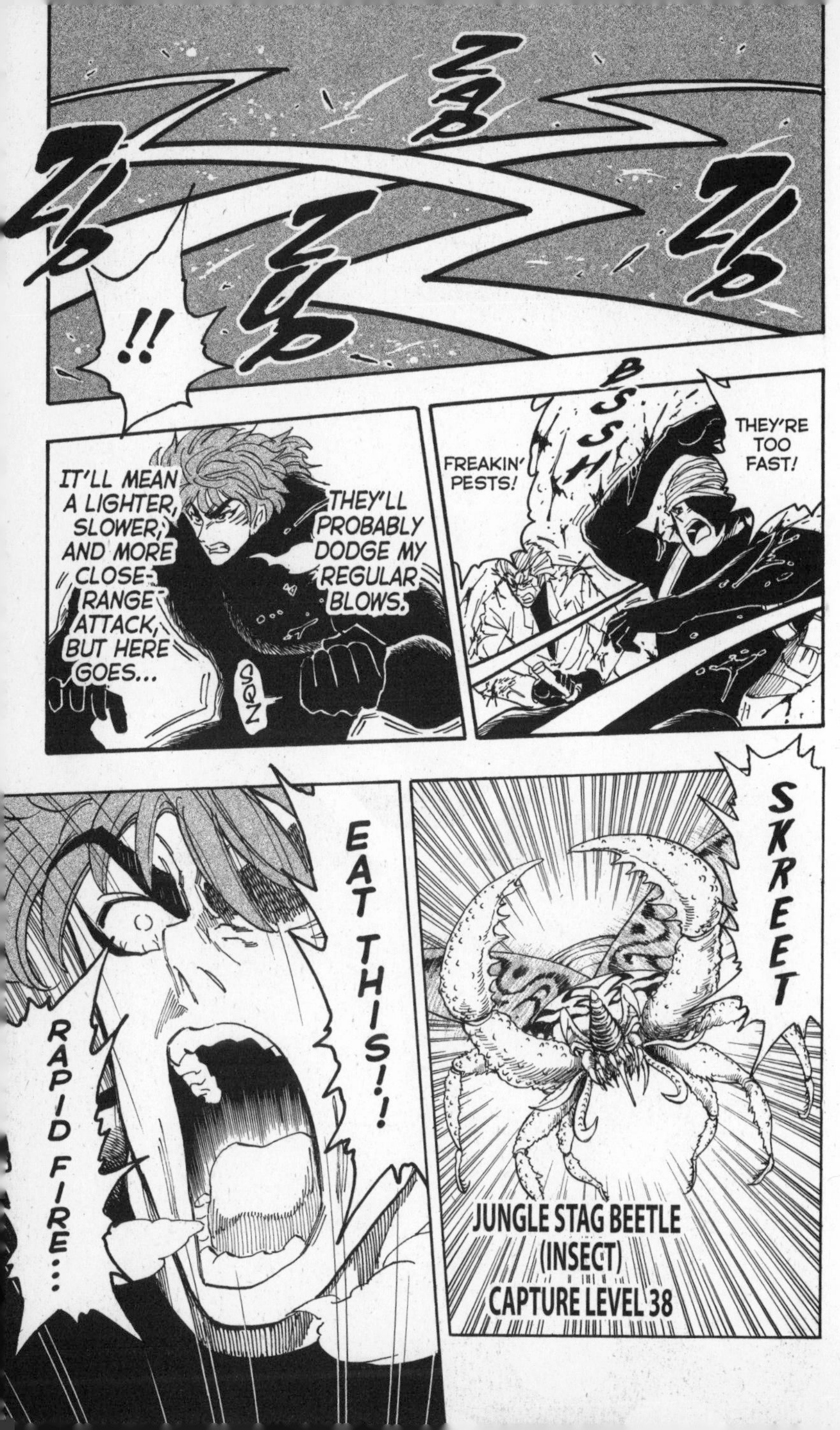
BSSH
THEY'RE TOO FAST!
FREAKIN' PESTS!
!!
THEY'LL PROBABLY DODGE MY REGULAR BLOWS.
IT'LL MEAN A LIGHTER, SLOWER, AND MORE CLOSE-RANGE ATTACK, BUT HERE GOES...
SQZ
SKREET
JUNGLE STAG BEETLE (INSECT) CAPTURE LEVEL 38
EAT THIS!!
RAPID FIRE...

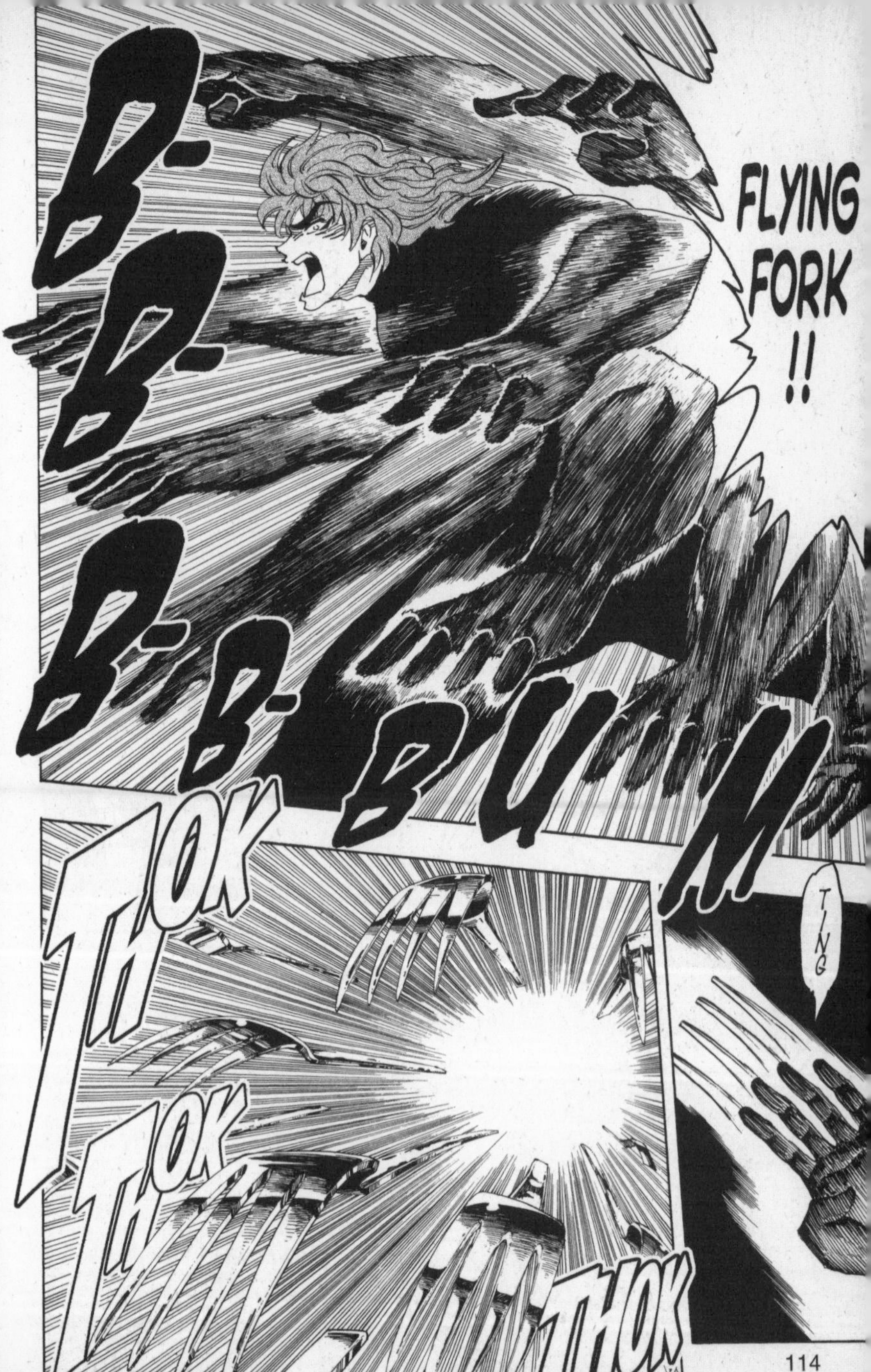
FLYING FORK!!
B-B-B-B-B-B-BUM
TING
THOK
THOK
THOK

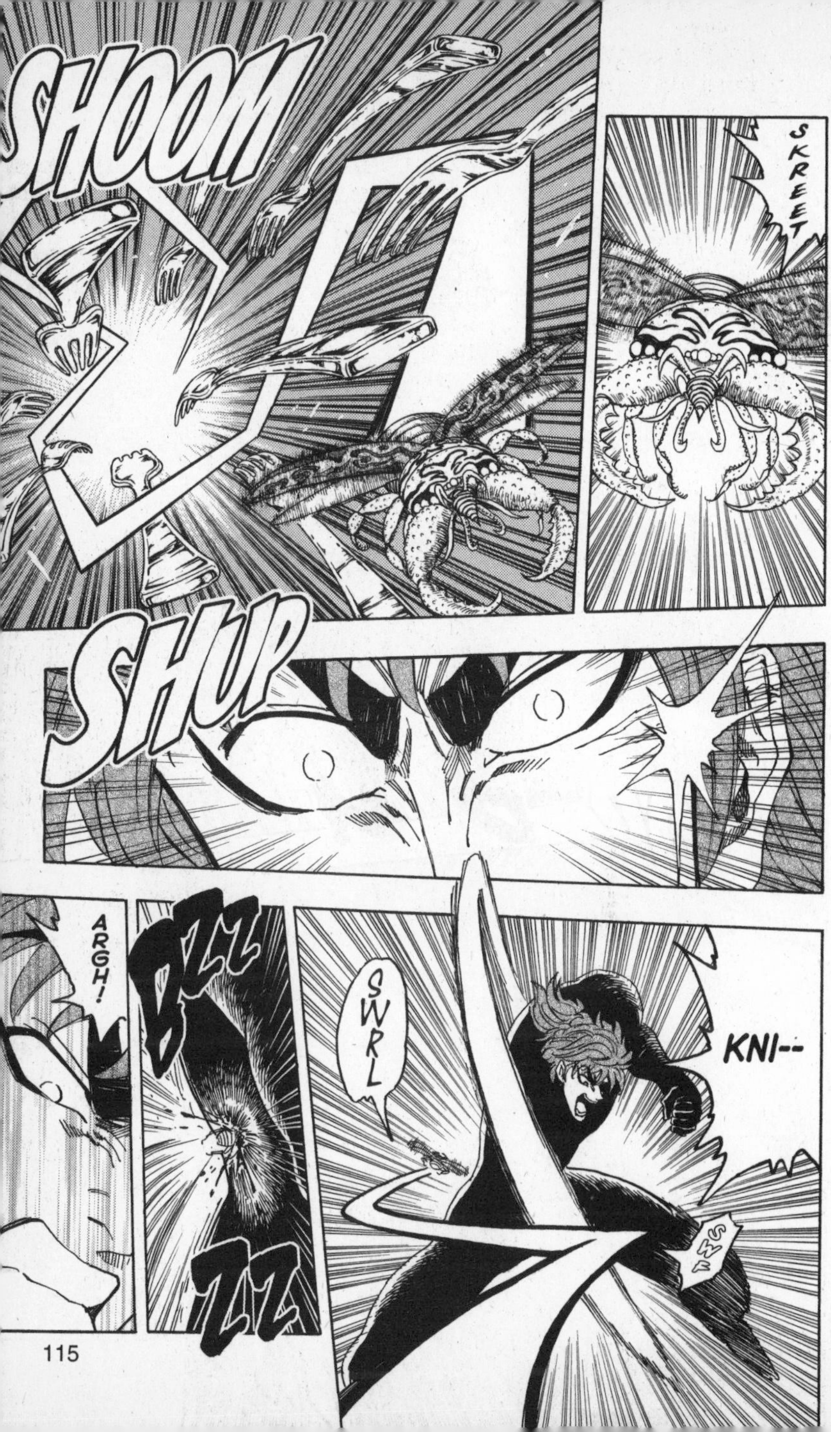
SKREET
SHOOM
SHUP
KNI--
SWRL
SWF
BZZZ
ZZZ
ARGH!

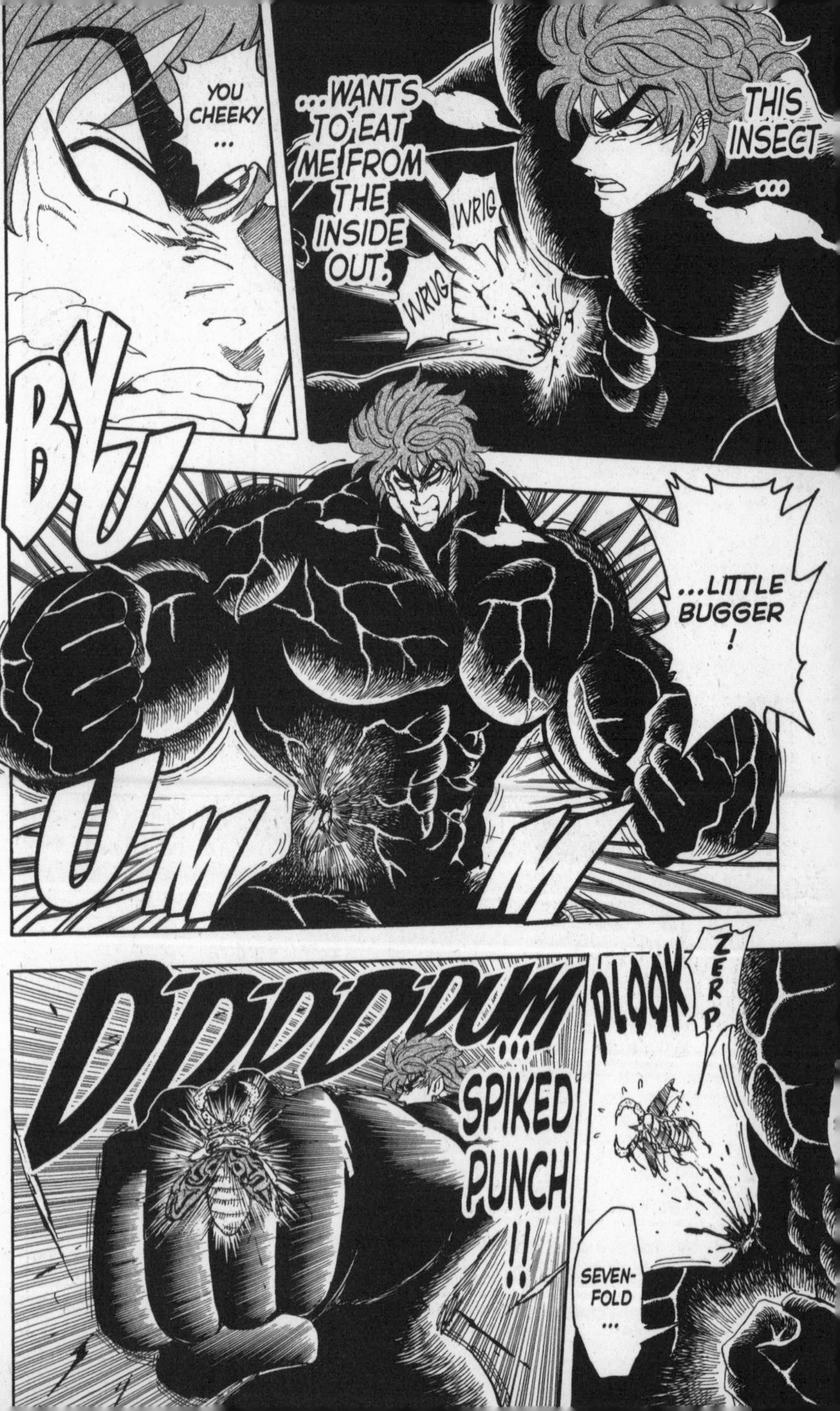
THIS INSECT...
...WANTS TO EAT ME FROM THE INSIDE OUT.
WRIG
WRUG
YOU CHEEKY ...
...LITTLE BUGGER!
BVUMM
PLOOK
ZERP
SEVEN-FOLD ...
D'D'D'DUM
...SPIKED PUNCH!!

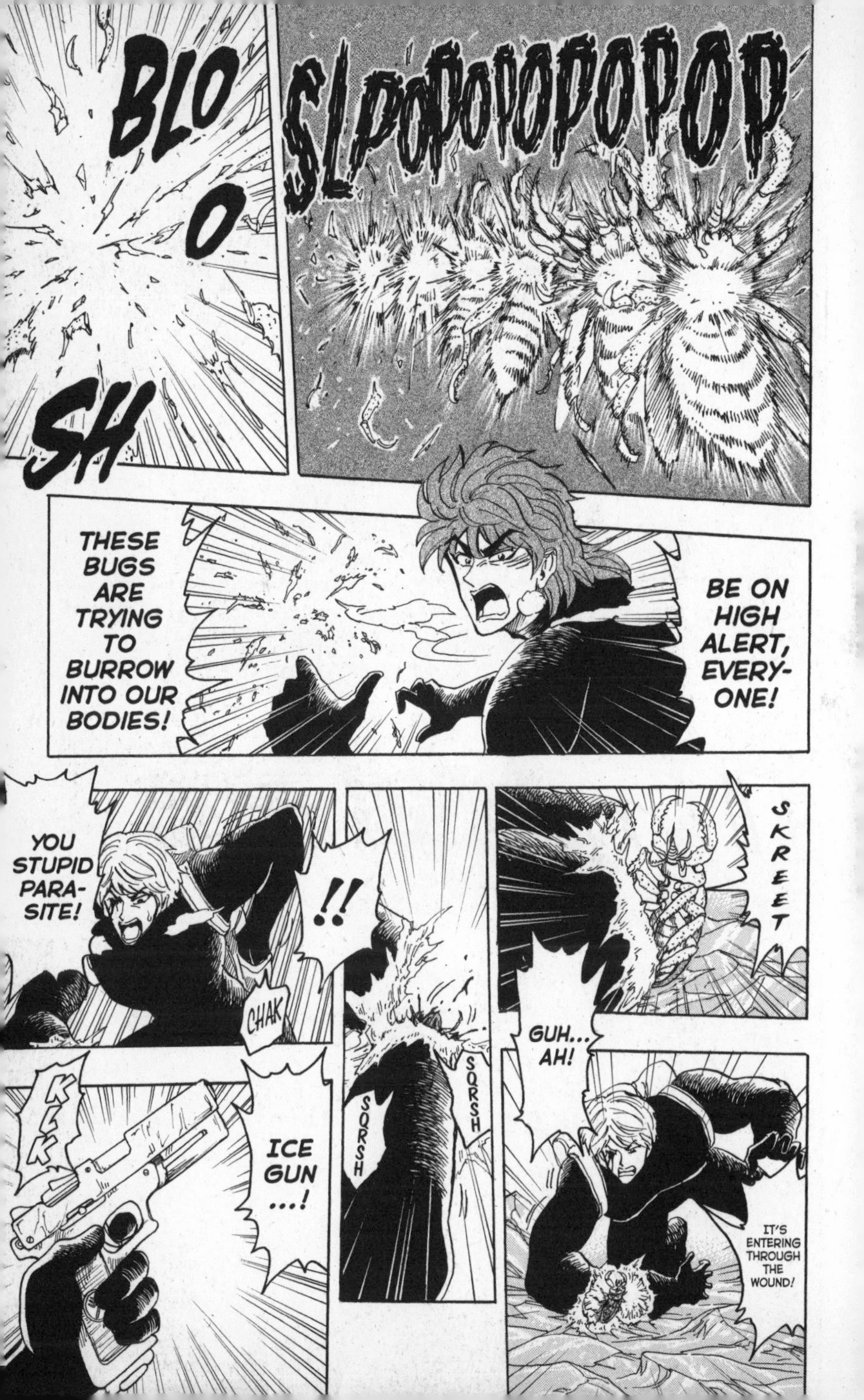
SLPOPOPOPOPOP
BLOOSH
BE ON HIGH ALERT, EVERYONE!
THESE BUGS ARE TRYING TO BURROW INTO OUR BODIES!
SKREET
GUH... AH!
IT'S ENTERING THROUGH THE WOUND!
!!
SQRSH
SQRSH
YOU STUPID PARASITE!
CHAK
ICE GUN ...!
KLK

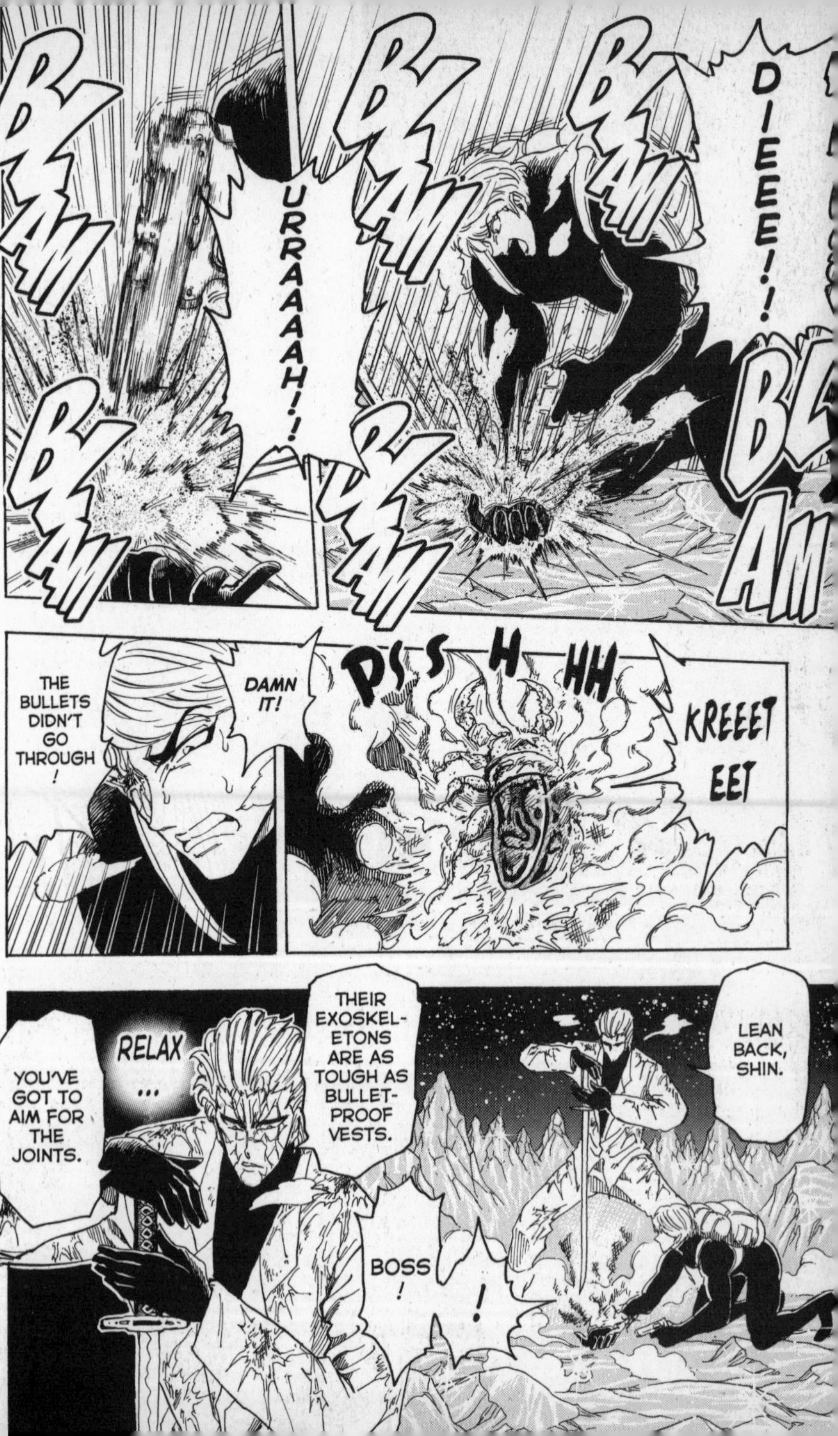

DIEEE!!
BLAM
BLAM
BLAM
BLAM
URRAAAAAH!!
BLAM
BLAM
PSSHHH
KREEEET EET
DAMN IT!
THE BULLETS DIDN'T GO THROUGH!
LEAN BACK, SHIN.
!
BOSS!
THEIR EXOSKELETONS ARE AS TOUGH AS BULLETPROOF VESTS.
RELAX...
YOU'VE GOT TO AIM FOR THE JOINTS.

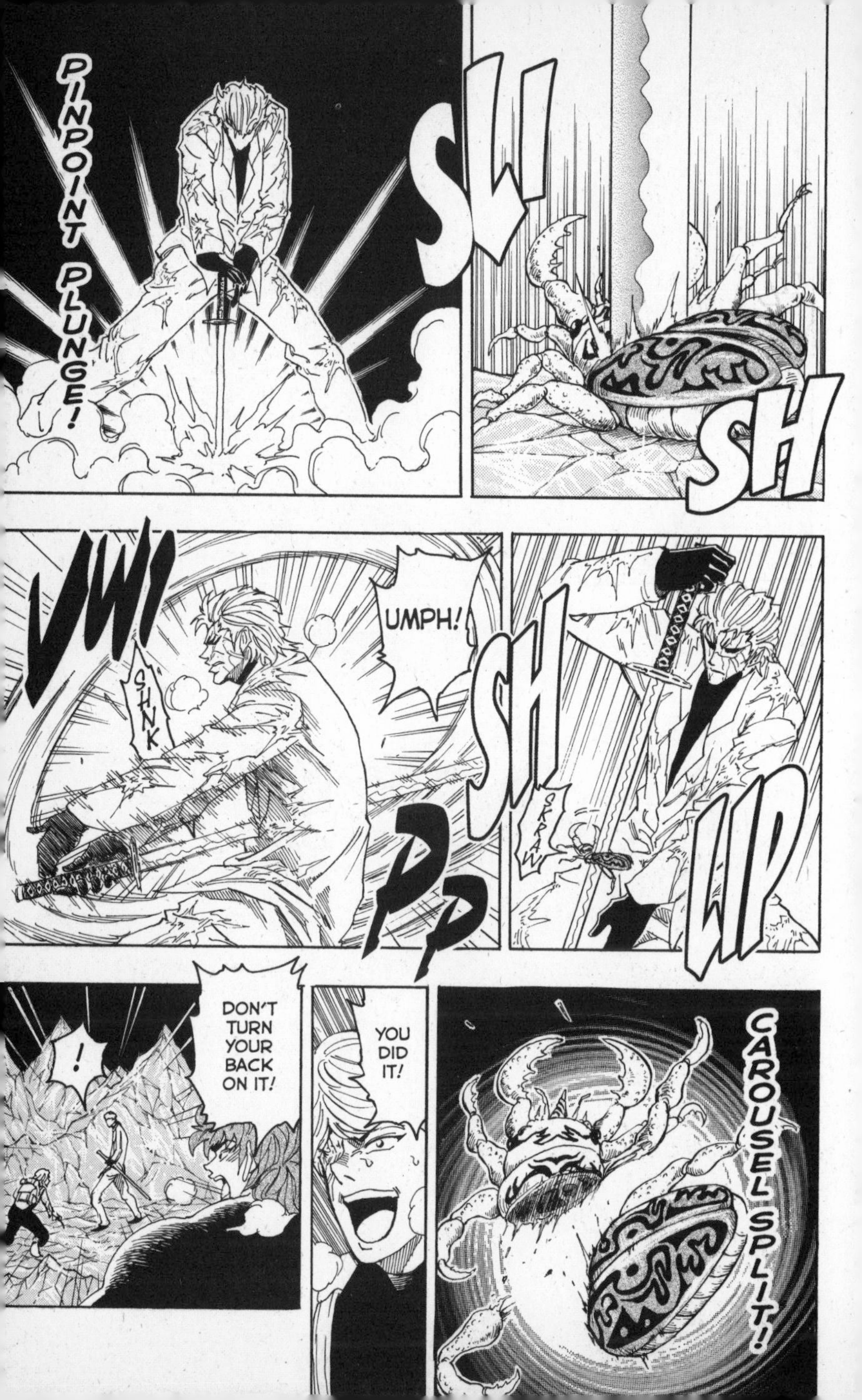
SLI
SH
PINPOINT PLUNGE!
SH
SKRAW
SHLIP
UMPH!
VWI
SHNK
PP
CAROUSEL SPLIT!
YOU DID IT!
DON'T TURN YOUR BACK ON IT!
!

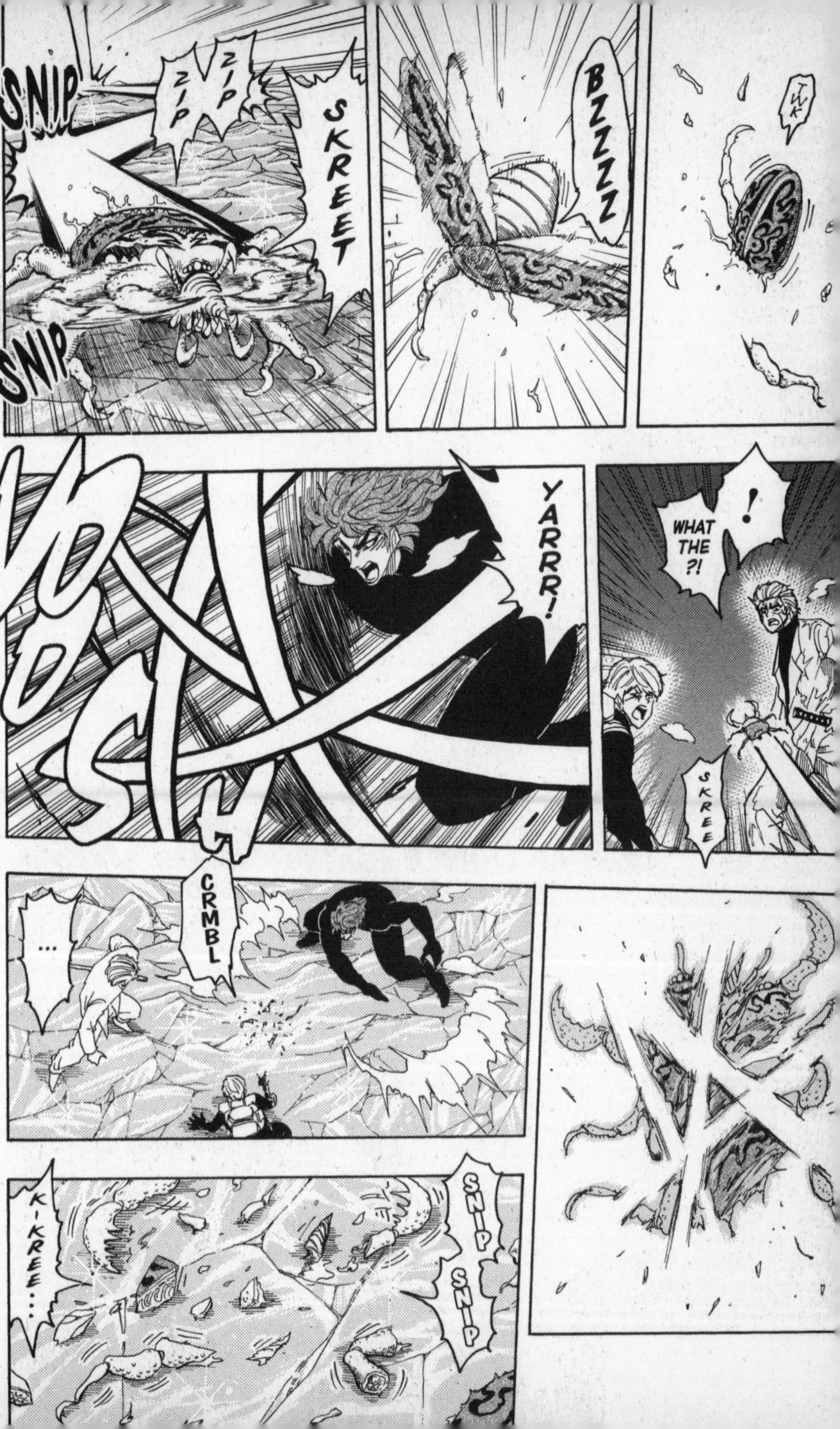
TWK
BZZZZZ
SKREEET
ZIP ZIP
SNIP
SNIP
!
WHAT THE ?!
SKREE
YARRR!
WOOSH
CRMBL
...
SNIP SNIP
KIKREE...

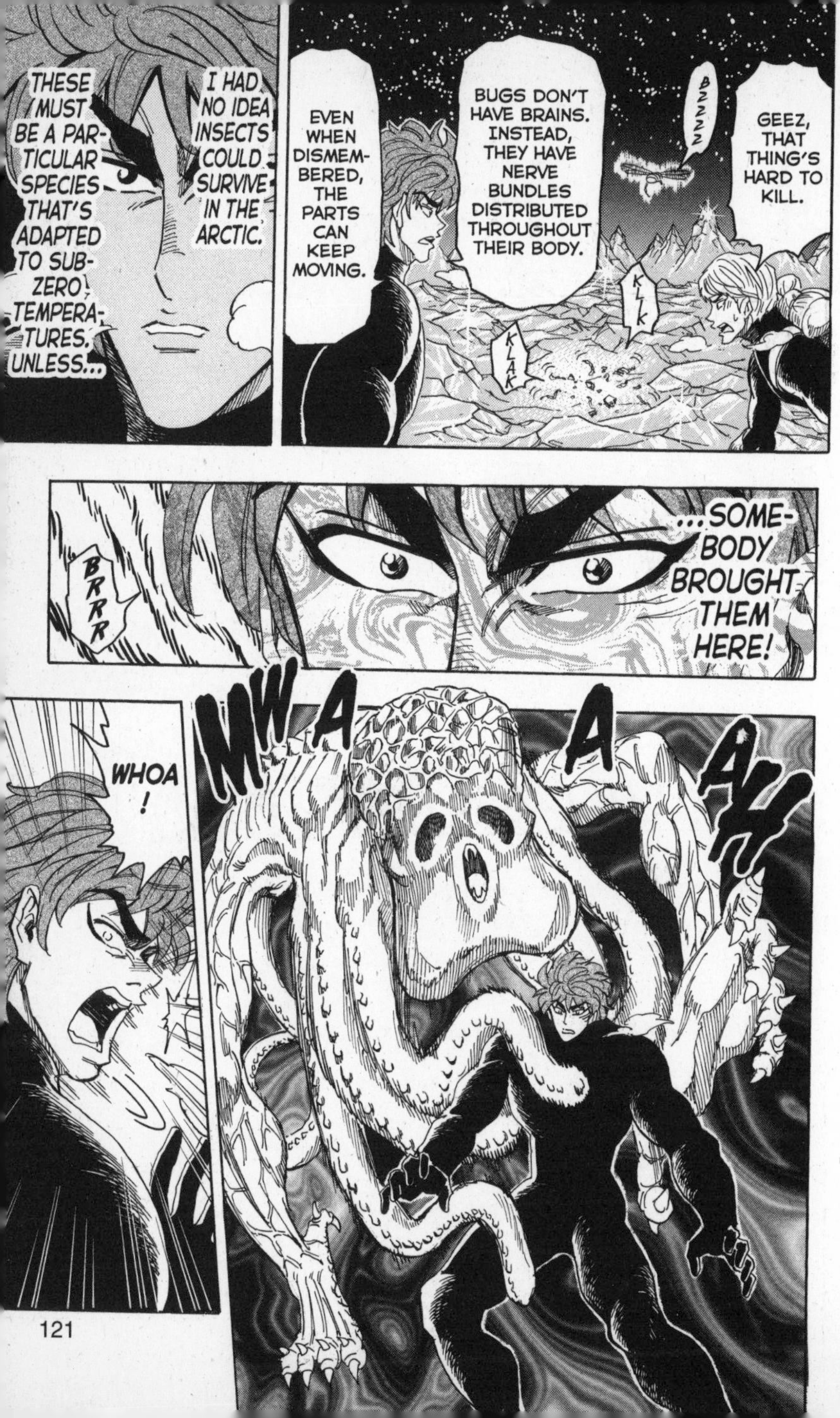

BZZZZ
GEEZ, THAT THING'S HARD TO KILL.
BUGS DON'T HAVE BRAINS. INSTEAD, THEY HAVE NERVE BUNDLES DISTRIBUTED THROUGHOUT THEIR BODY.
EVEN WHEN DISMEMBERED, THE PARTS CAN KEEP MOVING.
KLIK
KLAK
I HAD NO IDEA INSECTS COULD SURVIVE IN THE ARCTIC.
THESE MUST BE A PARTICULAR SPECIES THAT'S ADAPTED TO SUB-ZERO TEMPERATURES. UNLESS...
...SOMEBODY BROUGHT THEM HERE!
BRRR
MWAAAH
WHOA!

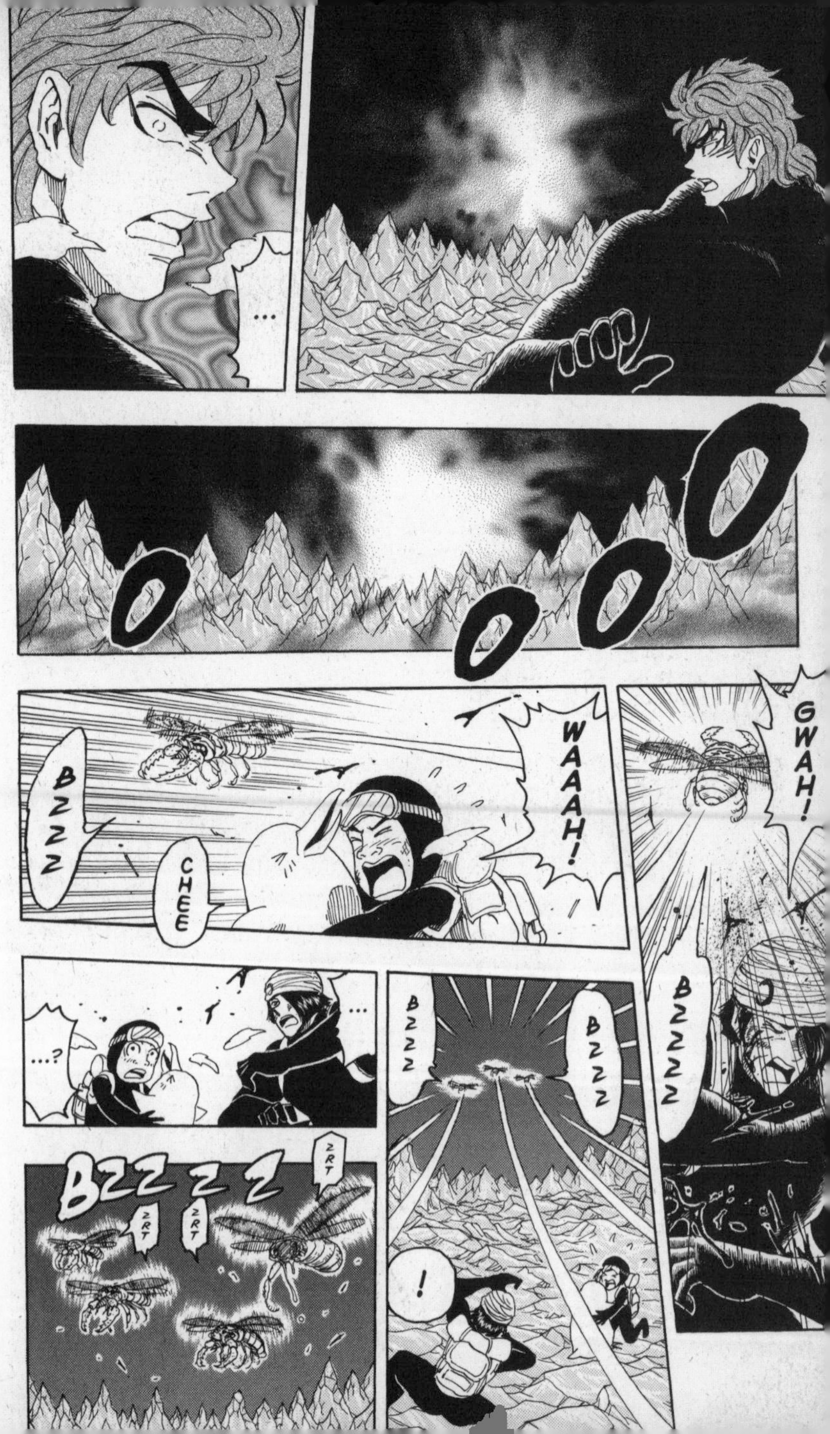
...
OOOOO
GWAH!
WAAAAH!
CHEE
BZZZ
BZZZZ
BZZZ
BZZZ
!
...
...?
BZZ Z Z
ZRT
ZRT
ZRT

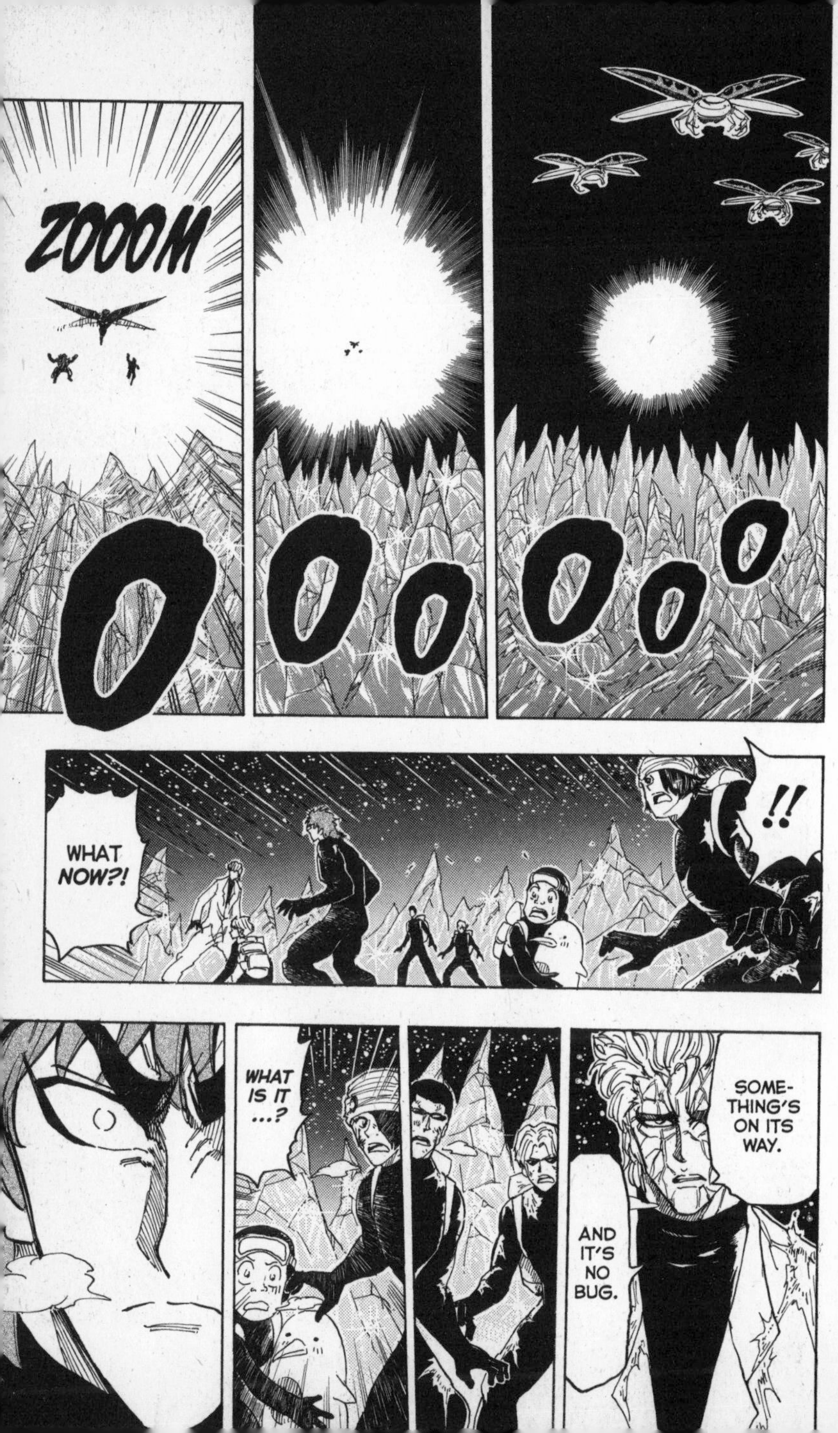
ZOOOM
OOOOOO
!!
WHAT NOW?!
SOME-THING'S ON ITS WAY.
AND IT'S NO BUG.
WHAT IS IT ...?

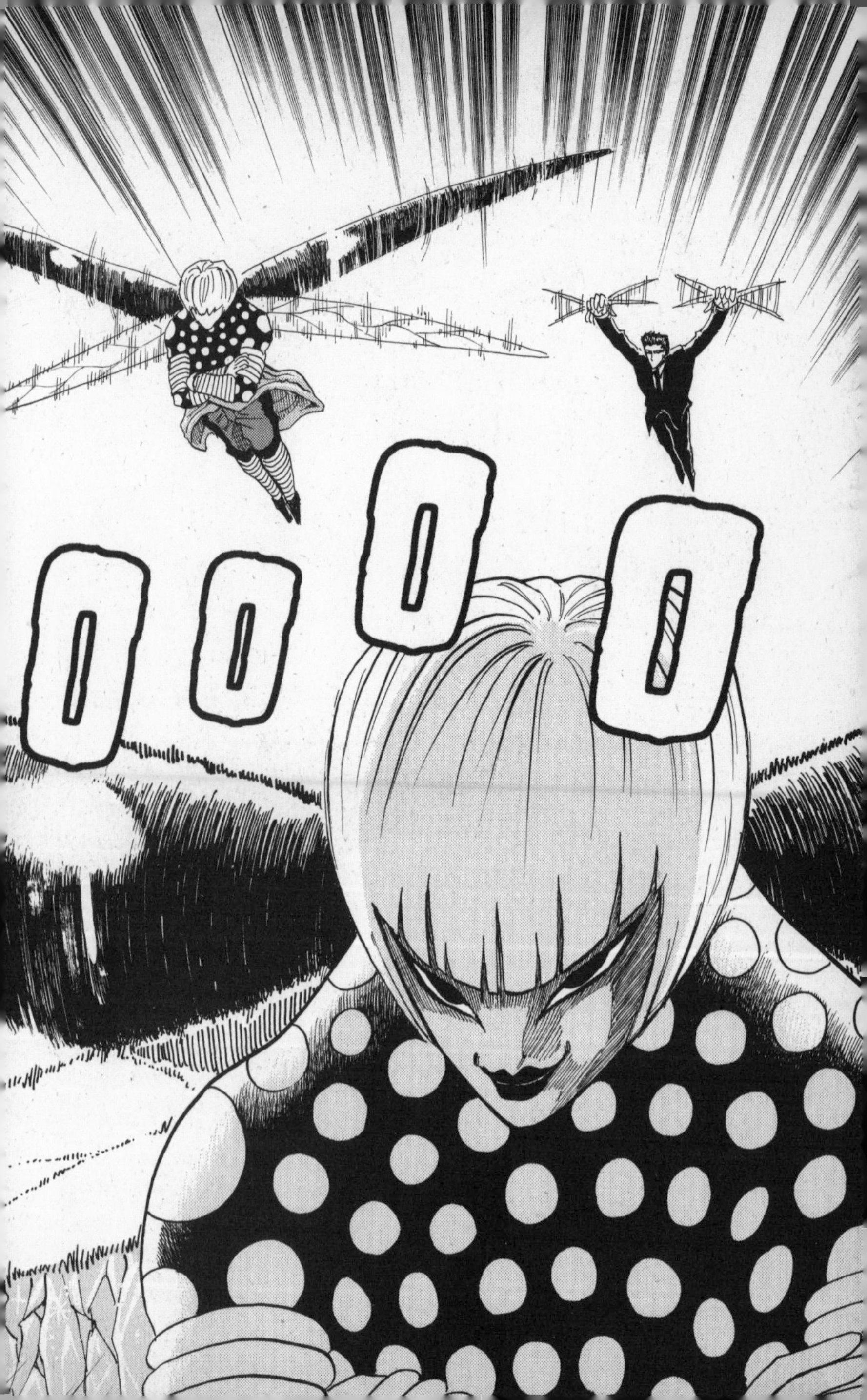
OOOO

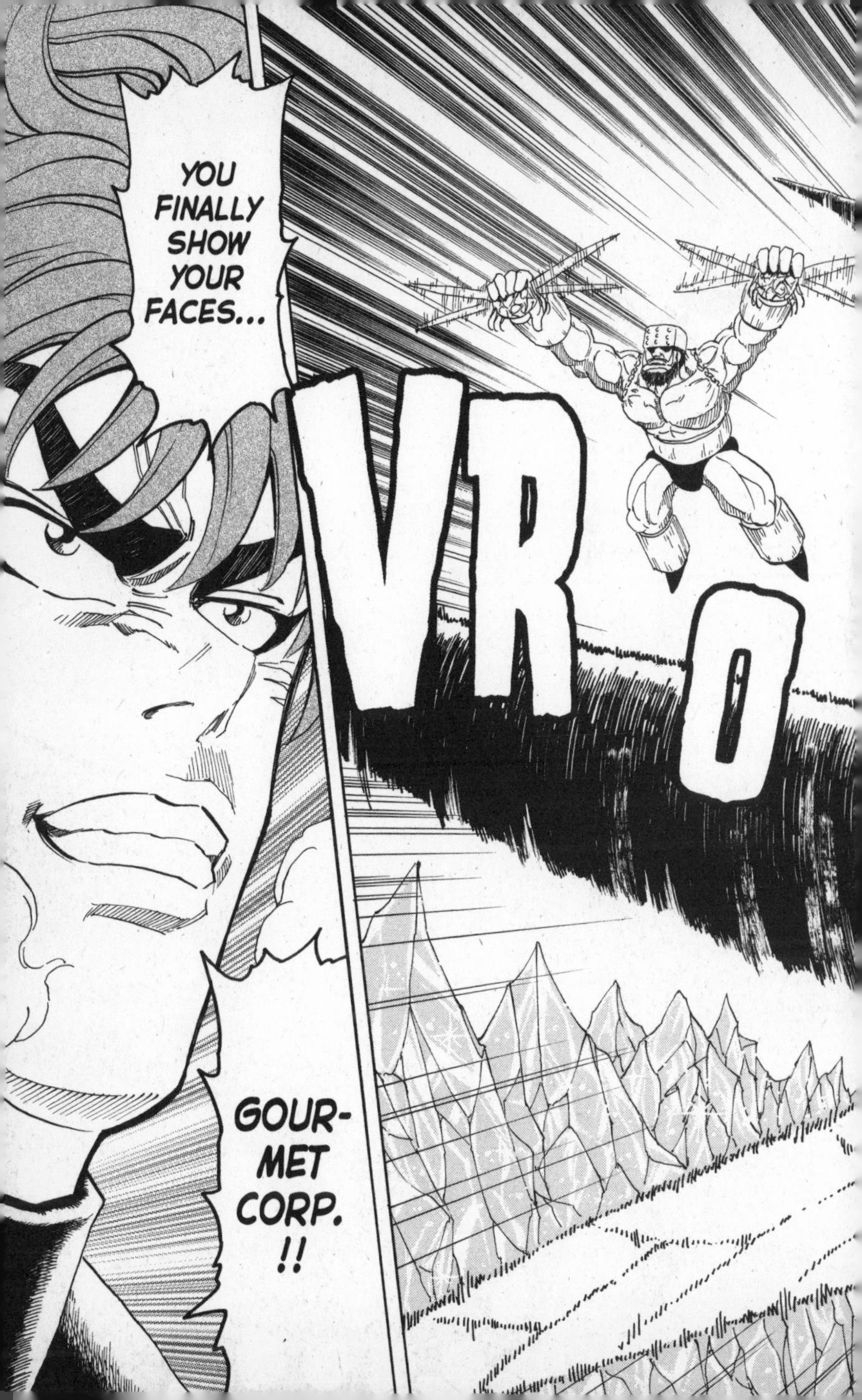
VRO
YOU FINALLY SHOW YOUR FACES...
GOUR-MET CORP. !!

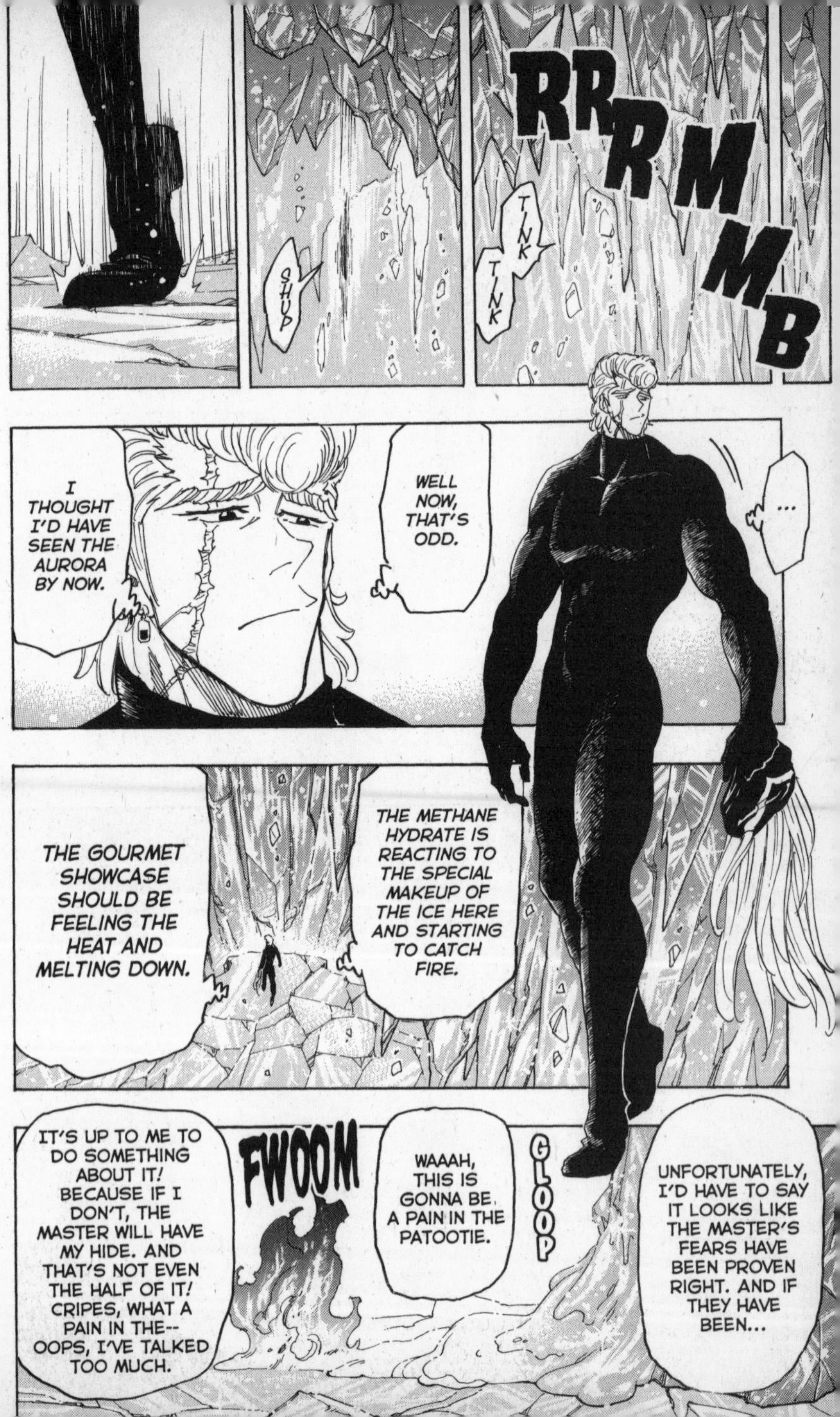
RRRMMMB
TINK TINK
SHUP
...
WELL NOW, THAT'S ODD.
I THOUGHT I'D HAVE SEEN THE AURORA BY NOW.
THE METHANE HYDRATE IS REACTING TO THE SPECIAL MAKEUP OF THE ICE HERE AND STARTING TO CATCH FIRE.
THE GOURMET SHOWCASE SHOULD BE FEELING THE HEAT AND MELTING DOWN.
UNFORTUNATELY, I'D HAVE TO SAY IT LOOKS LIKE THE MASTER'S FEARS HAVE BEEN PROVEN RIGHT. AND IF THEY HAVE BEEN...
GLOOP
WAAAH, THIS IS GONNA BE A PAIN IN THE PATOOTIE.
FWOOM
IT'S UP TO ME TO DO SOMETHING ABOUT IT! BECAUSE IF I DON'T, THE MASTER WILL HAVE MY HIDE. AND THAT'S NOT EVEN THE HALF OF IT! CRIPES, WHAT A PAIN IN THE-- OOPS, I'VE TALKED TOO MUCH.

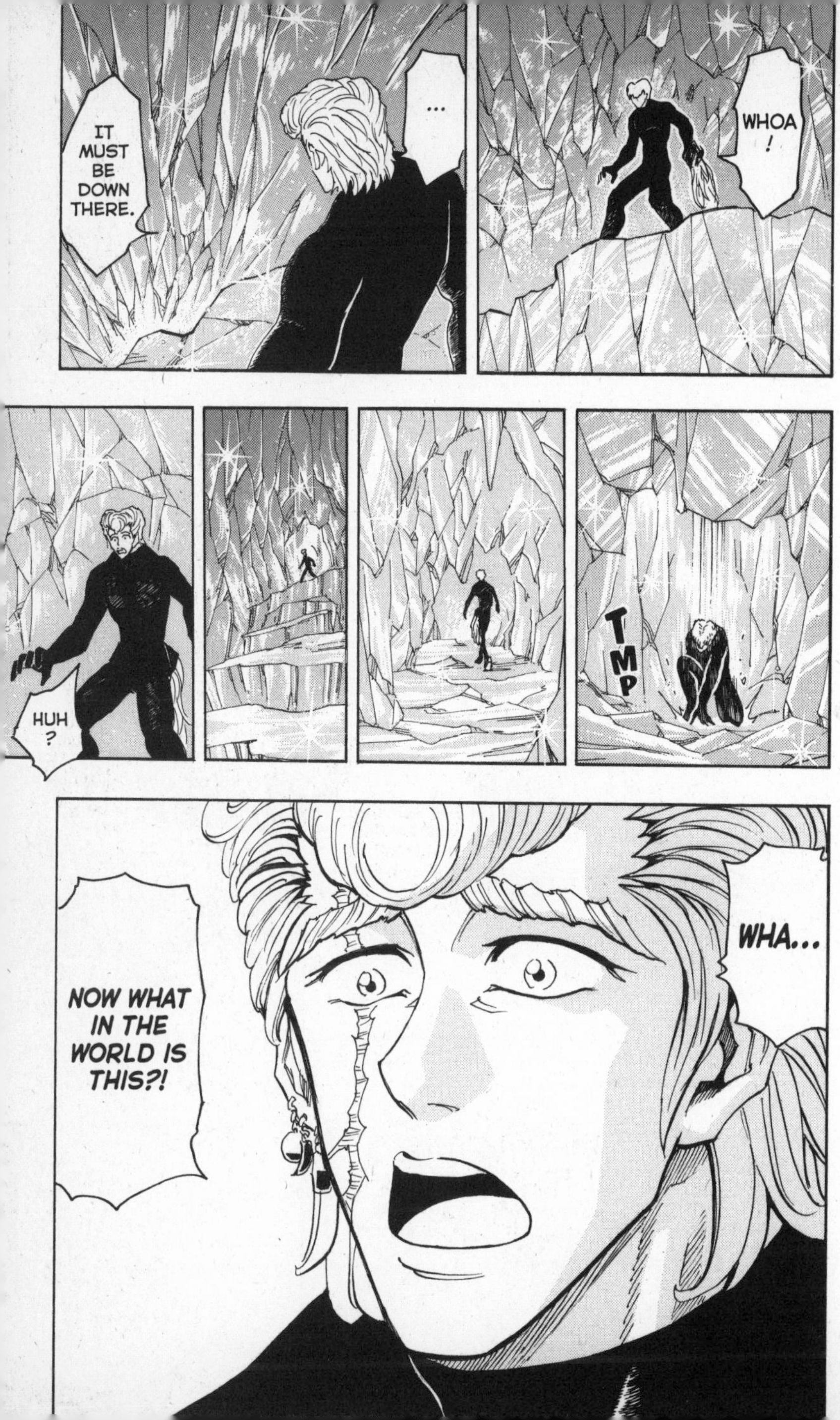
WHOA!
...
IT MUST BE DOWN THERE.
TMP
HUH?
WHA...
NOW WHAT IN THE WORLD IS THIS?!

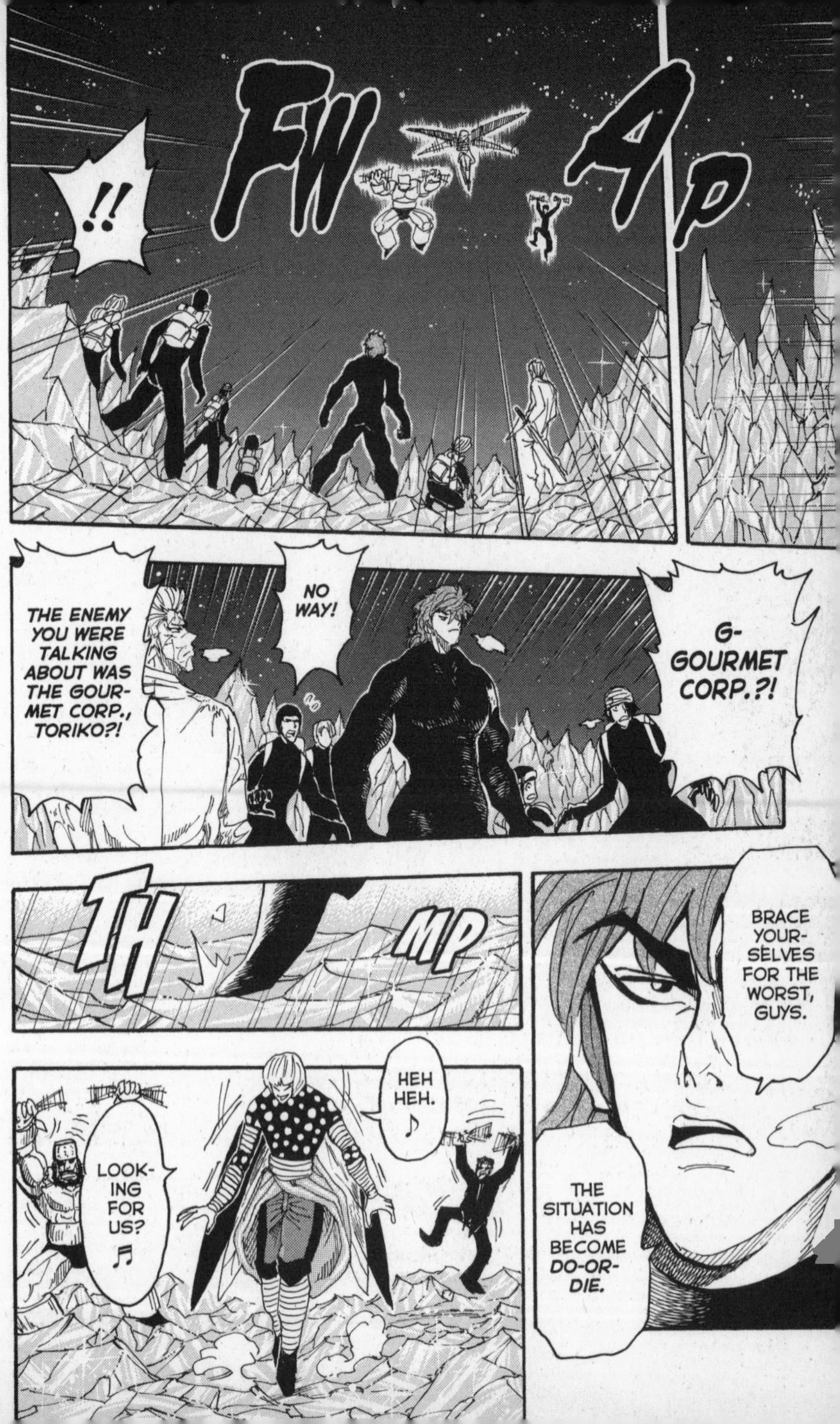
FWAP
!!
G- GOURMET CORP.?!
NO WAY!
THE ENEMY YOU WERE TALKING ABOUT WAS THE GOURMET CORP., TORIKO?!
BRACE YOURSELVES FOR THE WORST, GUYS.
THE SITUATION HAS BECOME DO-OR-DIE.
THUMP
HEH HEH. ♪
LOOKING FOR US? ♫

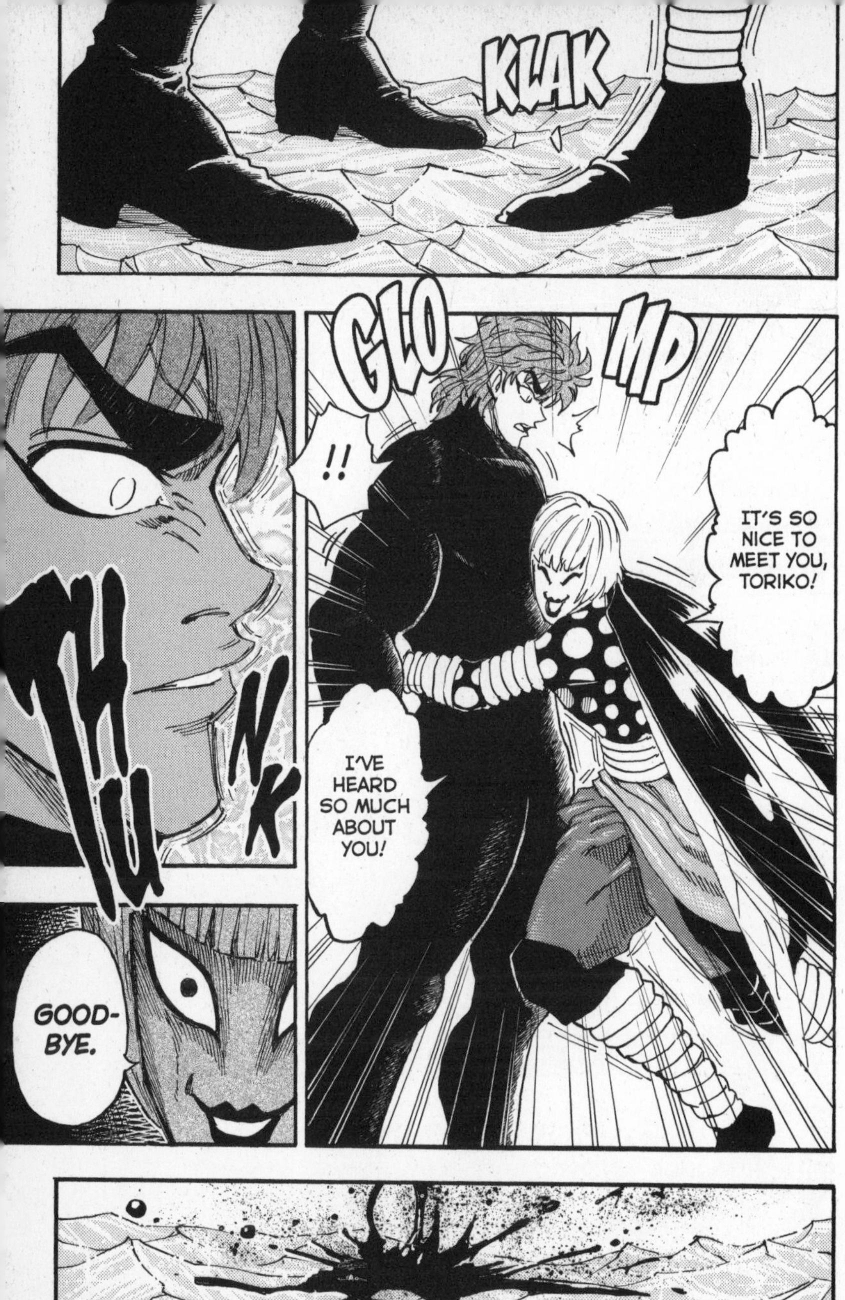
KLAK
GLOMP
!!
IT'S SO NICE TO MEET YOU, TORIKO!
I'VE HEARD SO MUCH ABOUT YOU!
THUNK
GOOD-BYE.

TORIKO

GOURMET CHECKLIST

Vol. 068

CHEESE RABBIT

(MAMMAL)

CAPTURE LEVEL: 12

HABITAT: GRASSY PLAINS

LENGTH: 180 CM

HEIGHT: ---

WEIGHT: 280 KG

PRICE: 100 G / 6,000 YEN

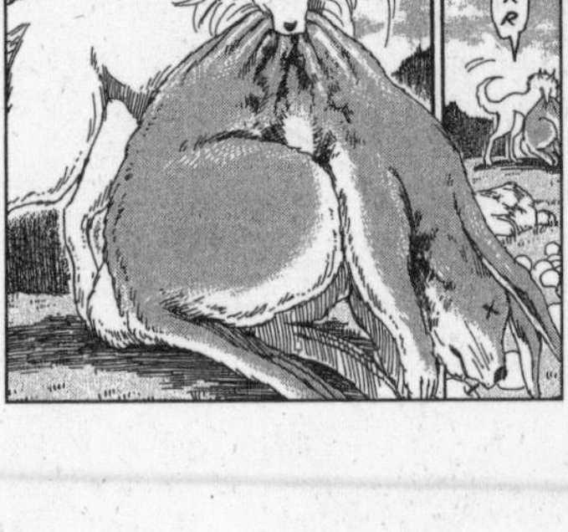
GRR

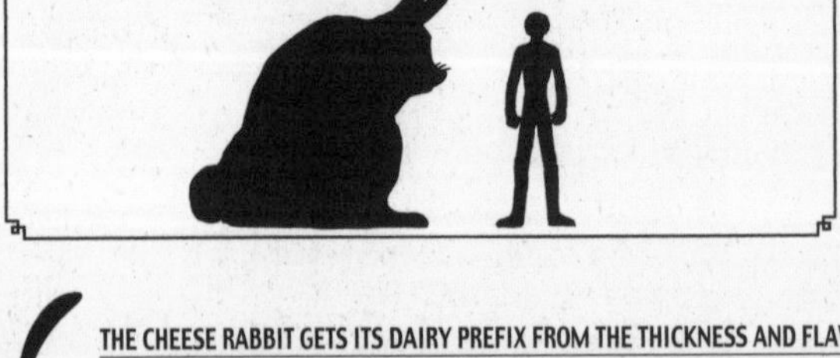

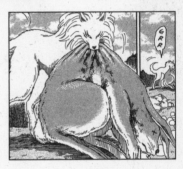

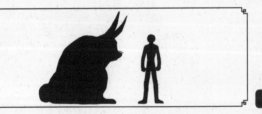

SCALE

THE CHEESE RABBIT GETS ITS DAIRY PREFIX FROM THE THICKNESS AND FLAVOR OF ITS MEAT--THE PROTEIN IN ITS BODY CONGEALS QUITE READILY. THIS BIG BUNNY LIVES IN BURROWS AND IS VERY TIMID, MEANING THAT IT RARELY SURFACES TO MAKE ITSELF AVAILABLE FOR CAPTURE. IN THE EVENT THAT ONE DOES VENTURE ABOVE GROUND, THE CHEESE RABBIT'S STRONG LEGS ENABLE IT TO SWIFTLY ESCAPE PREDATORS. IT IS THIS ANIMAL'S ABILITY TO FLEE, RATHER THAN ITS FIGHTING PROWESS, WHICH EARNS IT A RELATIVELY HIGH CAPTURE LEVEL.

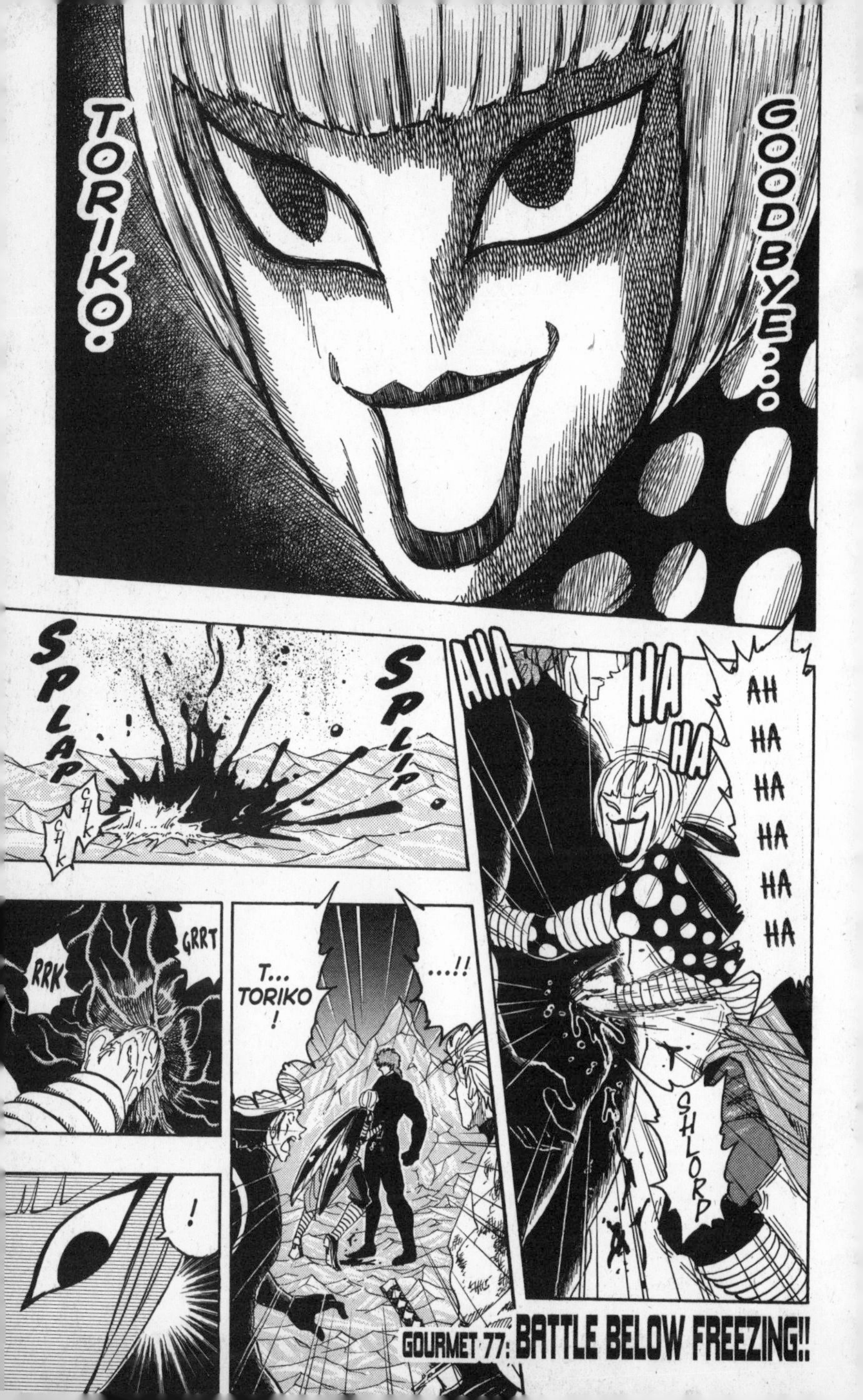
GOODBYE...
TORIKO.
AHA HA HA
AH HA HA HA HA HA HA
SHLORP
SPLIP
SPLAP
CHK CHK
...!!
T... TORIKO!
GRRT
RRK
!
GOURMET 77: BATTLE BELOW FREEZING!!

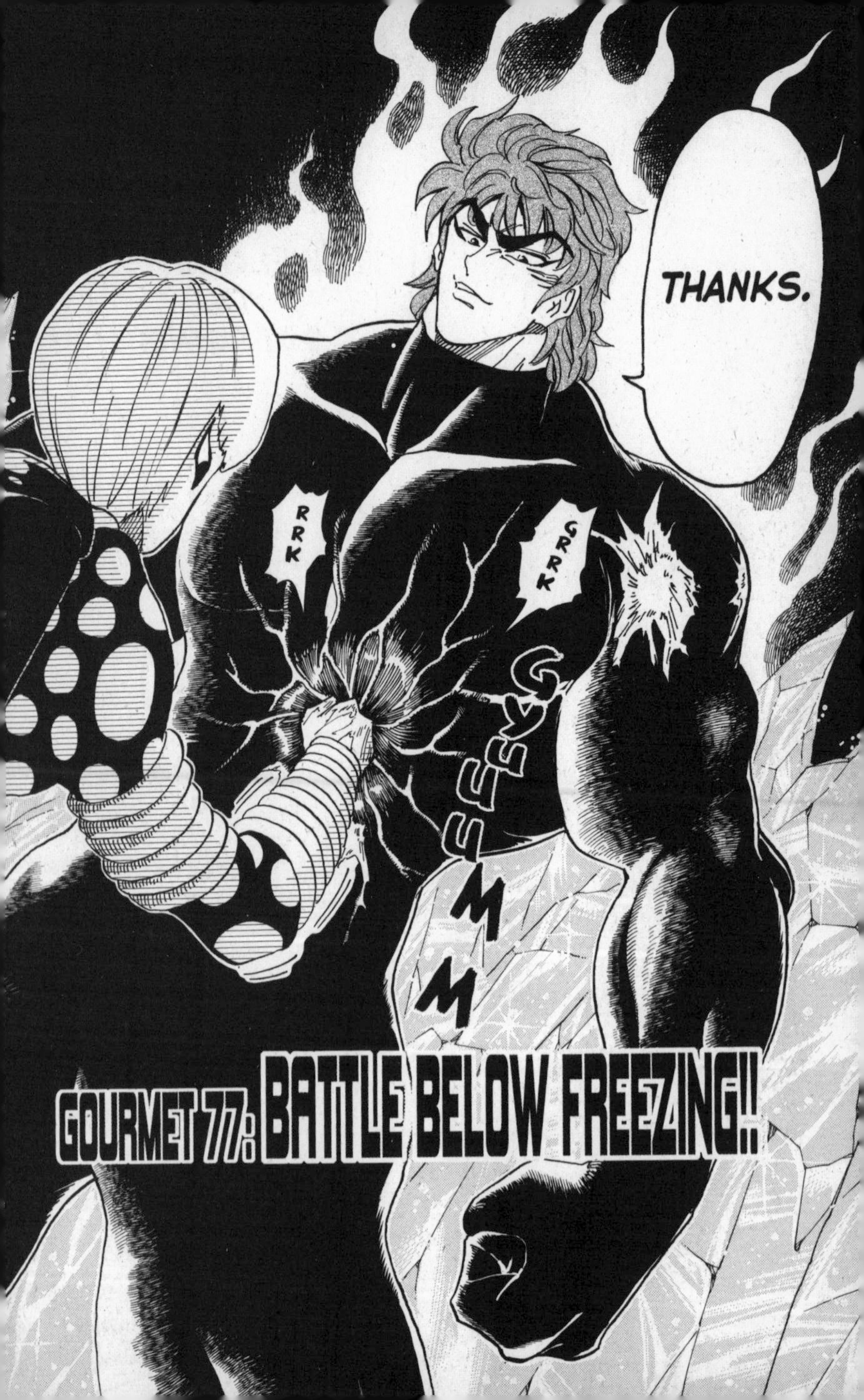
THANKS.
GRRK
RRK
GYGGGUMMM
GOURMET 77: BATTLE BELOW FREEZING!!

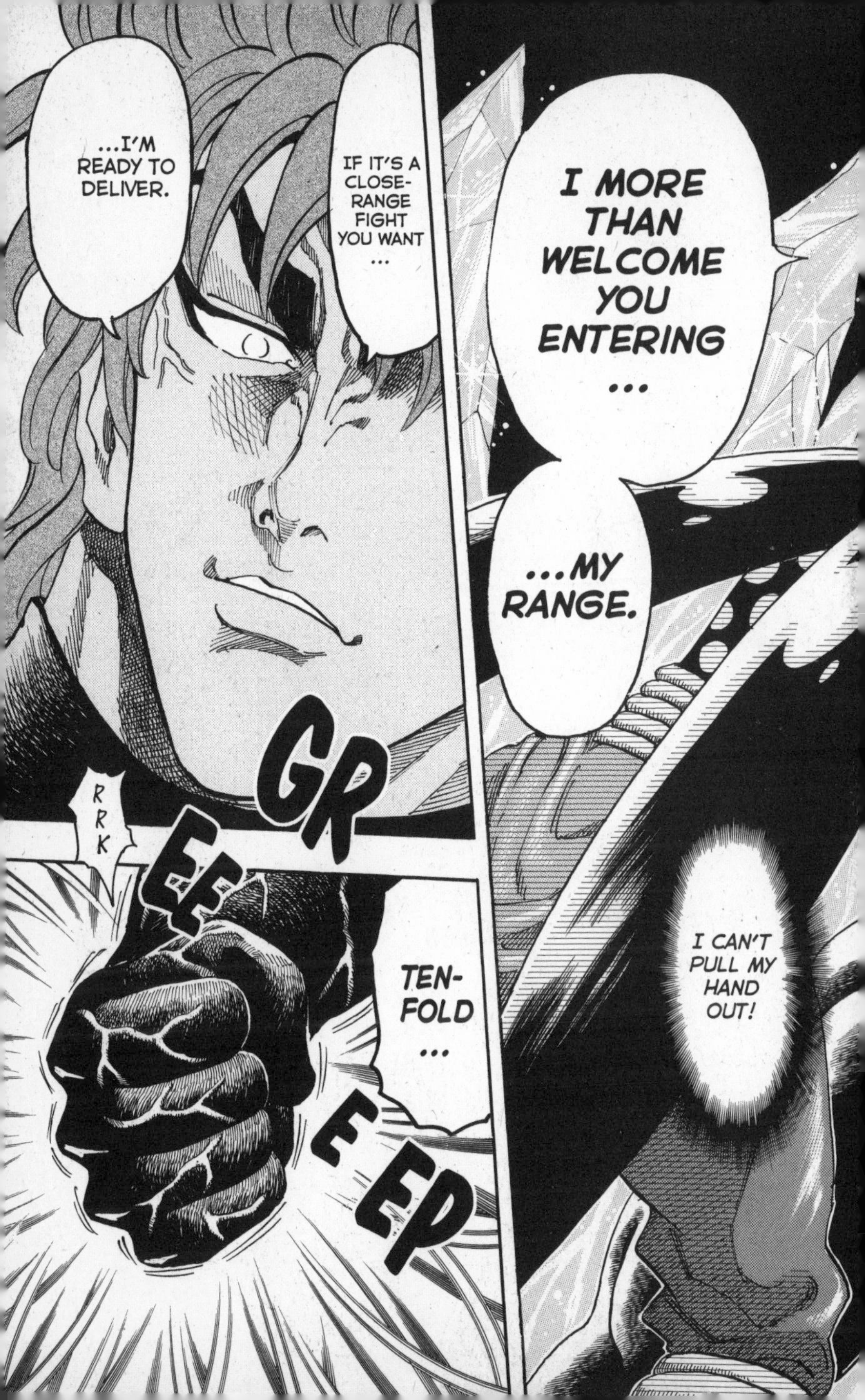
I MORE THAN WELCOME YOU ENTERING ...
...MY RANGE.
I CAN'T PULL MY HAND OUT!
IF IT'S A CLOSE-RANGE FIGHT YOU WANT ...
...I'M READY TO DELIVER.
RRK
GREEEEP
TEN-FOLD ...

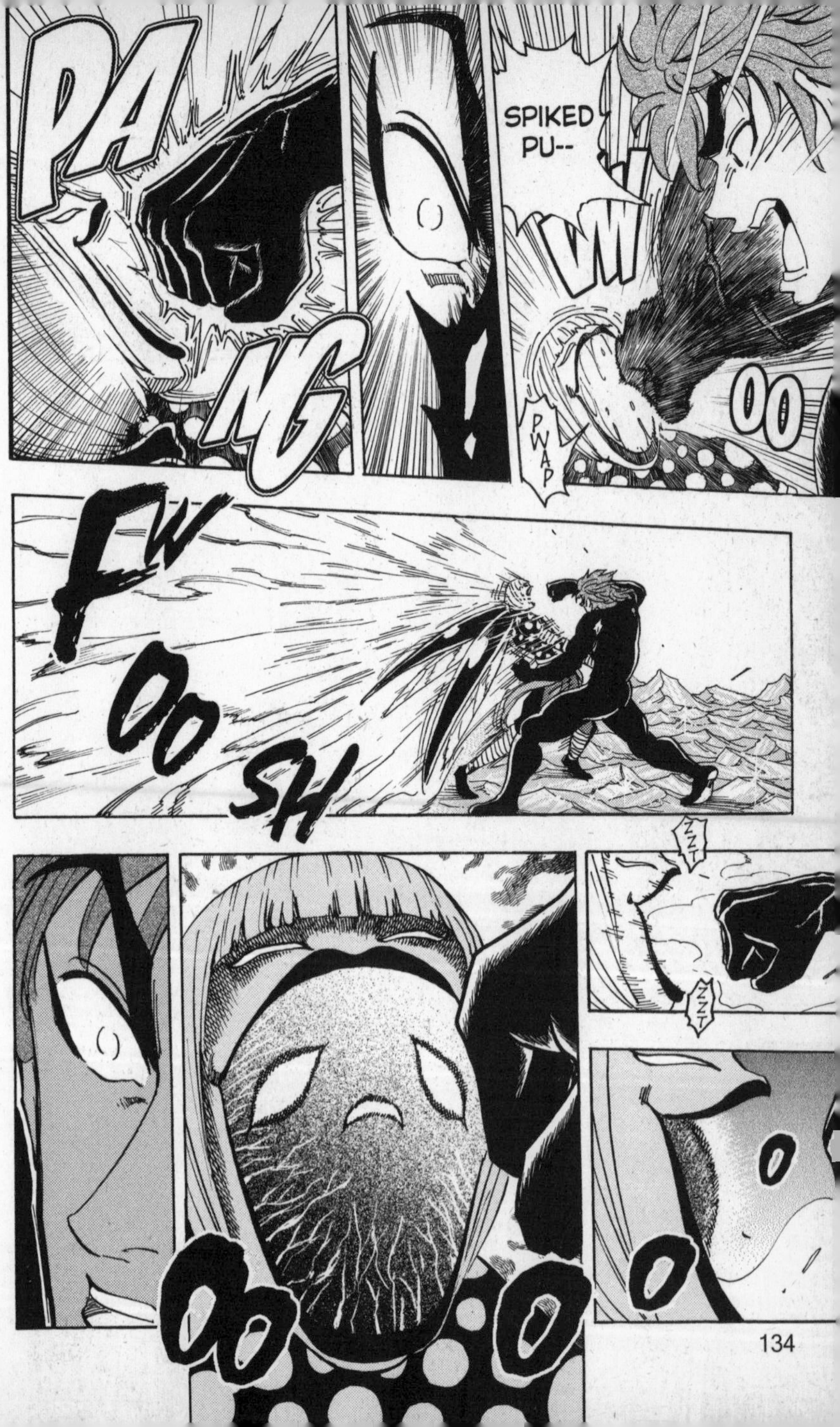
SPIKED PU--
PWAP
OO
PANG
FWOOSH
ZZZT
ZZZT
OOO
OOOO

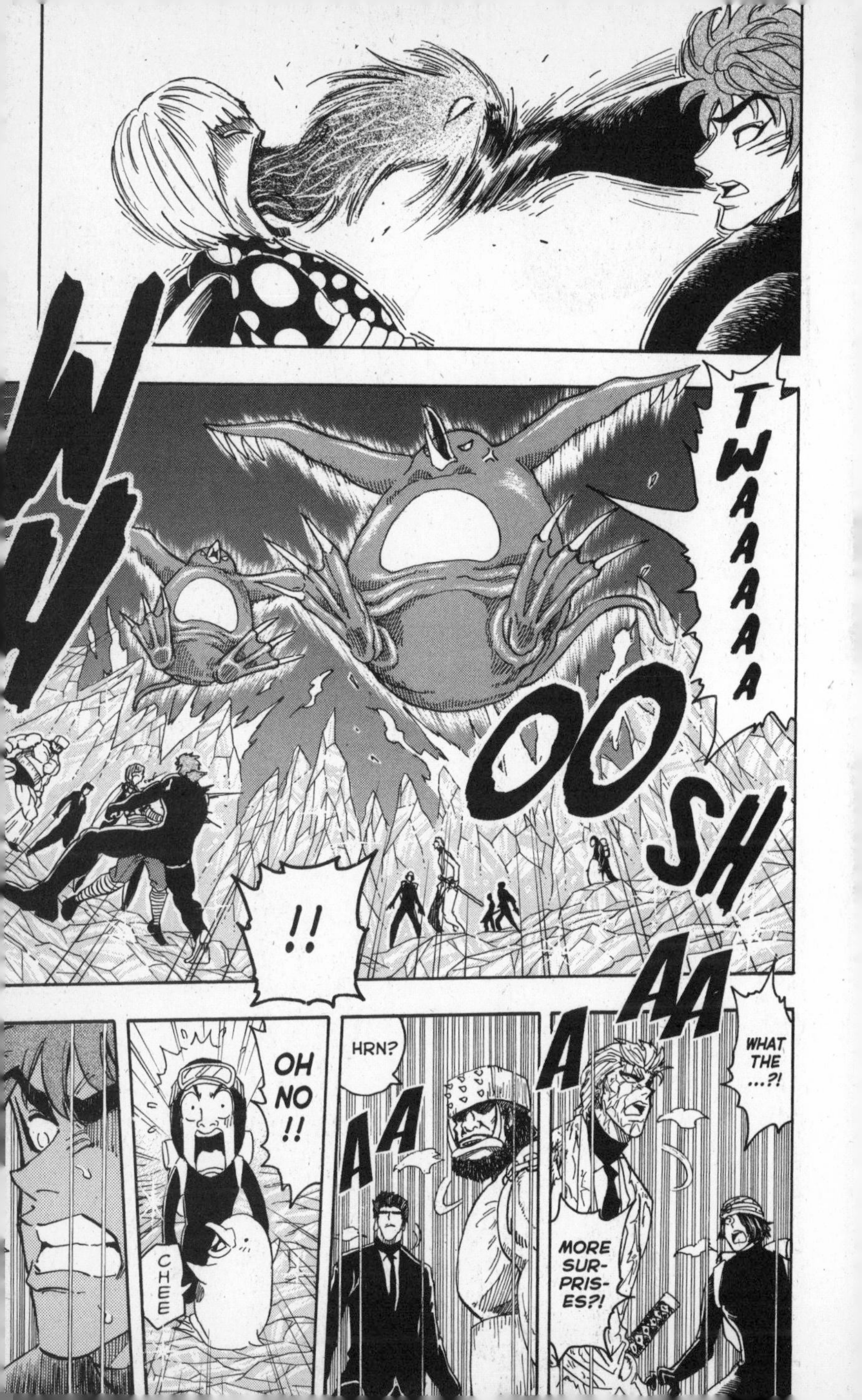
TWAAAAAA
OOSH
!!
AA
A
AA
WHAT THE ...?!
MORE SUR-PRIS-ES?!
HRN?
OH NO !!
CHEE

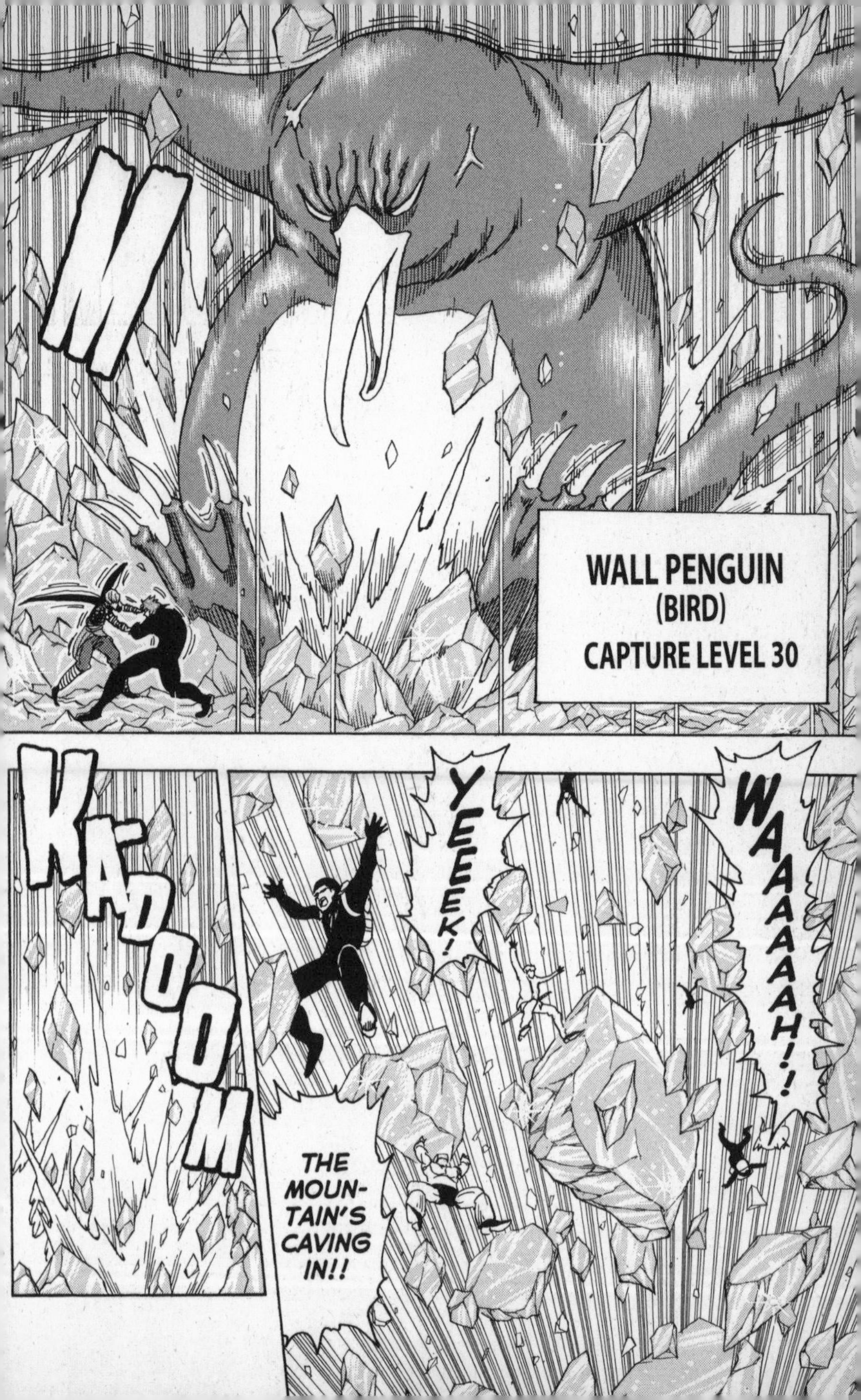
WALL PENGUIN
(BIRD)
CAPTURE LEVEL 30
WAAAAAAH!!
YEEEK!
THE MOUNTAIN'S CAVING IN!!
KA-DOOOM

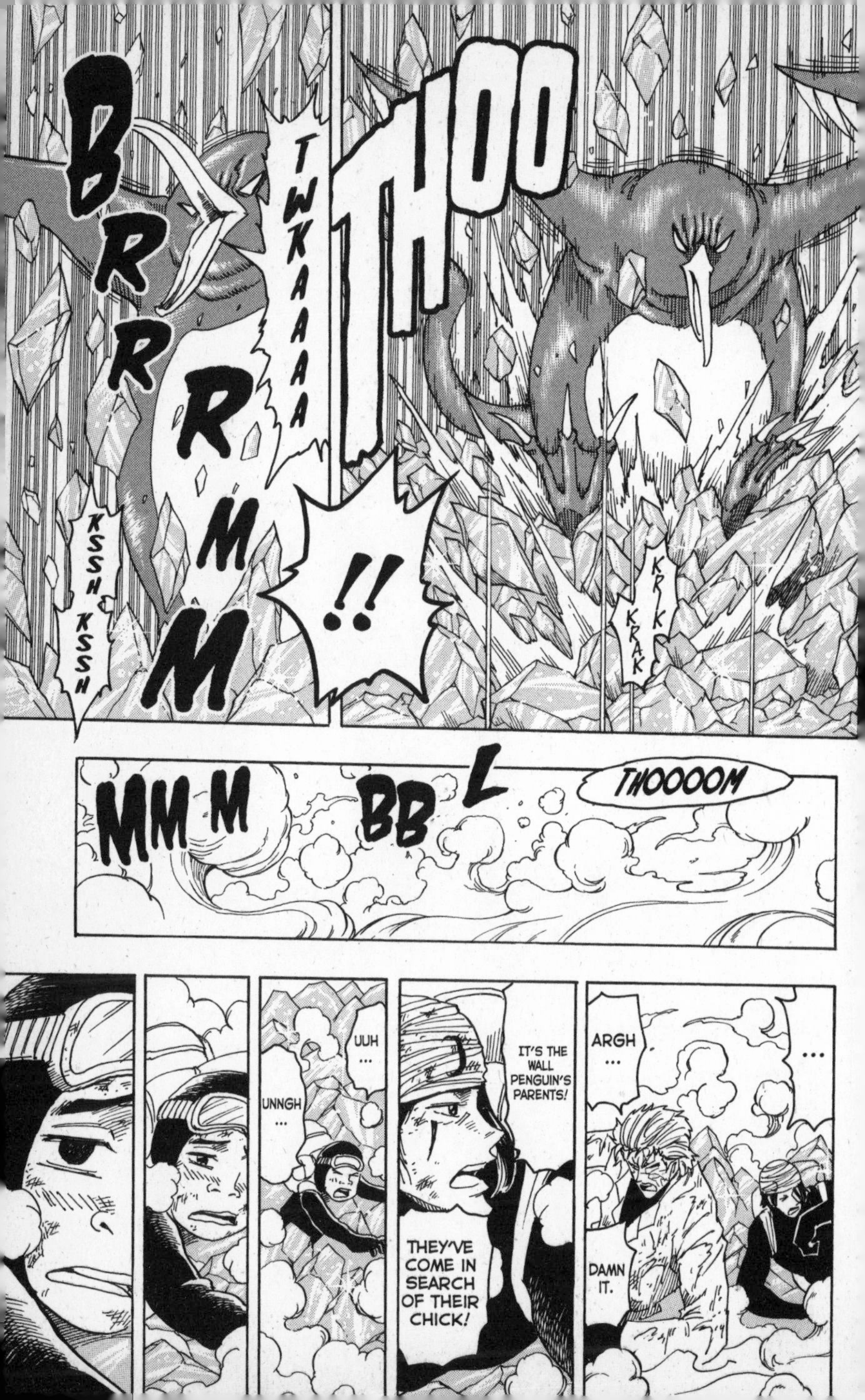
THOO
!!
KRIK KRAK
TWKAAAAA
BRRRMMM
KSSH KSSH
THOOOOM
MMMMBBL
...
ARGH ...
DAMN IT.
IT'S THE WALL PENGUIN'S PARENTS!
THEY'VE COME IN SEARCH OF THEIR CHICK!
UUH ...
UNNGH ...

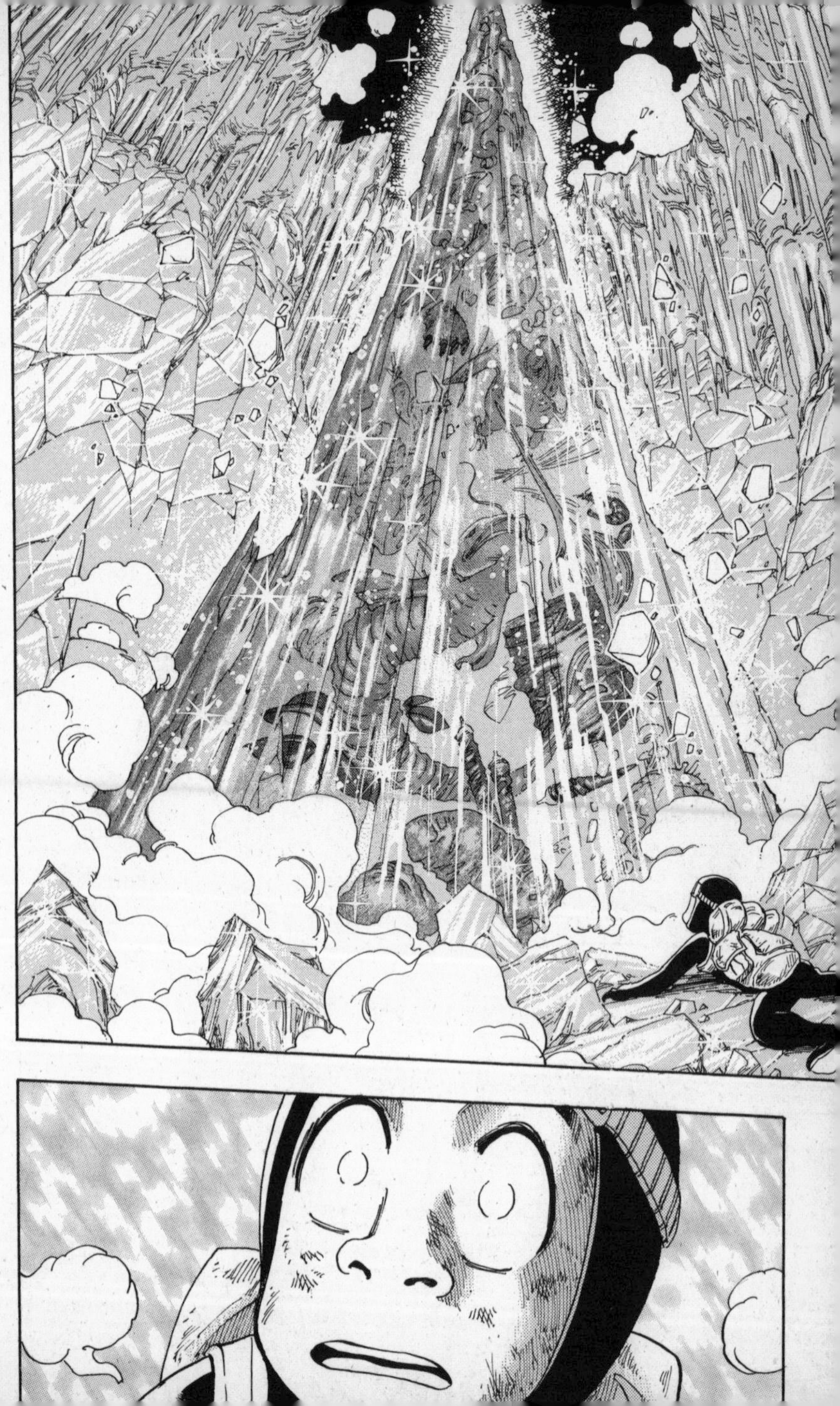

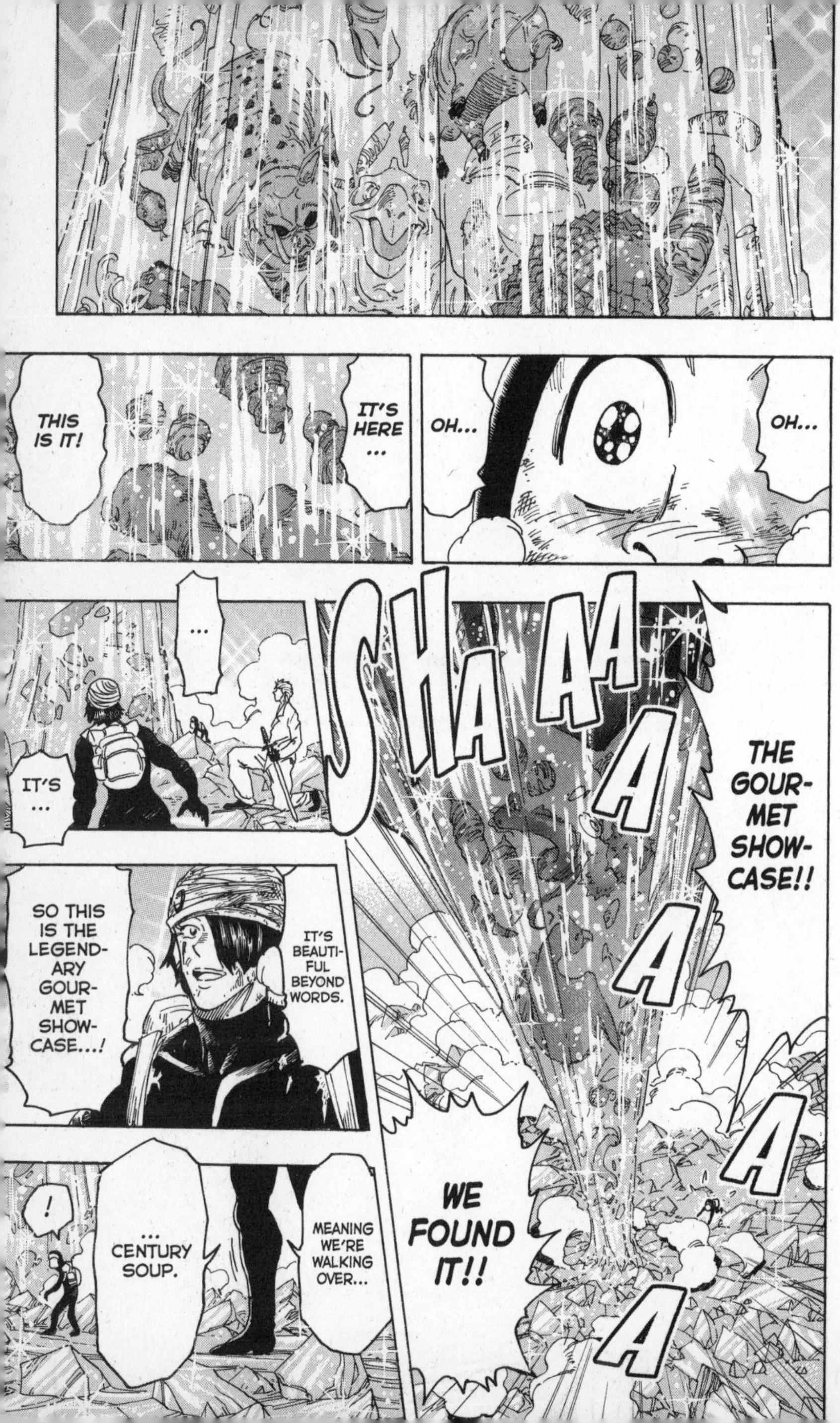
OH...
OH...
IT'S HERE ...
THIS IS IT!
SHAAAAAAA
THE GOURMET SHOWCASE!!
WE FOUND IT!!
...
IT'S ...
IT'S BEAUTIFUL BEYOND WORDS.
SO THIS IS THE LEGENDARY GOURMET SHOWCASE...!
MEANING WE'RE WALKING OVER...
... CENTURY SOUP.
!

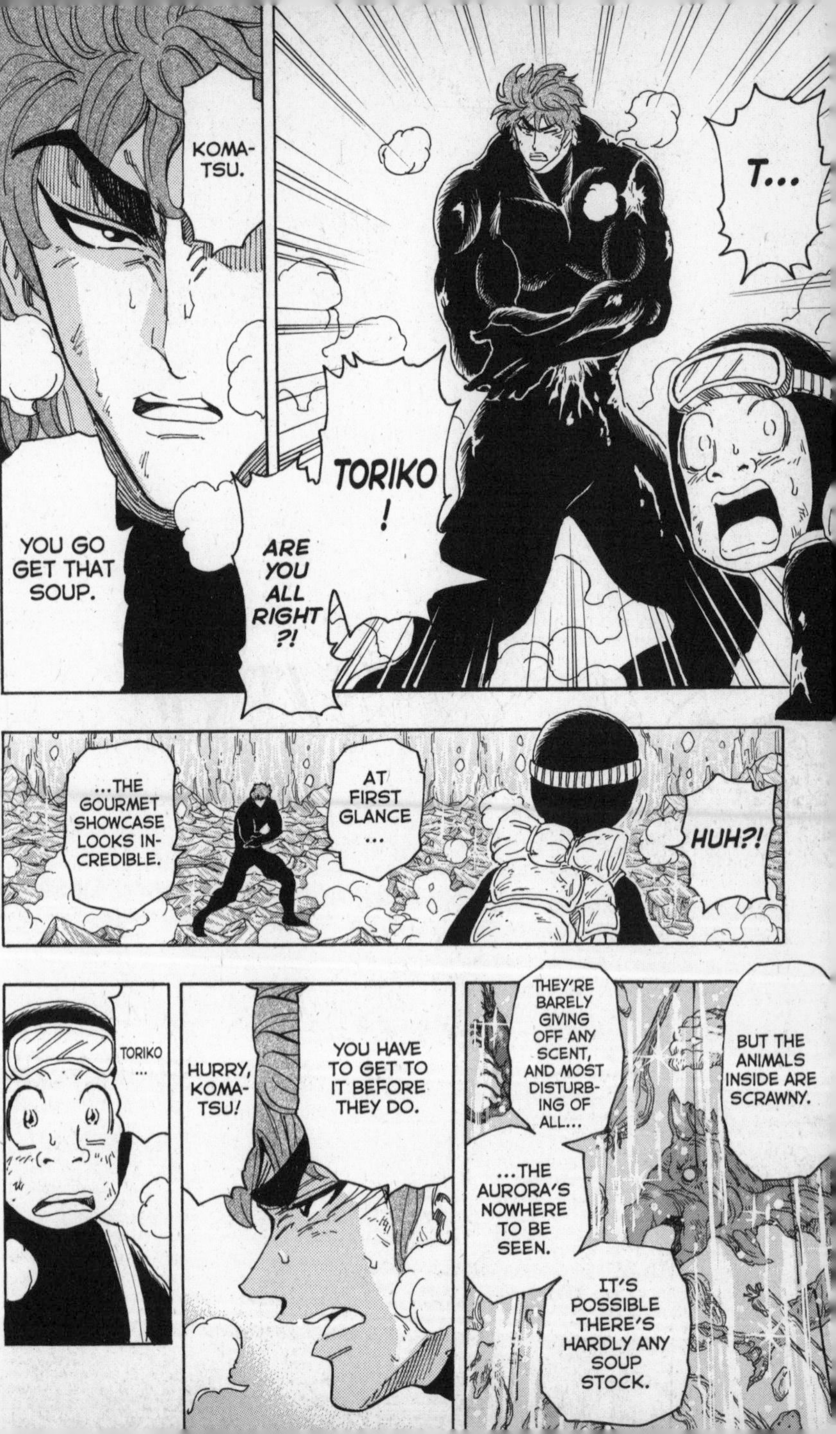
T...
TORIKO!
ARE YOU ALL RIGHT?!
KOMATSU.
YOU GO GET THAT SOUP.
HUH?!
AT FIRST GLANCE...
...THE GOURMET SHOWCASE LOOKS INCREDIBLE.
BUT THE ANIMALS INSIDE ARE SCRAWNY.
THEY'RE BARELY GIVING OFF ANY SCENT, AND MOST DISTURBING OF ALL...
...THE AURORA'S NOWHERE TO BE SEEN.
IT'S POSSIBLE THERE'S HARDLY ANY SOUP STOCK.
YOU HAVE TO GET TO IT BEFORE THEY DO.
HURRY, KOMATSU!
TORIKO...

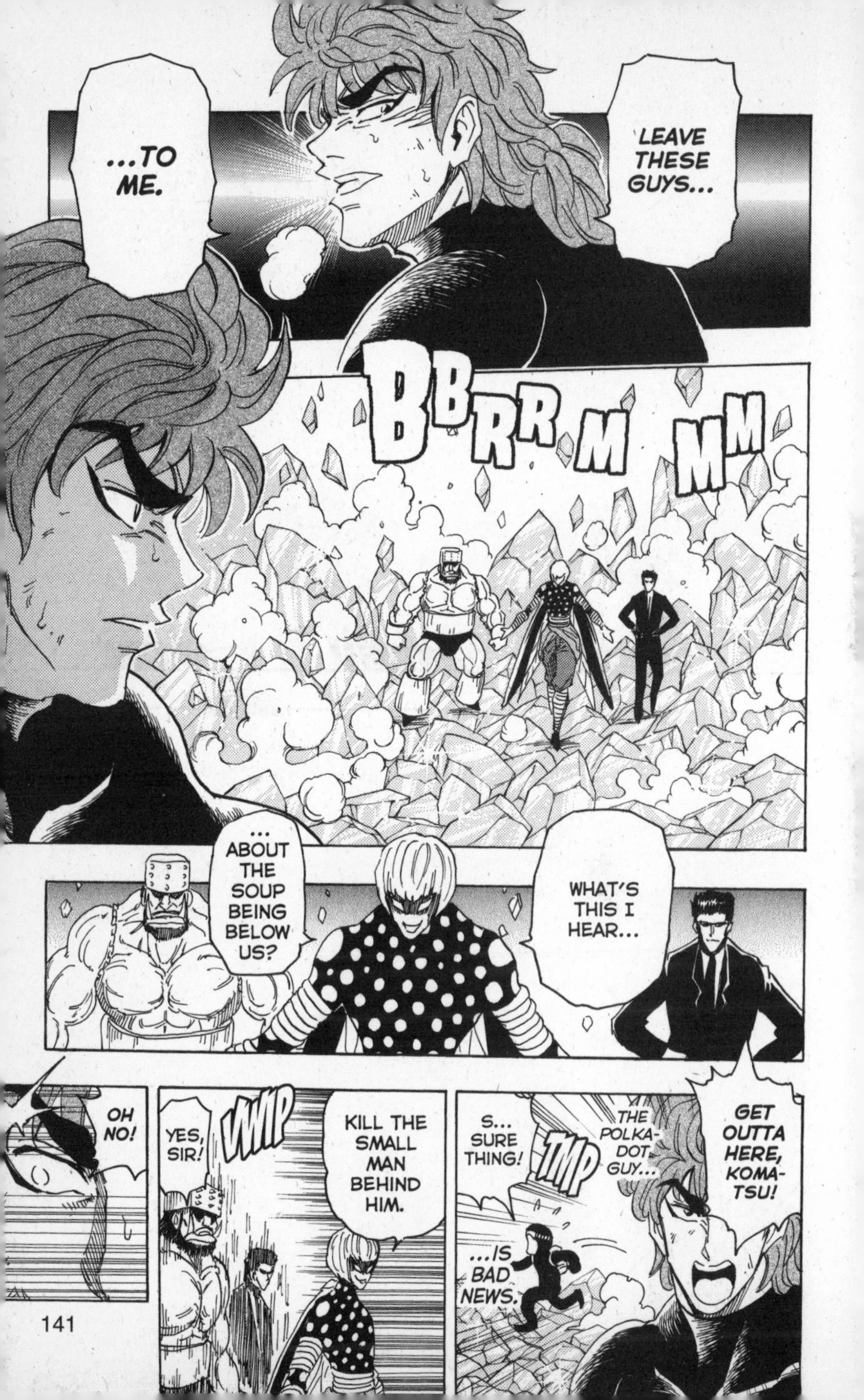
LEAVE THESE GUYS...
...TO ME.
BBRRRM MMM
WHAT'S THIS I HEAR...
...ABOUT THE SOUP BEING BELOW US?
GET OUTTA HERE, KOMATSU!
THE POLKA-DOT GUY...
S... SURE THING!
TMP
...IS BAD NEWS.
KILL THE SMALL MAN BEHIND HIM.
VWIP
YES, SIR!
OH NO!

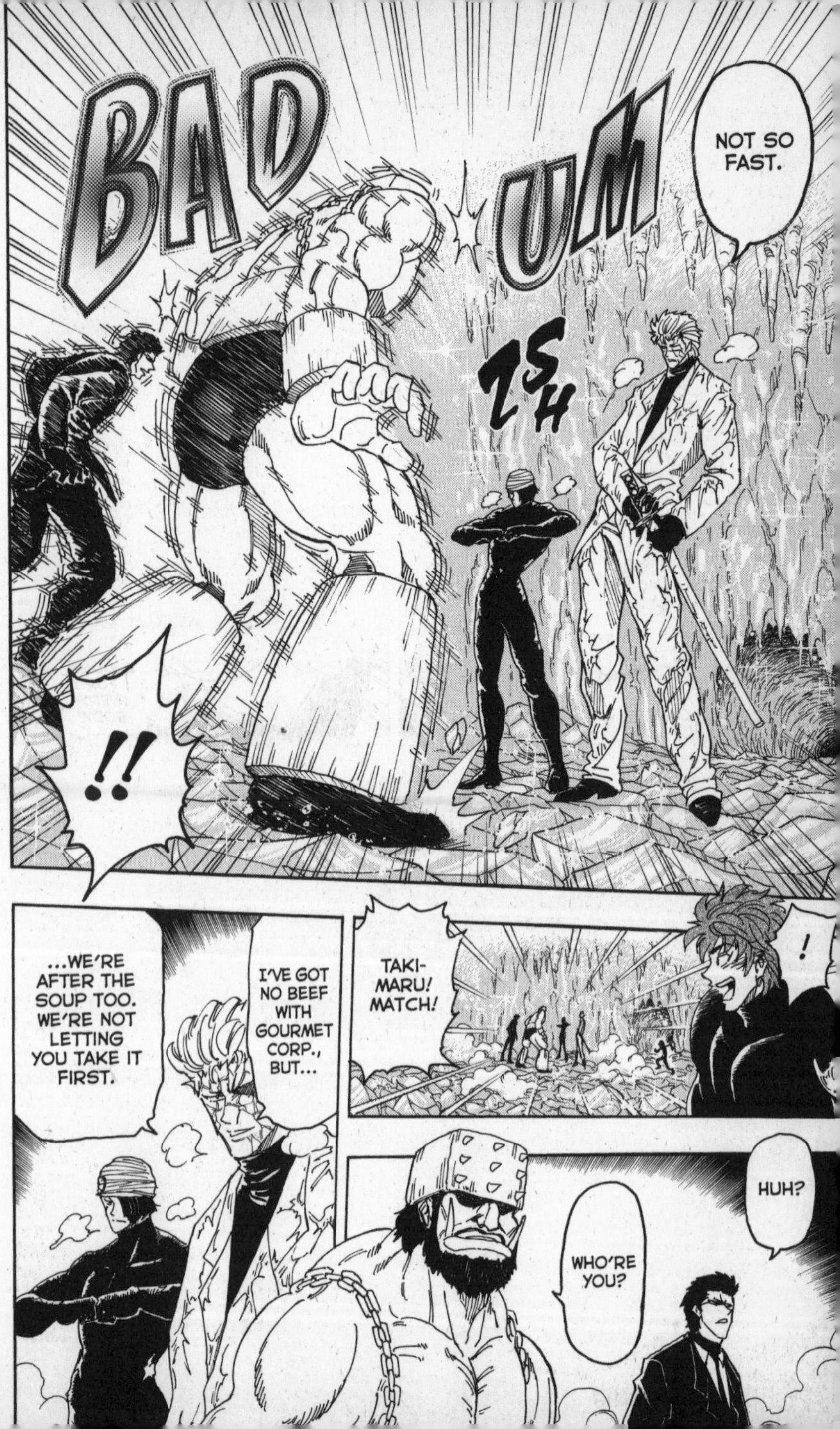
NOT SO FAST.
BADUM
ZSH
!!
!
TAKI-MARU! MATCH!
HUH?
WHO'RE YOU?
I'VE GOT NO BEEF WITH GOURMET CORP., BUT...
...WE'RE AFTER THE SOUP TOO. WE'RE NOT LETTING YOU TAKE IT FIRST.

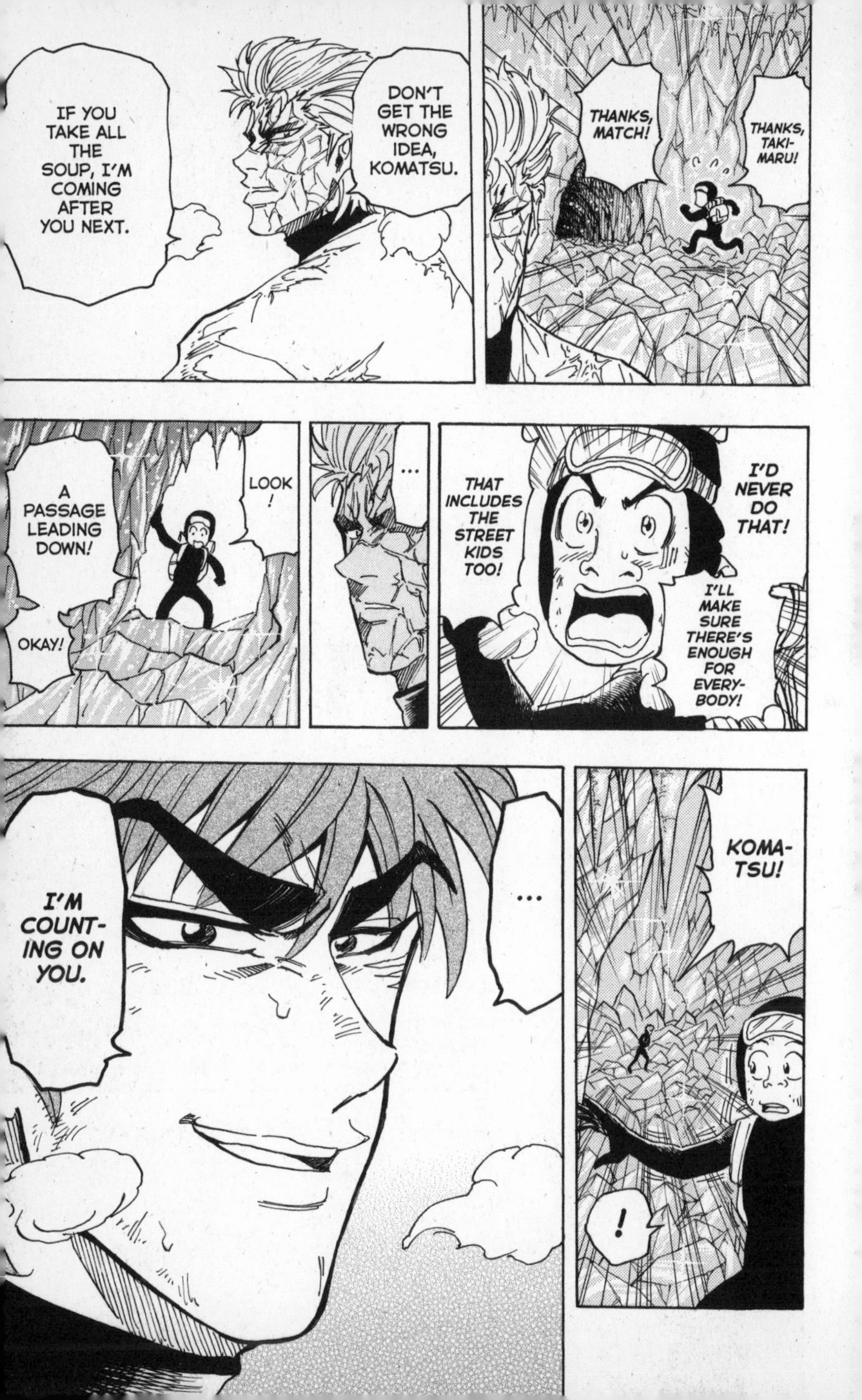
THANKS, TAKI-MARU!
THANKS, MATCH!
DON'T GET THE WRONG IDEA, KOMATSU.
IF YOU TAKE ALL THE SOUP, I'M COMING AFTER YOU NEXT.
I'D NEVER DO THAT!
I'LL MAKE SURE THERE'S ENOUGH FOR EVERYBODY!
THAT INCLUDES THE STREET KIDS TOO!
...
LOOK!
A PASSAGE LEADING DOWN!
OKAY!
KOMA-TSU!
!
...
I'M COUNTING-ING ON YOU.

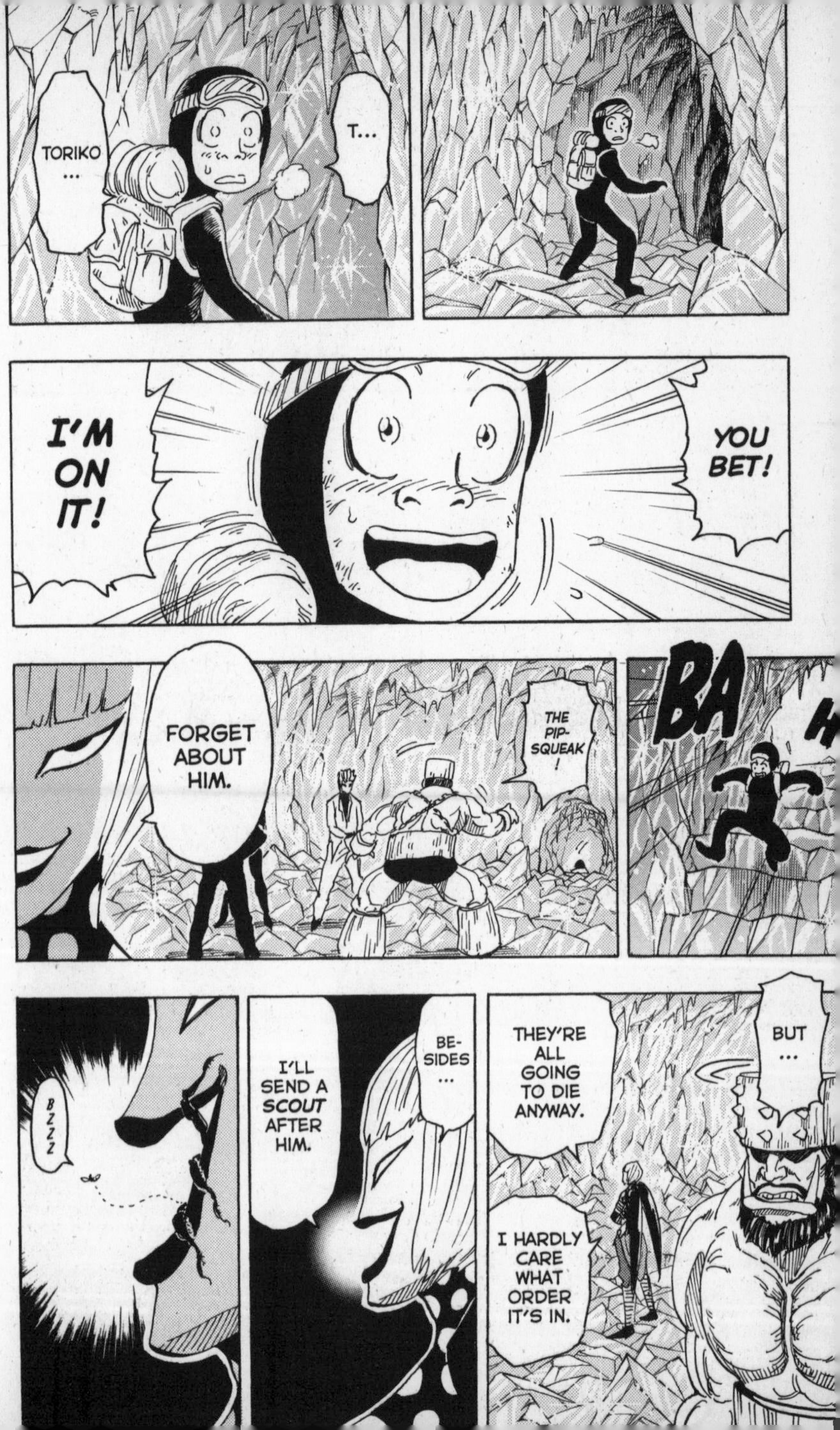
T...
TORIKO ...
YOU BET!
I'M ON IT!
BA
THE PIP-SQUEAK!
FORGET ABOUT HIM.
BUT ...
THEY'RE ALL GOING TO DIE ANYWAY.
I HARDLY CARE WHAT ORDER IT'S IN.
BE-SIDES ...
I'LL SEND A *SCOUT* AFTER HIM.
BZZZ

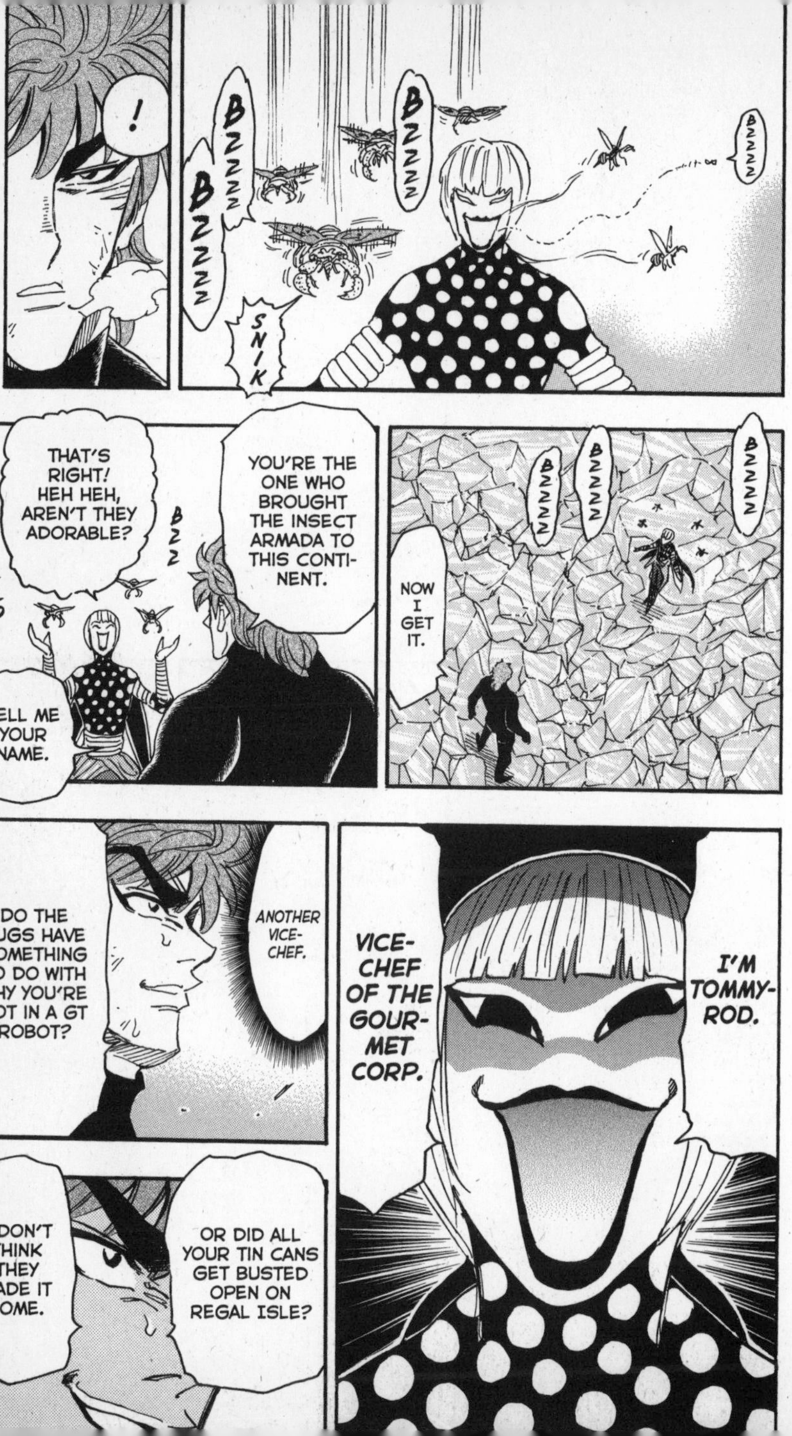
BZZZZ
BZZZZ
BZZZZ
SNIK
BZZZZ
!
BZZZZ
BZZZZ
BZZZZ
BZZZZ
NOW I GET IT.
YOU'RE THE ONE WHO BROUGHT THE INSECT ARMADA TO THIS CONTINENT.
THAT'S RIGHT! HEH HEH, AREN'T THEY ADORABLE?
BZZ
ZZP
TELL ME YOUR NAME.
I'M TOMMYROD.
VICE-CHEF OF THE GOURMET CORP.
ANOTHER VICE-CHEF.
DO THE BUGS HAVE SOMETHING TO DO WITH WHY YOU'RE NOT IN A GT ROBOT?
OR DID ALL YOUR TIN CANS GET BUSTED OPEN ON REGAL ISLE?
I DON'T THINK THEY MADE IT HOME.

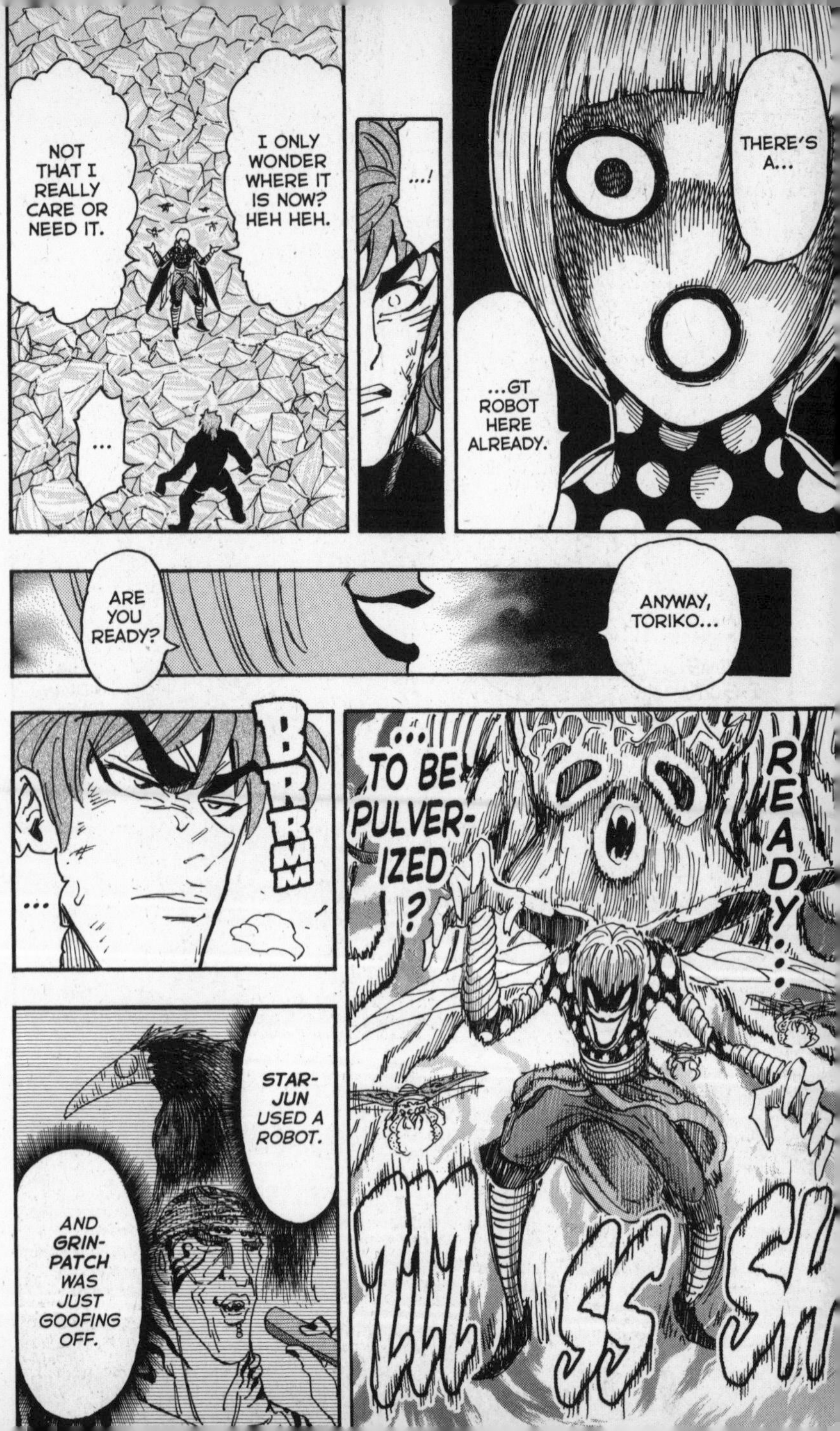
THERE'S A...
...GT ROBOT HERE ALREADY.
...!
I ONLY WONDER WHERE IT IS NOW? HEH HEH.
NOT THAT I REALLY CARE OR NEED IT.
...
ANYWAY, TORIKO...
ARE YOU READY?
READY...
...TO BE PULVERIZED?
BRRMM
...
STAR-JUN USED A ROBOT.
AND GRIN-PATCH WAS JUST GOOFING OFF.

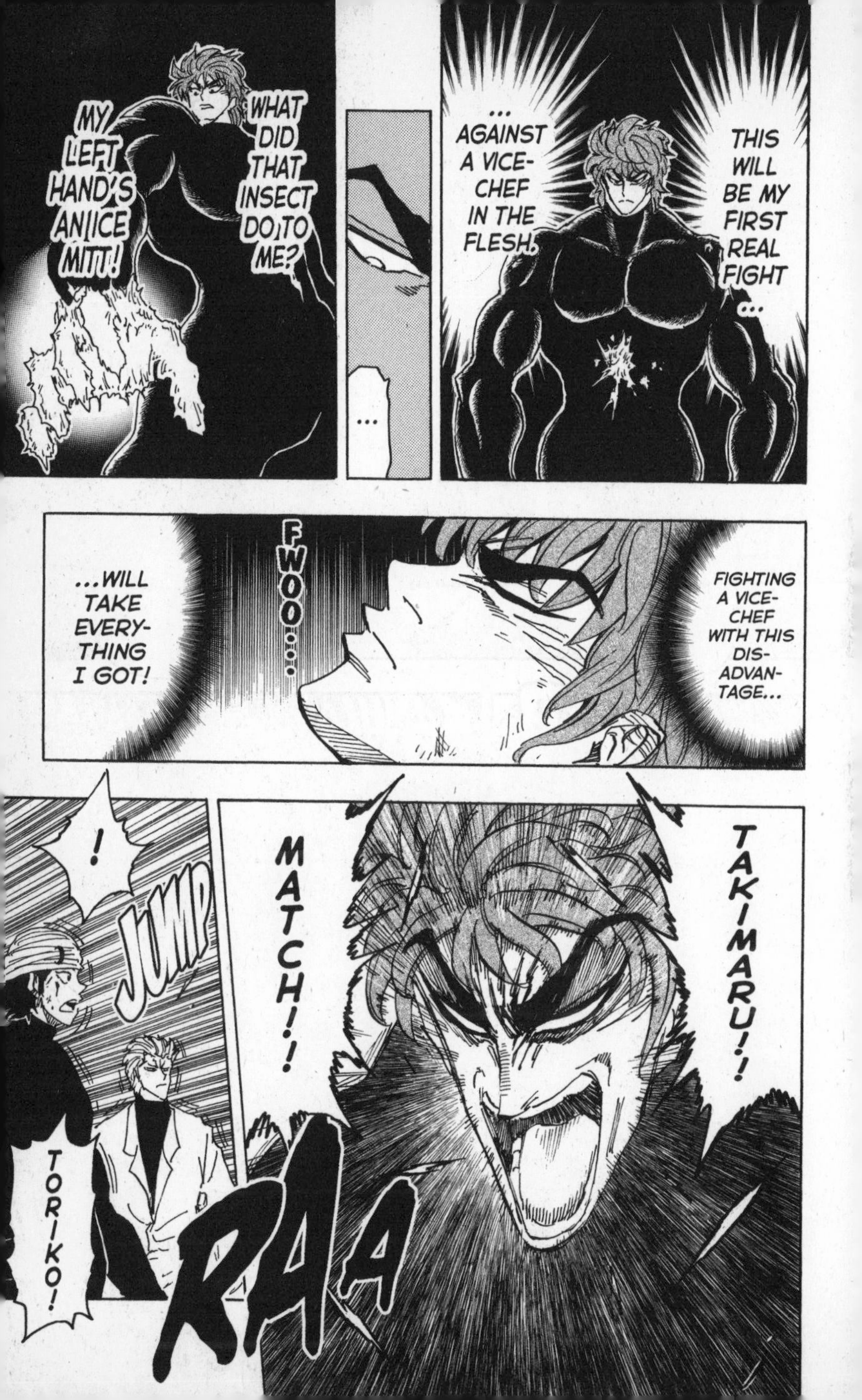
THIS WILL BE MY FIRST REAL FIGHT...
...AGAINST A VICE-CHEF IN THE FLESH.
...
WHAT DID THAT INSECT DO TO ME?
MY LEFT HAND'S AN ICE MITT!
FIGHTING A VICE-CHEF WITH THIS DIS-ADVANTAGE...
FWOO...
...WILL TAKE EVERY-THING I GOT!
TAKIMARU!!
MATCH!!
RAA
!
JUMP
TORIKO!

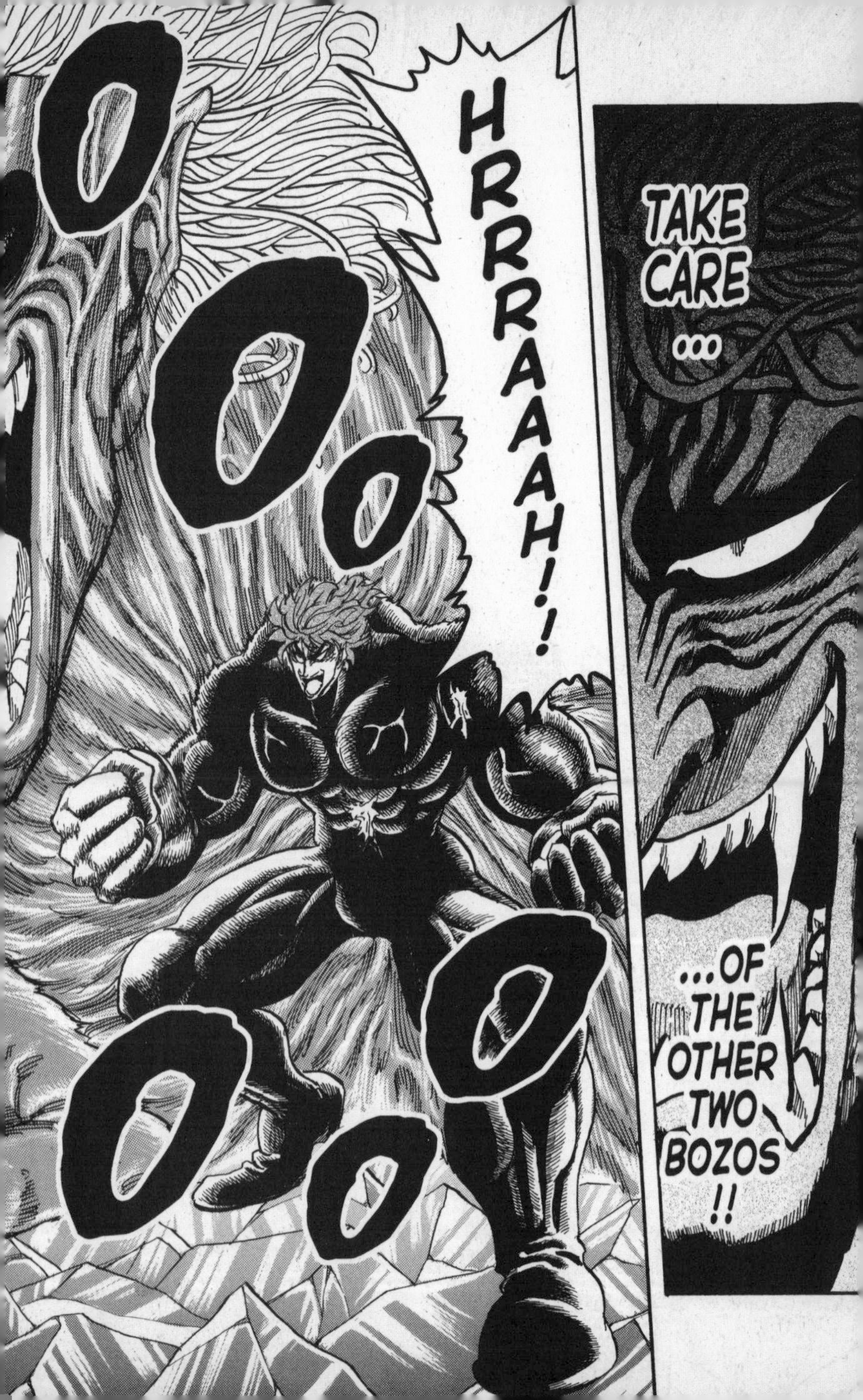
TAKE CARE...
...OF THE OTHER TWO BOZOS!!
HRRRAAAAH!!!
OOO
OOOO

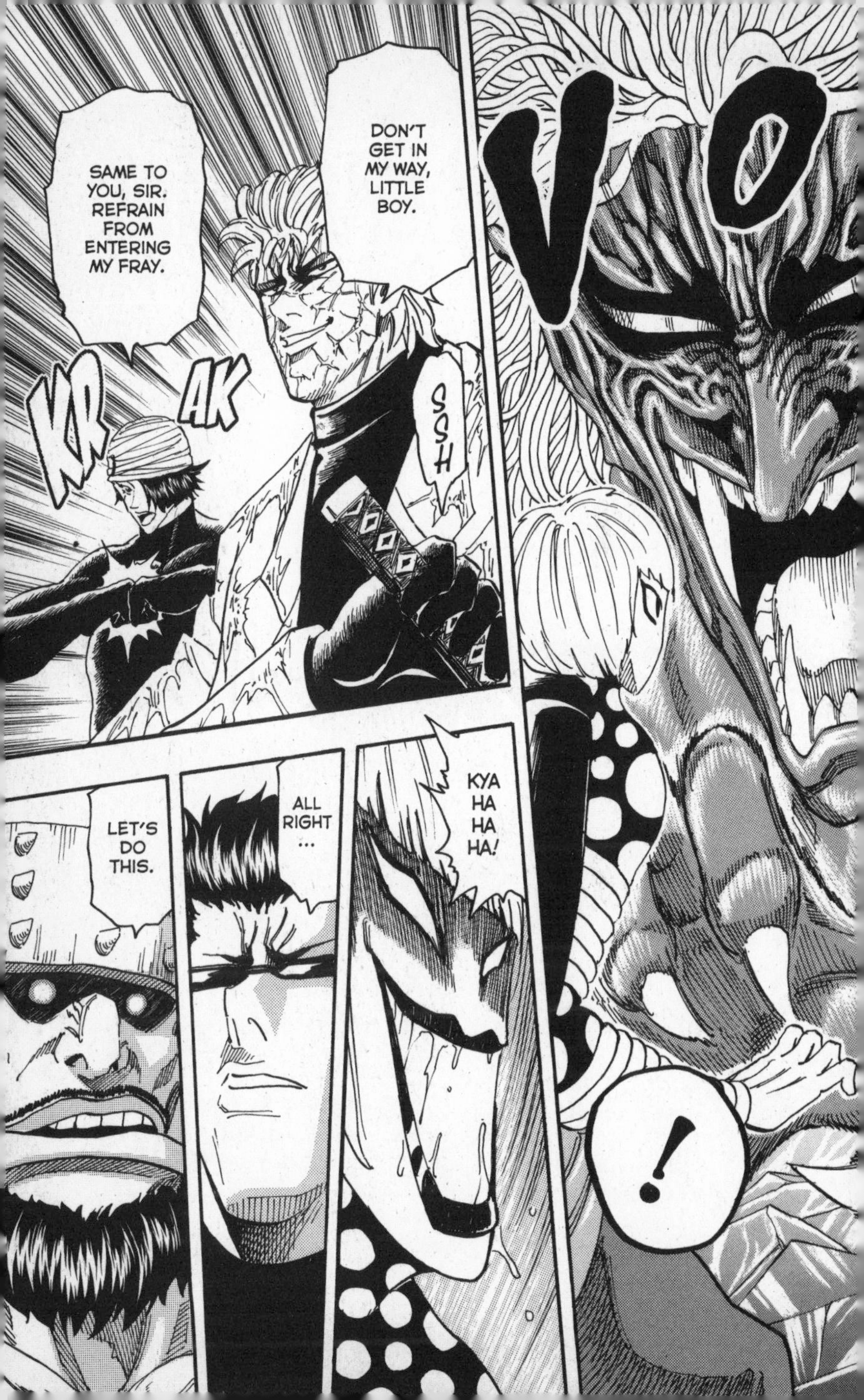
VO
!
DON'T GET IN MY WAY, LITTLE BOY.
SAME TO YOU, SIR. REFRAIN FROM ENTERING MY FRAY.
SSH
KRAK
KYA HA HA HA!
ALL RIGHT...
LET'S DO THIS.

TORIKO

GOURMET CHECKLIST

Vol. 069

PEACEFUL FLOWER
(PLANT)

CAPTURE LEVEL: LESS THAN 1

(CANNOT BE DOMESTICATED)

HABITAT: PEACEFUL ISLAND

LENGTH: ---

HEIGHT: 30 CM

WEIGHT: ---

PRICE: 500 YEN PER STALK

SCALE

THIS FLOWER BLOOMS ON THE WORLD'S MOST PEACEFUL ISLAND, THE ONE THAT THE GRINNING MANATEE AND OTHER GENTLE BEASTS CALL HOME. THE PEACEFUL FLOWER PREFERS TRANQUIL ENVIRONMENTS AND WILTS WHEN MENACING CREATURES ARE NEAR. THE NUMBER OF PETALS THAT WILT ARE IN DIRECT PROPORTION TO THE CREATURE'S CAPTURE LEVEL. THE PEACEFUL FLOWER CONTAINS SIX PETALS TOTAL AND IT TAKES A CAPTURE LEVEL OF TEN TO MAKE ONE PETAL WILT. A PEACEFUL FLOWER IS AN INDISPENSABLE ITEM FOR ANY BEGINNING GOURMET HUNTER.

GOURMET 78: VERMIN!!

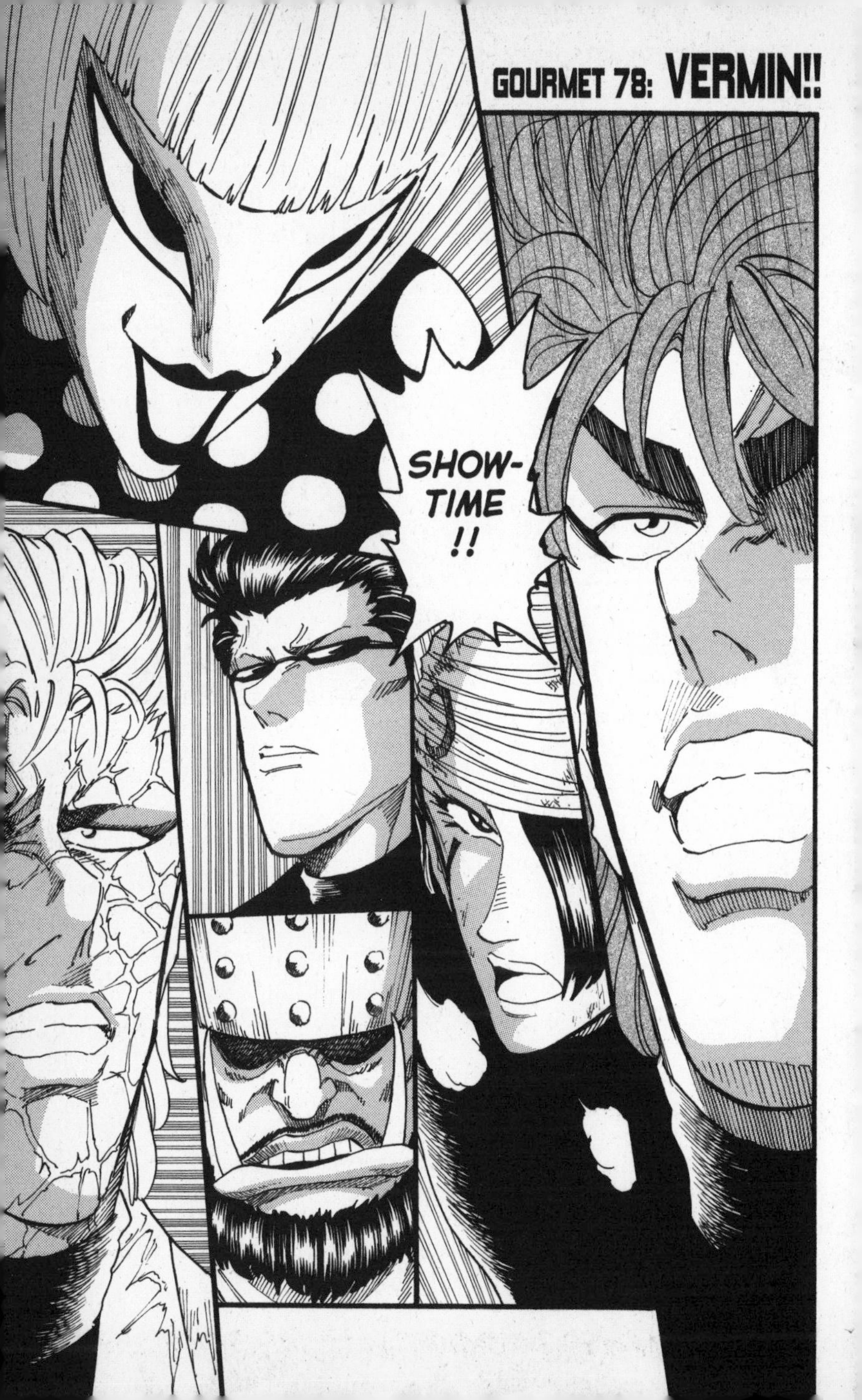
SHOW-
TIME
!!

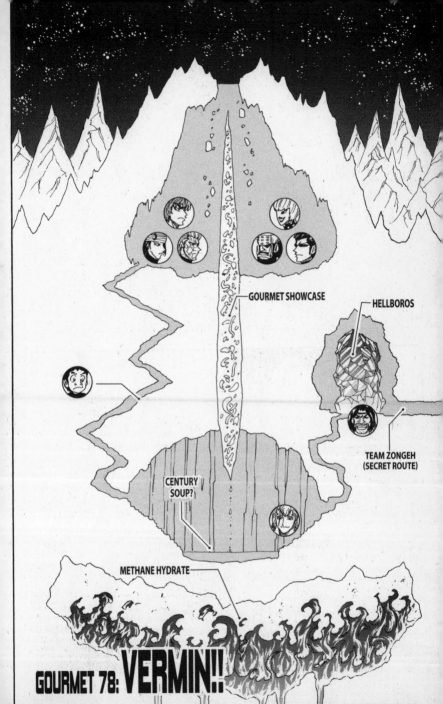

GOURMET SHOWCASE

HELLBOROS

TEAM ZONGEH
(SECRET ROUTE)

CENTURY
SOUP?

METHANE HYDRATE

GOURMET 78: VERMIN!!

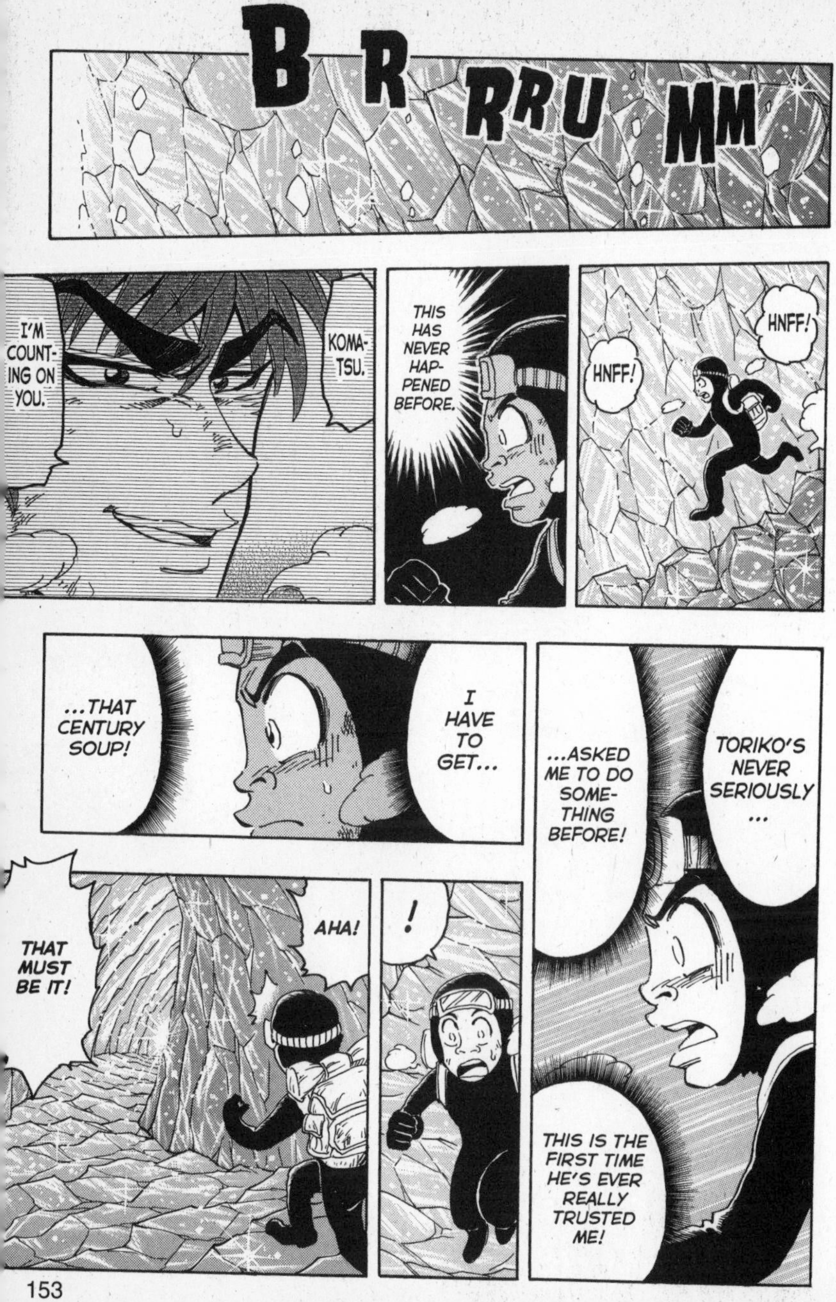
BRRRUMM
HNFF!
HNFF!
THIS HAS NEVER HAPPENED BEFORE.
KOMATSU.
I'M COUNTING ON YOU.
TORIKO'S NEVER SERIOUSLY ...
...ASKED ME TO DO SOMETHING BEFORE!
THIS IS THE FIRST TIME HE'S EVER REALLY TRUSTED ME!
I HAVE TO GET...
...THAT CENTURY SOUP!
!
AHA!
THAT MUST BE IT!

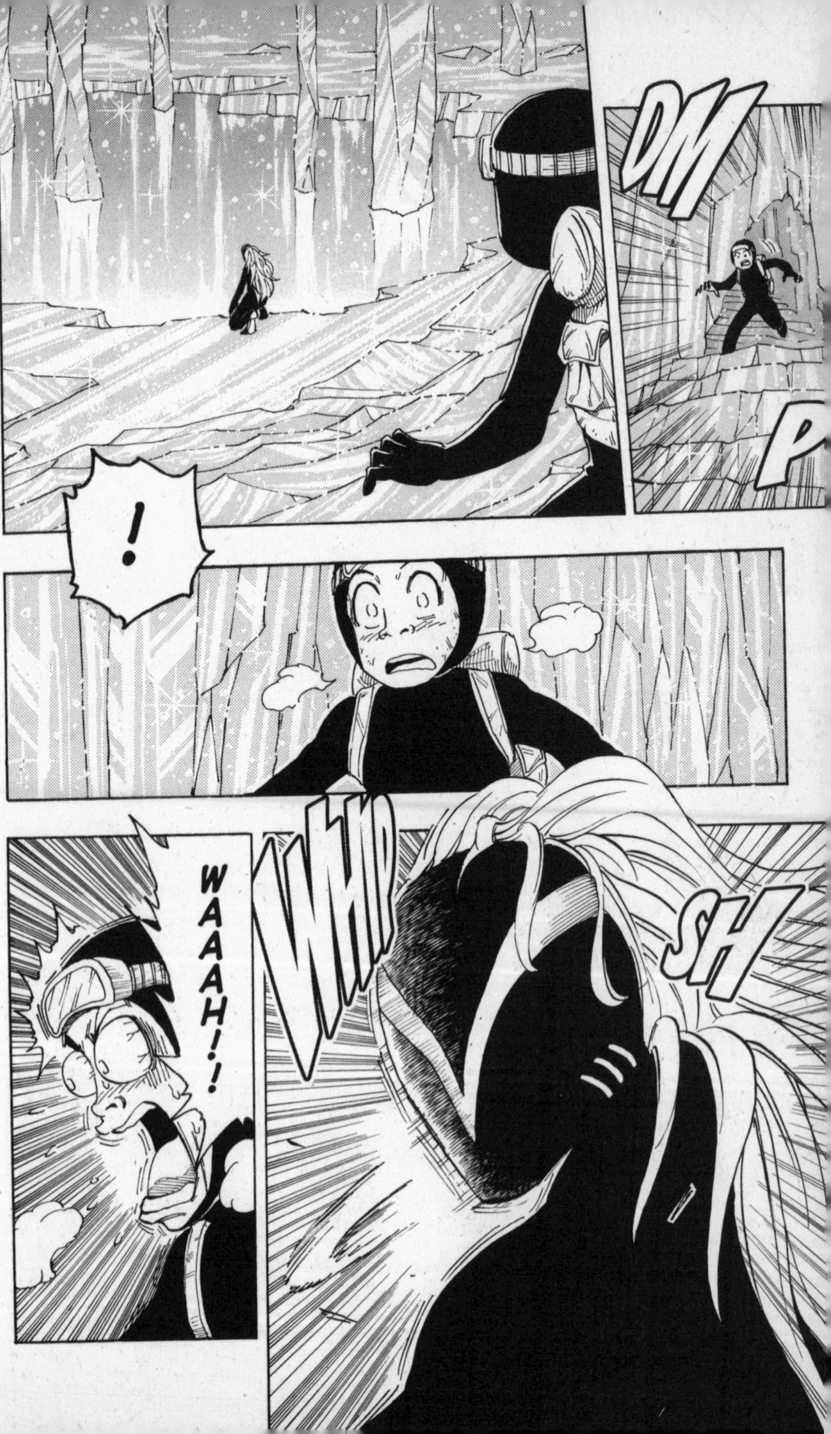
DM
P
!
WHIP
SH
WAAAAH!!!

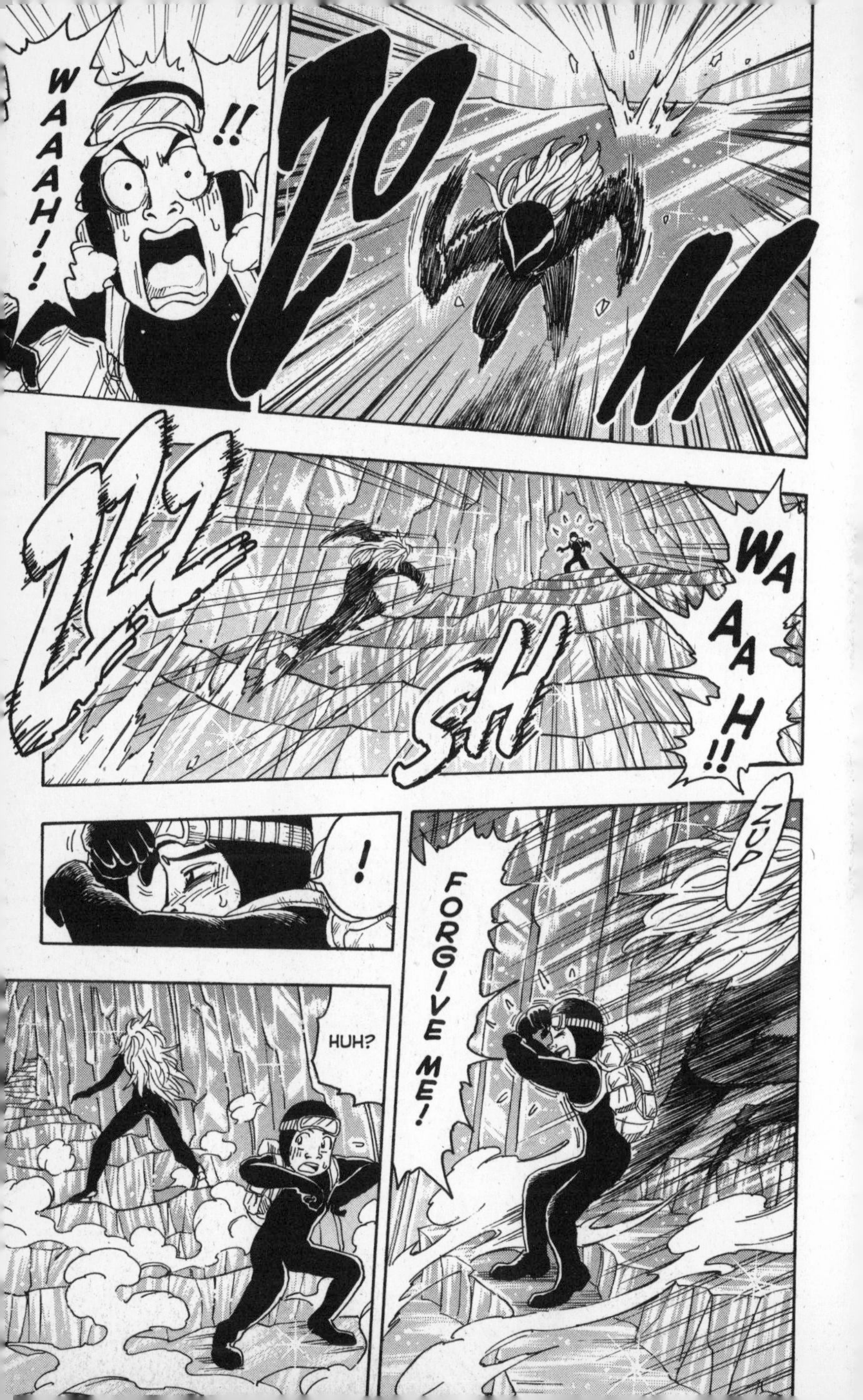
WAAAAH!!!
!!
WAAAH!!
ZZSH
ZUP
FORGIVE ME!
!
HUH?

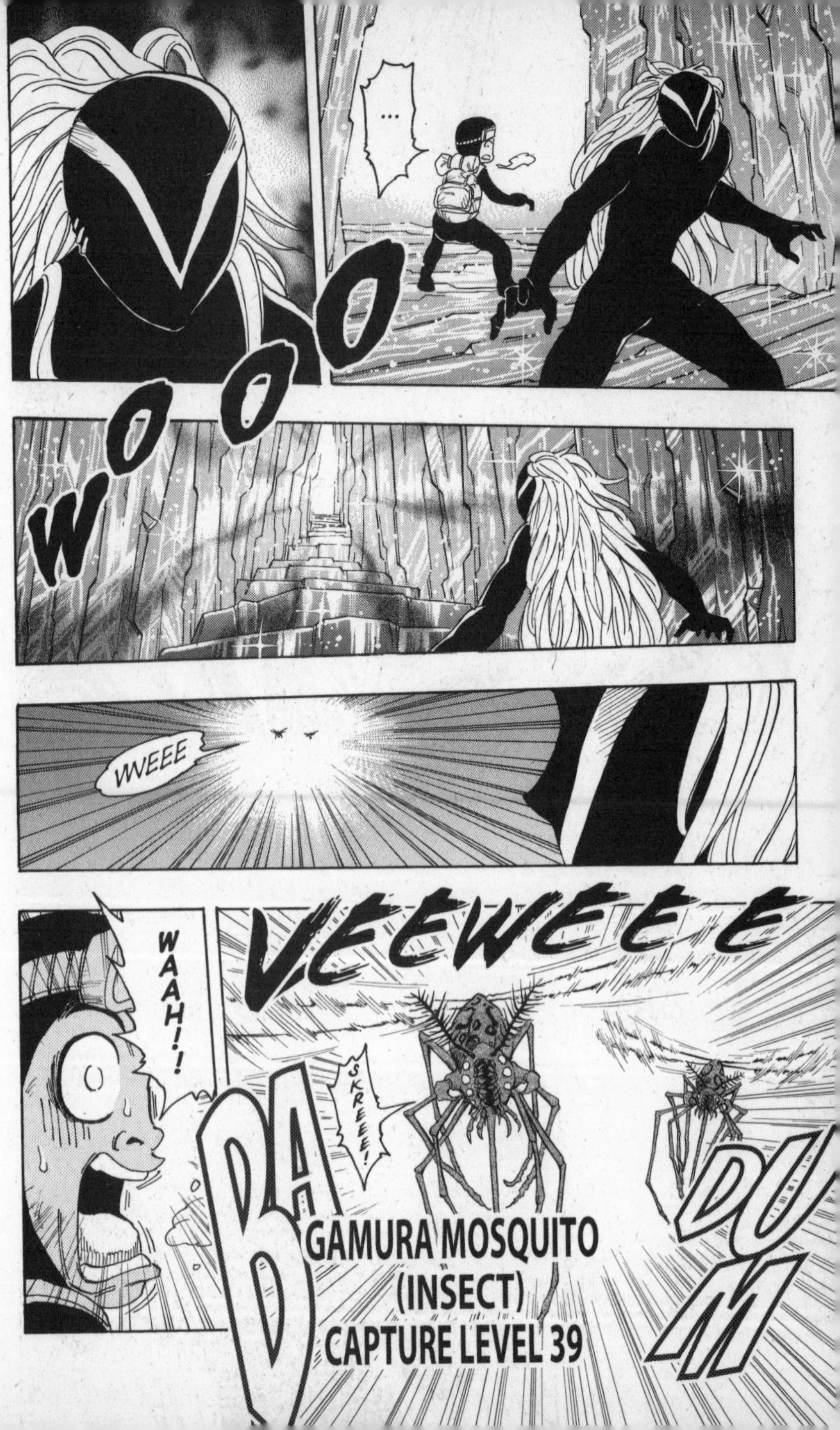
...
WOOO
VWEEE
VEEWEEE E
SKREEE!
BA
DUM
GAMURA MOSQUITO
(INSECT)
CAPTURE LEVEL 39
WAAAH!!

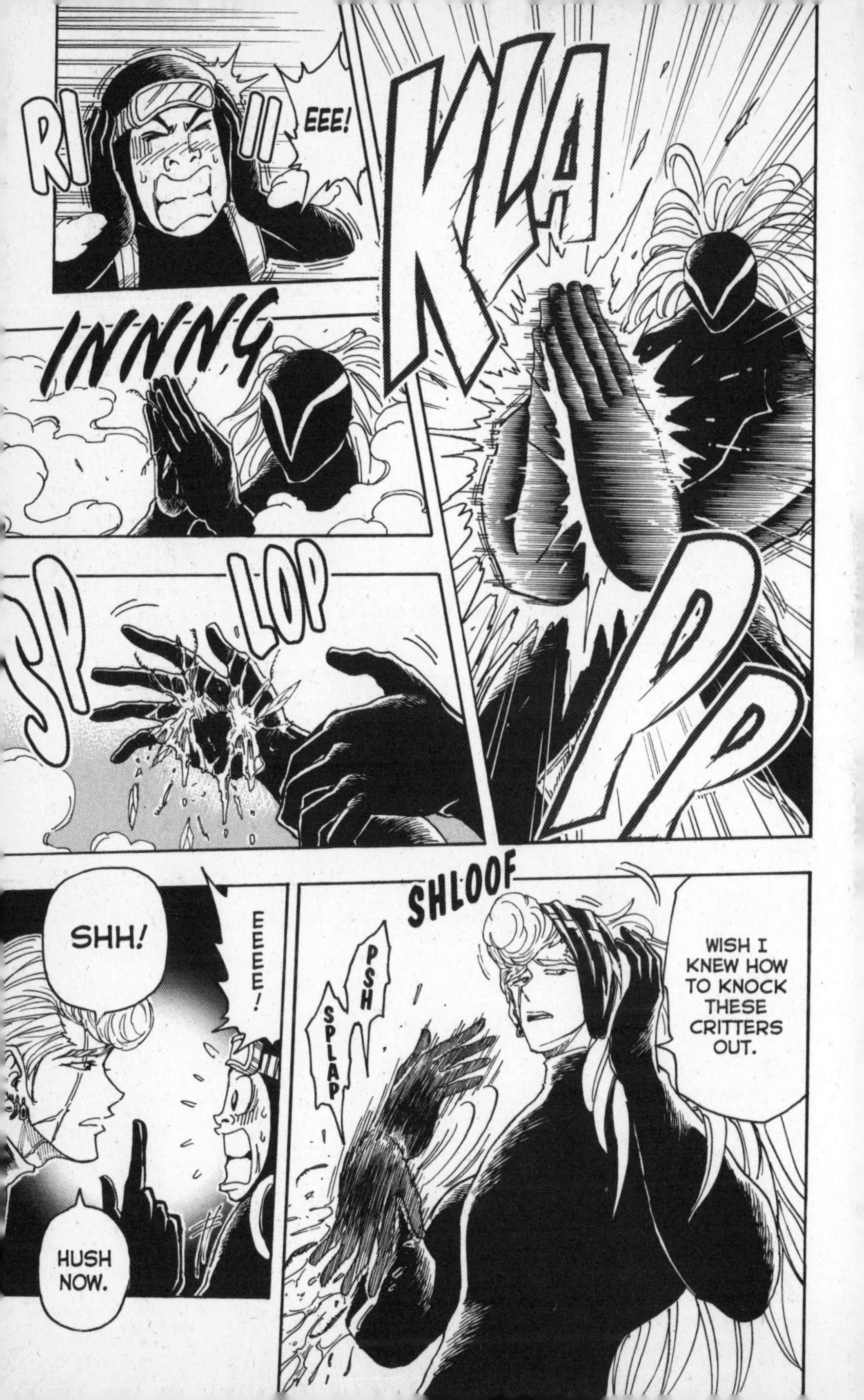
KLA
PP
RI II
EEE!
INNNG
SP LOP
SHLOOF
WISH I KNEW HOW TO KNOCK THESE CRITTERS OUT.
PSH
SPLAP
SHH!
EEEE!
HUSH NOW.

...

BZZ

...?

YOU'RE BETTER OFF NOT TALKING.

OTHERWISE YOU'LL NEVER LEAVE THIS CONTINENT.

BZZZ

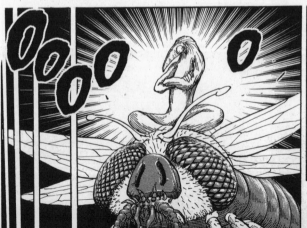

158

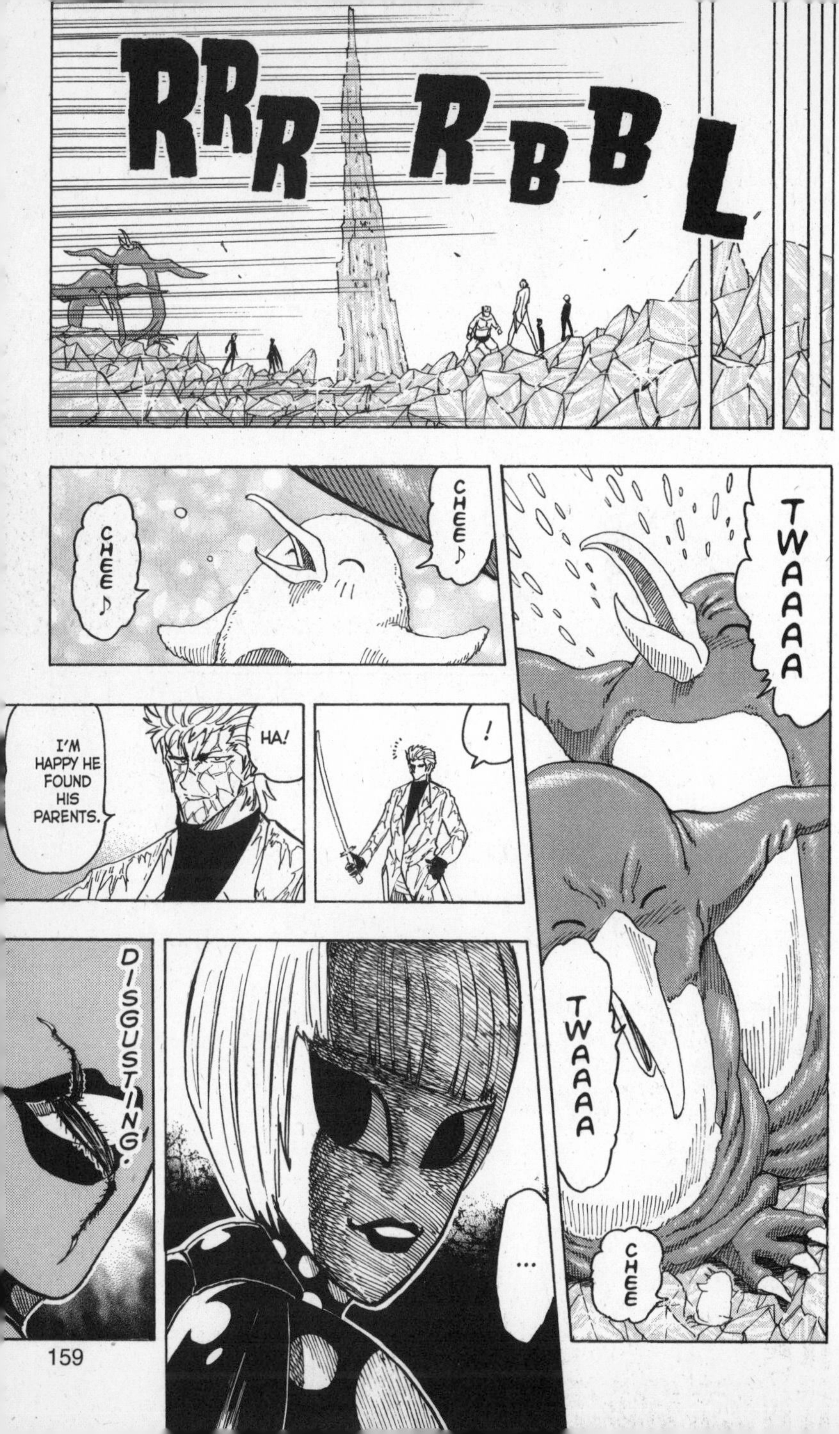
RRRRRBBBL
TWAAAAA
TWAAAAA
CHEE
CHEE♪
CHEE♪
!
HA!
I'M HAPPY HE FOUND HIS PARENTS.
...
DISGUSTING.

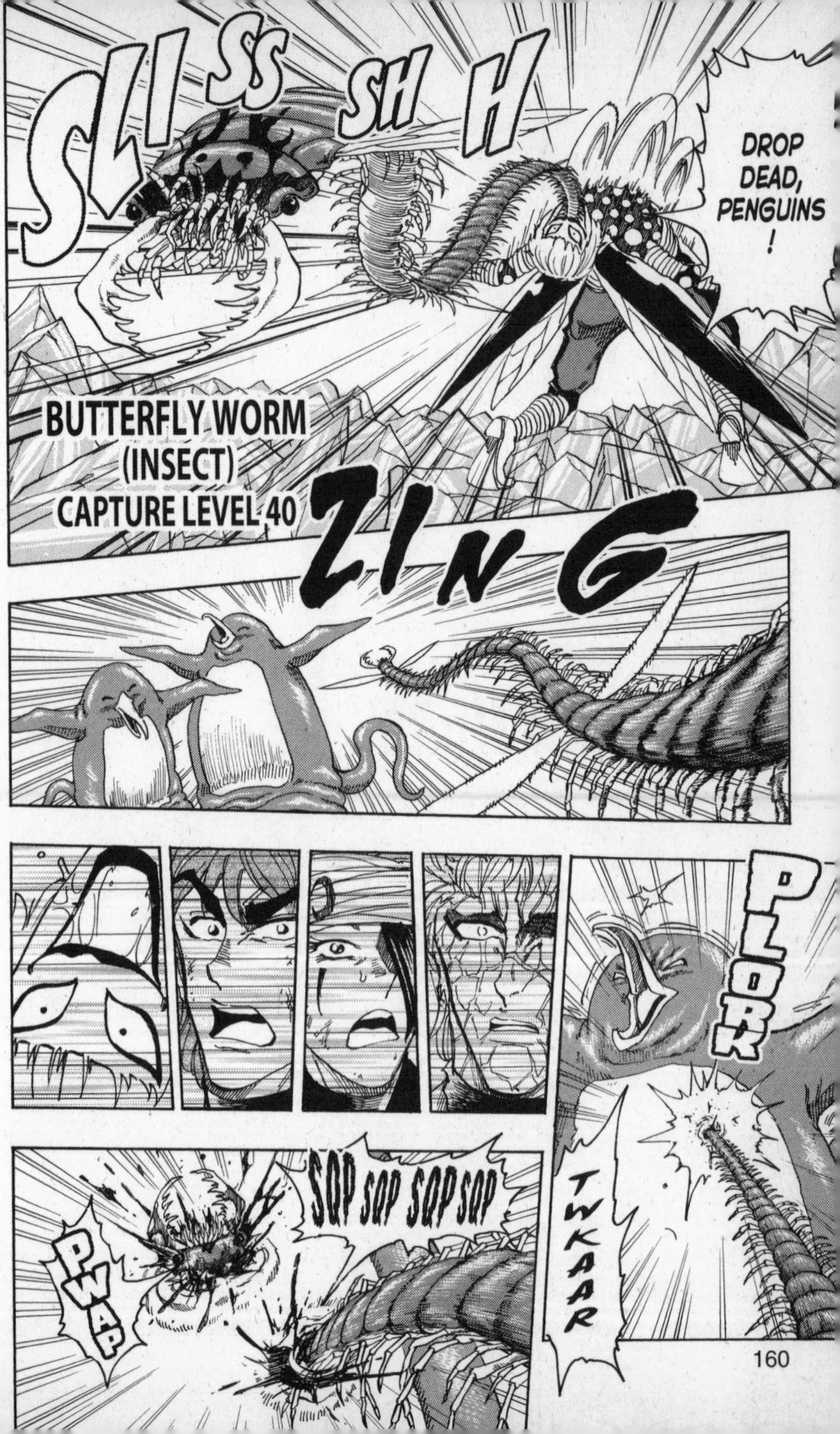
DROP DEAD, PENGUINS!
SLISSSHH
BUTTERFLY WORM (INSECT) CAPTURE LEVEL 40
ZING
PLORK
TWKAAR
SQP SQP SQP SQP
PWAP

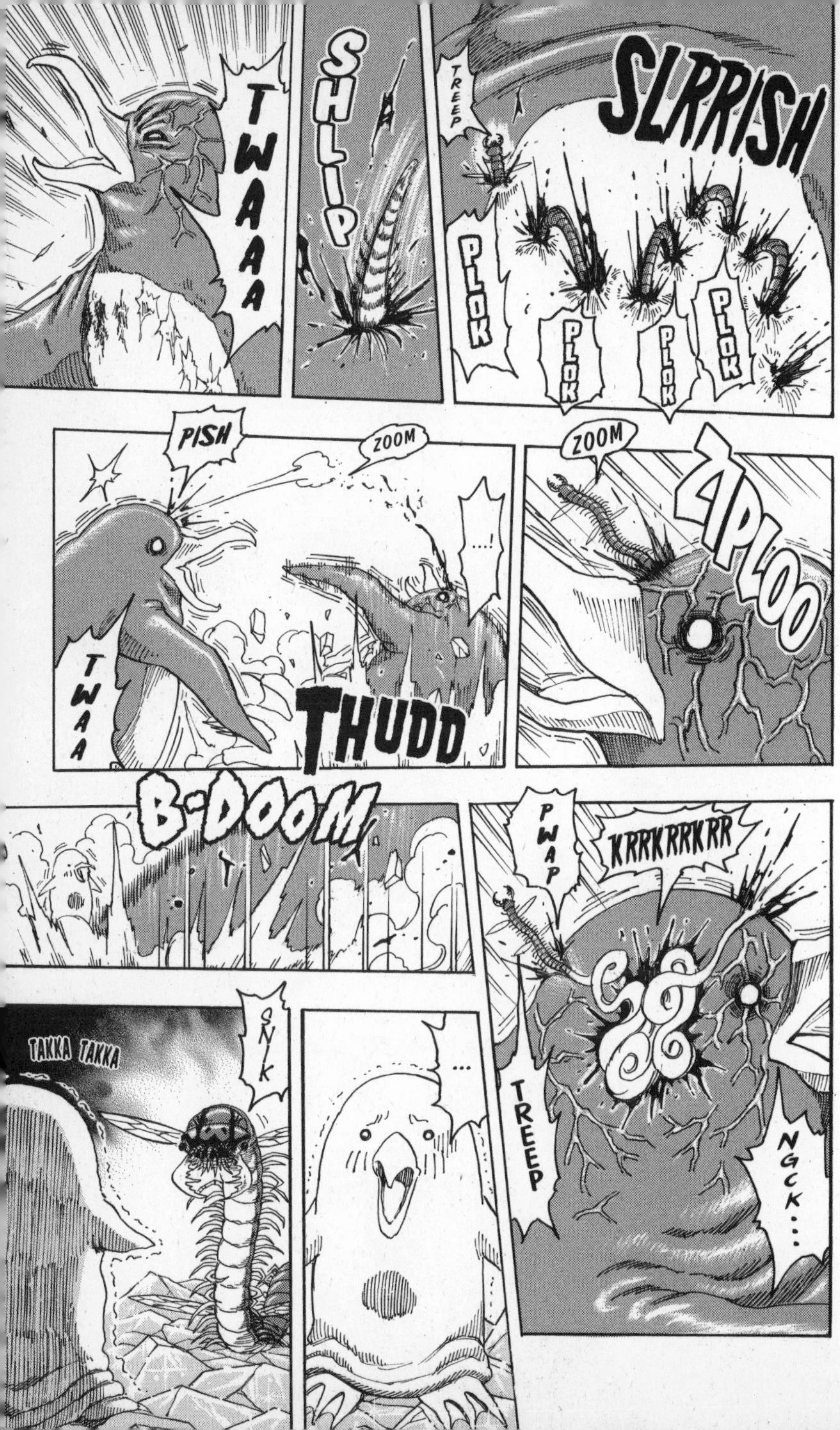
TREEP
SLRRISH
PLOK
PLOK
PLOK
PLOK
SHLIP
TWAAAA
ZOOM
ZIPLOO
PISH
ZOOM
...!
TWAAA
THUDD
PWAP
KRRKRRKRR
TREEP
NGCK...
B-DOOM
...
SNIK
TAKKA TAKKA

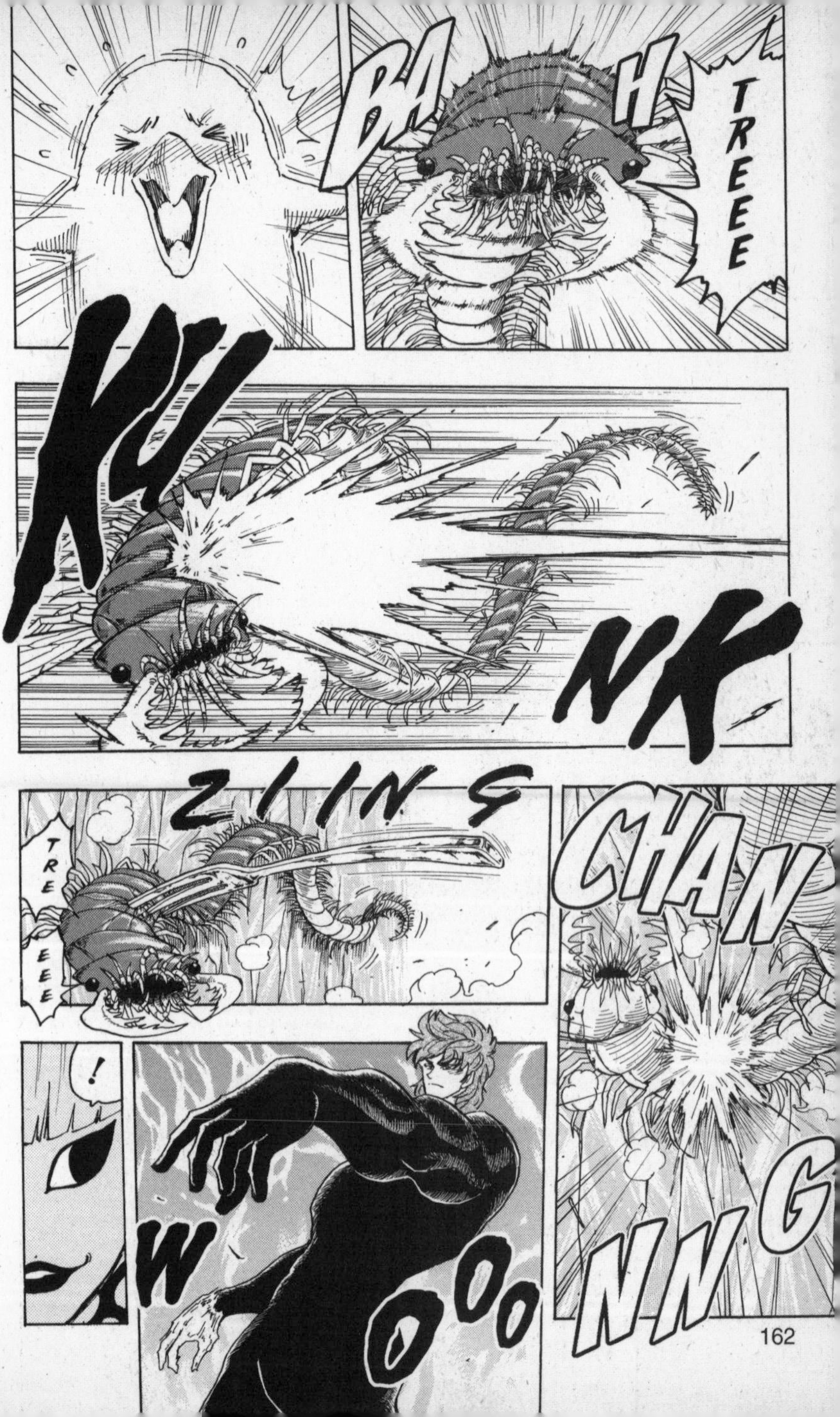
BAH
TREEEE
KUNK
CHANNG
ZIING
TREEEE
!
WOOO

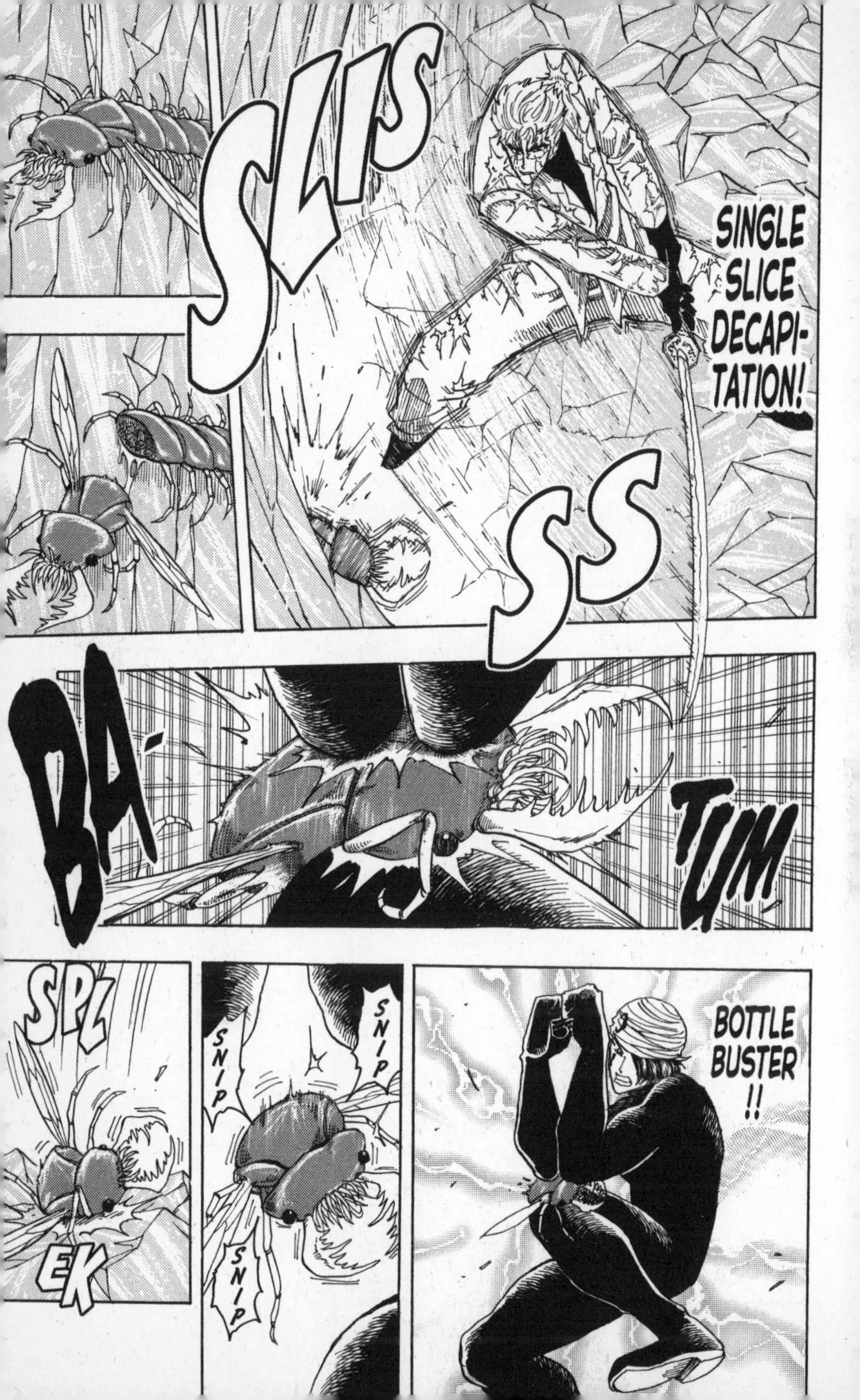
SINGLE SLICE DECAPITATION!
SLIS
SS
BA-
TUM
BOTTLE BUSTER!!
SNIP
SNIP
SNIP
SNIP
SPL
EK

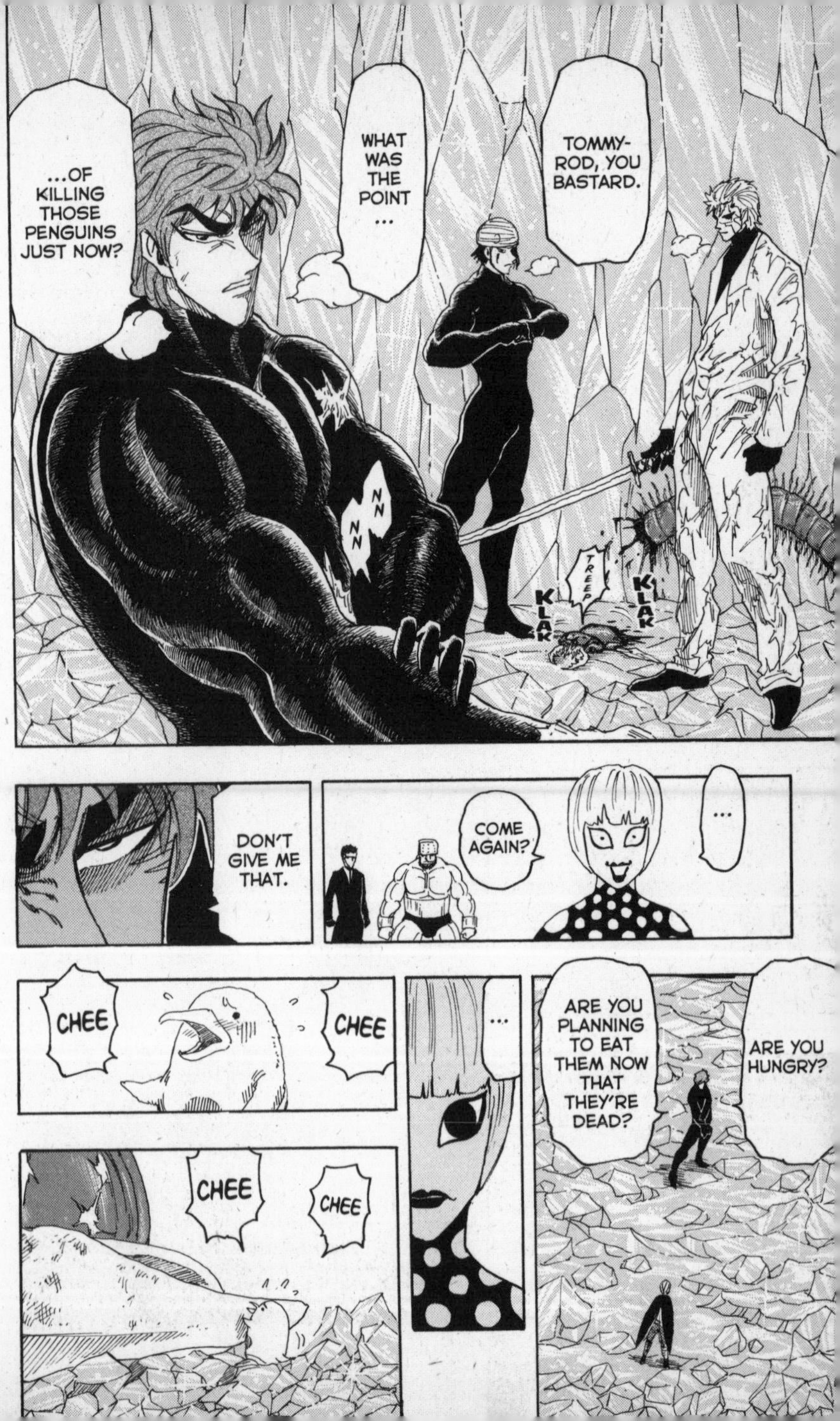
TOMMY-ROD, YOU BASTARD.
WHAT WAS THE POINT ...
...OF KILLING THOSE PENGUINS JUST NOW?
KLAK
TREEP
KLAK
NN NN
...
COME AGAIN?
DON'T GIVE ME THAT.
ARE YOU HUNGRY?
ARE YOU PLANNING TO EAT THEM NOW THAT THEY'RE DEAD?
...
CHEE
CHEE
CHEE
CHEE

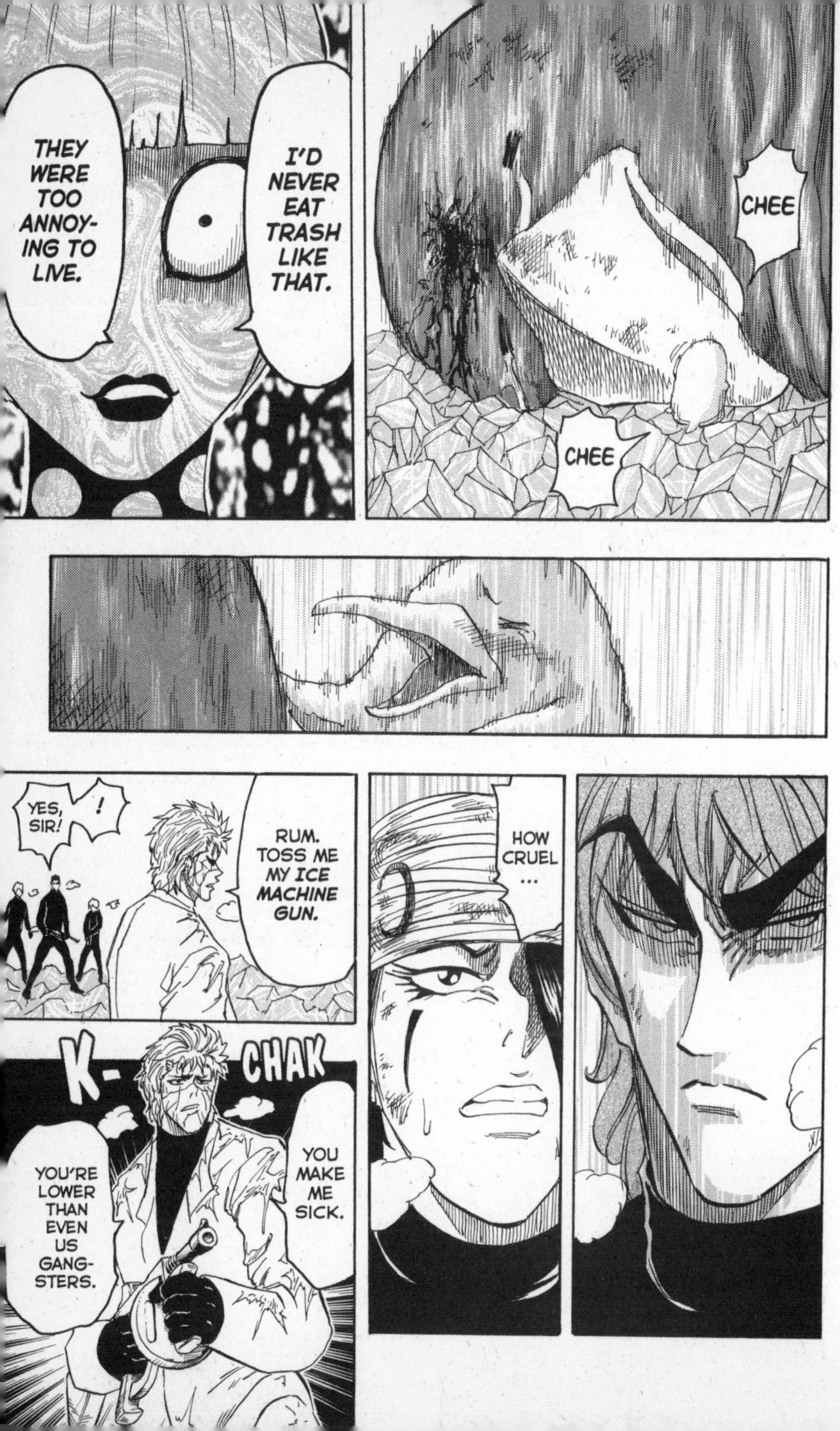
CHEE
CHEE
I'D NEVER EAT TRASH LIKE THAT.
THEY WERE TOO ANNOY-ING TO LIVE.
HOW CRUEL ...
RUM. TOSS ME MY ICE MACHINE GUN.
!
YES, SIR!
K-CHAK
YOU MAKE ME SICK.
YOU'RE LOWER THAN EVEN US GANG-STERS.

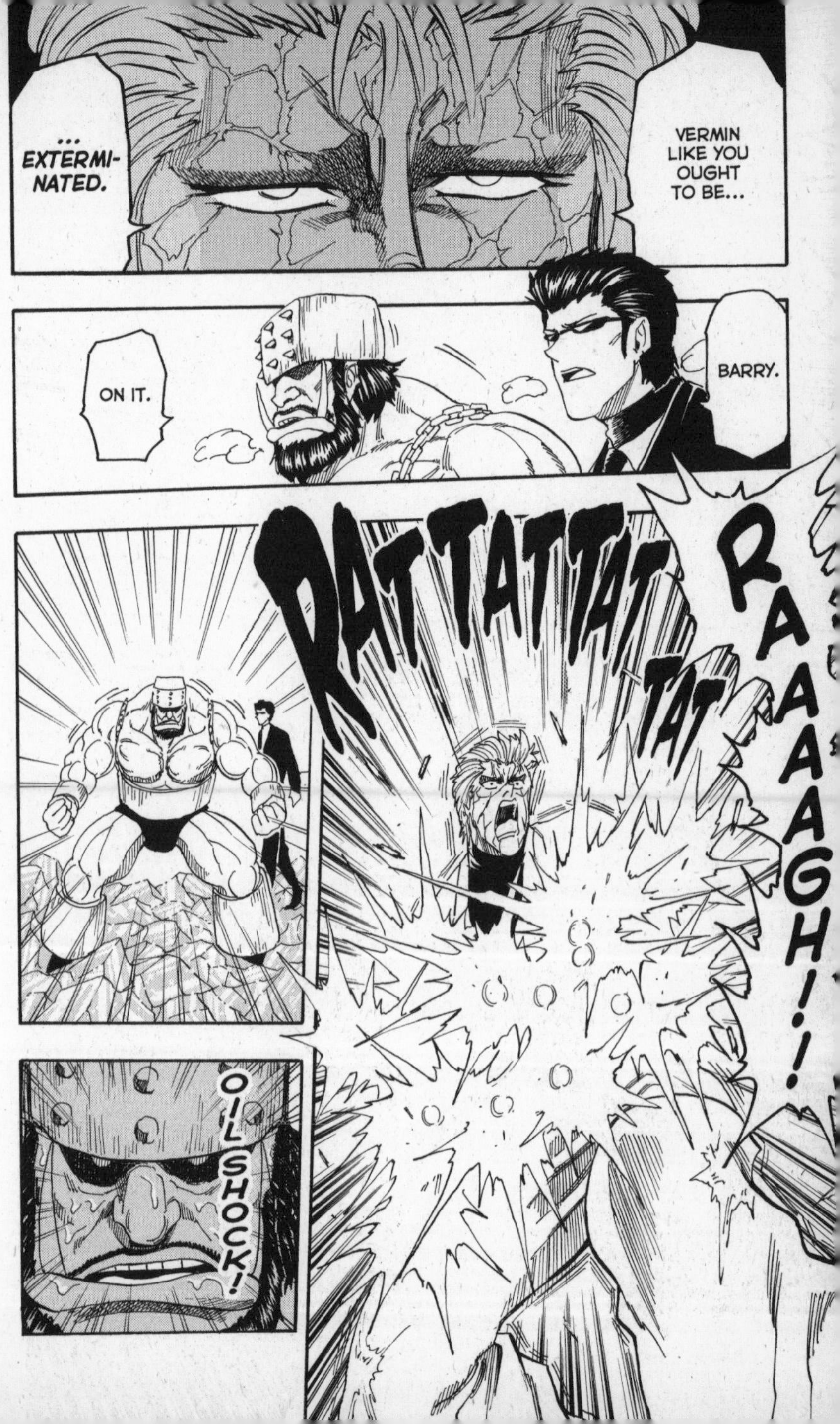

VERMIN LIKE YOU OUGHT TO BE...
... EXTERMINATED.
BARRY.
ON IT.
RAAAAGH!!!
RATTATTAT TAT
OIL SHOCK!

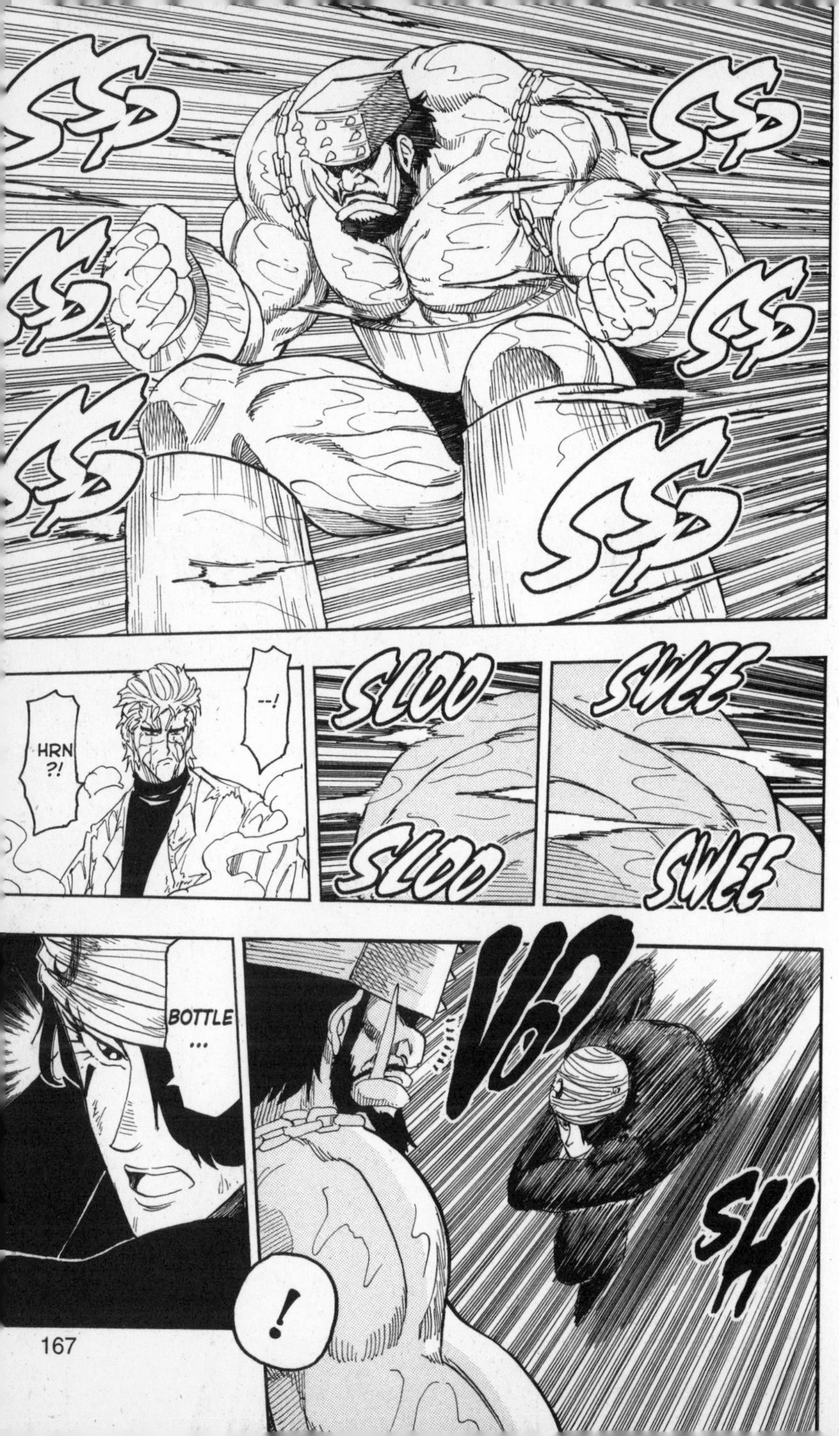
SSP
SSP
MSSP
MSSP
MSSP
MSSP
SWEE
SWEE
SLOO
SLOO
--!
HRN ?!
VOO
SH
!
BOTTLE ...

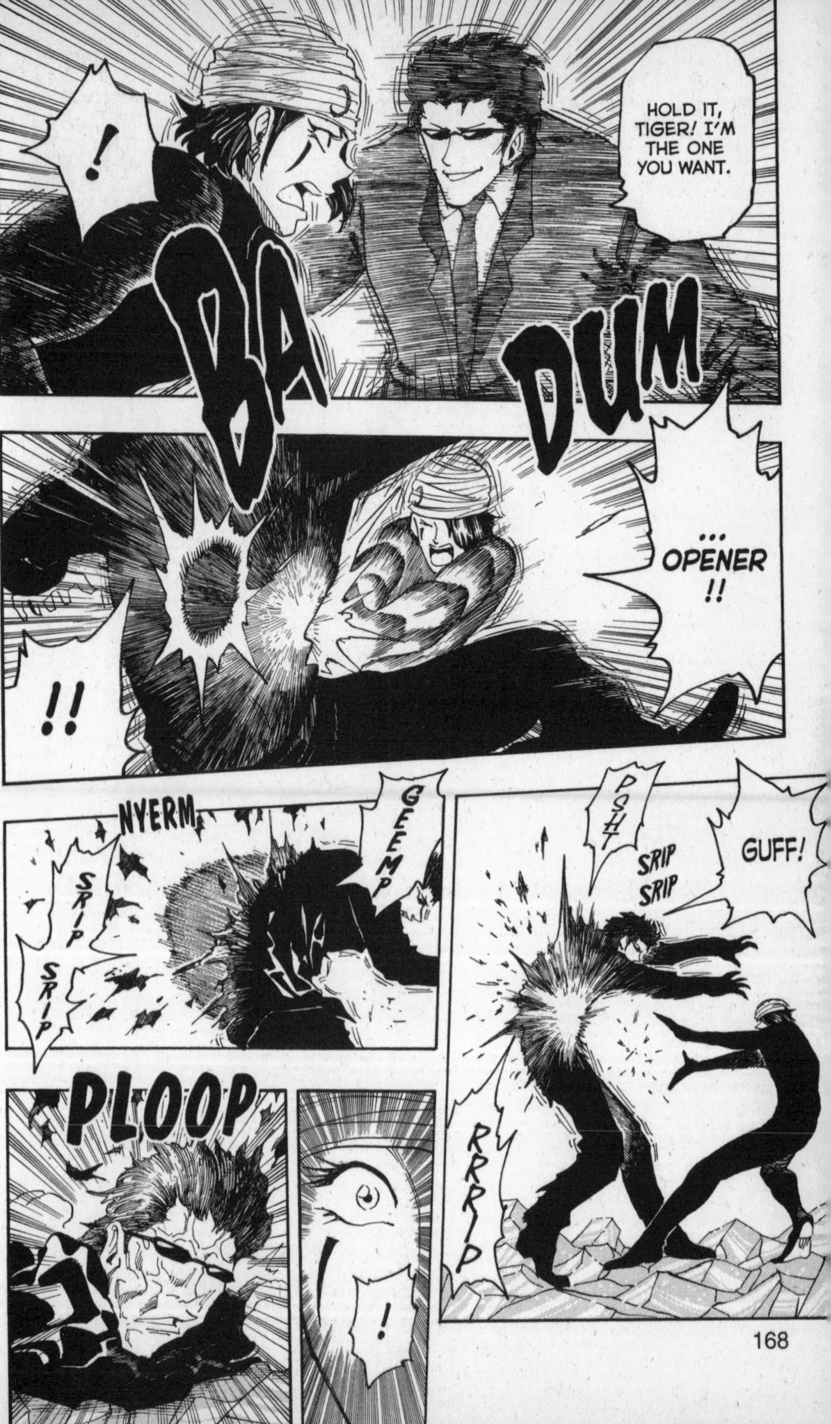
HOLD IT, TIGER! I'M THE ONE YOU WANT.
!
BA
DUM
... OPENER !!
!!
GUFF!
PSHT
SRIP SRIP
RRRIP
GEEMP
NYERM
SRIP SRIP
!
PLOOP

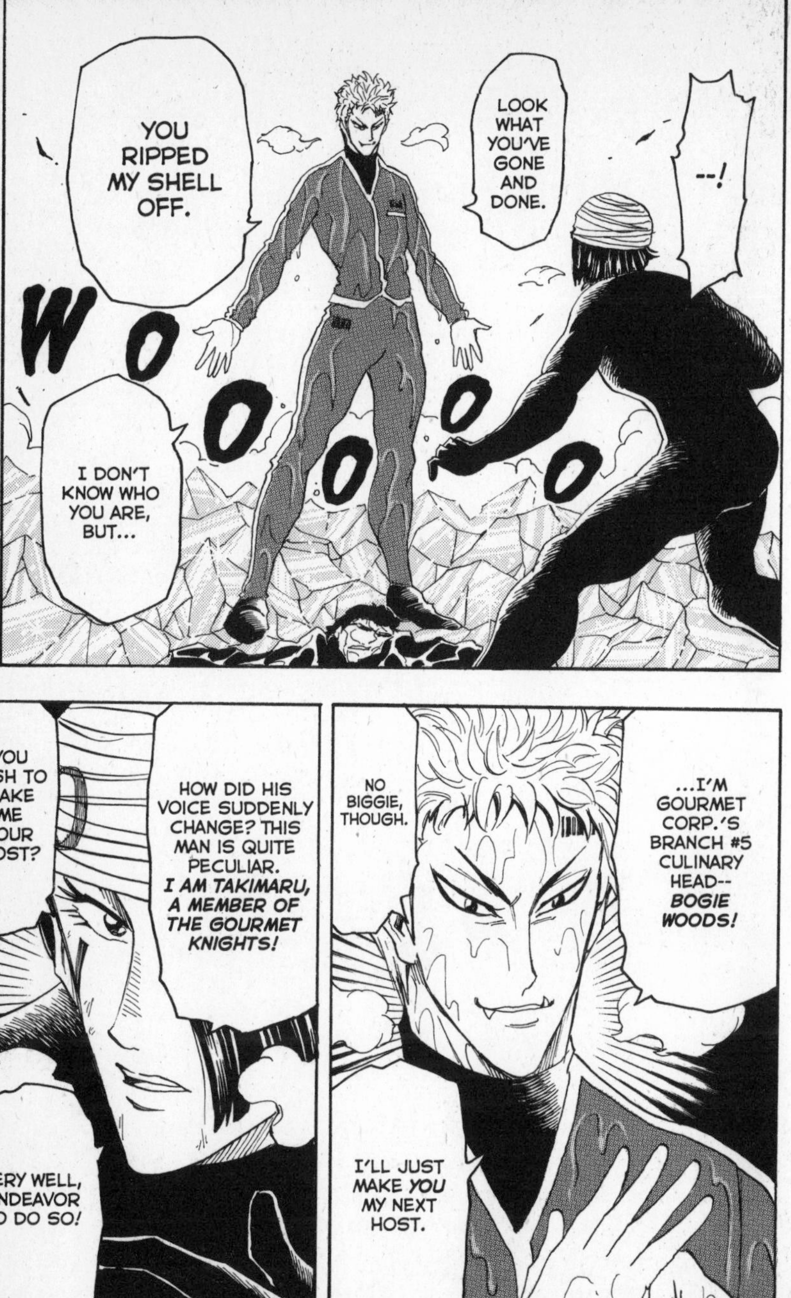
--!
LOOK WHAT YOU'VE GONE AND DONE.
YOU RIPPED MY SHELL OFF.
WOOOOOO
I DON'T KNOW WHO YOU ARE, BUT...
...I'M GOURMET CORP.'S BRANCH #5 CULINARY HEAD-- *BOGIE WOODS!*
NO BIGGIE, THOUGH.
I'LL JUST MAKE *YOU* MY NEXT HOST.
HOW DID HIS VOICE SUDDENLY CHANGE? THIS MAN IS QUITE PECULIAR. *I AM TAKIMARU, A MEMBER OF THE GOURMET KNIGHTS!*
YOU WISH TO MAKE ME YOUR HOST?
VERY WELL, ENDEAVOR TO DO *SO!*

TORIKO

GOURMET CHECKLIST

Vol. 070

SAKE COCONUT
(FRUIT)

CAPTURE LEVEL: 1

HABITAT: TROPICAL AND SUBTROPICAL REGIONS

LENGTH: 40 CM

HEIGHT: ---

WEIGHT: 6 KG

PRICE: 8,500 YEN PER COCONUT

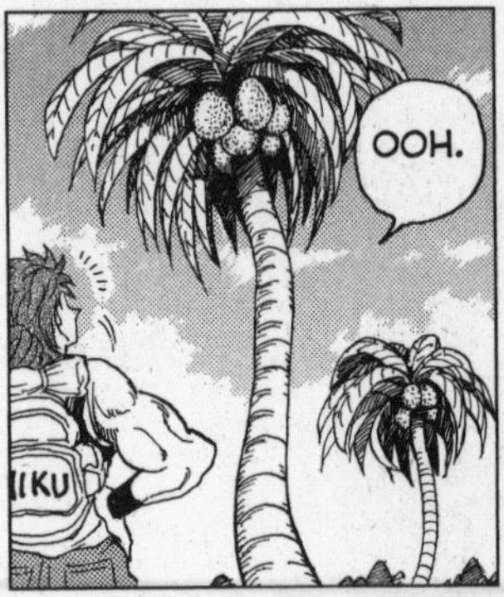
OOH.
IKU

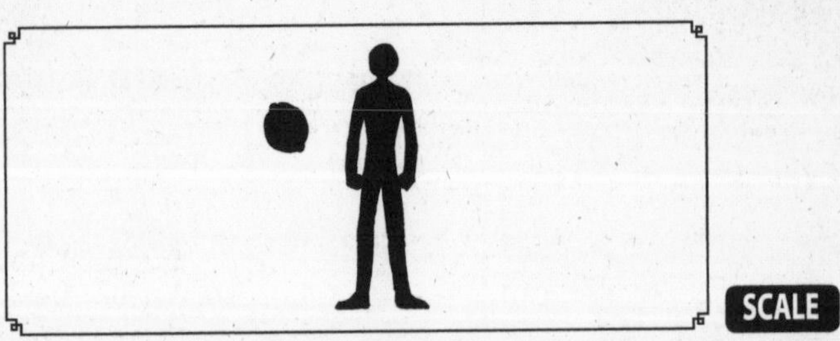
SCALE

SAKE COCONUT TREES GROW IN TROPICAL AND SUBTROPICAL AREAS ACROSS THE WORLD. CRACKING ONE OF THE NUTS OPEN REVEALS A SWEET ALCOHOL INSIDE. THE NATURALLY DISTILLED ALCOHOL IS SMOOTH AND MELLOW AS A FANCY LIQUEUR. IT'S VERY HIGH PROOF, SO THOSE WHO THINK THEY'RE DRINKING INNOCENT FRUIT JUICE CAN GET VERY DRUNK VERY FAST. THEREFORE, MINORS ARE PROHIBITED FROM CONSUMING IT.

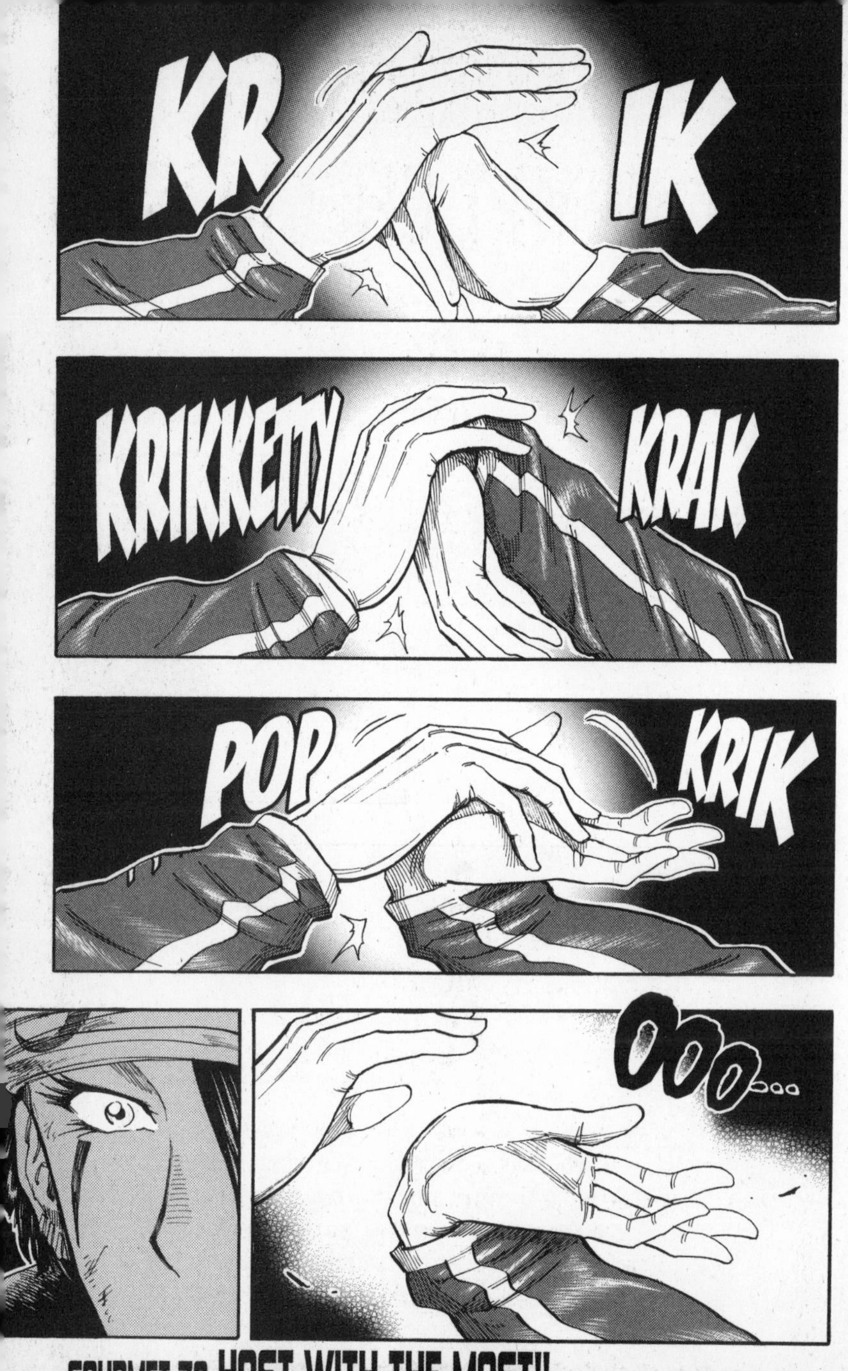
KR IK
KRAK
KRIKKETTY
KRIK
POP
OOO...

GOURMET 79: HOST WITH THE MOST!!

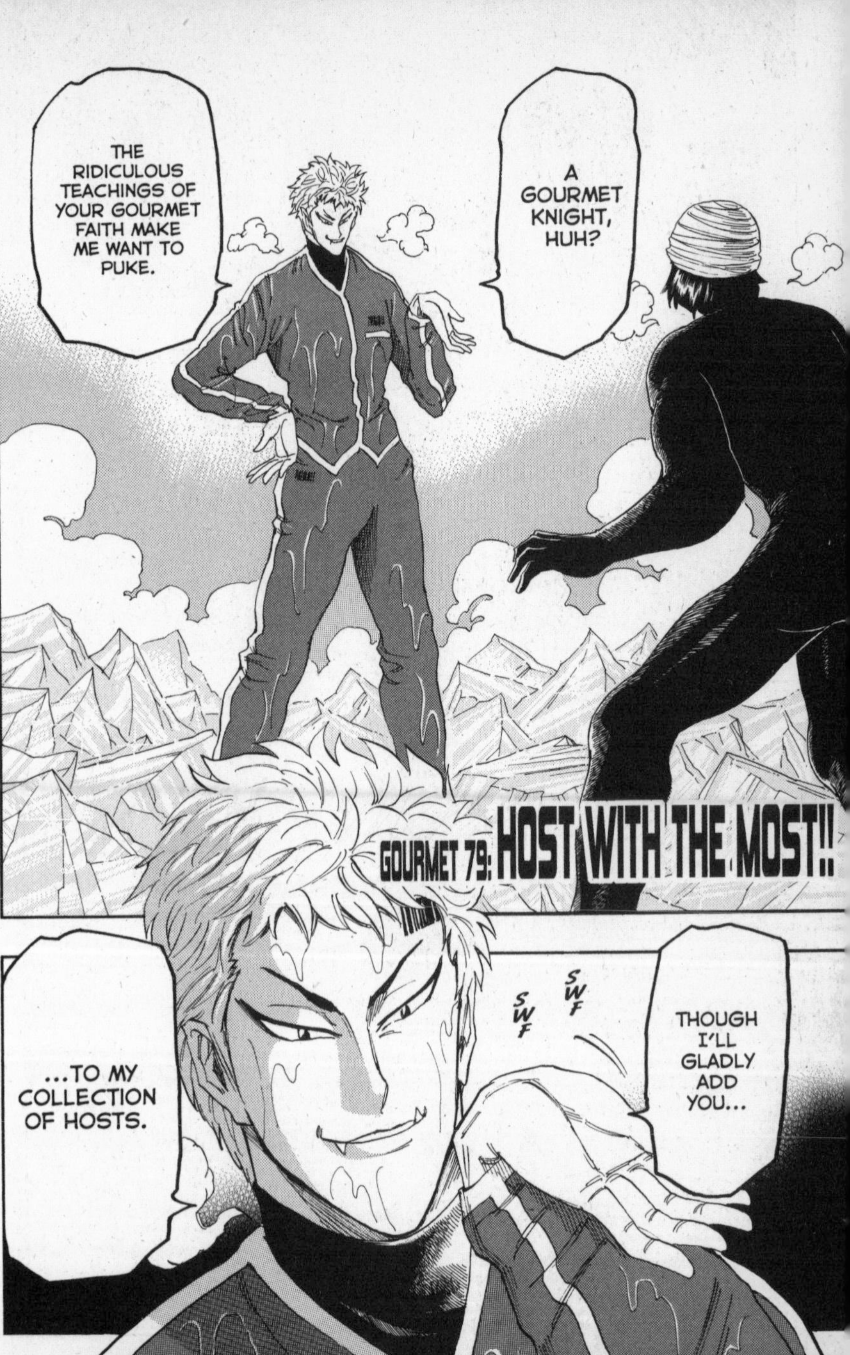
A GOURMET KNIGHT, HUH?
THE RIDICULOUS TEACHINGS OF YOUR GOURMET FAITH MAKE ME WANT TO PUKE.
GOURMET 79: HOST WITH THE MOST!!
THOUGH I'LL GLADLY ADD YOU...
SWF
SWF
...TO MY COLLECTION OF HOSTS.

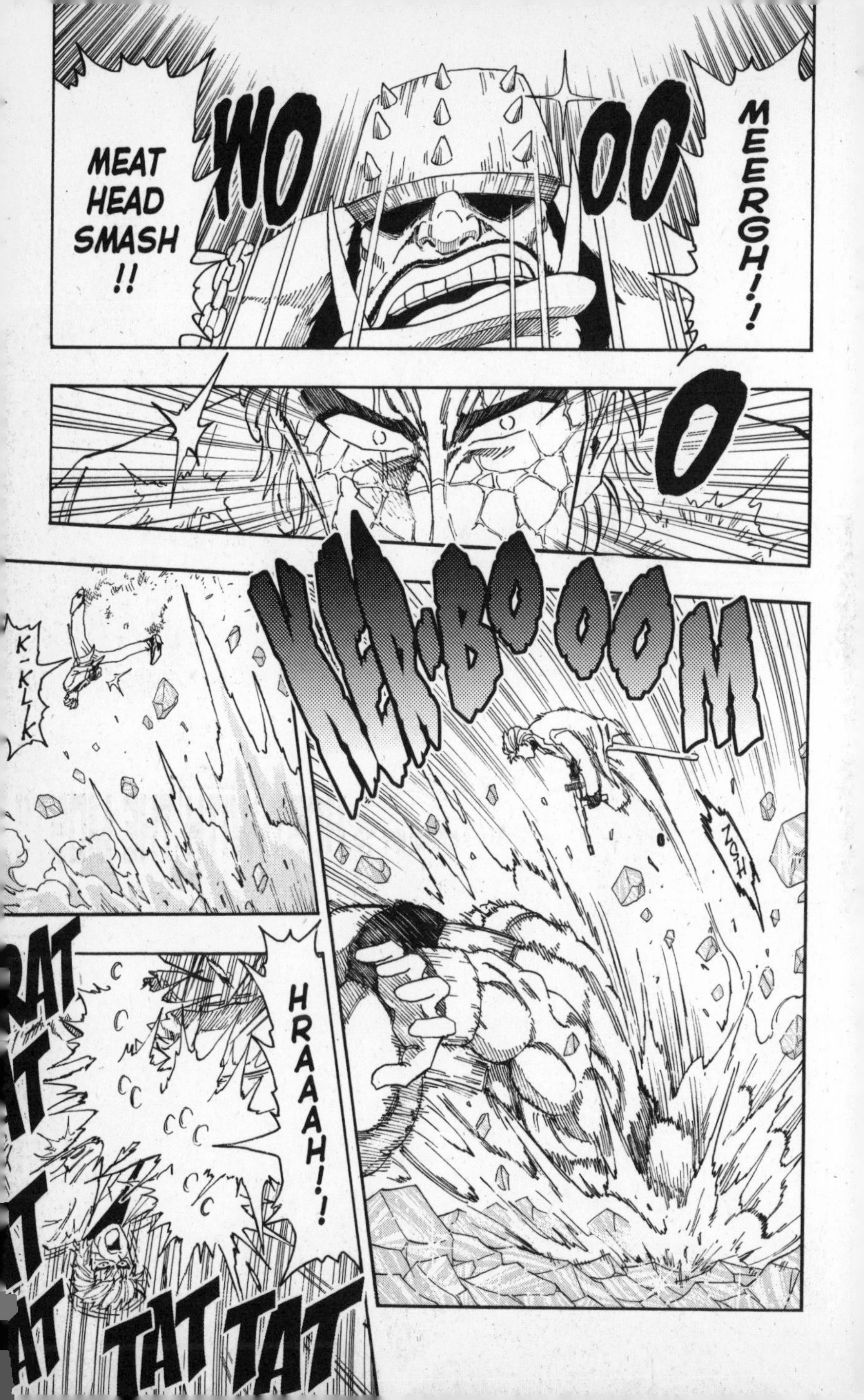
MEERGH!!
WO OO
MEAT HEAD SMASH!!
O
KA-BOOOM
ZSH
K-KLIK
HRAAAH!!
RAT TAT TAT TAT TAT

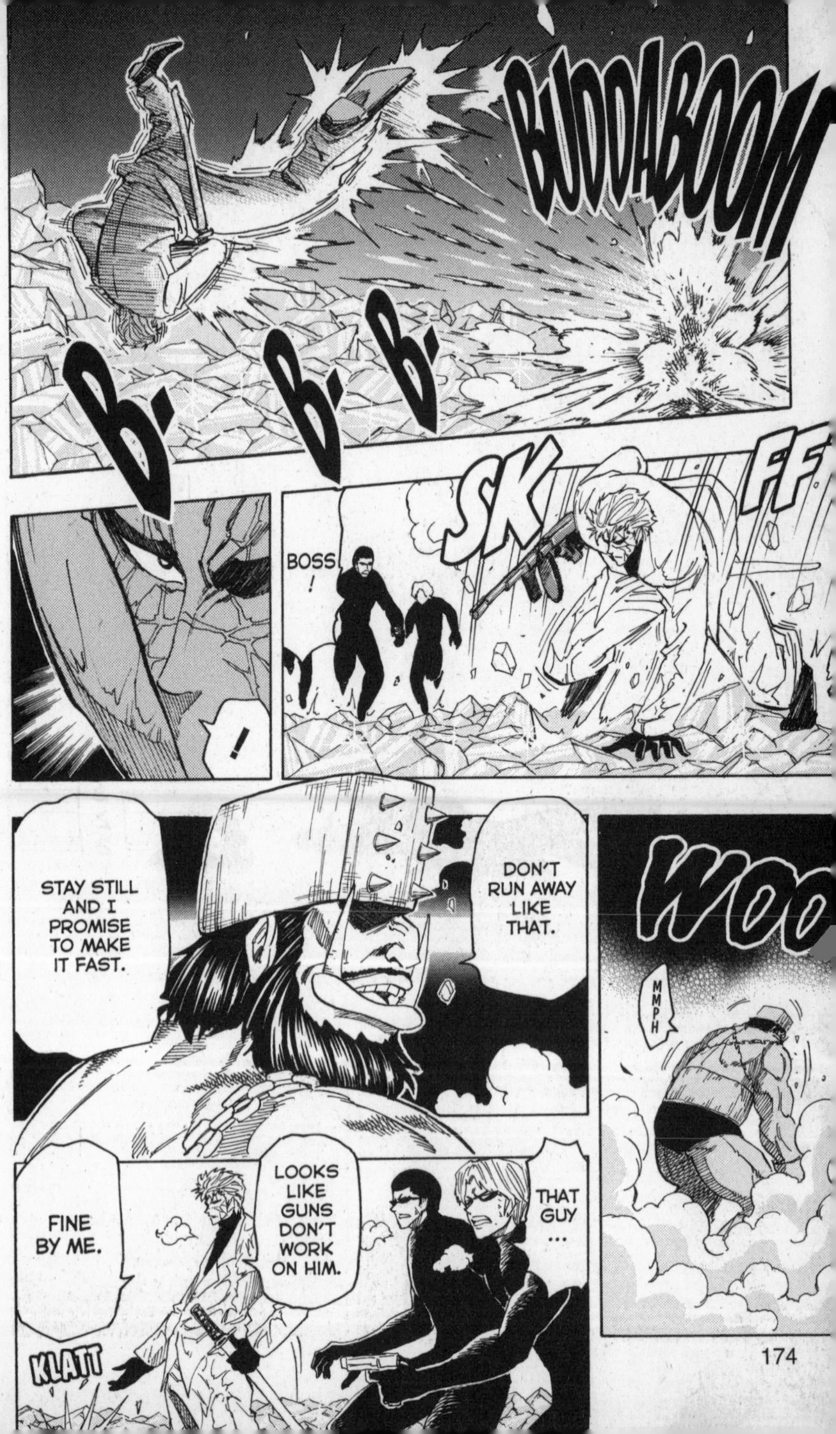
BUDDABOOM
B-B-B-
SK
FF
BOSS!
!
WOO
MMPH
DON'T RUN AWAY LIKE THAT.
STAY STILL AND I PROMISE TO MAKE IT FAST.
THAT GUY...
LOOKS LIKE GUNS DON'T WORK ON HIM.
FINE BY ME.
KLATT

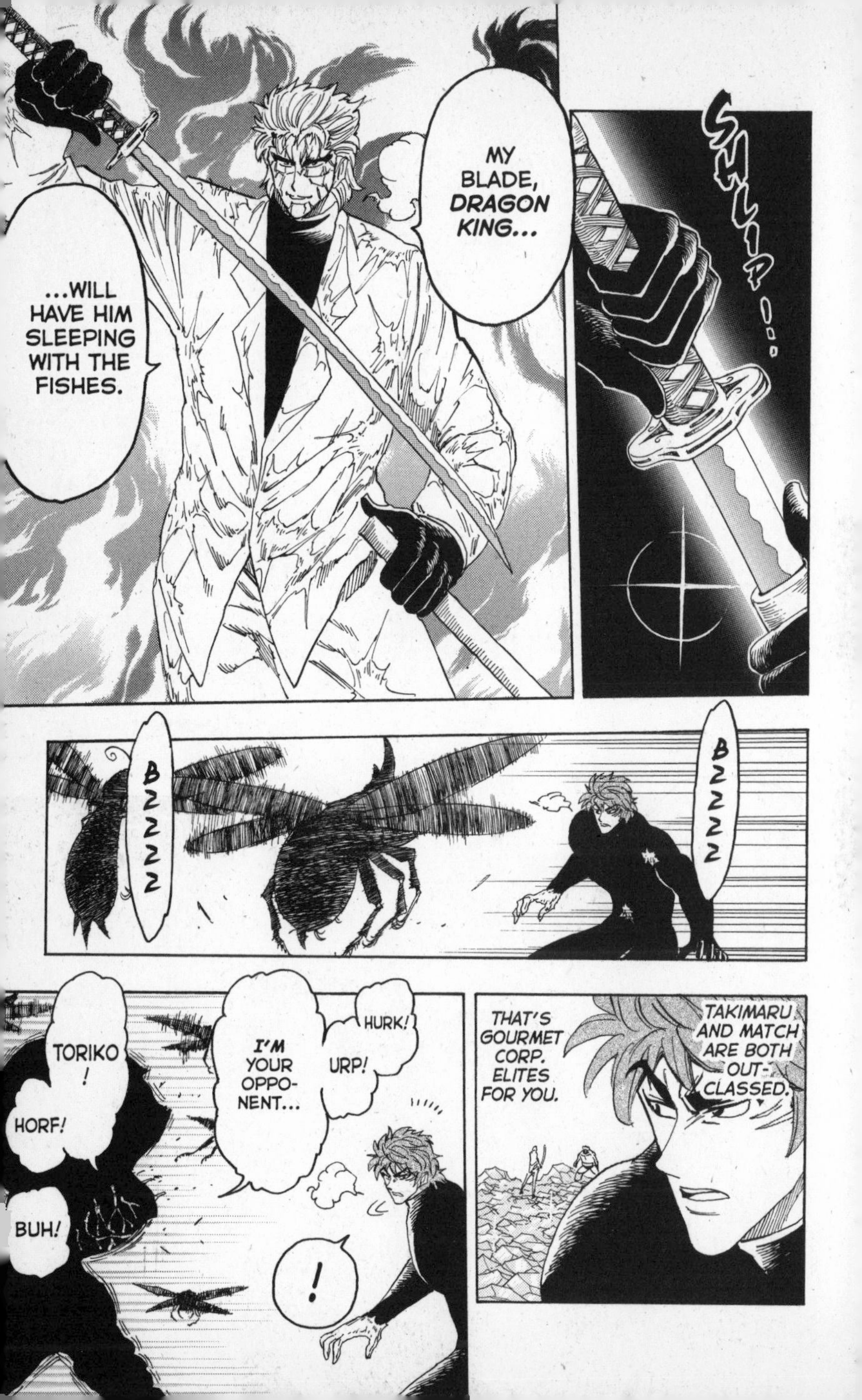

SHLIP!!
MY BLADE, DRAGON KING...
...WILL HAVE HIM SLEEPING WITH THE FISHES.
BZZZ
BZZZ
TAKIMARU AND MATCH ARE BOTH OUT-CLASSED.
THAT'S GOURMET CORP. ELITES FOR YOU.
HURK!
URP!
I'M YOUR OPPO-NENT...
TORIKO!
HORF!
BUH!
!

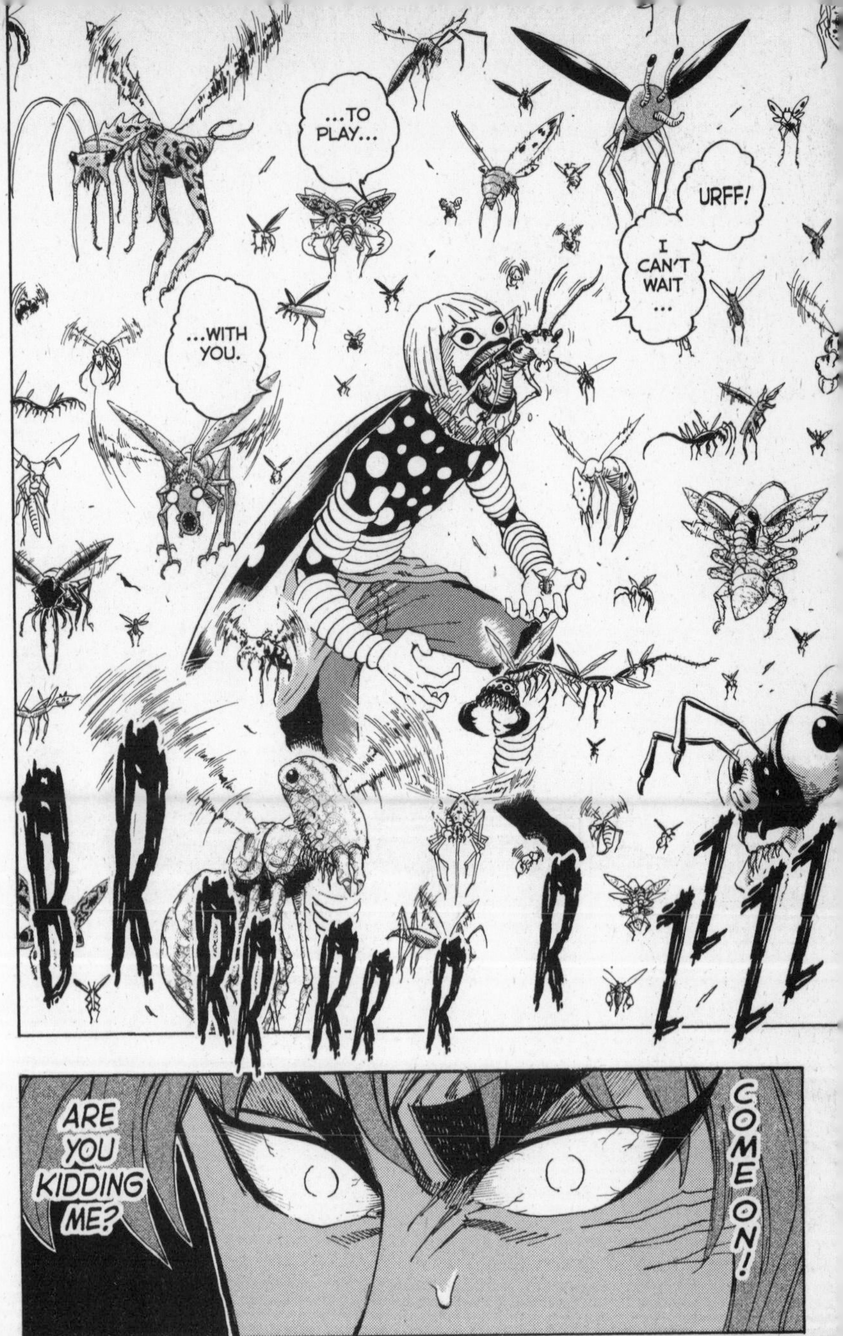
URFF!
I CAN'T WAIT...
...TO PLAY...
...WITH YOU.
BRRRRRRR RZZZZ
COME ON!
ARE YOU KIDDING ME?

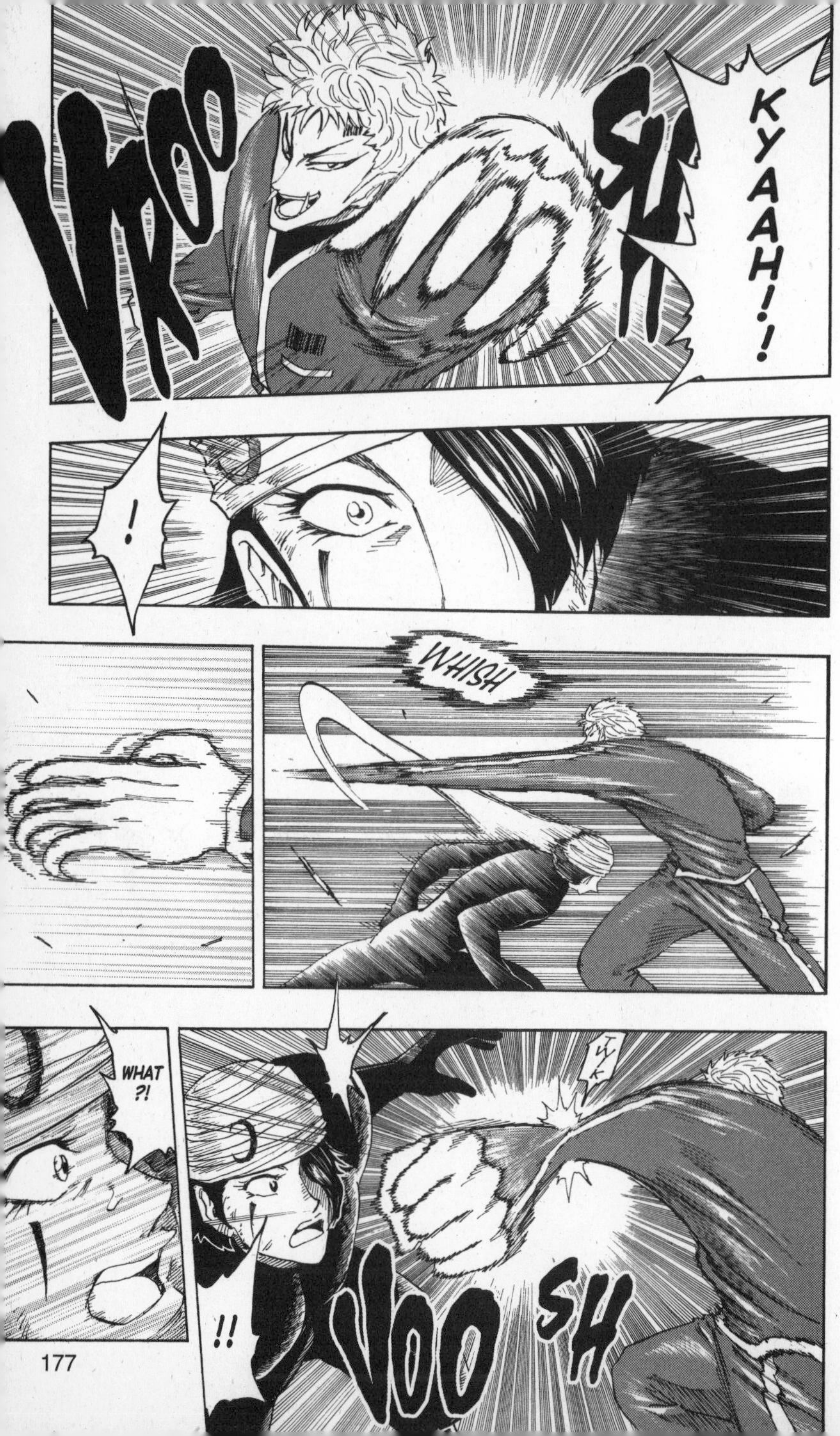
KYAAH!!!
!
WHISH
TWK
!!
VOOSH
WHAT ?!

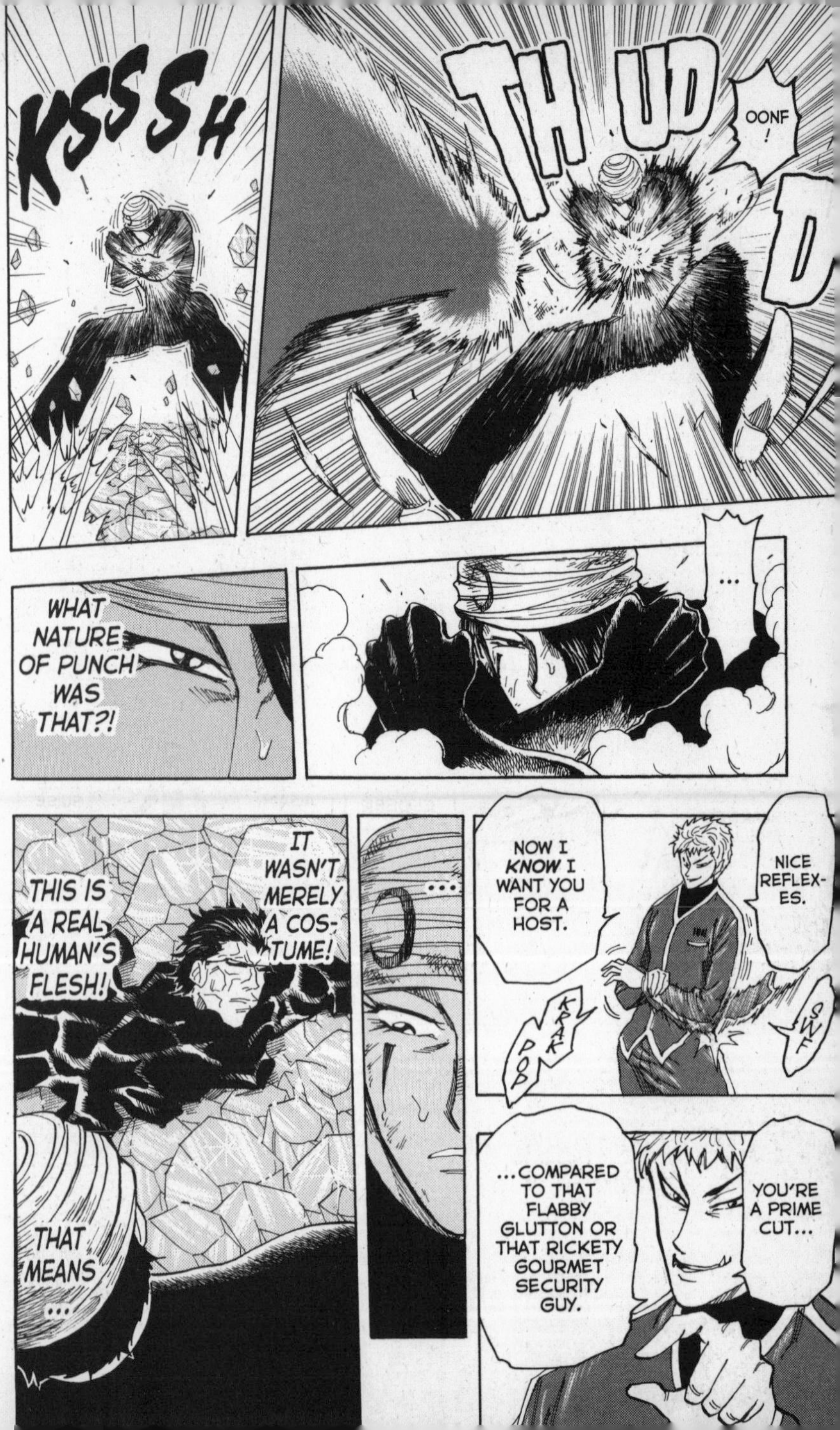
THUD
OONF!
D
KSSSH
...
WHAT NATURE OF PUNCH WAS THAT?!
NICE REFLEXES.
NOW I *KNOW* I WANT YOU FOR A HOST.
SWF
KRAK
POP
YOU'RE A PRIME CUT...
...COMPARED TO THAT FLABBY GLUTTON OR THAT RICKETY GOURMET SECURITY GUY.
...
IT WASN'T MERELY A COSTUME!
THIS IS A REAL HUMAN'S FLESH!
THAT MEANS...

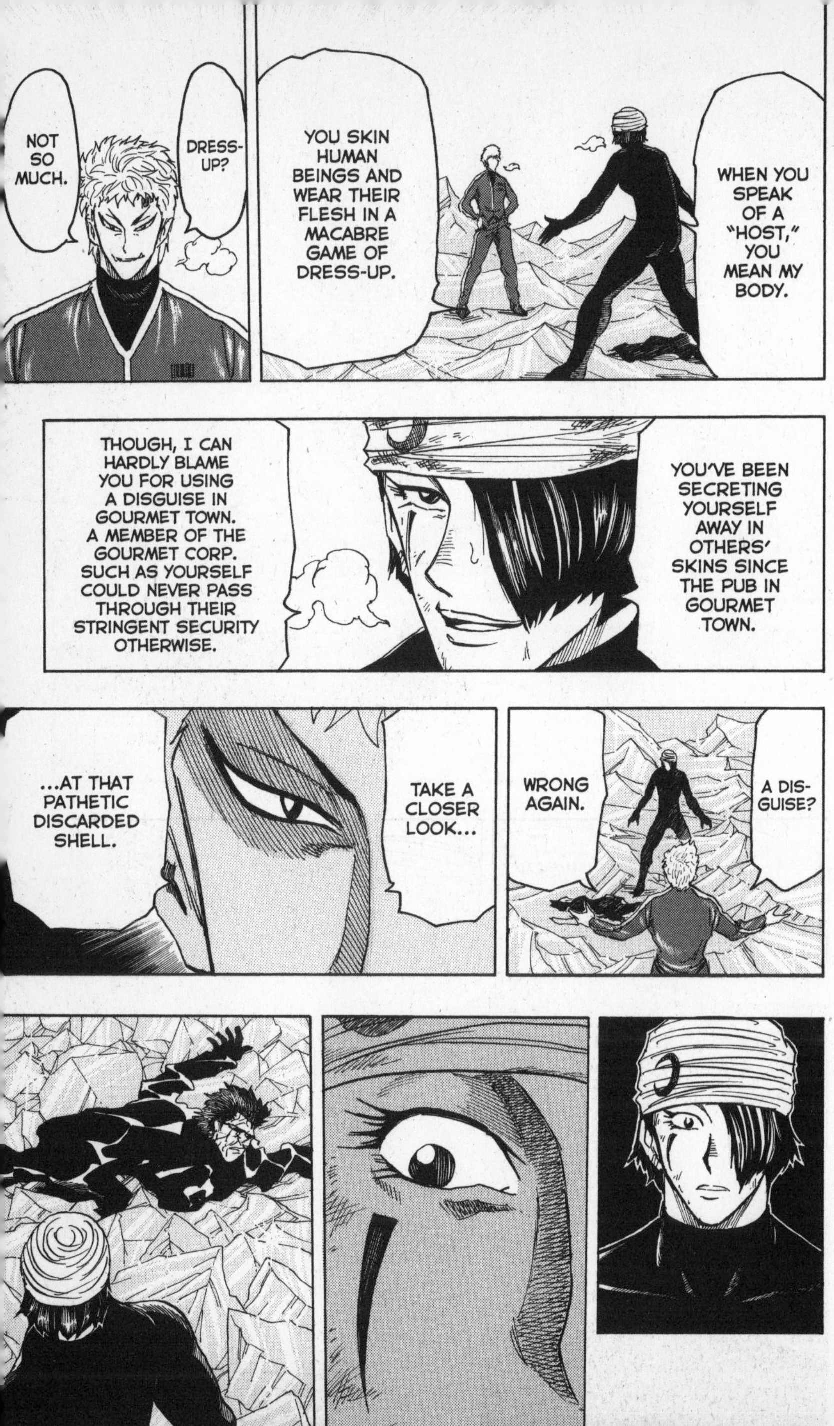
WHEN YOU SPEAK OF A "HOST," YOU MEAN MY BODY.
YOU SKIN HUMAN BEINGS AND WEAR THEIR FLESH IN A MACABRE GAME OF DRESS-UP.
DRESS-UP?
NOT SO MUCH.
YOU'VE BEEN SECRETING YOURSELF AWAY IN OTHERS' SKINS SINCE THE PUB IN GOURMET TOWN.
THOUGH, I CAN HARDLY BLAME YOU FOR USING A DISGUISE IN GOURMET TOWN. A MEMBER OF THE GOURMET CORP. SUCH AS YOURSELF COULD NEVER PASS THROUGH THEIR STRINGENT SECURITY OTHERWISE.
A DIS-GUISE?
WRONG AGAIN.
TAKE A CLOSER LOOK...
...AT THAT PATHETIC DISCARDED SHELL.

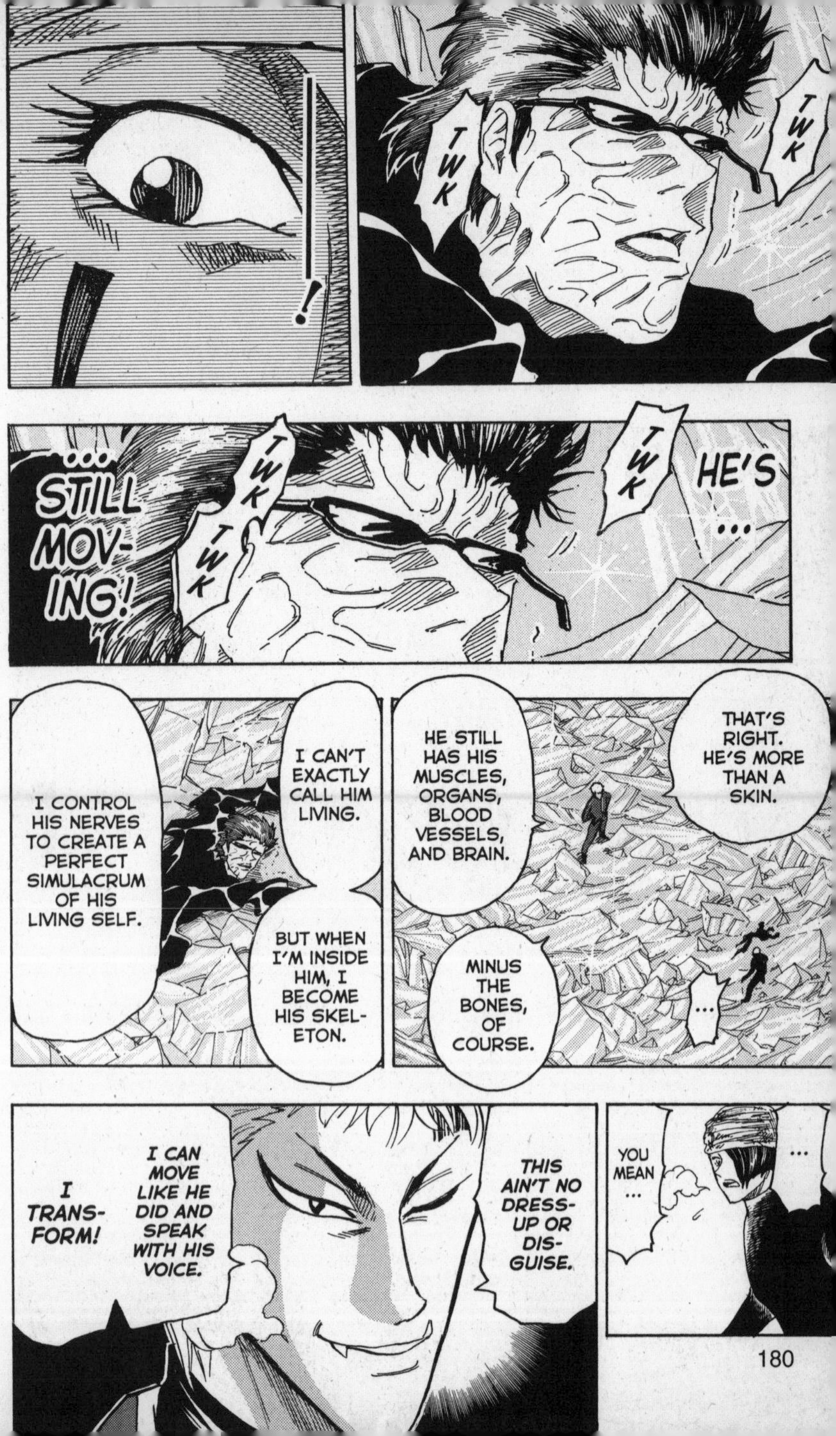
TWK
TWK
!
TWK
HE'S ...
TWK
TWK
... STILL MOV-ING!
THAT'S RIGHT. HE'S MORE THAN A SKIN.
HE STILL HAS HIS MUSCLES, ORGANS, BLOOD VESSELS, AND BRAIN.
MINUS THE BONES, OF COURSE.
...
I CAN'T EXACTLY CALL HIM LIVING.
BUT WHEN I'M INSIDE HIM, I BECOME HIS SKEL-ETON.
I CONTROL HIS NERVES TO CREATE A PERFECT SIMULACRUM OF HIS LIVING SELF.
...
YOU MEAN ...
THIS AIN'T NO DRESS-UP OR DIS-GUISE.
I CAN MOVE LIKE HE DID AND SPEAK WITH HIS VOICE.
I TRANS-FORM!

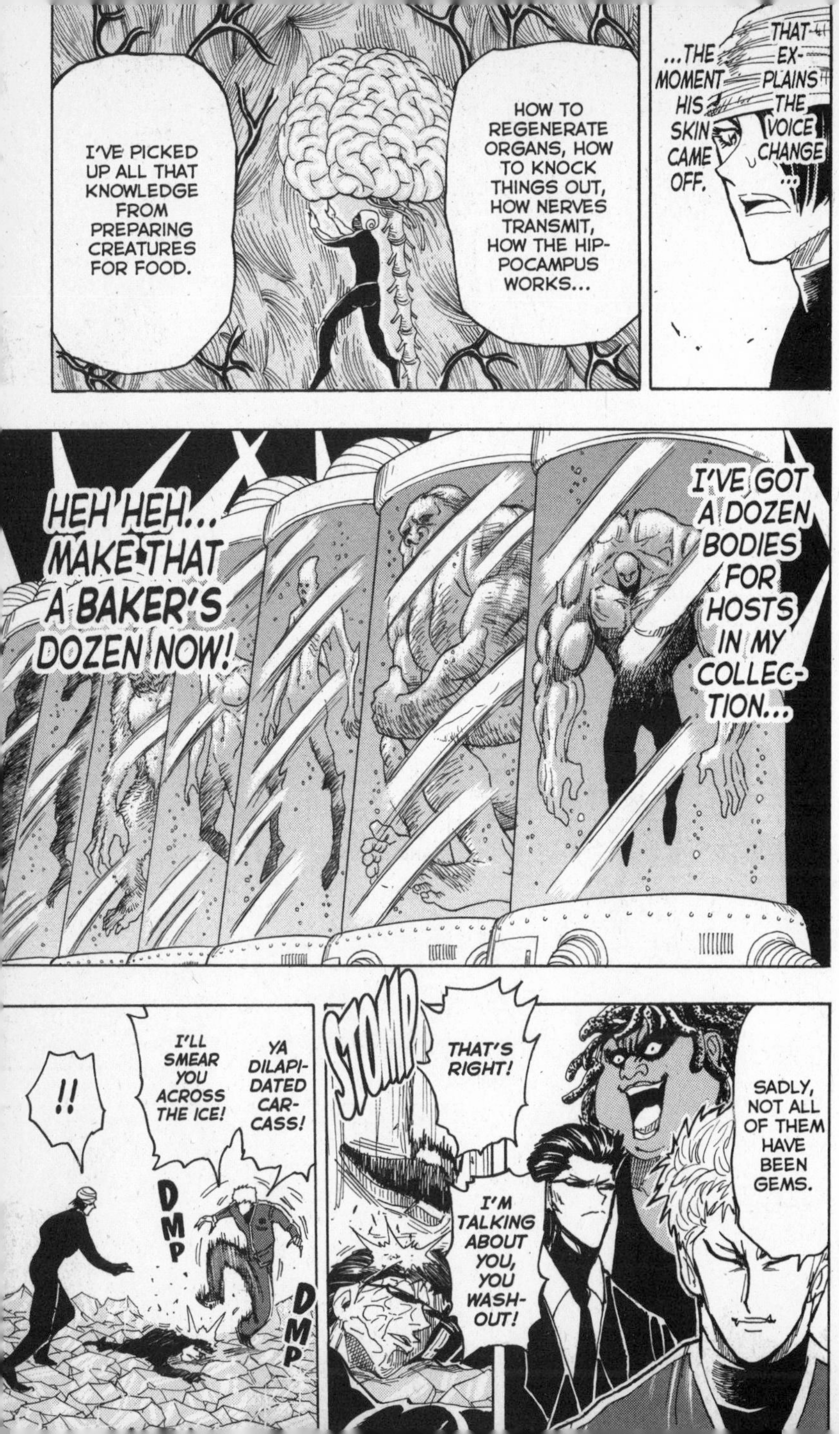
THAT EXPLAINS THE VOICE CHANGE...
...THE MOMENT HIS SKIN CAME OFF.
HOW TO REGENERATE ORGANS, HOW TO KNOCK THINGS OUT, HOW NERVES TRANSMIT, HOW THE HIPPOCAMPUS WORKS...
I'VE PICKED UP ALL THAT KNOWLEDGE FROM PREPARING CREATURES FOR FOOD.
I'VE GOT A DOZEN BODIES FOR HOSTS IN MY COLLECTION...
HEH HEH... MAKE THAT A BAKER'S DOZEN NOW!
SADLY, NOT ALL OF THEM HAVE BEEN GEMS.
THAT'S RIGHT!
STOMP
I'M TALKING ABOUT YOU, YOU WASHOUT!
YA DILAPIDATED CARCASS!
I'LL SMEAR YOU ACROSS THE ICE!
!!
DMP
DMP

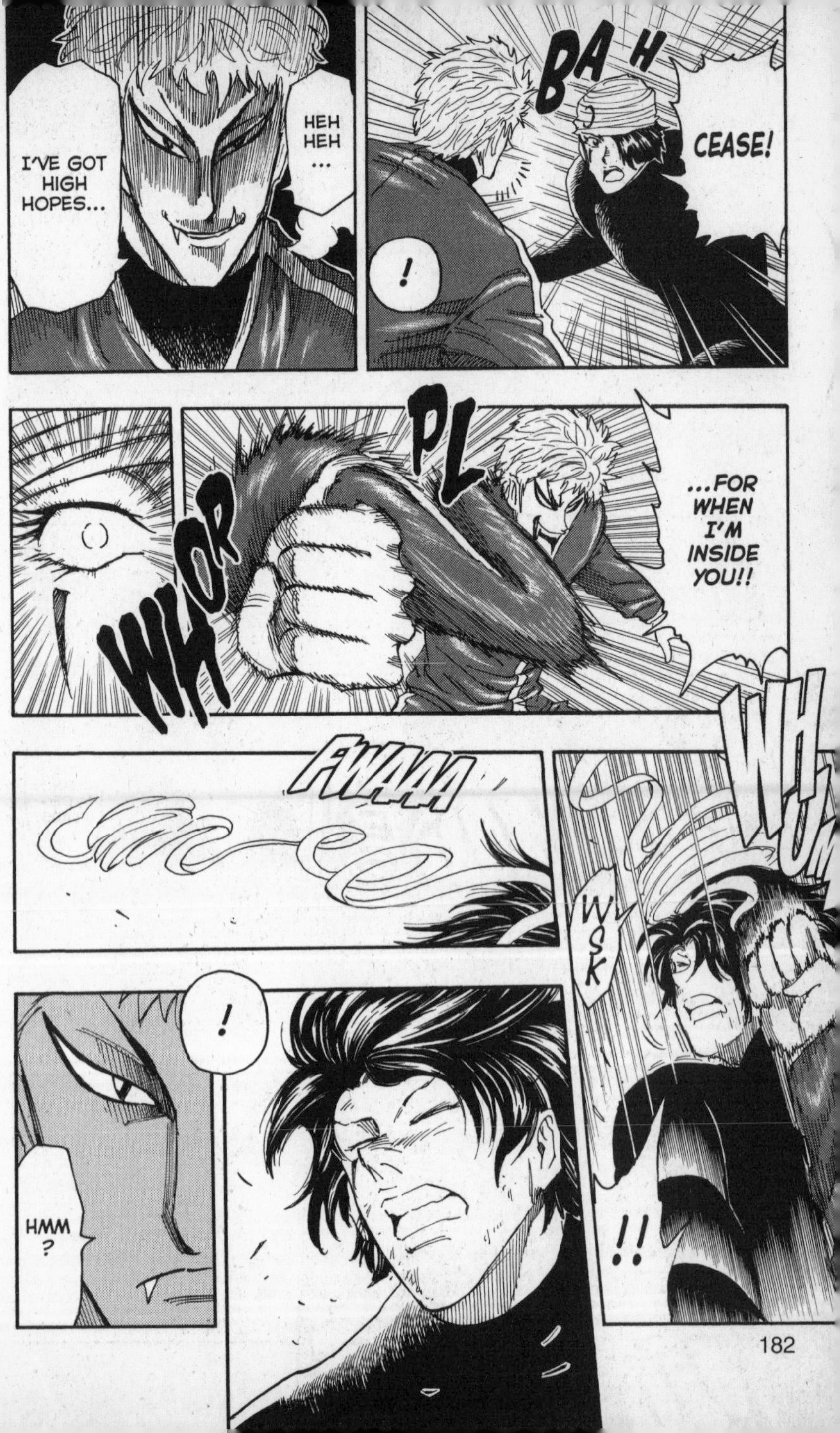
BAH
CEASE!
!
HEH HEH ...
I'VE GOT HIGH HOPES...
PL
...FOR WHEN I'M INSIDE YOU!!
WHOR
WH
UM
WSK
!!
FWAAA
!
HMM ?

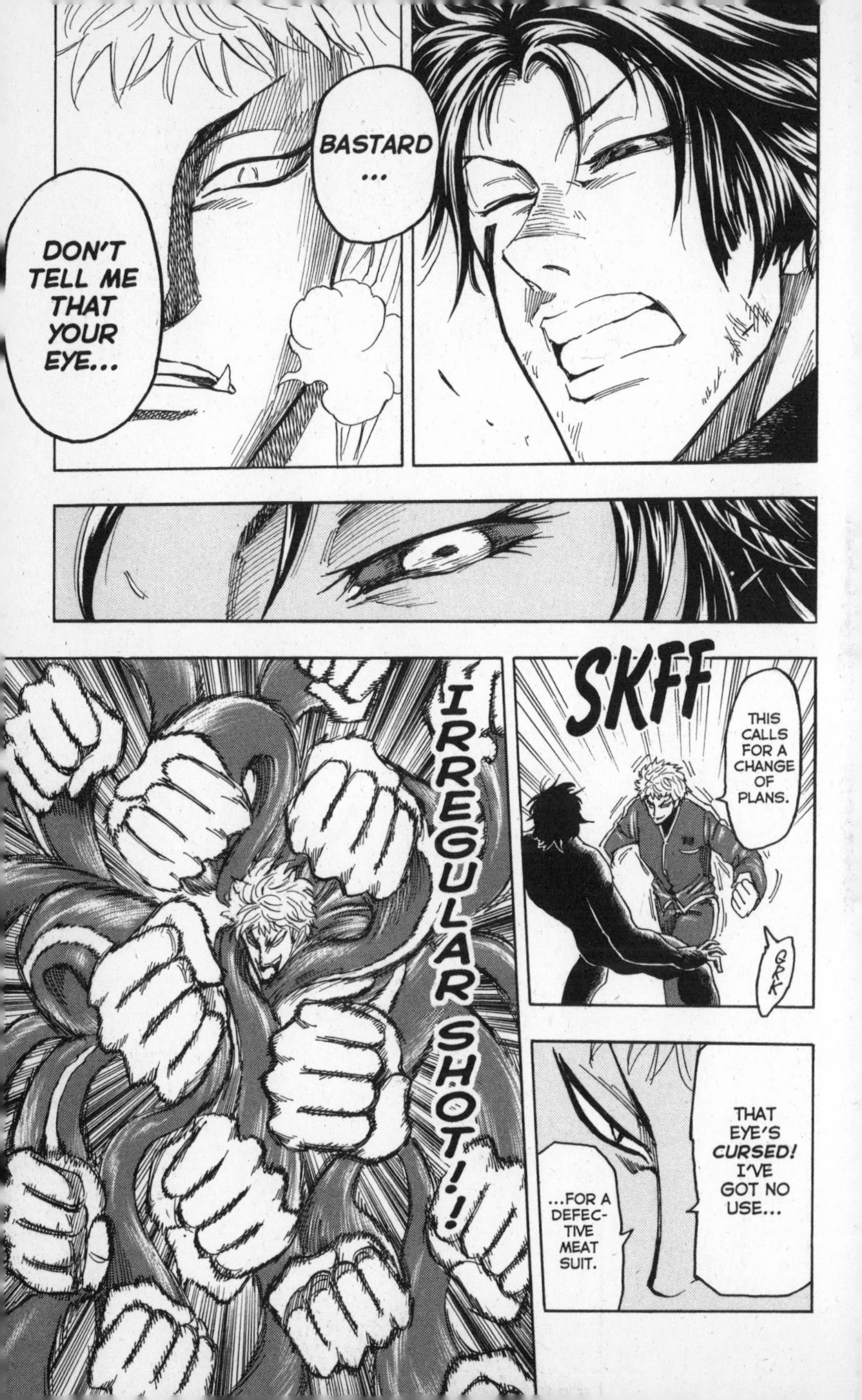
BASTARD ...
DON'T TELL ME THAT YOUR EYE...
SKFF
THIS CALLS FOR A CHANGE OF PLANS.
GRK
THAT EYE'S *CURSED!* I'VE GOT NO USE...
...FOR A DEFECTIVE MEAT SUIT.
IRREGULAR SHOT!!

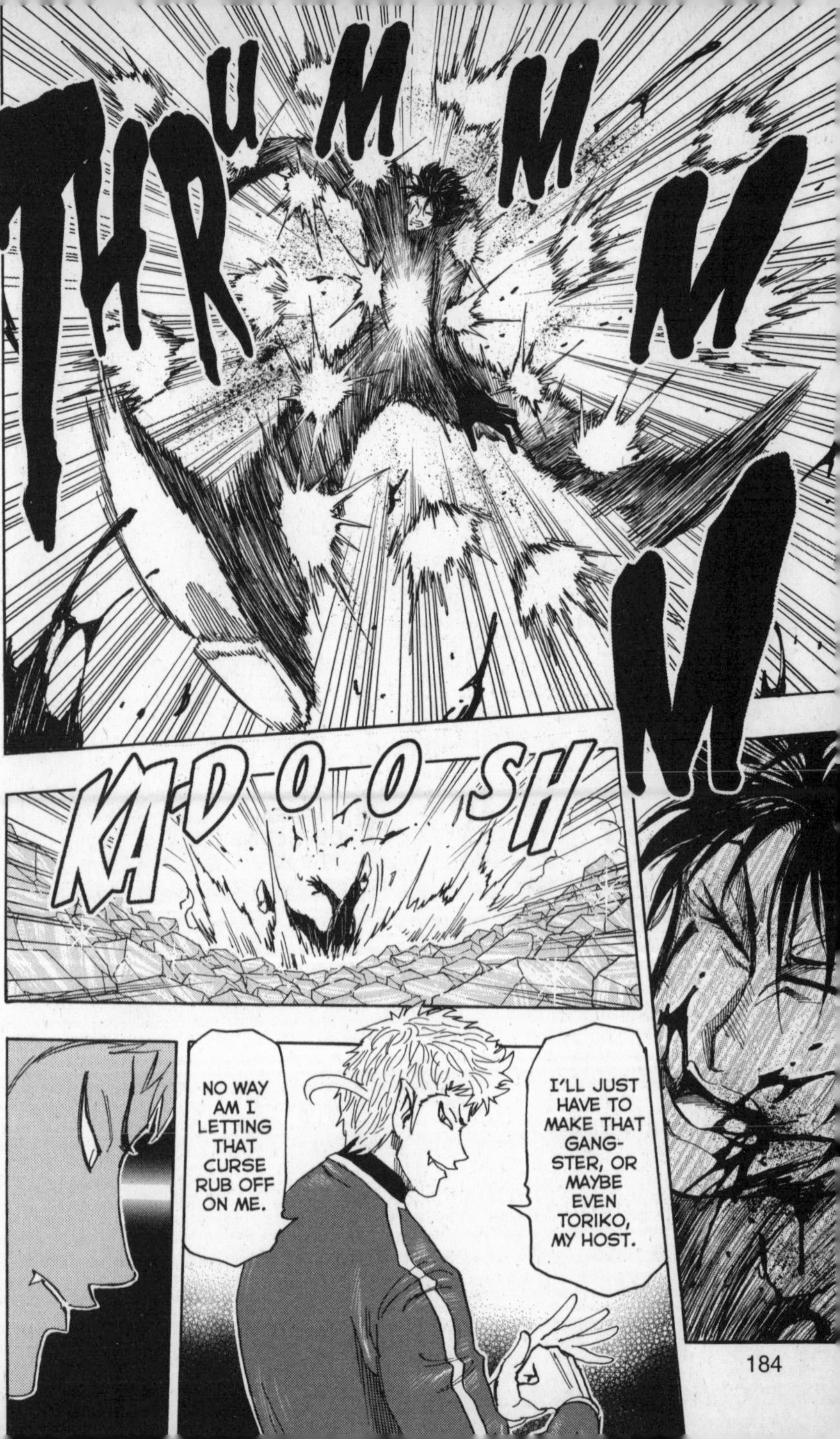
THRUMMMMM
KA-D-O-O-SH
I'LL JUST HAVE TO MAKE THAT GANG-STER, OR MAYBE EVEN TORIKO, MY HOST.
NO WAY AM I LETTING THAT CURSE RUB OFF ON ME.

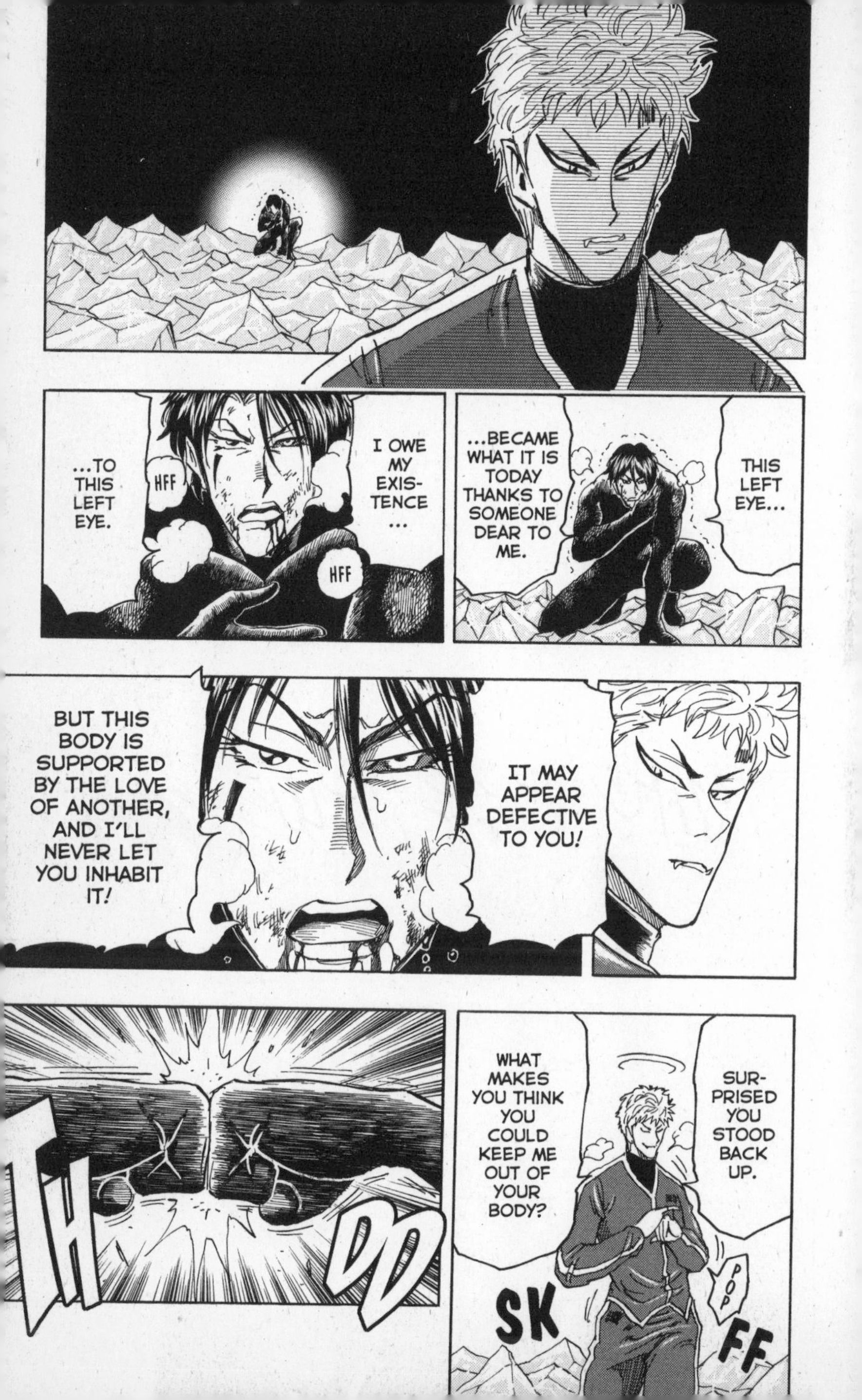

THIS LEFT EYE...
...BECAME WHAT IT IS TODAY THANKS TO SOMEONE DEAR TO ME.
I OWE MY EXIS-TENCE...
HFF
...TO THIS LEFT EYE.
HFF
IT MAY APPEAR DEFECTIVE TO YOU!
BUT THIS BODY IS SUPPORTED BY THE LOVE OF ANOTHER, AND I'LL NEVER LET YOU INHABIT IT!
SUR-PRISED YOU STOOD BACK UP.
WHAT MAKES YOU THINK YOU COULD KEEP ME OUT OF YOUR BODY?
POP
SKFF
THUDD

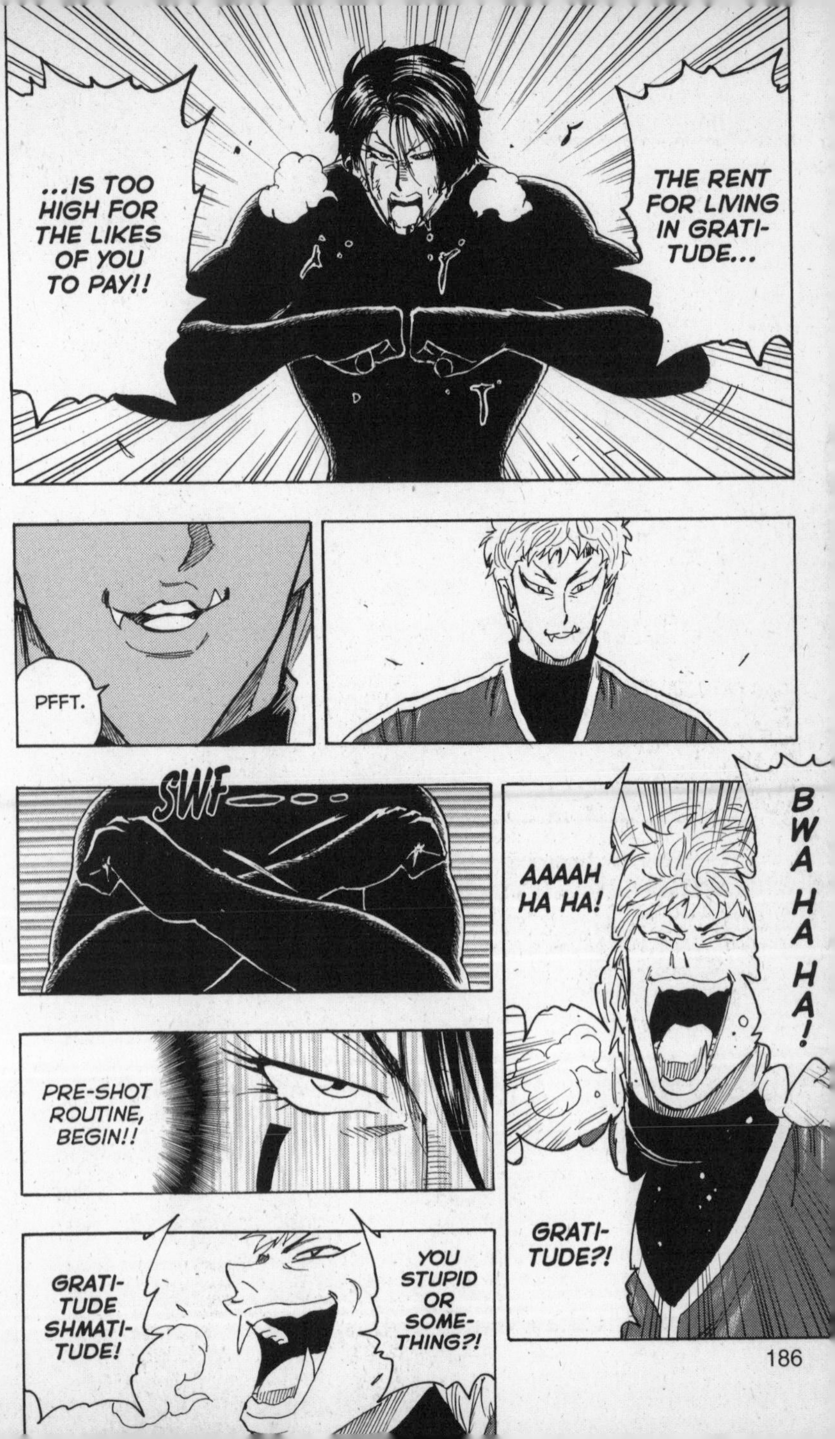
THE RENT FOR LIVING IN GRATI-TUDE...
...IS TOO HIGH FOR THE LIKES OF YOU TO PAY!!
PFFT.
BWA HA HA HA!
AAAAH HA HA!
GRATI-TUDE?!
SWF
PRE-SHOT ROUTINE, BEGIN!!
YOU STUPID OR SOME-THING?!
GRATI-TUDE SHMATI-TUDE!

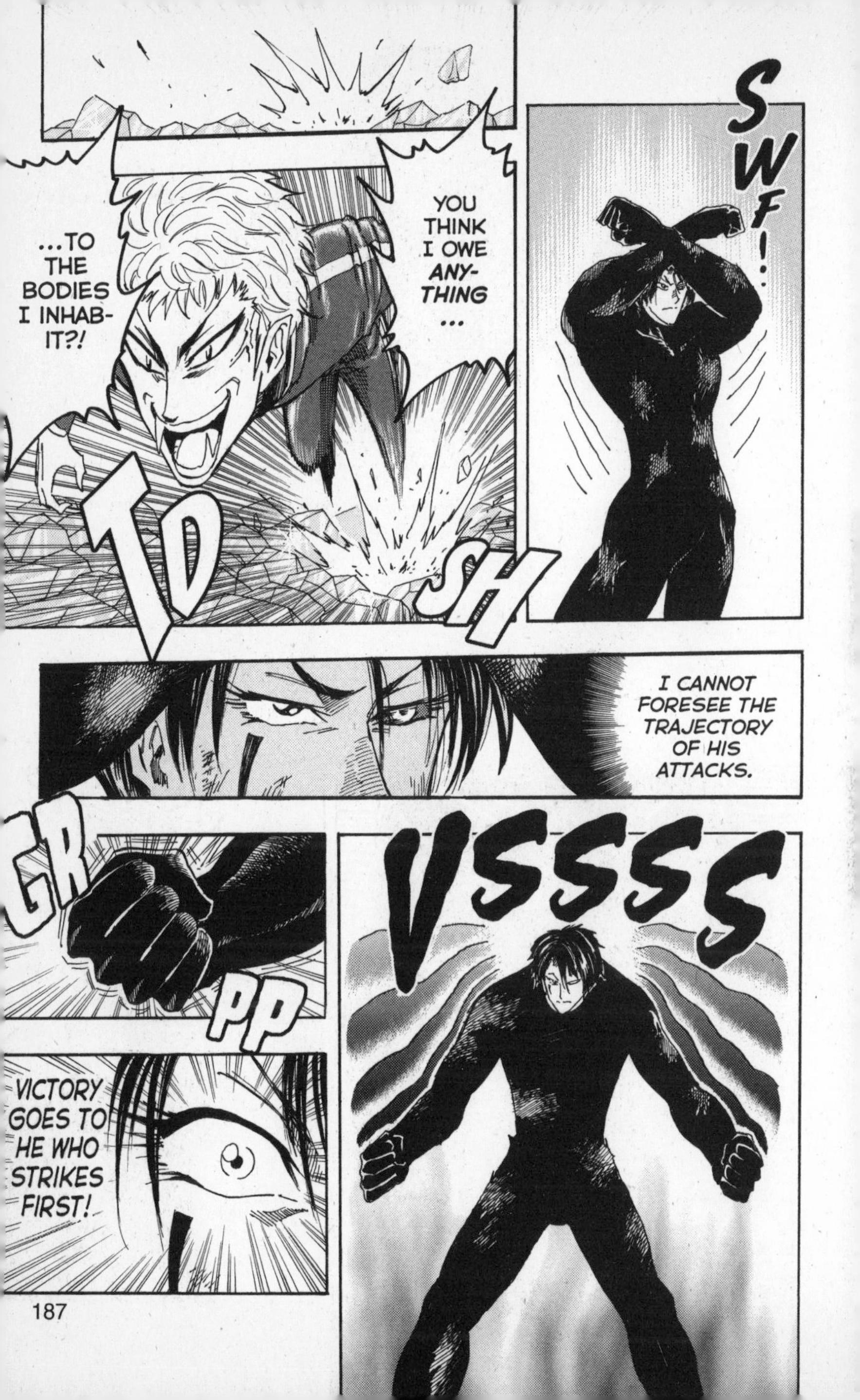
SWF!..
YOU THINK I OWE ANYTHING...
...TO THE BODIES I INHABIT?!
TOSH
I CANNOT FORESEE THE TRAJECTORY OF HIS ATTACKS.
VSSSS
GRIPP
VICTORY GOES TO HE WHO STRIKES FIRST!

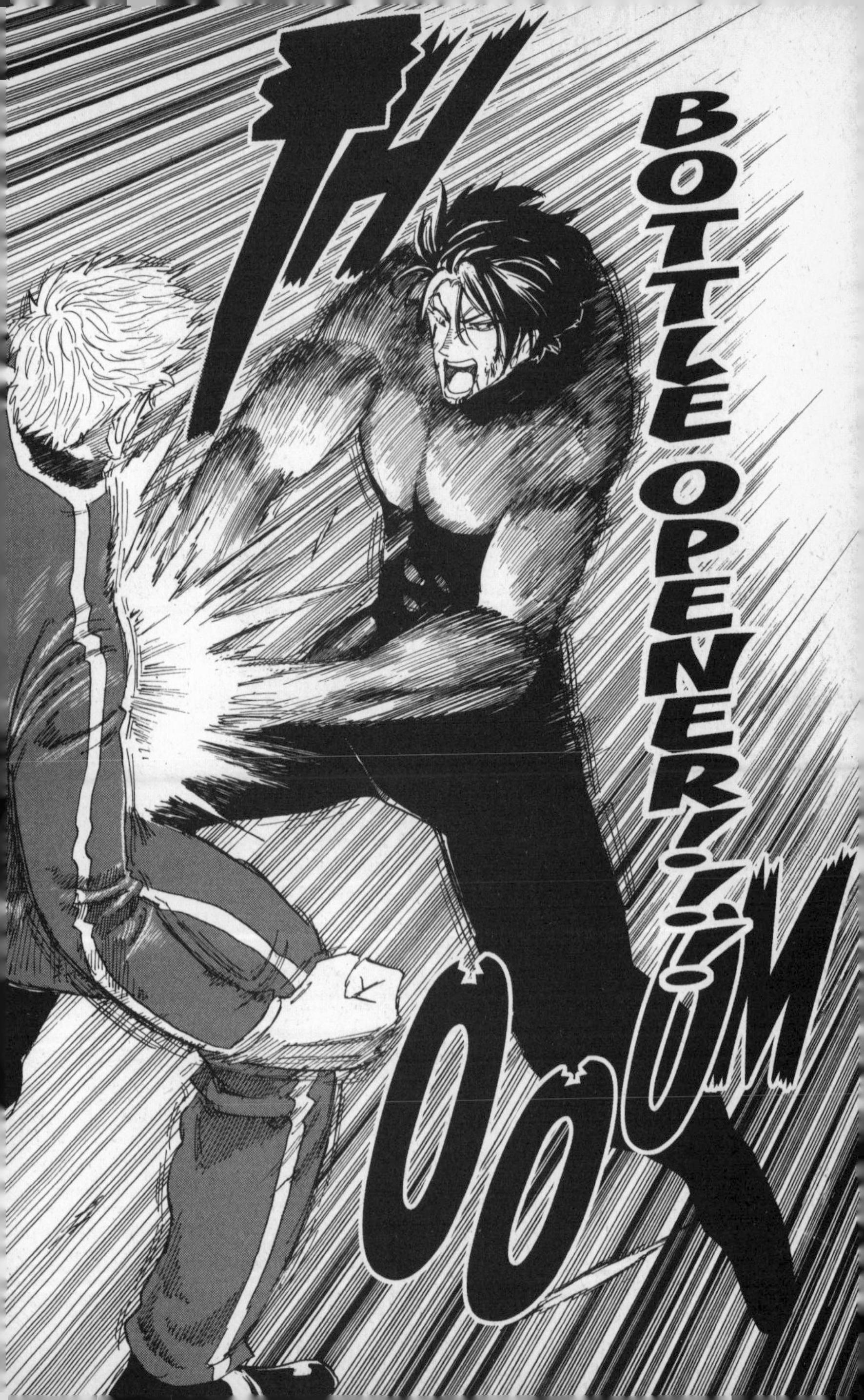
THWOOOOM
BOTTLE OPENER!!

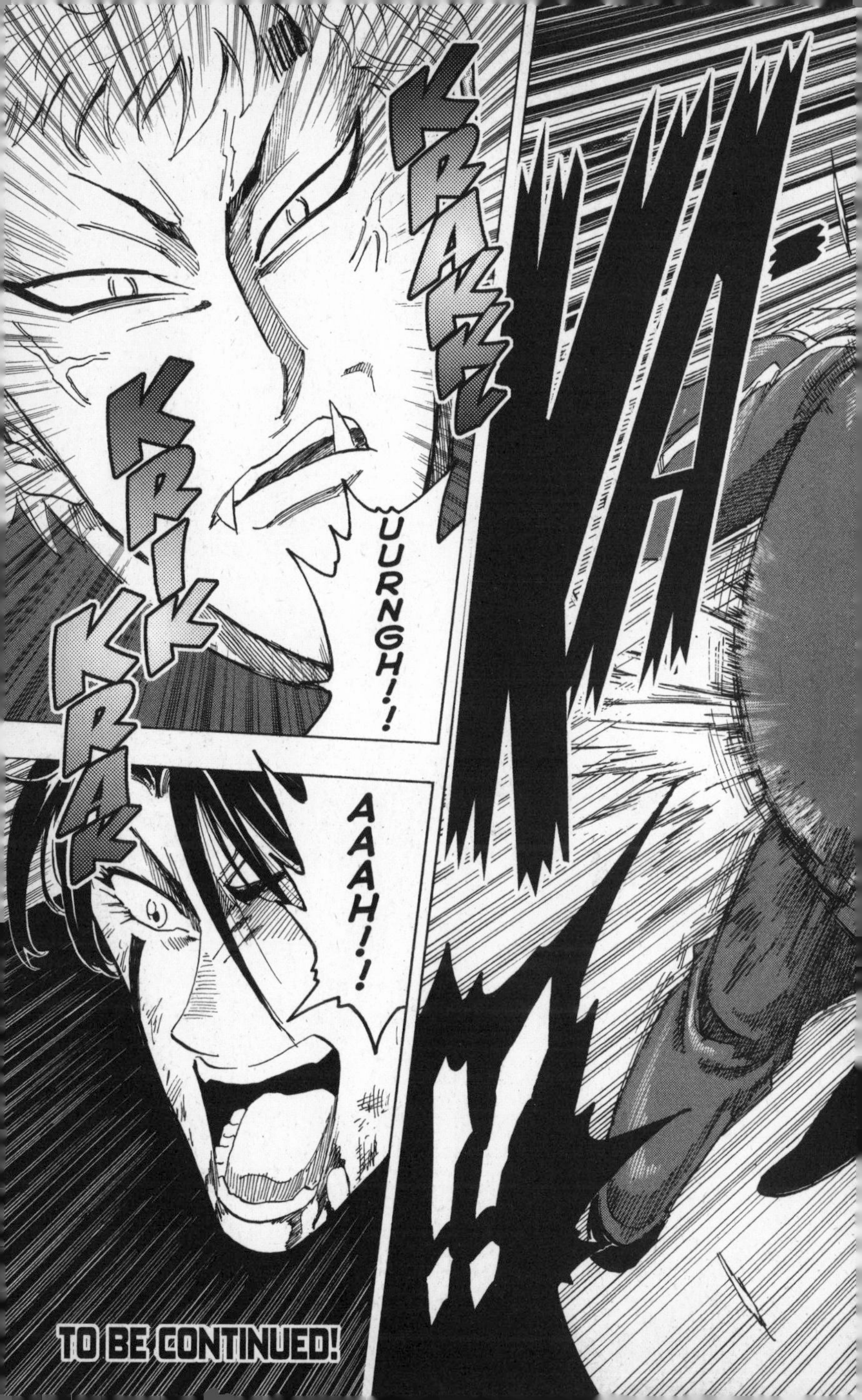

KRAKK
UURNGH!!
KRIKK
KRAK
AAAAH!!!
TO BE CONTINUED!

TORIKO

GOURMET CHECKLIST

Vol. 071

EYE-DAMAME

(PLANT)

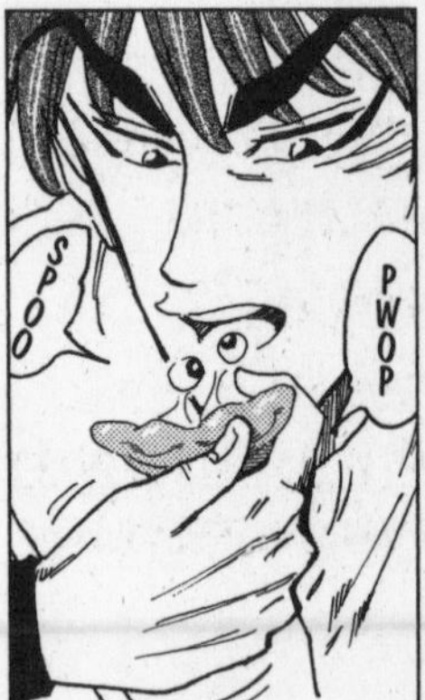
PWOP
SPOO

CAPTURE LEVEL: 1

HABITAT: RICH SOILS

LENGTH: 3 CM (1 BEAN)

HEIGHT: ---

WEIGHT: ---

PRICE: 1 POD (CONTAINS 6 – 8 BEANS) / 300 YEN

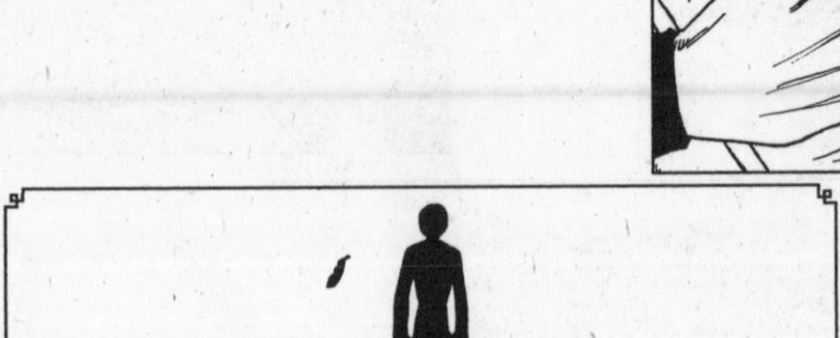

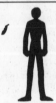

SCALE

A GROTESQUE STRAIN OF BEANS WHOSE PODS HOLD MINIATURE EYEBALLS! WELL, THEY JUST LOOK LIKE EYEBALLS, BUT THE EFFECT IS OFF-PUTTING ENOUGH THAT FEW WILL VENTURE TO TASTE THEIR PLEASANT SALTINESS. THEY'RE THE PREFERRED SNACK FOOD OF BOOZERS LIKE MANSOM.

TORIKO

GOURMET CHECKLIST

Vol. 072

FROBERRY
(AMPHIBIAN)

CAPTURE LEVEL: 6

HABITAT: PLAINS, SWAMPS, ETC

LENGTH: 7 METERS

HEIGHT: 3 METERS

WEIGHT: 5 TONS

PRICE: 100 GRAMS / 700 YEN (MEAT); 20,000 YEN (STRAWBERRY)

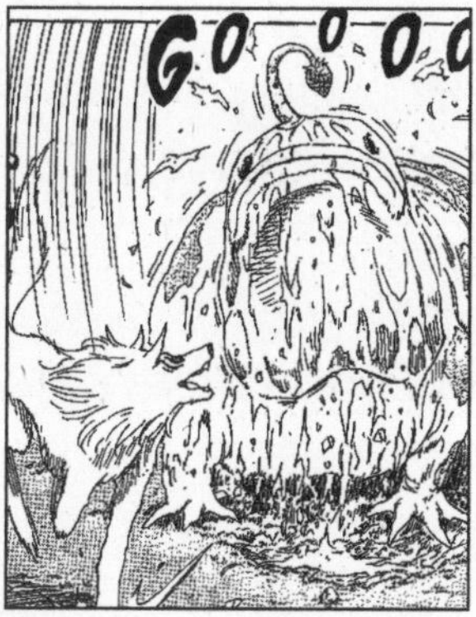
GOOOOO

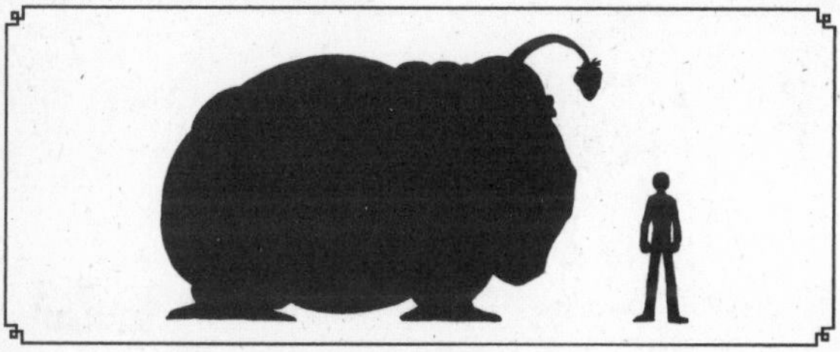

SCALE

TYPICALLY LIVES ON LAND, BUT WHEN IT'S ON THE HUNT, THIS AMPHIBIOUS BEAST WILL SUBMERGE ITSELF IN MURKY SWAMP WATERS. SINCE THE FROBERRY MOVES SLOWLY, IT LIES IN WAIT AND ENTICES ITS PREY TO APPROACH. OFTEN TIMES, IT WILL REACT TO EVEN THE SLIGHTEST STIMULATION, LOSING THE ELEMENT OF SURPRISE AND ITS DINNER. ITS MEAT IS UNREMARKABLE, BUT ITS SWEET STRAWBERRY IS BETTER THAN THE REAL THING!

TORIKO

GOURMET CHECKLIST

Vol. 073

GOBLIN PLANT
(PLANT)

CAPTURE LEVEL: 33

HABITAT: WU JUNGLE (PLANT HELL)

LENGTH: UNMEASURED

HEIGHT: ---

WEIGHT: ---

PRICE: NOT FIT FOR CONSUMPTION, BUT ITS

EMERALD-GREEN EYES ARE PRICED AT ONE

BILLION YEN EACH.

SCALE

THIS TREE'S UNBELIEVABLE SPEED AT PLANTING AERIAL ROOTS GIVES
THE IMPRESSION THAT IT CAN WALK. THE ROOTS ARE ALSO VERY
CLINGY AND WILL NAB CREATURES, DRAINING THEIR LIFEBLOOD AND
GROWING EVER STRONGER FROM IT. TAKING BITES OUT OF A GOBLIN
PLANT'S FUNKY TRUNK WON'T INFLICT THAT MUCH DAMAGE ON IT. IN FACT,
YOU'LL ONLY MAKE NEW ROOTS SPRING FORTH. RATHER THAN ATTACK IT
HEAD-ON, IT IS MORE EFFECTIVE TO BARRAGE IT WITH FIREARMS FROM
A DISTANCE. ITS EMERALD-GREEN EYES ARE CONSIDERED JEWELS.

TORIKO

GOURMET CHECKLIST

Vol. 074

BB CORN
(PLANT)

CAPTURE LEVEL: 35 (ONES IN THE GOURMET
REALM NOT YET MEASURED)

HABITAT: WU JUNGLE

LENGTH: 1 METER (UP TO 50 METERS)

HEIGHT: ---

WEIGHT: ---

PRICE: VARIES BY SIZE. GENERALLY 100,000
YEN (KERNEL); SEVERAL BILLION YEN (EAR);
3000 YEN (ONE SERVING OF POPCORN)

SCALE

THIS GRAIN GROWS PRIMARILY IN THE GOURMET REALM AND PROVIDED
ANCIENT GOURMET NOBLES WITH DELICIOUS POPCORN. POPPING JUST
ONE KERNEL TAKES AN ENORMOUS AMOUNT OF HEAT BUT WILL YIELD
ENOUGH POPCORN TO FEED A CROWD OF ONE HUNDRED. BB CORN'S SCIN-
TILLATING SCENT AND FINE FLAVOR MAKE IT HARD TO STOP EATING--
NO FOOD MAKES YOU HUNGRIER! PRICES START AT 100,000 YEN PER
KERNEL, WHILE A WHOLE EAR GOES FOR NO LOWER THAN ONE BILLION.
IT'S ONE OF TERRY'S FAVORITE FOODS AND THE HORS D'ŒUVRE IN
TORIKO'S FULL-COURSE MEAL. KING KONG HAS NOTHING ON KING CORN!

TORIKO

GOURMET CHECKLIST

Vol. 075

MAGMA RAT
(MAMMAL)

CAPTURE LEVEL: 3

HABITAT: WOOL VOLCANO

LENGTH: 90 CM

HEIGHT: ---

WEIGHT: 5 KG

PRICE: 100 G / 500 YEN

SCALE

A RODENT THAT THRIVES IN THE SWELTERING TEMPERATURES CREATED BY VOLCANIC HOT SPOTS AND MOLTEN LAVA. THEIR HIDES ARE PRIZED INSULATORS, AND THEIR MEAT IS A GODSEND IN PROTEIN-STARVED VOLCANIC REGIONS. EVERY PART OF A MAGMA RAT'S BODY CAN BE USED, MAKING IT A VERY VERSATILE FOOD.

TORIKO

GOURMET CHECKLIST

Vol. 076

DEVIL MOSQUITO
(INSECT)

CAPTURE LEVEL: UNKNOWN

HABITAT: UNKNOWN

LENGTH: 7 METERS

HEIGHT: ---

WEIGHT: 1 TON

PRICE: UNKNOWN

SCALE

A GIANT MOSQUITO WITH A PROBOSCIS CAPABLE OF POWERFUL SUCTION. GOURMET CORP. VICE-CHEF GRINPATCH USES A FLEXIBLE, DURABLE DEVIL MOSQUITO PROBOSCIS AS A STRAW TO AUGMENT HIS ALREADY INCREDIBLE LUNG CAPACITY.

TORIKO

GOURMET CHECKLIST

Vol. 077

GOD
(UNCLASSIFIED)

CAPTURE LEVEL: UNKNOWN

HABITAT: UNKNOWN

LENGTH: UNKNOWN

HEIGHT: UNKNOWN

WEIGHT: UNKNOWN

PRICE: UNKNOWN

SCALE

FIVE HUNDRED YEARS AGO, THE LEGENDARY GOURMET HUNTER ACACIA, SAID TO HAVE SAMPLED EVERY FOOD ON EARTH, SPENT HIS LIFE SEARCHING FOR THIS FOOD. THE DISCOVERY OF GOD IS SAID TO HAVE MARKED THE ADVENT OF THE AGE OF GOURMET. OTHER THAN ITS NAME, ALL OTHER DETAILS REGARDING THIS FOOD ARE SHROUDED IN MYSTERY. THE ONLY HINT TO ITS WHEREABOUTS SURFACES DURING THE GOURMET SOLAR ECLIPSE ONCE EVERY SEVERAL HUNDRED YEARS. IT'S THE DISH THAT TORIKO HAS DECIDED HE WILL MAKE THE ENTREE IN HIS FULL-COURSE MEAL. HE'S NOT THE ONLY ONE WHO WANTS IT--GOURMET RESEARCHERS, FAMOUS GOURMET HUNTERS, RETIRED PROFESSIONALS, GOURMET CORP., AND PRETTY MUCH EVERY SINGLE PERSON ON EARTH CRAVES A TASTE! ALSO CONSIDERED THE FINEST FOOD IN THE WORLD.

CHARACTER PROFILE

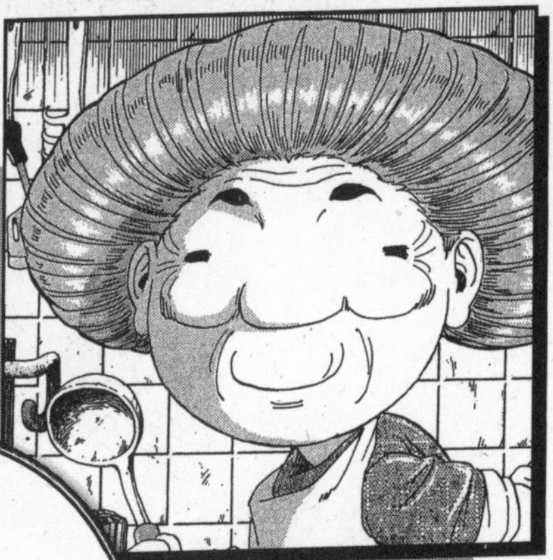

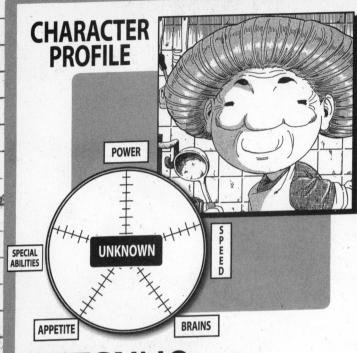

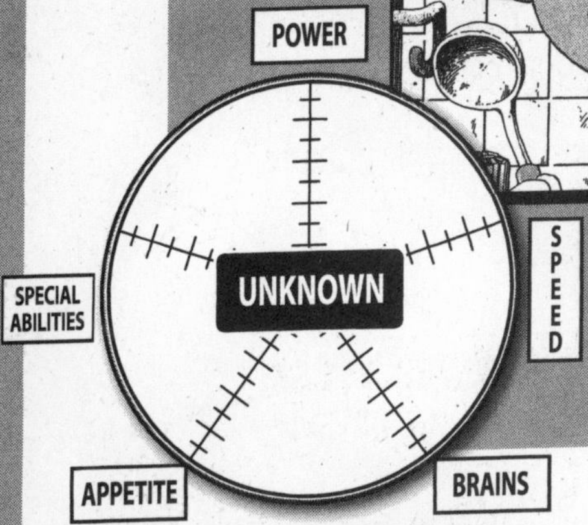
POWER
SPEED
BRAINS
APPETITE
SPECIAL ABILITIES
UNKNOWN

SETSUNO

AGE	UNKNOWN	BIRTHDAY:	DECEMBER 24
BLOOD TYPE	O	SIGN:	CAPRICORN
HEIGHT	148 CM	WEIGHT:	A LADY DOESN'T TELL
EYESIGHT	20/4	SHOE SIZE:	23 CM

SPECIAL MOVES/ABILITIES

- Food Preparation (specializing in foods that require "special handling")

One of only four Gourmet Living Legends. When this legendary chef was young, she was partnered up with Knocking Master Jiro. She has also sampled myriad foods and even stepped foot in the Gourmet World. At present, she runs a number of eateries and is so famous that her "Setsu Statues" are a common sight on any town's main drag.

COMING NEXT VOLUME

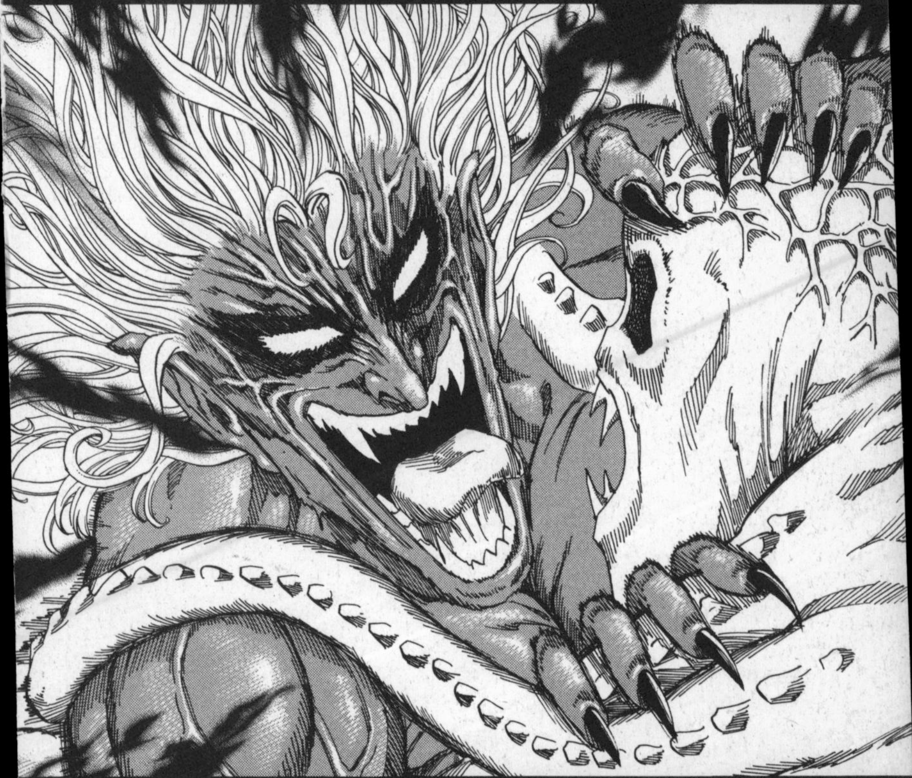

SUBZERO ZERO HOUR

The battle for the Century Soup continues as Toriko and friends face powerful members of Gourmet Corp.! Toriko will have to overcome the toughest foe of his life in Tommyrod, a diabolical freak who controls powerful insects.

AVAILABLE JUNE 2012!

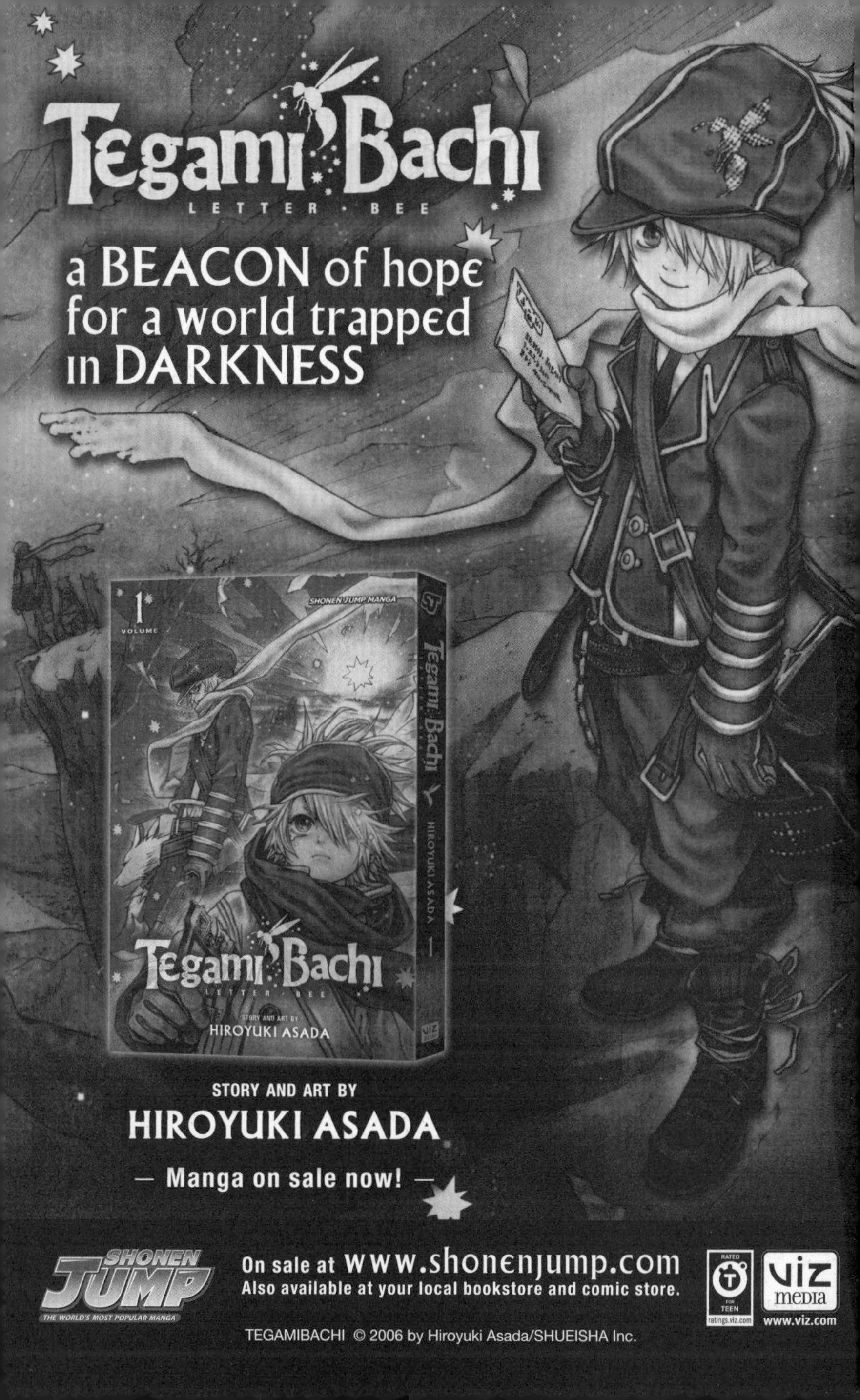
Tegami Bachi
LETTER · BEE
a BEACON of hope for a world trapped in DARKNESS
1 VOLUME
SHONEN JUMP MANGA
Tegami Bachi
LETTER BEE
STORY AND ART BY
HIROYUKI ASADA
STORY AND ART BY
HIROYUKI ASADA
— Manga on sale now! —
SHONEN JUMP
THE WORLD'S MOST POPULAR MANGA
On sale at www.shonenjump.com
Also available at your local bookstore and comic store.
RATED T FOR TEEN
ratings.viz.com
VIZ media
www.viz.com
TEGAMIBACHI © 2006 by Hiroyuki Asada/SHUEISHA Inc.